Whereas, We have noticed with pleasure the action taken in different parts of our Confederacy in response to the call of the President for the Soldiers to reenlist for the war, and whereas we feel with pride the interests that bind us together in a common brotherhood struggling for the same common rights and liberties, and earnestly desiring to emulate the example of those who have resolved to serve their Country until the last armed foe shall be driven beyond the borders of our land,

Therefore be it:

Resolved that having already enlisted unconditionally for the war, we take this method of renewing our pledge to stand by our brethren in the field, until we have achieved an honourable independence among the nations of the world, and have avenged the death of our gallant commanders, who have sealed their devotion to our Country's cause, and enriched the soil of every State in the Confederacy by their blood.

Captain L.A. Whilden
Company E, 5th Regiment, South Carolina Cavalry
1864

South Carolina's Military Organizations During the War Between the States

Volume I: The Lowcountry & Pee Dee
Volume II: The Midlands
Volume III: The Upstate
Volume IV: Statewide Units, Militia and Reserves

South Carolina's Military Organizations During the War Between the States

Statewide Units, Militia and Reserves

Robert S. Seigler

Published by The History Press
Charleston, SC 29403
www.historypress.net

Cover image: The Citadel in 1865. *Courtesy of The Citadel Archives & Museum, Charleston, South Carolina.*
Cover design by Marshall Hudson

First published 2008

Manufactured in the United States

ISBN 978.1.59629.195.9

Library of Congress Cataloging-in-Publication Data

Seigler, Robert S.
South Carolina's military organizations during the War between the States / Robert S. Seigler.
p. cm.
Includes bibliographical references and index.
ISBN 978-1-59629-195-9 (alk. paper)
1. South Carolina--History--Civil War, 1861-1865--Regimental histories. 2. United States--History--Civil War, 1861-1865--Regimental histories. 3. Confederate States of America--Armed Forces. I. Title.
E577.4.S45 2008
973.7'457--dc22

2007049670

Notice: The information in this book is true and complete to the best of our knowledge. It is offered without guarantee on the part of the author or The History Press. The author and The History Press disclaim all liability in connection with the use of this book.

In memory of:
Milledge Rivers Gunter
Company F
Palmetto Sharpshooters
Bratton's Brigade
Field's Division
Longstreet's Corps
A.N.V.

Joseph O'Hear Sanders
The Citadel Cadets, and
The Stono Scouts

Andrew Altman Seigler
Percival's Company
Colcock's Regiment
South Carolina State Troops

A.J. Bulkley
Company A, 17th Battalion, South Carolina Cavalry
Company D, 5th Regiment, South Carolina Cavalry

Contents

ACKNOWLEDGEMENTS

The following people offered invaluable assistance in the production of this work: John Mills Bigham, Curator of Education, South Carolina Confederate Relic Room and Museum, Columbia, South Carolina; Beth Bilderbeck, Visual Materials Archivist, South Caroliniana Library, University of South Carolina, Columbia, South Carolina; Suzanne Case, Supervisor, South Carolina Room, Greenville County Library System, Greenville, South Carolina; Doris Gandy, Director, Darlington County Historical Society, Darlington, South Carolina; Carl Hill, Director, The War Between The States Museum, Florence, South Carolina; Stephen L. Johnson, President, The State Printing Company, Columbia, South Carolina; Webster Jones, The 16th Regiment Museum, Greenville, South Carolina; Ola Jean Kelly, Director, Union County Museum, Union, South Carolina; Sidney R. Thompson, Executive Director, Greenville County Historical Society, Greenville, South Carolina; Jane Yates, Director, Archives and Museum, The Citadel, Charleston, South Carolina.

I deeply appreciate the expert editorial assistance of Ann Bowen of Greenwood, South Carolina, whose knowledge and guidance handmolded this work.

Finally and most importantly, I would like to thank my wife, Patti, and my children, Carrie and Robert, for their remarkable patience and encouragement throughout the fifteen or so years that I researched and wrote this book. I dedicate it to them.

INTRODUCTION

More than a century has passed since a comprehensive account of the organization of South Carolinians for military service in the War Between the States has appeared in print. In 1899 Professor William J. Rivers published *Rivers's Account of the Raising of Troops in South Carolina for State and Confederate Service 1861–1865*, and in the same year, Rivers's collaborator and then-state historian of Confederate records, John Peyre Thomas, issued an augmented version of Rivers's work as a report to the South Carolina legislature entitled *Annual Report of the State Historian of Confederate Records For The Year 1899.*[1] Since that time, a great many historical works dealing with South Carolina's Confederate history have been published. None, however, has attempted to update or expand upon Rivers's and Thomas's seminal works. This book attempts to do just that. It records the history of the infantry, cavalry, artillery and reserve units organized in South Carolina immediately before and during the War Between the States.

OVERVIEW

On November 13, 1860, the South Carolina General Assembly authorized the creation of a convention of the people to be called the South Carolina Secession Convention. In late 1860 and early 1861, both the General Assembly and the Secession Convention approved several acts and resolutions creating a significant state military force. The South Carolina General Assembly passed its first act related to the raising of troops for possible armed conflict on December 17, 1860, just three days before the Ordinance of Secession passed the Convention. In a precautionary move designed to arm ten thousand men, the legislature authorized the governor to call up troops for the defense of the state by "engrafting a volunteer system on the existing militia" thus creating an "Armed Military Force."[1] The act directed "that whenever it shall appear that an armed force is about to be employed against the State, or in opposition to its authority, the Governor be, and he is hereby, authorized to repel the same; and for that purpose to call into the service of the State…such a portion of the militia as he may deem necessary and proper."[2] It also directed the governor to call at once for one volunteer company of infantry from each militia infantry battalion, two rifle companies from each militia infantry brigade, one or more cavalry companies from each militia cavalry regiment and one regiment of artillery from Charleston. In addition, he was allowed to call for three artillery companies, one each from Columbia, Georgetown and Beaufort.[3]

This act also authorized the governor to receive into service any volunteer organization that had a full complement of officers and men and to draft men from any militia battalion that did not furnish its quota within thirty days.[4] These volunteer units were to be organized into battalions or regiments, which, in turn, were to be organized into four brigades. Then the entire organization was to be incorporated into a single division under the command of a major general. The men in ranks were to elect officers up to and including the rank of colonel. The governor, with the advice and consent of the Senate, was to appoint the four brigadier generals and the sole major general. The governor could call any or all elements of this organization into service for no more than twelve months. Governor Pickens duly appointed Milledge L. Bonham of Edgefield as major general; Patrick H. Nelson of Sumter, T.G. Rhett and Samuel McGowan of Abbeville and Albert C. Garlington of Newberry would be the four brigadier generals.

On December 26, 1860, Major Robert Anderson of the United States Army withdrew his troops from Fort Moultrie to Fort Sumter. On December 29, Governor Pickens responded by issuing the call to begin raising troops as authorized by the act of December 17.[5] The first regiments to be raised were called "South Carolina Volunteers." Initially there were to be ten of these volunteer regiments. They were given numeric designations—2nd Regiment Infantry, South Carolina Volunteers, for example—and were usually abbreviated "SCV." In 1860 South Carolina was divided into thirty districts.[6] These thirty districts were further divided into ten "regions" for the purpose of raising the ten regiments created by the December 17 act.[7] It is possible the first ten regiments were numbered based on their geographical origin. It is also possible that they were based on the dates of elections for field officers. In fact, Johnson Hagood said his regiment was the first to volunteer and for that reason was designated the 1st Regiment, SCV.[8]

While these volunteer regiments were being organized, the South Carolina legislature and the Secession Convention realized that the state militia, as it existed, was unable to meet the immediate needs of the state to defend itself. On January 1, 1861, the Secession Convention passed two resolutions. One created a Board of Ordnance and a Corps of Military Engineers. The other authorized the immediate enlistment of volunteer companies to be formed into a single regiment to serve for six months[9] and allowed the governor to accept volunteer companies attached to the South Carolina Militia to serve until they could be replaced by the forces raised under the legislature's December 17 act.[10] Acting on this resolution, the governor, on January 8, accepted Maxcy Gregg's regiment, known as the 1st Regiment Infantry, SCV, for six months' service as infantry support for Sullivan's Island and Fort Moultrie in the event of a Federal land attack.[11] He also employed the 4th Brigade, South Carolina Militia, as the primary military force in and around Charleston during the first few months of 1861.

The preceding day the Secession Convention had passed a resolution authorizing the creation of one or two regiments that would soon become known as the Regular Army of South Carolina. The first regiment was to have eight companies whose 640 privates who would enlist for twelve months. Company officers and field officers were to be appointed by the governor and confirmed by the Senate. The governor could enlist a second regiment following the same guidelines "whenever the public interest, in his opinion, may require it."[12] Originally, these "regular troops" were created to relieve the volunteers who were then in possession of the forts in the state, primarily in and around Charleston Harbor. On January 19, 23 and 28 the Senate confirmed Governor Pickens's recommendations for many of the field-grade and company-grade officers.

On January 28 the South Carolina legislature passed an act entitled "An act for creating a military establishment for the State of South Carolina, and for other purposes." This act modified the Secession Convention's resolution of December 31, 1860.[13] It created a state military establishment to be known as the Regular Army of South Carolina, and it extended the men's term of service to three years unless they were discharged earlier. All officers were to be approved by the governor and confirmed by the Senate. The organization was modified to comprise one infantry regiment, one artillery battalion and one cavalry squadron. Between them, the resolution of December 31 and the act of January 28 created the following units: the 1st Regiment, South Carolina Infantry, Regulars; the 1st Battalion, South Carolina Artillery, Regulars; and DeSaussure's Squadron, South Carolina Cavalry, Regulars. Brigadier General R.G.M. Dunovant commanded the Regular Army of South Carolina. Colonel R.H. Anderson commanded the infantry regiment, Lieutenant Colonel Roswell Ripley commanded the artillery battalion and Major W.D. DeSaussure commanded the cavalry squadron.[14]

In March 1861 the Secession Convention passed a resolution allowing the South Carolina Regular Army to be transferred to Confederate service for the remainder of its three-year term.[15] The intention was to have these troops form the nucleus of the Confederate Regular Army. Although these men enlisted in Confederate service as state volunteers, not regulars, they remained in and around Charleston Harbor until February 1865.[16] In December 1861, the legislature passed an amendment that augmented the artillery battalion to a regiment of eight companies and the cavalry to four squadrons.[17] Consequently, the 1st Battalion Artillery, South Carolina Regulars, was redesignated the 1st Regiment Artillery, South Carolina Regulars, on March 25, 1862. Although four cavalry squadrons were allowed, DeSaussure's Squadron was the only cavalry organization accepted into the South Carolina Regular Army, and it was converted to artillery within a few months of its organization. In fact, all three branches of the South Carolina Regular Army—infantry, artillery and cavalry—served as artillery units from shortly after their creation in 1861 until February 1865.

Meanwhile, South Carolinians were volunteering for twelve months' service under the act of December 17, 1860. By March 6, 1861, nearly nine thousand volunteers had enlisted in 104 companies. These companies of twelve-month volunteers were organized into the mandated ten regiments, four brigades and one division, with the ten regiments numbered one through ten.[18] The organization of the South Carolina volunteer infantry regiments numbered two through eight and ten was fairly straightforward. But it is easy to confuse some of the other regiments, especially the 1st, 9th and 11th. Johnson Hagood, for example, commanded one of the original regiments called the 1st Regiment, SCV. But Hagood's regiment should not be confused with either Colonel Maxcy Gregg's 1st Regiment (six-month), SCV; Colonel Butler's 1st Regiment, South Carolina Regulars; or Colonel Orr's 1st Regiment of Rifles, SCV. Colonel Nathaniel Heyward commanded the 9th Regiment, SCV, which was later redesignated the 11th Regiment, SCV, and it is usually referred to as such. Colonel J.D. Blanding's 9th Regiment, SCV, was not one of the original ten volunteer regiments, even though most of the companies of Blanding's regiment were among the initial 104 companies. The nucleus of Blanding's 9th Regiment was created by the consolidation of some of the original companies of the 2nd Regiment that refused to volunteer for service in Virginia in the spring of 1861 and some additional companies. In addition to these regiments, the 2nd Battalion, South Carolina Artillery, enlisted under the South Carolina General Assembly's act of December 17, 1860.[19]

On February 28, 1861, the Confederate Congress passed an act creating the Confederate States Provisional Army, usually abbreviated P.A.C.S. or C.S.P.A. After the bombardment of Fort Sumter in April 1861, President Davis called for eight thousand volunteers from South Carolina to enlist in the P.A.C.S., and Governor Pickens urged existing state troops to volunteer for Confederate service.[20] Though the response was generally positive, Davis's and Pickens's actions caused a great deal of disruption and confusion among South Carolina organizations. John Peyre Thomas wrote:

> *The Act of the Confederate States to raise provisional forces conferred upon the President the appointment of officers above the rank of Colonel. In transferring the enlisted troops of the state to the Confederate Government, the Governor was instructed by the Convention to endeavor to preserve the rank of State officers and obtain for them commissions of the same grade for at least the period of their enlistment. But many officers, natives of Southern states, were now resigning from the United States Army and seeking commissions in the Army of the Confederacy; and it was the policy of the government to hold in its own hands the appointment of all superior*

> *officers. Indeed, it was their desire to accept volunteers only by companies, and such alone as volunteered for the whole war; although, through the necessity of bringing large forces rapidly forward, it was accorded to the volunteer troops to retain their regimental organizations.*[21]

Every one of the original eleven regiments ultimately enlisted in part or in whole in Confederate service. Many of the men and companies who had enlisted for twelve months of state service, however, refused to enter Confederate service with their original regiments in the spring of 1861. Many South Carolina regiments were affected by this switch from state to Confederate service. Severely affected were Maxcy Gregg's reorganized 1st Regiment, Johnson Hagood's 1st Regiment, J.B. Kershaw's 2nd Regiment and J.D. Blanding's 9th Regiment. Moderately affected were the 3rd, 4th, 5th, 6th, 10th and 11th Regiments. Least affected were the 7th and 8th Regiments. On April 25, 1861, Governor Pickens, who believed the troops should be transferred under certain conditions, wrote: "Hardly any full regiment with all its companies was prepared to go suddenly [to Virginia]."[22] William W. East, a corporal in the 5th Regiment who wrote to the *Yorkville Enquirer* under the sobriquet "Our Corporal," explained the feelings of the men in May 1861: "Some think there is no danger and therefore, no need of us here [in South Carolina]; others wish to go to Virginia; others shrink from encountering the yellow fever or other disease during the idle garrison life…; and others still, feeling that the state is secure, are desirous of returning to their work-shops, their farms, or their merchandise."[23] At that time, many of the twelve-month volunteer companies, which had been in existence for only a few months, refused to enter Confederate service and were disbanded altogether, but the regiments quickly enlisted new companies to replace them. The 2nd Regiment, SCV, was split into two regiments—the 2nd Regiment, SCV, and Blanding's 9th Regiment, SCV. Another regiment, Johnson Hagood's 1st, SCV, was temporarily disbanded until the men and the governor could settle their differences. John Peyre Thomas wrote that in the summer of 1861, "the Governor exhorted the lately formed regiments from the upcountry to re-volunteer for Virginia. It was understood that such volunteering for Confederate service among the twelve months State troops would not bind them to the new service beyond the term of their first enlistment."[24] In June and July 1861, the 3rd, 4th, 5th, 6th, 7th and 8th Regiments, SCV, mustered in Confederate service and were sent to Virginia, where Maxcy Gregg's reorganized 1st Regiment and J.B. Kershaw's 2nd Regiment had been since April. The men of Johnson Hagood's 1st Regiment were still uncommitted and remained in South Carolina. Blanding's 9th Regiment, Manigault's 10th Regiment and Heyward's 11th Regiment also remained in the state. When the dust settled in the late spring and summer of 1861, the original ten regiments were intact. They had recruited back to full strength and had spawned one new regiment, Blanding's 9th. All eleven regiments had mustered in Confederate service. The eleven South Carolina Volunteer regiments, however, contained many new companies, which had replaced those that had refused to enter Confederate service.

Another organization, the Hampton Legion, mustered in Confederate service in 1861. In April, President Davis authorized its creation as a combined force of infantry, cavalry and artillery, which had originally enlisted for twelve months' service in the Provisional Army of the Confederate States.

On June 30, 1861, President Davis called for the creation of a thirty-thousand-man reserve army corps. This new call-up included an additional three thousand South Carolinians, who would enlist "for the duration of the war."[25] Under the plan, the three thousand men were to be organized into companies at two camps of instruction, and President Davis was to appoint the field officers for the new regiments. As the sites for the camps of instruction, Governor Pickens chose Lightwood Knot Springs, located about seven miles north of Columbia, and Camp Butler, near Polecat (now Montmorenci) in Barnwell District. A later modification of the terms of the call-up said a combination of ten companies could form a regiment, men could elect their field officers, and the regiment could enter service with this organizational structure.[26] In early September, there were forty-two infantry companies, three cavalry companies and two artillery companies at Lightwood Knot Springs. Except for one cavalry company, this contingent completed South Carolina's quota.[27] President Davis's call for three thousand new troops resulted in the creation of the 12th, 13th, 14th and 15th Regiments, SCV.

On July 1, 1861, President Davis called for two additional regiments to enlist for the duration of the war. This call resulted in the organization of two infantry regiments and one infantry battalion. The two regiments were Maxcy Gregg's 1st Regiment, SCV, which had reorganized for the duration after its initial six-month term of enlistment expired in early July 1861, and James L. Orr's 1st Regiment, South Carolina Rifles, the first South Carolina regiment to enlist for the duration of the war. Sixteen companies offered their services to Colonel Orr. He accepted ten; the remaining six were organized into the 5th Battalion Rifles, SCV, which was later augmented to become the 2nd Regiment Rifles, SCV.

By November 1, 1861, nineteen volunteer infantry regiments and one volunteer infantry battalion had been raised. One—Maxcy Gregg's 1st (six-month) Regiment—disbanded at the end of its term of enlistment in

July 1861, and it reorganized shortly thereafter. Gregg's regiment, along with five others and the 2nd Battalion, had enlisted for the duration of the war. Eleven regiments and the Hampton Legion signed on for twelve months. In addition, the South Carolina Regular Army, consisting of one infantry regiment, one artillery battalion and one cavalry squadron, had enlisted for three years. Several artillery batteries and about twenty-one independent companies of cavalry and mounted infantry were also organized during this period. Some of the cavalry companies were raised under a special resolution of the Secession Convention, with their terms of service limited to ten days after the adjournment of the regular session of the legislature.[28] It is difficult to determine exactly which company was which, but most likely they were the undersized companies of Martin's 1st Regiment Cavalry, South Carolina Militia. These troops were stationed along the South Carolina coast.

In November 1861, the South Carolina legislature met in special session to appoint electors for president and vice-president under the permanent Confederate Constitution. In response to the fall of Port Royal in early November and the subsequent threat to Charleston, the legislators passed a resolution authorizing the governor to call for volunteers to defend the state either against an actual invasion or against one he believed to be imminent.[29] Acting under a Confederate act entitled "an act to provide for local defense and special service" passed on August 21, 1861, the governor, on November 11, called for volunteers to enter Confederate service in special defense of the state. The response was slow.[30] As a result, the General Assembly amended the South Carolina Militia Law of 1841 on December 7, 1861, by passing an "Act to amend and suspend certain portions of the Militia and Patrol laws of the State."[31] This act stated that unless exempt, all free white males between the ages of sixteen and sixty years were liable to perform ordinary military duty during the war. In addition, it made eighteen- to forty-five-year-old men liable to be called for twelve months' service either in South Carolina or in any other Confederate state instead of the previously allowed three months' service inside and two months' service outside the state. The governor was authorized to call out these troops at any time.[32] If the South Carolina Militia did not furnish the allotted number of men, a draft would follow.[33] The law also tried to revitalize the South Carolina militia system by calling for new elections of officers and more frequent drilling. On December 9, 1861, Governor Pickens called for twelve thousand volunteers to enlist for twelve months' service, unless they were discharged before that time.[34] As a result, the 16th and 17th Infantry Regiments, SCV, and the 3rd Infantry Battalion, SCV, were organized. The 18th, 19th, 20th, 21st, 22nd, 23rd and 24th Infantry Regiments, SCV, were also organized under this call.

By the end of 1861, more than 7,000 men had enlisted "for and during the war" and 20,251 for shorter terms, usually either twelve or thirty-six months. A total of 27,362 men were in uniform, and an additional sixty-four companies were either in camp or under marching orders.[35] In 1861, a number of organizations enlisted for the duration of the war. These were the infantry regiments of Gregg's 1st SCV, the 12th SCV, 13th SCV, 14th SCV, 15th SCV and Orr's regiment of rifles; the 5th Battalion Rifles Infantry, Edward Manigault's Battalion, four companies of Hatch's Battalion of Coast Rangers and the 1st Battalion Cavalry; the artillery organizations of the 2nd Battalion, the 3rd Battalion (Palmetto Battalion) Light Artillery and the Chesterfield Light Artillery. Captain Boyce's Company, Captain Mangum's Company, Captain Boykin's Cavalry Company and Captain Shannon's Cavalry Company also signed on for the duration in 1861.

Many units enlisted in 1861 for shorter terms of service, usually for twelve months. Infantry regiments included Hagood's 1st SCV, the 2nd through the 11th SCV, the 16th SCV, the 17th SCV, the Hampton Legion and the Holcombe Legion. Infantry battalions were the 3rd (James's) Battalion and six companies of Hatch's Battalion of Coast Rangers. Artillery organizations were Bachman's Battery, the Beaufort Volunteer Artillery, Bonneau's Artillery, the Calhoun Light Artillery, the Santee Light Artillery, the Macbeth Artillery, the Marion Artillery and the Washington (Hart's) Artillery. Cavalry units were Boykin's Cavalry Troop, J.G. Harlan's Company, Lipscomb's Cavalry Troop, St. James Mounted Riflemen, Tucker's Squadron and Trenholm's Squadron. In addition, the 18th, 19th, 20th, 21st, 22nd, 23rd and 24th Regiments, SCV, along with some companies of Hatch's Battalion of Coast Rangers, were raised late in 1861 and early in 1862 for twelve months' service.

The South Carolina Regular Army, consisting of the 1st Regiment, South Carolina Infantry (Regulars), the 1st Battalion, South Carolina Artillery (Regulars) and the 15th Battalion, South Carolina Artillery (Regulars), also enlisted for three years in 1861. Other organizations enlisting for three years were the Pee Dee Legion Militia, Martin's Cavalry Regiment Militia, the 4th Brigade Militia, the Battalion of South Carolina Cadets and several independent cavalry companies.[36]

After the close of 1861, the record of the raising of troops for service in South Carolina is less clear. The accounts of both Professor Rivers and J.P. Thomas become ever more vague about which organizations were created under which act, resolution, law or authority in 1862.

On December 11, 1861, the Confederate Congress passed the first Confederate Conscription Act, also called the Bounty and Furlough Act. On February 19, 1862, the *Mercury* reprinted that act, along with subsequent orders from the War Department dated January 1, 1862.[37] The Conscription Act dictated a reorganization of existing Confederate military forces and provided for the following: (1) a bounty of fifty dollars would be paid to all privates, musicians and non-commissioned officers who would enlist in the Confederate States Provisional Army for three years, or for those men already enlisted for twelve months who would re-enlist for two additional years; (2) a furlough, not to exceed sixty days, would be granted "to all twelve months men now in service, who shall, prior to the expiration of their present term of service, volunteer or enlist for the next two ensuing years subsequent to the expiration of their present term of service, or for three years, or the war." The secretary of war would issue the furloughs at such times and in such number as he deemed most compatible with the public interest; (3) the act applied to any man who had already enlisted for twelve months or more in the service of any Confederate state; (4) all men who re-enlisted would be allowed, at the expiration of their original terms of service, to reorganize themselves into new companies and to elect new company officers. The new companies would be allowed to organize into new battalions or regiments, and the men would elect new field officers. Subsequent vacancies among the officer corps would be filled by promotion within the ranks of the existing officers of the unit. If the lowest ranking officer in a company had to be replaced, an election would be held to fill that vacancy. When a vacancy arose within the units of any state's Regular Army, new officers would be appointed and not elected; (5) further provisions were made for the reorganization of new companies into battalions and regiments.[38]

On February 2, 1862, the secretary of war called on Governor Pickens for South Carolina to fill its quota of troops to be furnished "for and during the war."[39] This quota—6 percent of the white male population of the state—translated to about 18,000 men.[40] An estimated 6,000 South Carolinians had already enlisted for the duration of the war. To meet the requisition of an additional 12,590 men, the secretary of war projected the need to enlist at least five new regiments and to re-enlist enough of the twelve months' troops whose terms were about to expire to make up the difference.[41] On February 20, 1862, the South Carolina adjutant and inspector general provided more accurate figures. His report showed that, of 30,670 South Carolinians currently in uniform, 9,349 had enlisted for the duration of the war and 21,321 had signed on for twelve months. At about the same time, by contrast, the secretary of war counted 6,260 South Carolinians enlisted for the duration and 23,975 enlisted for twelve months.[42] James Chesnut Jr., a member of the South Carolina Executive Council, urged the twelve months' troops to re-enlist for the duration to meet the quota of 18,000 men.

As a part of this call for additional troops, the *Mercury* reported on February 21, 1862, that President Davis had issued a call for 5,000 more men—approximately five regiments—from South Carolina. Another call for 5,000 men went out on March 5, 1862, with a notice that said until five regiments were raised, no man could enter any organization then in service for less than the duration of the war.[43] On March 6, 1862, the *Mercury* reprinted a proclamation from Governor Pickens stating that President Davis called for an additional 12,590 men from the state, a number that included the two previous calls for 5,000 men each.[44] To meet the state's quota, including the five new regiments called for, the governor and Executive Council, on March 5, 1862, adopted a system of conscription.[45] They also directed South Carolina Adjutant and Inspector General States Rights Gist to issue a statement in early March. Gist's proclamation, issued on March 7, declared a reorganization of the South Carolina Military System to bring it into compliance with the Executive Council's decision.[46] The statement contained several major points, among them: the system of volunteering by individuals or by companies would be in place until March 20, 1862, when all volunteering would be discarded and a system of conscription, as provided for by law, would be instituted; all male citizens between the ages of eighteen and forty-five would be required to enroll for active duty and would not be allowed to serve in the reserves; all eligible men must report for duty within ten days of being called or be liable for the draft; volunteer companies already in service would be required to re-enlist ten days before their term of service expired; any individuals who refused to re-enlist would be eligible for the draft; and the governor would appoint all field officers in new regiments and company-grade officers in new companies.[47] In addition, boards of exemption were to be created throughout the state, a system of conscription was to be established and a method for substitution was to be set in place.[48] Troops were to be received at Lightwood Knot Springs, north of Columbia.[49]

Even before the cutoff date of March 20, 1862, more than 22,000 South Carolinians had volunteered for the duration of the war, and an additional 17,210 men had enrolled for twelve months.[50] On March 21, the governor and Executive Council responded to this positive news by extending the deadline to April 15 and allowing the men to elect their officers, subject to approval by the Executive Council.[51] Under this proclamation, the 24th Regiment, SCV, was accepted for the duration of the war, and Lamar's 2nd Artillery Battalion was increased to regiment strength.

The Confederate Congress passed a new conscription law, entitled "An Act to further provide for the public defense," on April 16, 1862.[52] It contained even more details concerning re-enlistment of soldiers and distribution of conscripted men than had the law passed the previous December. And it authorized the president to call into service all white male residents of the Confederate States between the ages of eighteen and thirty-five years who were not legally exempted from duty. The term of service would be "three years, unless the war shall have been sooner ended."[53] In addition, all the twelve-month volunteers were to serve two additional years from the expiration of their original terms. Any men younger than eighteen and older than thirty-five were required to remain in service for ninety days unless their places were filled by recruits. Bounties were granted to the twelve-month men, and furloughs would be granted at the discretion of the secretary of war. Transfers from one organization to another and the creation of new organizations were cancelled unless they could be completed within thirty days. All the twelve-month men who re-enlisted were allowed to hold elections for their officers within forty days of April 16.[54] This act had little effect on the creation of new units in South Carolina because most eligible men were already in the service. About five thousand South Carolinians enlisted or re-enlisted in existing units in response.

According to estimates of the state's adjutant and inspector general, 39,274 South Carolinians were in the field by April 28, 1862. Of this number, 22,064—some 4,000 more than required—had enlisted for the duration and 17,210 had enlisted for twelve months.[55] By August 30, the number of men enlisted for service in all South Carolina military organizations had grown to 42,973. At that time, the infantry comprised twenty-eight regiments, two legions, eight battalions and two unattached companies. The artillery comprised two regiments, one battalion and eighteen unattached companies; the cavalry units numbered two regiments, five battalions and seven unattached companies.[56]

The conscription laws, especially the Conscription Act of April 16, set the stage for significant reorganization of the entire Confederate army in the spring of 1862; the laws greatly affected the organization of South Carolina troops as well. D.A. Dickert, captain of Company H of the 3rd Regiment, wrote of the Conscript Laws:

> *The Conscript Act was condemned in unmeasured terms in many places at the South, but its necessity and expediency was never doubted. To have allowed so great a number to absent themselves from the army at this time, in the face of an overwhelming enemy, and that enemy advancing upon our Capitol, was more than the morale of the army would admit. Not altogether would the absence of the soldiers themselves effect the army, but in the breaking up of organizations, for in some companies all had re-enlisted,*

> *while in others one-half, and in many cases none. New regiments would have to be formed out of the re-enlisted companies, and new companies out of the large number of recruits, now in camps of instruction. So by keeping up the old organizations, and filling up the ranks by the conscripts at home, the army would be greatly benefited.*[57]

The term of enlistment for most of the men who originally signed up for twelve months was set to expire in the spring of 1862. Twelve-month men not otherwise exempt were required to re-enlist "for three years or the duration of the war," meaning three years from their initial date of enlistment. Most men of eligible age who were exempt from re-enlistment in the spring of 1862 were those who had originally signed on for a term greater than twelve months; all new recruits were required to enlist "for three years or the duration of the war." This phrase caused some confusion. Some men interpreted it to mean three years, or for the duration of the war, whichever was shorter. Others interpreted it to mean the opposite—three years, or for the duration of the war, whichever was longer. In his discussion of the re-enlistment for "three years or the war," Douglas Southall Freeman wrote in *Lee's Lieutenants* that the soldiers took the phrase to mean a maximum of three years. This position is supported by the original wording, "three years, unless the war shall have been sooner ended."[58] D.A. Dickert, captain of Company H of the 3rd Regiment, held a similar view: "It was during our stay in winter quarters, March 1864, that the term of our second enlistment expired." Dickert explained that the troops who had originally enlisted for twelve months in the spring of 1861 and who had then re-enlisted for "three years" in the spring of 1862 were due to re-enlist a third time in the spring of 1864. He held that the men had re-enlisted in the spring of 1862 for three years, or for the duration of the war, whichever was the shorter of the two terms. Dickert wrote further that the re-enlistment in March 1864 was "only a form, no change in officers or organization."[59]

All but a few men voluntarily re-enlisted in March 1864, but because of the conscription laws, no one was allowed to leave the army or change his branch of service. An interesting example of the effect on the ranks lies in the 1st Regiment, South Carolina Infantry (Regulars). The men in that regiment clearly believed that their original term of service expired in early 1864, and they were right. On February 8, 1864, P.G.T. Beauregard published the following statement: "Soldiers of the Department of South Carolina, Georgia and Florida. The term of service of some of you is about to expire. You must have observed from the newspapers of your city that your brothers in arms of the veteran armies of Northern Virginia and of Tennessee have re-enlisted as was to be expected of such men, by entire companies, battalions, regiments and brigades, proudly retaining the organizations intact under which they have won renown. Will the men who have defended Forts Sumter and Moultrie, and Battery Wagner fail to follow these examples of soldierly patriotism?"[60] Beauregard's goal, of course, was to preserve the integrity of the 1st Regiment, and his method was to appeal to honor and patriotism. Left unsaid was the stark fact that, under the law, if the men did not re-enlist in the 1st Regiment, they would not be allowed to leave the service.[61]

Lieutenant J.F.J. Caldwell, historian of McGowan's Brigade, also discussed the issue of "three years or the duration of the war" and arrived at a different conclusion:

> *In February* [1864], *there was a general call for re-enlistment in the Confederate armies. It will be remembered that almost all the regiments organized in the summer of 1861 enlisted for "three years or the war." I always held the expression to mean a consent to serve three years, whether the war lasted so long or not; and to serve for the war, should it last for even longer than three years. But as there was doubt about it; as there were many originally twelve-month regiments, who reenlisted, it is said, for two years from the expiration of their first year, so making their term expire in the spring of 1864; and as, above all things, the weary citizens at home needed encouragement; a renewal of enlistment and of allegiance to the Confederacy was invited. The army adopted the suggestion most cordially, and declared afresh their determination never to lay down their arms until the independence of the South should be achieved.*[62]

To avoid a catastrophe of disorganization in early 1864 when the three-year terms would expire, and perhaps also to clarify the issue, the Confederate Congress, in early 1864, passed "A Bill to Organize Forces to Serve During the War."[63] This bill required all white males between seventeen and fifty years of age to serve during the war. All men between eighteen and forty-five currently in service were to remain in their units. Men between seventeen and eighteen and between forty-five and fifty would form companies and regiments of reserves, which would serve within the borders of their states. Consequently, in the first few months of 1864, most South Carolinians then in service either re-enlisted if their three-year term had expired or reaffirmed their commitment to the Confederacy if it had not; there were no major changes in organizational structure.

As a part of the reorganization in the spring of 1862, a Confederate soldier between eighteen and thirty-five years of age whose twelve-month term of enlistment had expired was required to re-enlist in the service. In the process, however, he could change to a different company or regiment, enlist in a new unit entirely, change to a unit from another state or even select a different branch of service. Men were also allowed to form new companies and regiments and re-elect both company-grade (lieutenants and captains) and field-grade (colonels, lieutenant colonels and majors) officers.[64] J.P. Thomas wrote: "The State Adjutant General reported that 'entire companies and even regiments were lost, and new companies and regiments formed; in most instances retaining their names, but the regiments in all instances were composed to a great extent of new company organizations. The original 9th [Blanding's] Regiment was, in this way, wholly lost; and the old 4th [Regiment] was reduced to a mere battalion.'"[65]

When the men were allowed to choose their own officers, many were not re-elected because they were judged either too old or too incompetent to perform their duties. It should be noted, however, that many efficient officers were not re-elected simply because they were unpopular. Thomas wrote that the reorganization act of February 1862 should have been named the disorganization act since it caused the loss of many of the Confederacy's best officers, the disciplinarian being turned out by the politician.[66]

Many new organizations were created in South Carolina during the first half of 1862. Infantry regiments created in early 1862 and not already mentioned were the 2nd (Moore's) Regiment of Rifles and the Palmetto Sharpshooters. Several infantry battalions were raised in the first half of 1862 as well, including the 1st (Charleston), the 1st Battalion Sharpshooters, the 13th (4th), the 6th (Byrd's), the 7th, the 9th (Pee Dee), the 11th (Eutaw) and Dunlop's Battalion of Sharpshooters. The only cavalry regiment created in the first half of 1862 was the 1st Regiment. Cavalry battalions created were the 1st (14th), the 2nd (10th), the 3rd (4th), the 6th (17th), the 8th (2nd Battalion Reserves) and the 12th (4th Squadron). Independent cavalry units created during this time were the German Hussars, the Rebel Troop, the Charleston Light Dragoons, Harlan's Company, the Yeadon Rangers, Whitner's Troop, Hough's Company, the Ripley Rangers, A.C. Earle's Company, M.J. Kirk's Squadron, Keitt's Mounted Riflemen and E.M. Boykin's Squadron. Two artillery regiments were created in early 1862: the 1st Regulars, an augmentation of the 1st Battalion, and the 2nd (Lamar's) Regiment. The 18th Artillery Battalion and several other batteries were also created, including the Brooks Guard Artillery, the Inglis Artillery, the Palmetto Light Battery, the German Artillery, the Gist Guards Battery and the McQueen Light Artillery. Still other batteries were the Lafayette Artillery, the Pee Dee Artillery, the Washington (Walter's) Artillery, the Waccamaw Light Artillery, Ferguson's Light Artillery, the Edisto Artillery, B.E. Dickson's Battery, the Carolina Artillery, the Silverton Artillery,

Willis's Battery and S.D. Lee's Battery. Thomas wrote, "In addition to these organizations, under the call for all arms-bearing men between eighteen and thirty-five years of age for Confederate service, many separate companies of infantry, artillery and cavalry were raised, most of which became merged into regiments or other organizations."[67]

Organizations created in the second half of 1862 or later were the 25th, 26th and 27th Regiments, SCV; Brooks's Partisan Rifles, later designated Company H of the 7th Battalion; and the 2nd Battalion Sharpshooters. Six of the seven South Carolina cavalry regiments, the 2nd–7th, as well as the 19th Cavalry Battalion, were created in July 1862 or were created later in the war.

The South Carolina militia played an important role in the organization of troops for military service. As an effective fighting force, the militia's role was limited to the first few months of 1861 when the 4th Brigade, South Carolina Militia, supplied most of the manpower around Charleston Harbor. Several militia regiments remained in active service until early 1862, but by that time the militia no longer existed as a fighting force. Its major contribution between late 1862 and late 1864 lay in providing an organizational structure upon which the governor could call for reserve troops as needed. The South Carolina Militia Law of 1841 had created forty-six regiments organized into ten brigades and five divisions, with the governor as commander-in-chief. Men between sixteen and sixty years of age were eligible for service, while those between eighteen and forty-five were liable to serve for three months in South Carolina and two months outside the state. Men elected their company and field officers, brigade officers elected brigadier generals and division officers elected major generals.[68]

The first Conscription Act of April 16, 1862, which claimed for active duty all white males between eighteen and thirty-five years of age, significantly depleted the ranks of the South Carolina militia.[69] The second Conscription Act, passed on September 27, 1862, further depleted the militia. The new law allowed the president to call up men between the ages of thirty-five and forty-five for three years unless the war ended sooner, an option that he implemented in stages.[70] These acts took "all the material of armies between the ages mentioned, from the control of the state."[71] The South Carolina Executive Council wrote: "To meet this new condition of things, it becomes necessary that the State shall adopt further measures to organize its forces and provide for its defence."[72] Soon after the passage of the conscription laws, the Executive Council decided to separate the remainder of the men between thirty-five and fifty from the militia and organize them into companies and regiments to be held in reserve for defense of the state or other service at the discretion of the governor.[73]

Consequently, on April 23, 1862, the Executive Council of South Carolina passed resolutions creating two corps of state reserves.[74] The 1st Corps was composed of thirty-five-year-old to fifty-year-old men conscripted from within the existing South Carolina militia regiments and battalions to be held for active service anywhere the state required, as the occasion dictated.[75] They were also subject to patrol and police duty until called to active service.[76] Men of the 1st Corps were allowed to elect their company officers—the lieutenants and captains. The governor and the Executive Council were to appoint field officers—the colonels, lieutenant colonels and majors.[77] When not on active duty, men of the 1st Corps of reserves were to perform patrol duty under the command of the officers of the 2nd Corps.[78]

On May 13, 1862, the governor and the Executive Council called for the organization of five regiments, each to consist of men between thirty-five and fifty years of age in one set of companies and men between sixteen and eighteen years of age in a second set. Each company would elect its own officers, and the Executive Council would appoint the field officers of any battalions or regiments formed from the companies.[79] These regiments were to be held in reserve until ordered into active service. At all times, one company was to remain in each regiment's camp of instruction without pay, with this duty rotating among companies every two weeks.[80] Unfortunately, whether these five regiments were ever actually organized is unclear. By August 30, 1862, the 1st Corps comprised ten regiments called regiments of reserves; these regiments consisted of about eight thousand men with elected company-grade officers. Each of the ten regiments was assigned a numeric designation of two through eleven.[81] To avoid confusion with the 1st Regiment, Charleston Reserves, which was organized in October 1861, none of these new regiments was designated the "1st Regiment." Originally, the Executive Council's resolution creating the reserve corps did not apply to the 1st Regiment of Charleston Reserves. By August 22, 1862, however, the Charleston unit was officially designated the 1st Regiment of the 1st Corps of Reserves, a modification that gave the 1st Corps of Reserves eleven regiments.[82]

Between October 4, 1862, and October 31, 1862, Governor Pickens reviewed nine of the eleven reserve regiments. On October 25, Secretary of War G.W. Randolph wrote James Chesnut that the Confederate States Government would accept four regiments—the 2nd, 3rd, 8th and 11th—for local service and that the remaining seven would be disbanded. Randolph also wrote that he would accept men over forty years of age for service in the reserve regiments, and that the men between thirty-five and forty, along with conscripts from the seven disbanded regiments, would be placed in existing South Carolina regiments. These four regiments, consisting of about three thousand men, were expected to be in camp in about twenty days.[83] On November 11, President Davis modified the plan to accept eight of the reserve regiments into service, with the result that, on November 18, eight of the ten new regiments of the 1st Corps Reserves entered Confederate service for state defense for ninety days.[84] These were the 2nd, 3rd, 5th, 6th, 7th, 8th, 9th and 11th. At least four of these regiments were ordered to report to Lightwood Knot Springs, north of Columbia, and then on to Charleston.[85] The 4th and the 10th Regiments were disbanded on November 7 because of disaffection among the men.[86]

The Secession Convention expired by its own ordinance on December 12, 1862. The very next day, the South Carolina General Assembly declared many of the Executive Council's decisions invalid.[87] In one action it revoked the Council's order to disband the 4th and 10th Regiments. On December 18, it passed an act forbidding the reserve regiments to serve more than ninety days. It also called for the replacement of council-appointed field officers through elections to be held on January 1, 1863.[88] P.G.T. Beauregard criticized this provision, and Governor M.L. Bonham requested and received an appeal. As a result, new elections were never held.[89] On February 10, 1863, after ninety days' service, the reserve regiments of the 1st Corps were disbanded.[90] The thirty-five- to forty-year-old men of the 1st Corps who had not been called to active service because of their age, however, were now required by the second Conscription Act of September 27, 1862, to enter active service. On February 18, 1863, Governor Bonham ordered the 1st, 4th and 10th Regiments back into the field. He held the remainder in reserve in anticipation of an immediate Federal assault.[91] On March 9, 1863, the governor suspended his order, and the reserves stayed at home.[92]

The 2nd Corps of Reserves was composed of men between sixteen and eighteen years of age, men between fifty and sixty-five years of age, alien residents and all others exempt from ordinary military duty. After organization into companies and regiments, the 2nd Corps was placed under the command of South Carolina militia officers, who were already commissioned but who could not, for some reason, serve in the 1st Corps. The 2nd Corps was used for patrol and police duty and for internal defense as required by the state. Since the 2nd Corps did not enter Confederate service, virtually no information about it appears in the *Compiled Service Records* (CSR). Additionally, little information about its organizational structure exists. On July 21, 1862, the Executive Council amended resolutions that said if the 1st and 2nd Corps of Reserves were brought into active service at the same time, the 1st Corps was to act as regulars and the 2nd Corps as militia.[93] When not under orders, both the 1st and 2nd Corps would perform patrol duty.[94]

To further shore up the South Carolina militia, the Executive Council passed a resolution on November 7, 1862, that contained the following directive: "the public safety imperiously demands that all white male residents of the State of South Carolina capable of bearing arms should be immediately placed into military organizations and armed." The Executive Council ordered the formation of companies to include practically all males between sixteen and sixty-five. Drill under pain of court martial was required every two weeks. The order included members of the legislature, doctors, ministers, millers and others; it exempted only a few groups like the Executive Council, judges and state treasurers. The force as a whole was designed as a district police with access to arms deposited at each courthouse.[95] To have troops available to serve as "alarm men" for military service in the South Carolina militia,[96] the commanding officer of each beat was ordered to keep a separate roll of men between forty and fifty years of age. Subject to the call of the commander in chief, these men would constitute a reserve force for the defense of the state.[97]

In the summer of 1863, Federal assaults were anticipated along the South Carolina coast. On June 6, and again on July 31, President Davis called on the governor of South Carolina to provide 5,384 volunteers for local defense and special service.[98] On June 16, Governor Bonham ordered South Carolina militia regiments to respond to President Davis's 5,000-man quota.[99] The president's authority was based on two acts passed by the Confederate Congress: the first, passed on August 21, 1861, was entitled "An act to provide for local defense and special service"; the other, passed on October 13, 1862, was called "An act to authorize the formation of volunteer companies for local defense."[100] The 1861 act authorized the president to accept volunteers to serve in a capacity and for a duration prescribed by him for the defense of exposed places or for special service.[101] Under this act, the volunteers would be mustered in Confederate service, and the president would appoint the field officers. Men were to be between forty and forty-five years of age and, beginning August 1, 1863, would serve in South Carolina for six months.[102] The governor was instructed to ask for volunteers from this age group. If the quota of 5,384 men went unmet, then the governor was authorized to draft men between forty and fifty years of age. Sixteen- and seventeen-year-old-men in the South Carolina militia were not subject to the draft. South Carolina militia regiments were ordered to assemble at their muster grounds on July 7 and to organize new companies either by volunteering or, if necessary, by means of a draft.[103] Each company was to carry between 64 and 125 privates on its roster, and each regiment was to contain ten companies.[104] The men elected their company-grade officers in early July.[105] Since all the men were volunteers, President Davis agreed on July 23 to allow them to elect their field officers as well. He set a date of July 31 for elections in all five regiments,[106] and he required the regiments to be ready for immediate service after elections were held.

As a result of the presidential call-up, about five thousand South Carolinians volunteered for service in five new regiments, known as the "South Carolina State Troops (Six Months)." It was understood that the regiments were raised only for local defense and special service—most importantly, the defense of Charleston.[107] The five regiments, numbered one through five, were ready for service on August 1. Beauregard, however, did not call them to active duty until September 5.[108] At that time, one regiment was sent to Pocotaligo, the other four to Charleston and their six months' service began.[109] In December 1863, Governor Bonham argued successfully that the six-month service should date from August 1; consequently, the five regiments of South Carolina state troops were mustered out on February 3, 1864.[110] Men between forty and forty-five years of age who were mustered out, however, were almost immediately conscripted into service again.[111]

The Conscription Act passed on February 17, 1864, was entitled "An act to organize forces to serve during the war."[112] On March 1, 1864, Adjutant General Samuel Cooper implemented the new law.[113] Under it, all white male citizens of the Confederate States between seventeen and fifty years of age were liable for service within their respective states for the duration of the war.[114] Men between eighteen and forty-five were to remain with their respective organizations. Seventeen-year-old men and forty-five- to fifty-year-olds were required to form a reserve corps and were allowed to elect their own company and field officers. They were ordered to organize themselves first into companies and then into either battalions or regiments.[115] Within thirty days from March 15, the men were required either to enroll in an existing local defense company or to organize a new company. "Those between seventeen and eighteen and between forty-five and fifty were organized and commanded by General (James) Chesnut under an appointment by President Davis; some were called into active service at Charleston, of course, at Confederate expense."[116] Camps of instruction were established and provisions were made for exemptions.[117]

Eight new battalions, designated the "1st to 8th Battalions, South Carolina Reserves," were created under this law. These battalions were later referred to as the Battalions of Senior Reserves to distinguish them from the regiments of Junior Reserves. The *Yorkville Enquirer* reported in late March that the new battalions were not to be called into active service "unless a greater emergency occurs."[118] In early April 1864, the *Daily South Carolinian* reported that all eligible men were to enroll before April 16 and that the new battalions were to serve as a "reserve for state defense" within the boundaries of the state.[119] The *Yorkville Enquirer* reported on June 15 that eight new battalions had been organized.[120] On June 24, General Chesnut ordered each battalion to elect a major to command it.[121] On July 13, he issued another order calling the reserve battalions to active duty "at once" because infantry support of the artillery on John's Island and James Island was needed.[122] By July 20, several of the reserve battalions were in the field.[123] Throughout the summer of 1864, the reserve battalions continued to muster in state service, and in December, they became part of the Confederate forces. Though some of the reserve battalions were disbanded shortly before the end of the war, others were merged into nonreserve South Carolina regiments on April 9, 1865.

In August and early September 1864 South Carolina required all white males between sixteen and sixty years of age to be liable for service in the South Carolina Militia.[124] Each regiment of militia provided one new company toward the creation of four new regiments designated the "1st, 2nd, 3rd and 4th Regiments, Junior Reserves, South Carolina State Troops." They were also called "Regiments of South Carolina Militia" and "Regiments of State Troops" and might also have been known as Battalions of State Troops.[125] These new regiments should not be confused with the 1st, 2nd, 3rd and 4th Regiments, South Carolina Militia, all of which had existed before and continued during the war. The Junior Reserves consisted of sixteen-year-old men. Before this call-up, the militia was a strictly local force, on duty as home guards and in other capacities.[126] All regiments of South Carolina Militia were ordered to rendezvous on September 12, 1864, so each could raise one company of Junior Reserves.[127] The men then went home and reassembled at Hamburg in late November. On March 29, 1865, Governor Magrath ordered militiamen who were between sixteen and seventeen years of age to assemble by April 1 in Spartanburg for the defense of the state. The Citadel and Arsenal cadets were to be placed in command of the camp of instruction.[128] By early April, all four of the regiments of Junior Reserves had been disbanded.[129] Older men were allowed to go home, but the "boys," called "State Troops, First Class Militia," were required to remain in service.[130] In early April, about seven hundred sixteen-year-olds were being held for state service and drilling at Spartanburg.[131] On April 3, they were ordered to reorganize immediately and report to Captain J.P. Thomas at Greenville. This move never took place, and on April 8, the State Troops, First Class Militia, was disbanded.

John Peyre Thomas offered an in-depth enumeration of South Carolinians who served in the War Between the States.[132] He estimated that 64,903 men were enrolled in Confederate service; of those, some 56,661 were considered effective. Thomas also estimated that 6,180 men were enrolled in state service, and that all but 3 of these were effective. Thus, of the 71,083 South Carolinians enrolled, a full 62,838 were effective. This service population of 71,083 men was drawn from an 1860 voting population of only 60,000 men.[133] In 1899 Thomas estimated that 20,101 South Carolinians were killed or died in service during the war. He noted that because many rolls were missing or incomplete, this number could run as high as 21,146. In a further breakdown, he estimated infantry deaths at 17,918, cavalry at 1,467 and artillery at 716. In his book *Broken Fortunes*, B.F. Kirkland records the deaths of South Carolinians as 18,666, but he suggests that the actual number could have been as high as 21,166 because the records of 2,500 men were missing.[134]

Thomas records a total of thirty-four infantry regiments and four infantry battalions; seven cavalry regiments, one cavalry squadron and one cavalry company; and three artillery regiments, two artillery battalions and nineteen unattached artillery batteries.[135] The accounting is actually somewhat more complicated because of duplications and other ramifications. Many independent companies, for example, were subsequently attached to battalions or regiments, and many battalions eventually merged into regiments. Additionally, a number of companies, battalions and regiments ceased to exist before the end of the war. If all duplications are avoided, the following summarizes South Carolina units in Confederate service during the war: thirty-six infantry regiments, seven infantry battalions, two artillery regiments, three artillery battalions, twenty-seven independent artillery batteries, seven cavalry regiments and one cavalry battalion. This listing includes neither the militia nor the reserves.

The basic building block of all military units during the War Between the States was the company. Men mustered in service as part of a company, and it was at the company level that all official records of individuals were kept. In the infantry, companies were referred to as such; in the cavalry, they were usually called a troop; and in the artillery, the words company and battery were used interchangeably. At the start of the war, a company was composed of 80 to 104 officers and men. Under the first Conscription Act passed in the spring of 1862, an infantry company consisted of 125 men, rank and file; each cavalry company consisted of 80 men; and a field artillery battery was made up of 150 men.[136] A captain commanded each company, with lieutenants as his immediate subordinates. Numerous independent companies were raised for local defense purposes early on, but most were consolidated into battalions or regiments before the end of the war.

Usually ten companies formed a regiment, and each regiment was commanded by a colonel, whose immediate subordinates were the lieutenant colonel and major. Four to eight companies normally formed a battalion, which was commanded by a lieutenant colonel or a major. Some battalions maintained their integrity throughout the war, but often two battalions or one battalion and several independent companies were merged to create a new regiment. Such mergers or consolidations typically occurred in South Carolina's cavalry regiments, and sometimes with the infantry and artillery as well—the creation, for example, of the 23rd, 24th, 25th, 26th and 27th Regiments, SCV, and the 2nd Regiment, South Carolina Artillery. In one instance the 4th Regiment, SCV, was raised as a regiment, but was downsized to the 13th Battalion at the reorganization as a result of losses from combat and disease. Subsequently, the 13th Battalion was disbanded and the remaining companies consolidated into just two that merged into the Hampton Legion. The cavalry branch of the service had a subdivision called the squadron, which was usually made up of two companies or troops. As the war progressed, most South Carolina cavalry squadrons were incorporated into cavalry regiments. Three to five regiments or battalions usually formed a brigade, which was commanded by a brigadier general. Three to five brigades usually formed a division, which was commanded by a major general. Three to five divisions usually formed a corps, which was under the command of a lieutenant general. Two or three corps usually formed an army.

This work concentrates on the company, battalion and regimental levels of South Carolina military organizations during the War Between the States. Companies were usually designated alphabetically, though several exceptions to this rule arose early in the war, when some regiments designated their companies numerically. The letter *J* was eliminated from military nomenclature because of the difficulty in distinguishing between the letters *J* and *I* when written by hand. An exception was that of the 4th Regiment, SCV, which had a Company J—the Confederate Guards. This company was composed of men from Anderson whose backgrounds were not military. Because other letter designations were already in use when they enlisted, these men innocently chose the letter *J* and opted to retain it even after they discovered their error.[137]

Early in the war, before many companies were attached to regiments, companies were designated by the name of their first captain; Captain Bill Smith's Company, SCV, for example. When companies became attached to a regiment or battalion, they were given an alphabetic designation, such as Company B, 3rd Regiment, SCV. A common practice in most companies was to allow the men to choose a company nickname, often some brief and colorful term, in addition to its alphabetic designation or its captain's name. Many of these nicknames reflected upon the men's hometown or district, their desire to defend their rights or some person whom they wished to honor. Nicknames included the Enoree Mosquitoes, the Meeting Street Saludas, the Horry Rough and Readys, the Lancaster Invincibles and the Bozeman Guards. Some companies had more than one popular name. This practice of nicknames was common among infantry companies and almost universal among cavalry companies and independent artillery batteries, but it was virtually nonexistent among companies of the South Carolina Regular Army. A good deal of evidence suggests that most of South Carolina's volunteer companies had a popular name or nickname. Many such names have been recorded in various newspapers, books and other records. Unfortunately, others probably existed but were not preserved and thus are lost forever. Multiple sources exist for the 14th Regiment, SCV, for example, and most of its companies' popular names are well documented. None of the known regimental records for Company G of the 14th Regiment, SCV, however, contain the company nickname—the McGowan Greys; the only known source that documents this popular name is an obituary in the *Due West Times*.[138]

Keeping track of companies and individuals throughout their service is usually straightforward but can sometimes be quite confusing. Some men whose original enlistments were for the duration never re-enlisted because the companies they first joined managed to maintain their integrity throughout the war. Many companies, however, had at least one opportunity, and some even a second, to re-enlist. The first such opportunity for many South Carolina companies came in the spring and summer of 1861 when they voluntarily left state service and joined the Confederate forces. This change of service offered at least three possibilities: men and officers could transfer individually to a different company; a company could remain intact, but it could transfer to a different regiment; and some companies could disband altogether. The second opportunity for many companies to re-enlist came when the army reorganized in the spring of 1862 at the expiration of the initial twelve-month term of enlistment. This reorganization offered many of the same possibilities for individuals and companies as had the changes of the preceding year. An extreme example of change can be found in the records of the Wee Nee Volunteers, which served with four different regiments and one battalion between 1861 and 1865.

At the reorganization of the Confederate army in the spring of 1862, many companies and regiments remained intact; some companies remained relatively intact but transferred to a different regiment; others disbanded completely and the men re-enlisted elsewhere. In some cases, most of the men from one company re-enlisted together in a new company. The 9th Regiment, SCV, was completely disbanded, and the 4th Regiment, SCV, was converted to a battalion. Further confusion arose from the practice of allowing individuals to transfer to a different company, though this did not happen on a large scale after the 1862 reorganization. Occasionally, companies were granted special permission to transfer to a different battalion or regiment, and sometimes regiments were transferred to a different brigade.

Every South Carolina company, squadron, battalion and regiment was provided with an official designation. While companies in Confederate service received alphabetic designations, regiments, battalions and cavalry squadrons were usually given numeric designations—the 1st Regiment, SCV, for example. In addition, most regiments were referred to unofficially by the name of their colonel—Gregg's regiment, for instance. Some, like the Eutaw Regiment (25th SCV) or the Pee Dee Regiment (8th SCV), had unofficial names. Three South Carolina regiments and one battalion in Confederate service received no numeric designation: the Hampton Legion, the Holcombe Legion, the Palmetto Sharpshooters and Manigault's Battalion.

Regiments and battalions in each service—infantry, cavalry and artillery—were given sequential numerical designations in 1861. All three services duplicated the use of numbers for regiments throughout the war. Numbering of battalions, on the other hand, was different. There was some duplication in the use of numbers among the three services during the first year of the war, and gaps in available information suggest that other numbers were probably skipped over and not used at all. In 1861, for example, infantry battalions were numbered the 1st, 3rd and 5th; cavalry battalions were designated the 1st, 2nd, 3rd and 4th; and artillery battalions used the designations 1st, 2nd and 3rd. At or shortly after the reorganization of the armies in 1862, all battalions in the state, regardless of service branch, seem to have been incorporated into a system of numerical designation that both avoided duplication of numbering among the various branches and started the numbering sequence all over again. There is, however, no documentation for this theory; it is simply an observation. At the reorganization, some battalions became full regiments, others remained unchanged and a few ceased to exist altogether. After that, the infantry battalions, some old and others new, were the 1st, 2nd, 3rd, 5th, 6th, 7th, 9th, 11th and 13th. The cavalry used the 4th, 8th, 10th, 12th, 14th, 16th, 17th and 19th. Artillery had the 15th and 18th Battalions. The artillery also carried the 3rd Battalion, which appears to duplicate the 3rd Infantry Battalion, but the artillery battalion, which failed in an effort to become a regiment, probably retained its designation for that reason.

An officer could lose his commission in several ways. Many, some excellent and some downright incompetent, were simply not re-elected at the reorganization of the Confederate armies in the spring of 1862 and were consequently dropped from the rolls of their respective organizations.

Such officers were then required to serve elsewhere unless they were overage or otherwise exempt. An officer could resign his commission by tendering a letter of resignation to the secretary of war through his commanding officer, who would either recommend approval or, rarely, denial and forward the letter up the chain of command. Most officers who resigned did so because chronic or severe illness, advanced age or the effect of wounds left them unable to perform their duties. A few resigned because they realized they lacked the intellect or leadership ability needed for their position. Confederate law gave an officer the option of resigning his commission if he held certain offices in the civil government, and some individuals resigned on those grounds. A few officers were cashiered or discharged by court martial, usually for drunkenness on duty or some other crime. The Invalid Corps was created by the Confederate Congress on February 17, 1864, to retain competent officers who wished to remain in the service but who had been disabled for further duty in the field. Many officers were retired to the Invalid Corps after approval from a medical examiners' board upon documentation by means of a surgeon's certificate. These men were usually assigned to light duty as officers in camps of instruction, at military posts or as enrolling officers.

This work will emphasize the company, battalion and regimental organization of South Carolina troops during the War Between the States. To obtain proper perspective, however, it is also necessary to present a basic outline of the relationship of battalions and regiments to higher levels of organization—brigades, divisions, corps and armies, as well as departments and their sub-units of military districts and subdivisions. This work gives a cursory overview of this relationship so readers can relate regiments and battalions to each other in their respective higher levels of organization. An excellent, and quite exhaustive, review of these higher levels of organization can be found in *Compendium of the Confederate Armies, South Carolina and Georgia* by Stewart Sifakis.

This work presents a history of South Carolina's military organizations in the War Between the States in four volumes. Within each volume, the order of presentation is: first, infantry, followed by cavalry and artillery. Volume I discusses those organizations whose men came from the Lowcountry and the Pee Dee; Volume II discusses those whose men came from the Midlands; Volume III discusses those whose men came from the Upstate; and Volume IV discusses those units that drew from all over the state, militia, reserves and miscellaneous organizations. Within each volume, each organization is set forth and described in numeric order—the 1st Infantry Regiment, for example. This order generally follows that of the *Compiled Service Records*, but, for the sake of clarity, there are exceptions. In numeric order, regiments are listed first, followed by battalions, squadrons and, finally, independent companies. The presentation of each regiment and battalion follows the same pattern. First, it gives a history of the organization of each unit followed by a brief wartime biography of each field officer (colonels, lieutenant colonels and majors). Next, it presents a synopsis of the origins and commanders (captains) of each company. Finally, it summarizes the brigade affiliations and the major movements and engagements of each regiment or battalion.

Unit Designation	When Organized	Under What Authority	Initial Enlistment
1st Regiment, SCV (Gregg's 6-month Regiment)	01/08/61	2	6 months
1st Regiment, South Carolina Infantry, Regulars	01/28/61	3 and 4	3 years
1st Battalion, South Carolina Artillery, Regulars	01/28/61	3 and 4	3 years
DeSaussure's Cavalry Squadron, Regulars	01/28/61	3 and 4	3 years
1st SCV Infantry (Hagood's)	04/12/61	1	12 months
2nd SCV Infantry	04/09/61	1	12 months
3rd SCV Infantry	04/14/61	1	12 months
4th SCV Infantry	04/14/61	1	12 months
5th SCV Infantry	04/13/61	1	12 months
6th SCV Infantry	04/11/61	1	12 months
7th SCV Infantry	04/15/61	1	12 months
8th SCV Infantry	04/14/61	1	12 months
9th SCV Infantry	07/12/61 to date from 04/08/61	1	12 months
10th SCV Infantry	~05/31/61	1	12 months
11th SCV Infantry	05/20/61	1	12 months
12th SCV Infantry	08/30/61	7	war
13th SCV Infantry	09/04/61	7	war
14th SCV Infantry	09/10/61	7	war
15th SCV Infantry	09/10/61	7	war
Gregg's (reorganized) 1st SCV Infantry	08–09/61	8	war
Orr's Regiment Rifles	07/20/61	8	war
5th Battalion Infantry	12/10/61	8	war
1st Battalion Cavalry	10/31/61	25	war

Unit Designation	When Organized	Under What Authority	Initial Enlistment
2nd Battalion Artillery	10/61	1	war
3rd Battalion Artillery	07–12/61	7	war
Manigault's Battalion	12/61	17	war
Chesterfield Light Artillery	08/25/61	—	war
16th SCV Infantry	12/12/61	10	12 months
17th SCV Infantry	12/18/61	6	12 months
Holcombe Legion	11/21/61	22	12 months
Hatch's Battalion Coast Rangers	09/61	—	mixed
3rd Battalion Infantry	12/04/61	10	12 months
Pee Dee Legion, South Carolina Militia	12/60–01/61	—	12 months
1st (Martin's) Cavalry Regiment, South Carolina Militia	11/61	2	90 days
4th Brigade, South Carolina Militia	1861	2	—
Stono Scouts	11/10/61	—	—
W.F. Percival's Company	11/61	—	—
South Carolina College Cadets	01/19/61	—	—
German Light Artillery	08/22/61	—	5 years
Beaufort Volunteer Artillery	05/61	1	12 months
Bonneau's Artillery	10/01/61	—	—
Calhoun Light Artillery	~04/26/61	—	~90 days
Santee Light Artillery	10/30/61	prob. 17	war
Macbeth Artillery	09/16/61	—	war
Marion Artillery	09/61	—	—
Washington (Hart's) Artillery	05/18/61	6	12 months
1st Regiment Charleston Guards	—	—	—
1st Regiment Reserves, South Carolina Militia	11/11/61	—	—
A.H.Boykin's Cavalry Troop	06/26/61	—	war
J.G.Harlan's Company	12/30/61	—	—
Lipscomb's Cavalry Troop	12/61	—	—
St. James Mounted Riflemen, Company A	04/15/61	9	war
Marion Men of Winyah	05/05/61	—	—
Trenholm's Squadron	09/09/61	—	12 months
Battalion South Carolina Cadets	01/28/61	24	—
6th Battalion Infantry	05/29/62	prob. 18	war

Unit Designation	When Organized	Under What Authority	Initial Enlistment
18th SCV Infantry	01/02/62	10	12 months
19th SCV Infantry	01/03/62	10	12 months
20th SCV Infantry	01/11/62	10	12 months
21st SCV Infantry	11/12/61	10	12 months
22nd SCV Infantry	12/61	10	12 months
23rd SCV Infantry	11/15/61	10, 39	mixed
24th SCV Infantry	12/61–04/62	10, 11	war
25th SCV Infantry	07/22/62	11 and 38	war
26th SCV Infantry	09/09/62	20	mixed
27th SCV Infantry	09/30/63	21	war
2nd Regiment Rifles	04/27/62	35	war
2nd Battalion Sharpshooters	09/01/62	prob. 10	—
4th (13th) Battalion Infantry	04/21/62	36	3 years or war
15th Battalion Artillery Regulars	summer 1861	37	3 years
18th Battalion Artillery	05/01/62	—	war
Palmetto Sharpshooters	04/16/62	23	2 years or war
1st Regiment Artillery Regulars	03/25/62	5	war
2nd Regiment Artillery	04/12/62	34	war
1st Regiment Cavalry	06/25/62	26	war
2nd Regiment Cavalry	08/22/62	27	war
3rd Regiment Cavalry	08/62	29	war
4th Regiment Cavalry	12/16/62	30	war
5th Regiment Cavalry	01/18/63	31	war
6th Regiment Cavalry	11/01/62	32	war
7th Regiment Cavalry	03/18/64	33	war
7th Battalion Infantry	02/22/62	19	war
1st (Charleston) Battalion Infantry	02/17/62	15	12 months
1st Battalion Sharpshooters	06/62	16	—
11th Battalion Infantry	~02/22/62	10	12 months
9th Battalion Infantry	01–03/62	prob. 10	12 months
1st (14th) Battalion Cavalry	01/62	—	12 months
3rd (4th) Battalion Cavalry	01–02/62	prob. 10	12 months
2nd (10th) Battalion Cavalry	01/19/62	—	12 months
6th (17th) Battalion Cavalry	03/62	—	mixed
Brooks Guard Artillery	01/28/62	17	2 years and 3 months
Inglis Light Artillery	03/20/62	17	war

Unit Designation	When Organized	Under What Authority	Initial Enlistment
Palmetto Light Battery	~04/08/62	—	—
German Artillery	02/12/62	prob. 10	—
Gist Guards Artillery	02/62	prob. 10	3 years
McQueen Light Artillery	04/14/62	—	—
Lafayette Artillery	03/13/62	prob. 10	12 months
12th Battalion (4th Squadron Cavalry)	01/01/62	—	mixed
16th (6th) Battalion Cavalry	07/21/62	prob. 10 and 11	war
19th Battalion Cavalry	12/20/64	—	war
Pee Dee Artillery	03/62	—	war
Washington (Walter's) Artillery	02/20/62	prob. 10 or 11	3 years or war
Waccamaw Light Artillery	01/20/62	prob. 10	war
Ferguson's Light Battery	04/62	—	—
Edisto Artillery	03/19/62	—	war
B.E. Dickson's Battery	03/19/62	—	war
Carolina Artillery	04/12/62	—	war
Silverton Artillery	04/09/62	—	2 years or war
Willis's Battery	spring 1862	—	—
S.D. Lee's Battery	~05/12/61	—	—
South Carolina Reserve Regiments	11/62	12, 40	90 days
South Carolina State Troops	08/04/63	14	6 months
South Carolina Reserve Battalions	09/64	13	war
South Carolina Junior Reserves	summer 1864	41	—
Brooks Foreign Battalion	10/10/64	—	—
Dunlop's Battalion Sharpshooters	05/03/62	—	—
8th Battalion (2nd Battalion Reserves) Cavalry	05/30/62	28	war
St. Peters Guards	1861	9	—
German Hussars	1861	prob. 9	—
Rebel Troop	01/17/62	prob. 10	—
Charleston Light Dragoons	04/61	prob. 10	—
Yeadon Rangers	07/27/62	—	war
Whitner's Troop	—	—	—
Hough's Company	01/01/62	—	war

Unit Designation	When Organized	Under What Authority	Initial Enlistment
Ripley Rangers	04/03/62	—	war
A.C. Earle's Company	04/15/62	—	war
M.J. Kirk's Squadron	07/11/62	—	war
Keitt's Mounted Riflemen	06/10/63	—	—
E.M. Boykin's Squadron	11/05/62	—	—
Brooks Infantry Partisan Rangers	07/14/62	17	war

1. South Carolina legislature act of December 17, 1860.
2. South Carolina Convention resolution of January 1, 1861.
3. South Carolina Convention resolution of December 31, 1860.
4. South Carolina legislature act of January 28, 1861.
5. South Carolina legislature act of December 1861.
6. President Davis authorized the Hampton Legion on April 27, 1861.
7. President Davis called for three thousand men to enlist for the duration of the war on June 30, 1861.
8. President Davis called for two regiments to enlist for the duration of the war on July 1, 1861.
9. Special resolution of the South Carolina Convention in 1861 calling for twenty-one cavalry companies to serve until the end of the legislative session.
10. South Carolina legislature resolutions of November 1861 and December 7, 1861, and Governor Pickens's calls on November 11, 1861, and December 9, 1861, for special local defense troops.
11. Confederate Congress act of February 28, 1862.
12. South Carolina Executive Council created two corps of reserves in the summer of 1862.
13. Confederate Conscription Act of February 17, 1864.
14. Confederate Congress act of August 21 1861, and Confederate Congress act of October 13, 1862 and President Davis's call for troops.
15. Arose from a failed scheme of John Pemberton to raise a battalion of sharpshooters in late 1861 and early 1862.
16. Primarily compulsory draft and a few volunteers.
17. Special permission from the Confederate War Department.
18. A series of calls in 1862 (February 2, 21 and 28, 1862, and March 5, 1862) for eighteen thousand South Carolinians to enlist for the duration of the war.
19. Confederate Congress called for twenty-five hundred men for the duration of the war.

20. Consolidation of the 6th and 9th Infantry Battalions.
21. Consolidation of the 1st (Charleston) Battalion and the 1st Battalion Sharpshooters.
22. Governor Pickens authorized the Holcombe Legion in the fall of 1861.
23. Act of Congress and permission of the secretary of war.
24. South Carolina legislature created the South Carolina Military Academy (The Citadel and The Arsenal) as well as the Battalion State Cadets.
25. Governor Pickens called up the 1st Battalion in the fall of 1861.
26. Augmentation of the 1st Battalion Cavalry.
27. Alignment of the Hampton Legion Cavalry Battalion with the 4th (3rd) Cavalry Battalion, Lipscomb's Company and A.H. Boykin's Company.
28. Consolidation of eight independent companies.
29. Consolidation of the 8th Cavalry Battalion (2nd Battalion Reserves) with three independent companies.
30. Augmentation of the 10th and 12th Cavalry Battalions with B.H. Rutledge's Company and Thomas Pinckney's Company.
31. Augmentation of the 14th and 17th Cavalry Battalions with Harlan's Company and Whilden's Company.
32. Augmentation of the 16th (6th) Cavalry Battalion with three companies.
33. Augmentation of the Holcombe Legion Cavalry Battalion with Tucker's Squadron, Trenholm's Squadron and E. Boykin's Squadron.
34. Augmentation of the 2nd (Lamar's) Artillery Battalion with six companies when the secretary of war called for additional troops on February 2, 1862.
35. Augmentation of the 5th Battalion Infantry.
36. Abatement of the 4th Regiment Infantry.
37. Formed from DeSaussure's Cavalry Squadron Regulars.
38. Augmentation of the 11th Battalion Infantry.
39. Augmentation of Hatch's Battalion Coast Rangers.
40. Confederate Conscription Act of September 17, 1862, and South Carolina Executive Council resolutions of April 23, 1862 and November 7, 1862.
41. South Carolina Militia Laws, not Confederate States troops.

1.

The 1st Regiment, South Carolina Infantry Regulars

The 1st Regiment, South Carolina Infantry Regulars, was also called the 1st Regiment, South Carolina (Regulars) Infantry; the 1st Butler's South Carolina Infantry; 1st South Carolina Infantry Regulars or Enlisted Men; the 1st Regulars; Butler's regiment; and the 1st Regiment Regular Infantry, Confederate States Provisional Army.[1] In May 1863, the regiment became the 3rd Regiment, South Carolina Artillery; it was also called the 3rd Heavy Artillery Regiment. Because of its status as the original infantry regiment of the South Carolina Regular Army, the word volunteer was not part of its name. On December 31, 1860, the South Carolina Secession Convention passed a resolution authorizing the creation of one or two regiments of regulars, each of which would consist of 640 enlisted men who would serve for twelve months. Governor Pickens was to appoint company and field officers, and the Senate was to confirm the appointments. With only one exception, every captain the governor chose had either been an officer in the Mexican War, or had attended West Point and served as an officer in the United States Army.[2] The South Carolina General Assembly passed an act on January 28, 1861, modifying the Secession Convention's resolution. This act changed the term of enlistment to three years; it also authorized the formation of the South Carolina State Army, Regular State Service, to comprise one infantry regiment, one artillery battalion of five companies and one squadron of cavalry. Anderson's regiment of infantry, Ripley's battalion of artillery and DeSaussure's squadron of cavalry soon became the three original components of the South Carolina Regular Army. Thus it was that Butler's regiment began its three-year enlistment as part of the South Carolina Regular Army under an act of the General Assembly dated January 28, 1861.

Butler's regiment began its service with ten companies numbered one through ten.[3] The regiment adopted the more common method of designating companies alphabetically sometime before it entered Confederate service on May 18, 1861. At that time, two companies were lost. The *CSR* shows that the regiment mustered in Confederate service on May 18, 1861, at Sullivan's Island with eight companies and that Companies I and K were added in early 1862; the *Memory Roll* indicates that only Company K became part of the regiment after it mustered in Confederate service. It is possible that both sources are correct. Company I was created about January 1, 1862, though there might easily have been a different Company I early in 1861 before the regiment entered Confederate service. The possibility also exists, however, that this earlier Company I was not mustered in Confederate service with the others and was finally replaced by a new Company I in January 1862. Other changes were probably made in May 1861 as well, since the *CSR* indicates that only five of the original companies could be identified after the regiment enlisted in Confederate service. The *CSR* and the *Keowee Courier* named five company commanders from the original regiment who cannot be associated with a company after May 1861.[4] Butler's regiment was organized as an infantry unit but served as a heavy artillery regiment until the evacuation of Charleston in February 1865.[5]

On February 6, 1863, Senator James L. Orr introduced a bill before the Confederate Senate that would redesignate this regiment as the 2nd Regiment South Carolina Artillery.[6] The Senate and the House passed it, but the president vetoed it.[7] The House failed to override the veto, and the bill died.[8] The regiment was redesignated the 3rd Regiment South Carolina Artillery in May; people, however, persisted in calling it at various times the 1st or the 2nd Regiment, South Carolina Artillery, a situation that both confused the public and provoked the officers, who preferred the designation of either 1st Infantry or 3rd Artillery.[9] In January 1864, there was serious disaffection among some of the men because they believed their enlistment expired that month; a few, whose conduct was mutinous, were confined.[10] Even so, on February 8, 1864, P.G.T. Beauregard asked the men to re-enlist; most of them complied.[11]

FIELD OFFICERS

Richard Heron Anderson of Sumter District was appointed the first colonel of the regiment and was confirmed by the Senate on January 28, 1861. An 1842 graduate of West Point, Anderson served in the United States Army until February 16, 1861.[12] He was promoted to brigadier general on July 19, and in February 1862, he was given a brigade comprising the 4th, 5th, 6th and 9th Regiments, SCV.

Barnard Elliott Bee was appointed the first lieutenant colonel and was confirmed by the Senate on January 28, 1861. The *Memory Roll* incorrectly shows him as the second lieutenant colonel. Bee was promoted to brigadier general on June 17 and was mortally wounded on July 21 while in command of the 3rd Brigade, Army of the Shenandoah, at First Manassas. Bee died on July 22, 1861. He is buried at St. Paul's Episcopal Church in Pendleton, South Carolina.

John Gore Dunovant, a Chester native, had served as both captain in the 10th Infantry Regiment, United States Army, and major in the South Carolina Militia.[13] He was appointed the first major of the 1st Regiment and was confirmed by the Senate on January 19, 1861.[14] Dunovant was promoted to colonel on July 22 upon Anderson's promotion to brigadier general.[15] As Federal troops moved across John's Island on June 10 and June 11, 1862, in preparation for the assault on Secessionville, Dunovant was intoxicated. The general in charge of Confederate forces on John's Island at the time, Nathan G. Evans, brought charges against Dunovant, possibly to deflect criticism from his own culpability in failing to attack the Federals as they marched in an exposed position across the island. A subsequent court-martial found Dunovant guilty of drunkenness and dismissed him from the service in November 1862. The record is slightly conflicting in that it indicates that the adjutant and inspector general of the Confederate States of America dismissed Dunovant on November 7, 1862, and that Governor Pickens dismissed him on the eighth. Dunovant was given command of the 5th Regiment, South Carolina Cavalry, on July 28, 1863, and was promoted to brigadier general on August 22, 1864. He was killed on October 1, 1864, along Vaughn Road, and is buried in a family cemetery near Chester, South Carolina. Johnson Hagood wrote that Dunovant "was an excellent officer, save for this unfortunate failing."[16]

William Butler was promoted to lieutenant colonel on July 21, a date also shown as July 22, 1861, replacing Lieutenant Colonel Bee.[17] Butler was promoted to colonel on November 7, a date also shown as November 8, 1862, when Dunovant was dismissed. On May 18, 1864, the *Edgefield Advertiser* reported incorrectly that Butler had been promoted to brigadier general, stating: "No appointment in the war has been more fully merited."[18] Butler remained in command of the 1st Regiment until March 1865, when he was detached from the 1st Regiment and given command of Rhett's Brigade.[19] He was wounded in the abdomen in North Carolina, in 1865, and his name appears on the roll of parolees at Greensboro, but he was detached from the 1st Regiment and was commanding Rhett's Brigade then. William Butler was the older brother of Major General Matthew C. Butler, a cavalry commander during the war.

John Calhoun Simkins of Edgefield was promoted to major on July 22, 1861, when Dunovant was named colonel.[20] With prior service as an officer in the Mexican War, Simkins was captain of Company B at the time he was promoted to major. He was promoted to lieutenant colonel on November 8, 1862, and was in command of the artillery at Battery Wagner when he was killed during the Federal assault there on July 18, 1863.[21] Shell Point, a new battery near Fort Johnson on James Island, was renamed in Simkins's memory on August 21.[22] He is buried in the cemetery of Trinity Episcopal Church in Abbeville. Simkins "was a gentleman of the very first tone, a patriot of the very purest type, and a soldier of the very highest mettle."[23]

Thomas McDonald Baker, a physician from Claremont in Sumter District, was promoted from captain of Company F to major on November 8, 1862. Baker had served as an officer in the Palmetto Regiment during the Mexican War and as a brigadier general in the South Carolina Militia.[24] He was named lieutenant colonel on July 18, 1863, to replace Simkins.[25] Baker had been granted sick leave on April 19, 1863, and the leave was extended for thirty days on December 12. Though promoted to lieutenant colonel, he never returned to the regiment to serve in his new rank. Baker died of tuberculosis at the home of his father-in-law, F.J. Moses, on January 20, 1864.[26] His obituary reads in part: "As an officer, his gallant bearing and impartiality endeared him to his command, and officers and men regaled him with affection and respect."[27]

Robert DeTreville Jr., a Charleston lawyer and former lieutenant governor, was captain of Company C until he was promoted to major with rank to date from July 18, 1863. About July 6, 1864, he was named lieutenant colonel with rank from January 20.[28] On April 23, 1864, DeTreville received a three-month suspension for being absent without leave. He was killed on March 16, 1865, while in command of the regiment at the battle of Averasboro, North Carolina. Shortly after DeTreville's death, Brigadier General W.B. Taliaferro called him one of "our best officers."[29]

Warren Adams, previously captain of Company H, was promoted to major about July 6, 1864, with rank from January 20, 1864.[30] During the evacuation of Cheraw in 1865, Adams was wounded in the chest while engaged in a rear guard action on the east bank of the Pee Dee River.[31] He was wounded again in the left breast, probably at Averasboro, and was admitted to General Hospital #11 in Charlotte on March 18. The *CSR* indicates that Adams was promoted to lieutenant colonel on March 18, 1863, though 1865 is more likely the correct year. He was paroled at Greensboro in 1865.

Thomas Abraham Huguenin of Beaufort was captain of Company A until he was promoted to major on March 16, 1865.[32] Huguenin graduated from The Citadel in 1859 and remained there as a math professor. John Mitchel, captain of Company I of the 1st Artillery Regiment Regulars and commander of Fort Sumter, was killed at Fort Sumter on July 20, 1864. Captain Huguenin arrived that evening to assume command of the fort and remained there until February 1865.[33] Huguenin also served as acting adjutant for the regiment. Slightly wounded on four occasions, Huguenin was paroled at Greensboro. John Johnson, the engineer of many of Charleston's defensive works, wrote that Huguenin was "a well-trained and gallant soldier."[34] He was also described as "an able and gallant officer."[35]

COMPANIES

The ten companies listed below were attached to the 1st Regiment in February 1861:[36]

Company #1: Captain L.W. O'Bannon
Company #2: Captain William Butler (captain of Company A after May 1861)
Company #3: Captain J.L. Corley (captain of Company C after May 1861)
Company #4: Captain B.F. Sloan
Company #5: Captain J.C. Simkins (captain of Company B after May 1861)
Company #6: Captain Thomas M. Baker (captain of Company F after May 1861)
Company #7: Captain S.W. Ferguson
Company #8: Captain Sebastian Sumter
Company #9: Captain A.E. Latimer
Company #10: Captain George T. Andrews (captain of Company E after May 1861)

The following are the ten companies attached to the 1st Regiment after May 1861:

Company A was originally Company #2 and was also known as Company B before the regiment mustered in Confederate service at Sullivan's Island on May 18, 1861. After that time, the company was designated Company A. William Butler was confirmed by the Senate as captain of the second company of regulars on January 19, 1861, and was promoted to lieutenant colonel on July 22, 1861.[37] The same day, Thomas Abraham Huguenin was named captain to replace Butler.[38] Huguenin was promoted to major on March 16, 1865. L.W. Perrin, previously an officer in Companies C, D, E and H of the 1st Regiment, was promoted to captain between March 16 and March 22. Perrin was captain of Company A when he was captured at Bentonville. He was sent first to New Bern and was transferred on April 10 to Hart's Island in New York Harbor. On April 15, he was sent to Fort Delaware for two months and was released on June 17.[39] The men of this company came from as far away as Memphis, Tennessee, and Charlotte, North Carolina. Most, however, were from Edgefield, Laurens, Chesterfield, Lancaster, Columbia, Sullivan's Island, Charleston, Darlington, Spartanburg, Abbeville and Calhoun.

Company B was organized on March 4, 1861. The company, originally Company #5, was also designated Company E before May 1861.[40] It mustered in Confederate service on May 17, 1861, at Sullivan's Island. John C. Simkins was appointed captain of the fifth company of regulars—hence the original designation of Company E—and was confirmed by the Senate on January 19, 1861.[41] Simkins was promoted to major on July 22, and William J. Davis was named captain the same day.[42] Davis was placed under arrest in August 1862 for charges not specified in the *CSR* and resigned on January 19, 1863, with his trial pending. J. Hamilton Warley, previously first lieutenant of Company A, was promoted to captain of Company B on February 1, 1863, with rank from January 19. The last captain of Company B, Warley was admitted to General Hospital #3 at Greensboro, on March 19, 1865. Though he was probably wounded at Averasboro, neither the *CSR* nor the *Memory Roll* indicates the reason for hospitalization. The men of Company B were primarily from Greenville, Columbia and Anderson, though a few came from other areas around the state.

Company C, originally Company #3 and also called Company C before May 1861, was organized on March 12, 1861, and mustered in Confederate service on May 17 at Sullivan's Island.[43] W.D. DeSaussure was appointed captain of the third company and was confirmed by the Senate on January 19, 1861. Governor Pickens was then making recommendations to the Senate for officers in the Regular Army but had not yet indicated who would serve in which branch. DeSaussure was confirmed as major of the Cavalry Squadron on January 28 and left Company C soon afterward.[44] J. Laurens Corley was captain of the company by February 16 but failed to report for duty.[45] A.S. Salley wrote that Corley's name appears on the muster roll for April 30, 1861, but not on the one for May 17.[46] Robert DeTreville Jr. became the third captain on May 15 and was promoted to major in 1863, the rank dating from July 18. Bartlett "Bart" J. Witherspoon, previously first lieutenant of Company F, replaced DeTreville as captain on July 18. Ill during the surrender at Greensboro,

Witherspoon was paroled on May 3, 1865. L.W. Perrin commanded the company as lieutenant, but was never promoted to captain. Perrin later became captain of Company A. James Harrington Powe, MD, raised Company C and served in the company with the rank of second lieutenant in 1861. Powe served as an officer in several companies of the 1st Regiment and was captain of Company D in 1863. The men of Company C came from South Carolina, Virginia and Memphis, Tennessee.

Company D, the Calhoun Light Infantry, was known as Company D from its organization in March 1861. The company mustered in Confederate service on May 24, 1861, at Sullivan's Island. Charles "Charley" Thomson Haskell Jr., a Citadel graduate and one of several brothers from Abbeville who distinguished themselves during the war, was appointed the first captain.[47] His commission dated from May 18, 1861, but he was probably in command of the company even before that time. A.S. Salley wrote that Haskell was promoted from first lieutenant of Company B to captain of Company D on May 15, 1861.[48] During the Federal assault on the south end of Morris Island on July 10, 1863, Haskell was standing in a rifle pit shouting encouragement to his men when he was pierced by nine balls and killed.[49] His last words were, "Tell my mother I died for her and my country."[50] A battery at Legare's Point on the east side of James Island was named in his memory. The same James Harrington Powe who helped raise Company C also served in Company D, Company F and Company H from 1861 to 1864, rising from second lieutenant to captain. The *Memory Roll* records that Powe was named assistant quartermaster general of South Carolina with the rank of major in April 1861. On July 18, 1863, an exploding shell at Battery Wagner hurled a plank at Lieutenant Powe, wounding him in the right arm and leg and throwing pieces of wood in all directions. One piece struck him in the neck hard enough to fracture his skull behind the left ear, resulting in paralysis on the right side.[51] Powe was promoted to captain of Company D on August 4, 1863, with rank dating from July 10. He received a thirty-day furlough four days after his promotion, but the severity of his wounds kept him from returning to active duty. Powe retired to the Invalid Corps on October 19, 1864. Thus, though Powe was promoted to captain of Company D, he never actually assumed command at that rank. He did, however, survive the war and lived until August 1, 1898. Duff G. Calhoun was the third and last captain of Company D. Calhoun was promoted from first lieutenant of Company E to captain of Company D on October 19, 1864. He was wounded at Averasboro on March 16, 1865, and was admitted to General Hospital #3 at Greensboro on March 19.[52] The men of Company D were from South Carolina, Memphis and Nashville, Tennessee, and Georgia.

Company E was originally Company #10 and was also known as Company K and Captain Black's Company before May 1861. It was organized on March 4, 1861, and it mustered in Confederate service on May 17 at Sullivan's Island. On January 1, 1862, Company E was divided to form two companies: E and K. Though not so stated in the *Memory Roll*, George T. Andrews was appointed the company's first captain. On March 26, 1861, Andrews left the company on detached service and lost his commission, probably when the company entered Confederate service. On July 24, 1863, while serving as a private in Company G, Andrews was killed at Battery Wagner. The second captain of Company E, John L. Black, joined the company on March 6, 1861, but the records are unclear as to the precise date of his appointment. Black resigned his commission sometime between August 31 and October 23, 1861. Most likely, this is the same John Logan Black who was elected lieutenant colonel in command of the newly created 1st Battalion, South Carolina Cavalry, on October 31, 1861. R. Press Smith Jr. was promoted to captain of Company E on October 23, 1861.[53] Smith was wounded at Averasboro on March 16, 1865, and was admitted to General Hospital #3 at Greensboro on the nineteenth.[54] The *Memory Roll* erroneously indicates that both John C. Simkins and Charles T. Haskell served as captains of this company. Company E drew men from throughout the state, especially from Charleston and its environs.

Company F was originally Company #10 and was also called Company F before May 1861. The company was organized on March 2, 1861, and it mustered in Confederate service on May 17 at Sullivan's Island. Thomas McDonald Baker was appointed the first captain, and the Senate confirmed the appointment on January 19, 1861. Baker took command of the company on March 1 and was promoted to major on November 8, 1862. Charlestonian Burgh Smith Burnet, also spelled incorrectly as Burnett in the *CSR*, succeeded Baker as captain on November 8. Before then, Burnet had served as an officer in Companies C, E and H. Burnet was mortally wounded in the right thigh on March 16, 1865, at the battle of Averasboro, and died of his wounds on March 29 at High Point. Both Kirkland and the *Roll of the Dead* give the date of his death as March 28. The men of Company F were from across the state and from Memphis, Tennessee.

Company G was known as Company G before May 1861. It mustered in Confederate service on June 6, 1861, at North and South Islands, near Georgetown. The first captain, Robert Martin, was the only one of the original captains in the South Carolina Regular Army who had neither been an officer in the Mexican War nor attended West Point. Even so, Governor Pickens described him as "a very intelligent and thorough officer of great merit."[55] Martin resigned on October 1, 1861, a date also shown in the records as October 7. Jacob Valentine, previously first lieutenant in Company F, was promoted to captain on October 1, 1861, a date also shown as October 8. Valentine was wounded in the groin at Fort Moultrie on November 28, 1863.[56] He was still suffering from the wound in May 1864, and he retired to the Invalid Corps on January 12, 1865.[57] Pierre Bacot, previously first lieutenant in Company K, was promoted to captain of Company G around January 12, 1865. Bacot was wounded in the knee at Averasboro on March 16, 1865, and was admitted to General Hospital #3 at Greensboro three days later.[58] The men of Company G came from all over South Carolina and from as far away as Memphis and Baltimore.

Company H was also Company H before May 1861. The company mustered in Confederate service on May 24, 1861, at Sullivan's Island. W.D. Smith was appointed captain and the Senate confirmed him on January 19, 1861.[59] Smith was originally appointed captain of the first company of regulars, but these appointments were generic in nature, and most of the original captains did not command the company to which they were first appointed. First Lieutenant Warren Adams was appointed captain on May 18, 1861. Slightly wounded at Battery Wagner on July 18, 1863, Adams was promoted to major on January 20, 1864. Mitchell King Jr., previously an officer in Companies A, B, C, D and E, as well as adjutant of the regiment, was promoted to captain of Company H on January 20, 1864. King was captured on the picket line at Bentonville on March 22, 1865.[60] He was taken to New Bern and on April 10 was sent to Hart's Island in New York Harbor. On April 15, 1865, King was taken to Fort Delaware, where he was released on June 17, 1865. Most of the men of Company H were from the upper part of South Carolina; a few were from Memphis.

Company I was organized about January 1, 1862, when the number of companies was increased from eight to ten. Probably, however, a different Company I existed before May 1861 and was disbanded when the regiment entered Confederate service. William "Poss" T. Tatom of Abbeville, previously a first lieutenant in Company D, was promoted to captain of Company I on January 1, 1862.[61] One day in the spring of 1863, Tatom appeared drunk at the office of the commanding general. Subsequently, he submitted a written pledge of abstention but soon broke it by becoming intoxicated while serving as officer of the day. Informed that charges of drunkenness would be brought unless he resigned, Tatom complied on June 29 and wrote, "My position in this regiment is embarrassing in the extreme." During the night assault on Battery Wagner on July 18, Tatom was killed on the parapet of the battery while leading a few men in a charge.[62] The record shows that his resignation was revoked on July 29, 1863.[63] A battery at Point of Pines on Lighthouse Creek on the east side of James Island was subsequently named in Tatom's memory.[64] K.G. Billings, previously a lieutenant in Companies A, F and G, was promoted to captain of Company I on July 18, 1863. In September, Billings requested a transfer to the Quartermaster's Department, but it was not approved, and he remained with the company.[65] Billings tendered his resignation on December 22, 1864, because he had recently been elected commissioner in equity, an exempted office. His resignation was accepted on January 7, 1865. Jacob Youngblood, who had been wounded at Sullivan's Island on September 8, 1863, replaced Billings as captain. Youngblood was paroled at Greensboro at the rank of captain. The men of Company I were from across the state, especially Anderson District, and from Georgia as well.

Company K, known as Rivers's Battery, was formed about January 1, 1862, when Company E split into Companies E and K.[66] Constantine H. Rivers, previously a first lieutenant in Company E, was promoted to captain of the new company then.[67] Rivers was paroled on April 28, 1865, while in a Greensboro hospital. Company K men came from throughout the state.

BRIGADE AFFILIATIONS

Butler's regiment was part of R.G.M. Dunovant's Brigade in March 1861. From January 1861 to December 1864, the regiment was assigned successively to Charleston Harbor, the Department of South Carolina, the Department of South Carolina and Georgia and the Department of South Carolina, Georgia and Florida.[68] In late November 1864, it was attached to Brigadier General Roswell Ripley's Brigade.[69] A.M. Rhett's Brigade was formed on December 28, 1864, from the 1st Regiment, South Carolina Artillery (Regulars); the 2nd Regiment, South Carolina Artillery; and the 1st Regiment, South Carolina Infantry (Regulars).[70] By late January 1865, Rhett's Brigade comprised the 1st Regiment, South Carolina Artillery (Regulars); the 1st Regiment, South Carolina Infantry (Regulars); the 19th Battalion, South Carolina Cavalry; the 1st and 19th Regiments, South Carolina Militia; Parker's Battery; the Orleans Battery; and a detachment of the 32nd Georgia.[71] By the end of March, it was made up of the original South Carolina Regular Army—1st Regiment, South Carolina Artillery (Regulars); the 1st Regiment, South Carolina Infantry (Regulars); and J.J. Lucas's 15th Battalion, South Carolina Artillery.[72] William Butler commanded the brigade after Rhett's capture on March 15, 1865.[73]

MAJOR MOVEMENTS AND ENGAGEMENTS

The 1st South Carolina Infantry Regulars served on the coast from January 1861 to February 1865. The various companies functioned primarily as artillery, though occasionally as infantry, and some companies often carried out detached duty elsewhere. The regiment was stationed at Sullivan's Island in January 1861. Company F was stationed there as early as January 16, and it engaged the enemy as artillery on April 12 and April 13.[74] Most of the other companies were engaged in various batteries on Sullivan's Island during the bombardment of Fort Sumter on April 12 and April 13. Company A was based at the Five Gun Battery as artillery during the engagement with Fort Sumter.[75] Company E, then designated Company K, was detached on March 3 for artillery service and sent to the Enfilade Battery on Sullivan's Island. There it saw action on the twelfth and thirteenth. Company G was sent to the Mortar Battery at Mount Pleasant as artillery on April 2 and was engaged there on April 12 and April 13.[76] Company G returned to Sullivan's Island on April 18. In late April, Company E was sent to the Moffit Channel Battery on Sullivan's Island, but by May, it had been transferred to the Moultrie house. In June 1861, all but three companies remained on Sullivan's Island. Company D was stationed at Fort Palmetto on Cole's Island. Company G was on South Island at Winyah Bay, where it had been since April 24. Company H was at Fort Pickens on Battery Island, where it had been since May 29. Company G returned to Sullivan's Island from Georgetown on August 8. From about September 14 to November 20, Companies B, C, D, E, F and G were stationed at Camp Barnard E. Bee on Edisto Island. Company A and probably Company F were stationed at the batteries on North Edisto River, and Company H was at South Edisto River. On November 19 and November 20, the regiment returned to Fort Moultrie on Sullivan's Island. Company E was stationed at Battery Beauregard in November 1861. Company F was based at Fort Moultrie from November 1, 1861 until the spring of 1864.

The regiment was still stationed at Sullivan's Island in early 1862.[77] Companies I and K were based at Fort Moultrie from their creation on January 1 to April 30, 1862. In late April or early March, Companies B, C, E and H were sent to Camp Buist at John's Island Ferry below Charleston, and on March 2, they were transferred to nearby Camp Evans at Church Flats (Rantowles). Company D was sent to the Breech Inlet on Sullivan's Island in March 1862, but Companies A, F, G, I and K remained at Fort Moultrie. Companies I and K were sent to Church Flats about May 7, 1862. Eight companies of the 1st Regiment were sent to John's Island on May 22.[78] They made several marches there in late May and from June 4 to June

11 without once engaging the enemy. By September 9, the entire regiment was back on Sullivan's Island. Companies B, C, H and I were stationed on Sullivan's Island at the Enfilade Batteries (also called the Cove Batteries) in September, while Company D was still at the Breech Inlet Battery, and Companies E and I were at Fort Moultrie. On September 30, Company D engaged a Federal gunboat. By November 1862, Companies A, E, F, G and K were stationed at Fort Moultrie; Companies B, C, H and I were at Battery Bee; and Company D was at Battery Marshall. Later the same month, Company K was stationed at the Bee Battery and remained there until February 1864. Company H served at Battery Bee and other batteries on Sullivan's Island from November 1862 to June 1864.

On January 1, 1863, fifty men of Company D under Captain C.T. Haskell were engaged in a skirmish on Bull Island with about one hundred Federal troops from the blockading gunboat *Flambeau*.[79] Company B was at Battery Beauregard in January and February 1863. During the Federal ironclad attack on Fort Sumter on April 7, the regiment engaged the enemy from Sullivan's Island. During that battle, Companies A, E, F, G and K garrisoned Fort Moultrie, and Companies C, H and I garrisoned Battery Bee.[80] Company B was also engaged on April 7 as part of the garrison at Battery Beauregard, along with Company K, 1st Regiment, South Carolina Artillery (Regulars). Company B served at Battery Marshall from May 1863 until December 1864, except for a three-week tour at Fort Sumter. Company E served at the Brooks Gun Battery on Sullivan's Island from June 1863 until February 1864, except for one week at Battery Wagner. By June 14, 1863, four companies of the 1st Regiment were based at Fort Moultrie, three at Battery Bee, two at Battery Marshall and one at Battery Beauregard.[81] A small detachment of men from Companies B and D were engaged at Battery Wagner on July 10 and probably also on July 11, 1863.[82] About forty men from Company D under the command of Charles T. Haskell were engaged during the Federal assault on the south end of Morris Island on July 10.[83] About twenty men of Company D were engaged at Battery Wagner the next morning.[84] Company H was sent to Battery Wagner on July 15.[85] During the night assault on Battery Wagner on July 18, Companies H and I were engaged at the battery.[86] Company C was at Battery Gregg at Cummings's Point on Morris Island on July 31.[87] Except for its service at Morris Island, the regiment was stationed on Sullivan's Island and in Christ Church Parish as artillery until September 1863.[88]

On August 6, 1863, Company A moved to Battery Beauregard on Sullivan's Island and was engaged with Federal monitors there on August 31. Company E was sent to Morris Island on August 27 and remained there until September 5.[89] Company E was engaged at Battery Wagner and

Battery Gregg for nine days, from August 27 to September 5. On September 3, Company A arrived at Morris Island to relieve Company E; about half of the company went to Battery Gregg and the rest went to Battery Wagner. During the evacuation of Morris Island and the concomitant night attack on Battery Gregg on September 5, the detached troops of Company A were engaged as part of the rear guard.[90] Company A returned to Battery Beauregard on September 7. On September 6, Company C was sent to Fort Moultrie. Companies A, C, D, E, F, G, H, I and K were at Battery Beauregard and Fort Moultrie, where they engaged Federal ironclads on September 7 and September 8. In a bizarre accident on September 8, a shell from the grounded USS *Weehawken* glanced off the muzzle of an eight-inch Columbiad, struck an ammunition chest and exploded, killing sixteen and wounding twelve men of Company E. Company F was quickly moved from Battery Beauregard to Fort Moultrie during the battle to replace Company E. The regiment was engaged again during the night assault on Fort Sumter on September 8. Company I was stationed at Battery Rutledge from September 7, 1863, until about September 1864 and again in November and December. The entire regiment was based on Sullivan's Island on September 20, and several companies were engaged with Federal land batteries on Morris Island on October 26.[91] Companies C and G at Fort Moultrie engaged four ironclads and land batteries on Morris Island on November 16.[92] Companies C, F and G were garrisoning Fort Moultrie during the engagement with the *Lehigh* on November 17. Some companies of the 1st Regiment at Fort Moultrie were engaged during the Federal boat assault on Fort Sumter on November 20.[93] The regiment remained on Sullivan's Island throughout the rest of 1863 and into the new year.[94]

Company E was sent to Battery Marion on Sullivan's Island in March 1864 and served at various batteries on the island from May 29 to October 6, 1864. On April 9, four companies were stationed at Fort Moultrie, two at Battery Beauregard, two at Battery Bee and one each at Battery Rutledge and Battery Marshall.[95] On May 3, Company D was sent to Battery Rutledge on Sullivan's Island, and on May 25, Company A was sent to Battery Marshall. From June 16 to June 24, sixteen men of Company A scouted Bull's Bay and the adjacent islands. Company K was sent to Battery Ramsay in Charleston in July 1864 and remained there until at least December 31. On July 2, Companies C, D, E, F, K and probably B were sent to the New Lines on James Island to resist the Federal assaults on John's Island and James Island, a siege lasting from July 2 until July 11. While on picket duty on July 5 and 6, they were continually under shellfire from one gunboat, two monitors and two mortar boats.[96] On July 12, Company C was sent back to Fort Moultrie, where it remained until at least December. The entire regiment had returned to Sullivan's Island by July 31.[97] Elements of the regiment were stationed at Fort Sumter from April 30 to November 26, 1864. On June 28, one detachment of the 1st Regiment relieved another at Fort Sumter.[98] Company F served at Fort Sumter from July 28 until August 18, when it was sent back to Battery Beauregard.[99] Company G served at Fort Sumter from July 26 to August 20, when it returned to Fort Moultrie.[100] Company A performed garrison duty at Fort Sumter from July 18 to September 14, and Company B was there from September 14 until October 7. Company I served at the fort in September 1864. On September 14, Company A returned to Battery Marshall and remained there for the remainder of the year. Company E served at Fort Sumter from October 6 to November 12, when it returned to Battery Marshall. On October 31, eight companies of the 1st Regiment were stationed on Sullivan's Island, and two were on detached duty in nearby Christ Church Parish.[101] Company D served at Fort Sumter from November 21 to November 26 and then returned to the Two Gun Battery on Sullivan's Island. Company H was at Fort Sumter for part of September 1864; it returned to Fort Moultrie on September 15 and was sent to Battery Rutledge on October 1. On December 7, Company H was engaged at the battle of Tullifinny River.[102]

In January 1865, after serving as artillery for four years, the regiment reverted to infantry. Two companies of the 1st South Carolina Infantry Regulars and three companies of the 32nd Georgia Volunteers were the last to evacuate Fort Sumter on the night of February 17, 1865.[103] Rhett's Brigade, of which the 1st Regiment was a part, acted as the rear guard during the withdrawal through South Carolina and into North Carolina in February and March 1865. The regiment was engaged on the east bank of the Pee Dee River during the evacuation of Cheraw in 1865.[104] It was also engaged at Averasboro, North Carolina, on March 15 and March 16 and was present at Bentonville. The 1st Regiment, South Carolina Infantry (Regulars), surrendered with the Army of Tennessee on April 26, 1865.

2.

The 1st Battalion, South Carolina Sharpshooters

The 1st Battalion, South Carolina Sharpshooters, was also called the 1st Battalion Sharpshooters and Abney's Battalion of Sharpshooters. In July 1862, the Confederate Congress passed an "act for organizing battalions of sharpshooters."[1] These were to be organizations of regulars, not volunteers, with officers appointed by division or department commanders. Major General J.C. Pemberton's interpretation was that men were to be conscripted from existing organizations.[2] Both officers and recruits disliked the compulsory nature of the law. Many felt the law was enacted to help advance young aspirants who lacked the ability to secure promotion on their own merits to higher command. All believed they had enlisted with the right to choose their own organizations and officers. "The whole scheme was looked upon as disgraceful tyranny by every officer whose regiment or company was affected."[3] Most of those officers protested the new law—without success. Their objections proved ungrounded, however, because Pemberton picked good officers, especially J.B. Allston, captain of Company B. Though men were allowed to volunteer for the battalion, no existing company was permitted to drop below sixty-four privates.[4] Few volunteers came forward, and the order was made peremptory on July 27. Twenty-four men from the 25th Regiment—two or three from each company—were ordered into the new Battalion of Sharpshooters. Though there was no overt resistance among the officers, they showed resentment in other ways: captains chose worthless men, some companies paid men to go and some companies tapped individuals unlikely to succeed in sharpshooter roles. The bad news was that Pemberton's Sharpshooter Battalion was a rival for "Falstaff's Army," but there were good results as well; after the "blind, halt, and maimed" were excluded, enough good men were left to fill two companies.[5] On June 27, 1862, South Carolina cavalrymen without horses were ordered to form a new company and were given the option of joining the Battalion of Sharpshooters.[6] Johnson Hagood wrote that while the War Department's plan to raise a special corps of sharpshooters failed, the effort resulted in the formation of some excellent companies. These companies acted not as sharpshooters but instead performed the normal duties of any other line company.[7] Several sources record that Pemberton's efforts to create a battalion of sharpshooters failed, and the companies that were created were attached to the Charleston Battalion. This probably refers to the merger of Abney's Battalion of Sharpshooters and the Charleston Battalion in September 1863. The 1st Battalion, South Carolina Sharpshooters, was raised in June 1862 in Columbia, partly by compulsory draft from other regiments and partly from volunteers from other companies.[8] The three companies, designated A to C, mustered in Confederate service on June 23 or June 24, 1862. In June 1862, the 2nd Battalion of Sharpshooters was organized as well.[9] On September 30, 1863, the 1st Battalion Sharpshooters merged with the Charleston Battalion to create the 27th Regiment, SCV.

FIELD OFFICERS

Joseph Abney of Edgefield District was appointed major of the 1st Battalion Sharpshooters on June 21, 1862. A lieutenant in the Palmetto Regiment during the Mexican War, Abney had been colonel of the 22nd Regiment, SCV, in early 1862.[10] He was not re-elected at the reorganization and was dropped from the rolls on May 5, 1862. Poor health may have prevented Abney from offering himself for re-election. When the 1st Battalion of Sharpshooters merged into the 27th Regiment on October 2, 1863, Abney was appointed major of the 27th Regiment. He was called a "gallant and efficient officer."[11]

COMPANIES

Company A, the Union Light Infantry and German Fusiliers, was apparently composed of men from each of the two companies of the 17th Regiment, South Carolina Militia, with the same names. There were also a number of men in Company A who transferred from other organizations. Robert Chisolm was appointed captain on July 23, 1862, with rank from June 22. He retained command of the company when it became Company E in the 27th Regiment.[12] Company A men were from districts as diverse as Charleston, Lexington, Newberry, Orangeburg, Sumter, Spartanburg,

Laurens, Barnwell, Edgefield, Pickens, Anderson, Richland and York. This company became Company E of the 27th Regiment, SCV.

Company B, the Sumter Guards, was composed of men who transferred from various organizations. They came from the following districts: Georgetown, Beaufort, Charleston, Edgefield, Marion, Laurens, Clarendon, Sumter, Barnwell, Lexington, Anderson, Darlington, Greenville and Richland. Joseph Blyth Allston was appointed captain on June 23, 1862.[13] The *CSR* gives his middle name as Blythe and last name as Alston, but his signature reads Joseph Blyth Allston. Previously captain of Company D, 9th Battalion, Allston was not re-elected at the reorganization in May 1862. He was slightly wounded by a Minié ball in the right forearm at the battle of Pocotaligo on October 22, 1862, and, again, in the fleshy part of the right buttock, by buckshot. He retained command of the company when it became Company F of the 27th Regiment in September 1863.

Company C, the Charleston Sharpshooters, was also called the Palmetto Guards. This company was also composed of men who transferred from various organizations. Most were from Spartanburg, Orangeburg, Laurens, Union and Charleston Districts, but a few were from Newberry, Marion, Barnwell and Lexington Districts. Henry Buist was appointed captain on June 24, 1862, and retained command when the company became Company G in the 27th Regiment.

Brigade Affiliations

The battalion was assigned to the Department of South Carolina, Georgia and Florida for its entire existence.

Major Movements and Engagements

The Battalion of Sharpshooters was stationed at points along the South Carolina coast during its fifteen-month existence. It was at McPhersonville in Beaufort District in August 1862 and from September to December 1862 at Grahamville, also in Beaufort District. Company B was sent from Grahamville to McPhersonville on October 13, 1862, and to Pocotaligo on November 1; Companies B and C saw action there on October 22.[14] Company A missed the engagement because it was en route by rail with the 11th Regiment, SCV, at the time. The battalion continued to serve in the vicinity of McPhersonville, Coosawhatchie, Pocotaligo, Combahee Ferry and on James Island during the first half of 1863. In January and

February, the battalion was stationed at Coosawhatchie in Beaufort District. Company B was sent to the Combahee Ferry to serve as artillery on March 6, and on May 12, the battalion was ordered to James Island, where it remained until about the seventeenth. On May 31, four companies of the 25th Regiment, along with Abney's Battalion of Sharpshooters, pursued two hundred Federal troops near Legare's House on James Island but were not actively engaged.[15] On June 6, 1863, the battalion left Secessionville on James Island for Georgetown to support Battery White. The battalion served in Georgetown and at Battery White from early June until mid-September 1863.[16] According to a sketch in *Recollections and Reminiscences*, the battalion was engaged at Grahamville, Bee's Creek, Coosawhatchie, Pocotaligo, Combahee Ferry, John's Island, Wadmalaw Island, James Island and Winyah Bay.[17] The men were sent to Legare's Point on James Island in late September 1863 and merged into the 27th Regiment on September 30.

3.

Dunlop's Battalion of Sharpshooters

Dunlop's Battalion of Sharpshooters was also called Dunlop's Battalion and actually had two distinct iterations. The battalion was never a truly independent organization; it was designed to serve as a separate body of sharpshooters for McGowan's Brigade. Its officers always retained their previous company rank within the various regiments of the brigade. The battalion was first organized on June 3, 1863, by the adjutant and inspector general's general order #34, but was never assigned a numeric designation.[1] Thirty-six men from each regiment of McGowan's Brigade—Gregg's 1st SCV, Hagood's 1st Rifles, 12th SCV, 13th SCV and 14th SCV—were formed into three companies. At least one man from each company in the brigade was chosen for the battalion; it was composed of handpicked men—young, active and good shots. W.T. Haskell commanded the first battalion until his death on July 2, 1863. The battalion was dissolved in the autumn of 1863, but in early 1864, a corps of sharpshooters was once again needed, and the battalion was reorganized with three companies of about sixty men each. Dunlop gives the date of reorganization as about March 1, but Benson records it as April 6.[2] At that time, the battalion consisted of six commissioned officers, ten non-commissioned officers and one hundred and sixty privates. Each company in the brigade provided three or four men for the battalion. Captain William Simpson Dunlop of the 12th Regiment was placed in command of the revived battalion in March 1864.

J.F.J. Caldwell wrote that the battalion's men were to serve as skirmishers, as pickets and on special duty in general engagements. The battalion marched at the head of the brigade.[3] Dunlop wrote: "During the winter and intervals of rest [the sharpshooter battalion's] position was in front of the outposts and picket lines; and in the active campaigning of the summer they occupied the front in the advance and the rear on a retreat, as skirmishers. When the opposing armies met upon the field it became their duty to open and bring on the fight, or to stand like ushers on the vestibule of battle and receive and welcome our friends in blue whenever they choose to visit our lines."[4]

FIELD OFFICERS

William Thomson Haskell of Abbeville commanded the battalion with the rank of captain from January 1863 until his death while leading the battalion at Gettysburg on July 2, 1863. Brigade Commander Colonel Perrin wrote: "This brave and worthy officer fell while boldly walking along the front line of his command, encouraging his men and selecting favorable positions for them to defend."[5] Haskell was captain of Company H, Gregg's regiment, at the time of his death. There is no documentation that Haskell was ever promoted to major.

Thomas Pinckney Alston was in command from the time of Haskell's death until the battalion was dissolved in the fall of 1863. Alston continued to serve as captain of Company F of Gregg's regiment during this period. Though he was promoted to major of Gregg's regiment in January 1864, there is no evidence that Alston held that rank while in command of the battalion.

William Simpson Dunlop of York commanded the battalion when it was reorganized on March 1, 1864. Dunlop was captain of Company B of the 12th Regiment at the time. He was wounded and captured along the Appomattox River on April 3, 1865. There is no evidence that Dunlop was ever promoted to the rank of major.

COMPANIES

Company A was commanded by James Y. McFall of the 13th Regiment from January to July 1863. McFall was a second lieutenant in Company D of the 13th Regiment in January 1863. He was promoted to first lieutenant on June 10 and to captain of the company on July 1, 1863. N. Ingraham Hasell of Charleston commanded Company A, also called Company 1, in 1864. Hasell, who was wounded at Gettysburg, was a corporal in Company L of Gregg's regiment until he was elected junior second lieutenant of that company on January 1, 1864.[6] He was promoted to first lieutenant the same day and commanded Company A of Dunlop's Battalion with that rank. Hasell went to Charleston on a leave of absence on January 28, 1865, and because of

Sherman's advance through South Carolina, he did not return to the battalion until April 4.[7] Hasell was paroled at Appomattox Court House with the rank of first lieutenant in Company L of the 1st Regiment, SCV.

Adam Washington Ballenger was promoted from sergeant in Company C of the 13th Regiment to second lieutenant in command of Company H of the 13th Regiment on July 28, 1864. Ballenger commanded Company A of Dunlop's Battalion from January 28 to March 27, 1865.[8] As he was lying in front of the breastworks near Petersburg on March 27, Ballenger was wounded in the left arm and leg but managed to avoid capture by crawling away.[9] He was captured later, on April 3, while a patient in the Jackson Hospital in Richmond and was sent to Point Lookout, Maryland.

Company B was commanded by Lieutenant Mike R. Sharp of the 12th Regiment from January to July 1863. Sharp was promoted from second to first lieutenant of Company D, 12th Regiment on February 20, 1863. Sharp was wounded on July 1, 1863, at Gettysburg and left in the hands of the enemy when the Army of Northern Virginia withdrew on the fifth. Sharp's arm was amputated sometime between July 1 and December 26, 1863; he was paroled by September 27, 1864. Sharp was permanently disabled and retired to the Invalid Corps on February 14, 1865. William Henry Brunson of Edgefield commanded Company B, also called Company 2, in 1864.[10] Brunson was promoted from second to first lieutenant in Company D of the 14th Regiment in July or August 1863. He was wounded several times: in the mouth and neck at Gaines's Mill on June 27, 1862; in the hand at Chancellorsville; and in the left arm and leg at Gettysburg on July 1, 1863. He returned to duty and commanded Company B of Dunlop's Battalion in 1864. Brunson was wounded again, this time in the left foot, during an engagement along the Weldon Railroad near Petersburg on June 21, 1864.[11] Brunson was paroled at Appomattox Court House on April 9, 1865.

Company C was commanded by Lieutenant A.W. Poag of the 12th Regiment from January to July 1863. Poag was promoted from second lieutenant to first lieutenant of Company H of the 12th Regiment on September 18, 1862. He was killed at Gettysburg on July 3, 1863. Charles E. Watson commanded Company C, also called Company 3, in 1864. Watson was promoted to first lieutenant of Company B, Orr's regiment, on August 2, 1864, and was paroled at that rank at Appomattox Court House on April 9, 1865.

Brigade Affiliations

The battalion was part of McGowan's Brigade.

MAJOR MOVEMENTS AND ENGAGEMENTS

The battalion participated in its first engagement at Gettysburg from July 1 to July 3, 1863. The only elements of McGowan's Brigade engaged on July 2 were the sharpshooters and McCreary's regiment.[12] The battalion, along with rest of the brigade, was engaged at Hagerstown, Maryland, on July 11. It fell into disuse during the winter of 1863 to 1864 but was revived in March or April 1864. The battalion covered the left flank of the brigade during an eight- to ten-mile march on May 5, and the men were deployed as skirmishers in front of the brigade at the Wilderness later that day. On May 6, the sharpshooters and the entire brigade were forced to give ground before Longstreet's corps arrived on the field. The sharpshooters were engaged again later that afternoon. The brigade remained on the field on the seventh, and the sharpshooters advanced to find the Federal lines abandoned. They advanced farther the next day and found the Federal works empty. That evening, the entire brigade marched toward Spotsylvania Court House.[13]

McGowan's Brigade was not engaged at Brock's Crossroads on May 8 and arrived at Spotsylvania Court House about noon on the ninth. As the sharpshooters skirmished, the brigade entrenched itself on the extreme right of the Confederate line. The brigade experienced light skirmishing and some shelling on May 10, moved to its left on the eleventh and saw more light skirmishing that day. McGowan's Brigade was quickly moved farther to the left on May 12 and was heavily engaged in recapturing Confederate trenches overrun earlier that morning. The Battalion of Sharpshooters fought in the line of battle with the brigade on the twelfth; firing went on until after midnight. The brigade remained in the lines around Spotsylvania Court House, where the sharpshooters skirmished from May 19 to May 21. The brigade pulled out and marched toward the North Anna River on May 22.

During the Overland campaign, the battalion was engaged at Jericho Ford on May 23, 1864.[14] The men marched that evening to Hanover Junction and faced light skirmishing there. The sharpshooters drove in the Federal advanced line and were engaged as rear guard on the morning of May 24, while the brigade lay in the lines at Hanover Junction under some shelling that day and the next. Marching and skirmishing occupied the brigade from May 27 until it arrived in the vicinity of Cold Harbor on the thirty-first. The men were not engaged, except for brief skirmishes, during the battle of Cold Harbor from June 1 to June 3, 1864. The Battalion of Sharpshooters guarded the front but was not heavily engaged at Cold Harbor. The brigade crossed the Chickahominy River on June 13 and moved toward the old battlefield of

Frayser's Farm; it was lightly engaged, and the Battalion of Sharpshooters fought as skirmishers at Riddell's Shop that day. The sharpshooters, along with the brigade, crossed the James River at Drewry's Bluff on June 18 and moved by rail and foot to Petersburg. The men were placed on the extreme right of the Confederate lines, with the sharpshooters forming the brigade skirmish line, but none saw action that day. The brigade was lightly engaged on June 21, but the sharpshooters were heavily engaged as skirmishers near the Weldon Railroad. On June 22, the men were held in support on the field. The Battalion of Sharpshooters provided the rear guard for the brigade as it withdrew from the battlefield that day and narrowly escaped being completely cut off. The brigade occupied the Petersburg lines for the following week, facing only light skirmishing, while the sharpshooters took positions in the advanced rifle pits and suffered some casualties. McGowan's men were withdrawn from the Petersburg lines after dark on June 30 and marched all night, crossing to the north side of the James River at Chaffin's Bluff the next morning and entering the lines near Fort Harrison, where they remained for several weeks.

The brigade, including the sharpshooters, was engaged at Deep Bottom on July 28 and remained on the north side of the James River in the fortifications near Fort Harrison during late July and early August. On August 11, the brigade moved toward Dutch Gap, where it drew artillery fire the next day. Both brigade and sharpshooters endured skirmishes and shellfire on August 13, shelling on the fourteenth and an engagement at the battle of Fussell's Mill on the sixteenth.[15] The sharpshooters were also engaged as skirmishers the next day. The brigade crossed to the south side of the James River on August 20, and on the twenty-second, it was posted on the extreme right of the Confederate lines on the Weldon Railroad below Petersburg; the sharpshooters formed the skirmish line. The brigade marched down the Weldon Railroad on August 24 and was lightly engaged at Reams Station about nine miles below Petersburg on the twenty-fifth. The Battalion of Sharpshooters saw heavy action at the battle of Reams Station on August 25 both as skirmishers and on the battle line; 160 rounds per man were fired over five hours. The brigade returned to the trenches on August 26 and enjoyed a period of relative quiet, carrying out picket duty and daily work on the entrenchments until September 30. The sharpshooters performed picket duty about six hundred yards in advance of the main line during this period. On September 16, the Battalion of Sharpshooters demonstrated on the Federal main line to divert attention from Wade Hampton's Beef Steak Raid. The brigade was withdrawn from the trenches on the thirtieth and marched through Petersburg, but its course was reversed between Petersburg and Richmond, and the men were sent instead to the

Boydton Plank Road about four miles south of Petersburg. The brigade was engaged at Poplar Spring Church, also called Jones's Farm, Peebles's Farm and Pegram's Farm, on September 30. The Battalion of Sharpshooters opened the engagement there on September 30 and captured the Jones's house from Federal sharpshooters. The sharpshooters were engaged again near the Pegram house on October 1. The brigade entrenched itself near Jones's Farm on the second. The Battalion of Sharpshooters occupied the advanced rifle pits every other day during this time.

The brigade was not engaged during the battle near Hatcher's Run on October 27. It marched down the Boydton Plank Road toward Dinwiddie Court House on December 8 and unsuccessfully pursued a body of Federal infantry and cavalry. On December 12, the brigade returned to its winter quarters, performed picket duty and improved breastworks and field fortifications. The battalion performed picket duty every third or fourth day during the winter of 1864 to 1865, charging the Federal picket several times to capture prisoners. The Battalion of Sharpshooters was augmented during the winter months by two non-commissioned officers and seventy-five privates, raising it to a total force of about one hundred and twenty-five men and officers. The sharpshooters were ordered relieved from picket duty in late December. To capture enough supplies to make conditions more livable, both Dunlop's and Young's Sharpshooter Battalions attacked the Federal picket line on December 31 and took the supplies they needed and a number of Federal prisoners as well. The battalion performed picket duty at intervals before moving into winter quarters on January 15, 1865.

The brigade marched toward the right of the Confederate line on February 5 but was not engaged at Hatcher's Run from February 5 to February 7. Near the end of February, the Battalion of Sharpshooters resumed its position on the picket line. Though the brigade did not participate in the attack on Fort Stedman on March 25, both the Battalion of Sharpshooters and the brigade were engaged in the lines around Petersburg on that day and the next. The four battalions of sharpshooters of the Light Division successfully stormed McIlwaine's Hill on March 27, though the remainder of McGowan's Brigade was not engaged there. The brigade marched toward Hatcher's Run on the evening of March 29 and skirmished alongside the sharpshooters about a mile and a half south of that place on the thirtieth. They were also heavily engaged at Gravelly Run the following day. The brigade left the works on April 1 and marched toward Dinwiddie Court House, but it soon returned and was not engaged at Dinwiddie Court House that day. The brigade participated in picket firing that was light that afternoon but grew heavier as night fell. The battalion performed picket duty in front of the works on April 1. On April 2, the brigade was engaged in the works before evacuating and marching across Hatcher's Run toward Sutherland's Station on the South Side Railroad. The Battalion of Sharpshooters was the last unit of the brigade to leave Hatcher's Run. Later that day as the brigade and sharpshooters were engaged as skirmishers near Sutherland's Station, overwhelming Federal odds forced the men to a disorderly withdrawal from the battlefield. They rested along the Appomattox River on the night of April 2 and moved, still in a disorganized manner, along the Appomattox River toward Amelia Court House the next day. On April 4, the brigade became more organized and marched toward Amelia Court House. The men marched all day and most of the night on April 5. On the sixth, the brigade was met with skirmishing and shellfire as it neared Farmville. The Battalion of Sharpshooters also skirmished near Farmville on April 6. The men marched all night on April 6, reaching Farmville on the seventh. The brigade was not engaged on the seventh; it crossed to the north side of the Appomattox River at Farmville, marched most of that night toward Lynchburg and bivouacked about four to five miles east of Appomattox Court House on the morning of April 8. On April 9, the brigade resumed its march toward Appomattox Court House. The Army of Northern Virginia surrendered that day. The Battalion of Sharpshooters "were ordered from one flank to the other, and from front to rear, as occasion required, until—Appomattox and the end. The sharpshooters were deploying for another advance when the white flag was seen to meet Gen. Longstreet."[16] "On the morning of the 12th day of April, 1865, the battalion of Sharpshooters of McGowan's brigade laid down their arms and in the afternoon of the same day marched through the Federal lines and took the road for their distant homes."[17]

4.

THE 2ND BATTALION, SOUTH CAROLINA SHARPSHOOTERS

The 2nd Battalion, South Carolina Sharpshooters, was also called Smith's Battalion Sharpshooters. It was created early in the war as a special corps of marksmen in response to heavy casualties sustained in battle at the hands of Federal sharpshooters.[1] The *Mercury* ran advertisements in March 1862 calling for men to volunteer for service in a sharpshooter organization under B.B. Smith and Edward Rhett.[2] Smith continued the advertising campaign into the summer, urging men to transfer from existing regiments to his battalion.[3] On June 14, Major General John C. Pemberton called for 192 volunteers for Smith's Battalion.[4] He asked for an average of 2 men from each company of Hagood's 1st Regiment, SCV; the 11th, 15th, 18th, 21st and 23rd Regiments, SCV; the Charleston Battalion; the 11th (Eutaw) Battalion; Smith's 9th Battalion; Brown's Battalion; and the 6th (Byrd's) Battalion.[5] Three companies—A, B and C—were organized in June 1862; their captains' commissions dated from the twenty-second and twenty-third.[6] Company C was ordered into camp at McPhersonville on July 16, and all three companies mustered in service on September 1. The battalion was disbanded on December 28, 1862. Enlisted men returned to their former commands, and officers reported to the Commandant of Conscripts of South Carolina.

FIELD OFFICERS

Benjamin Burgh Smith Jr., a graduate of the South Carolina Military Academy, commanded the battalion as major in the Provisional Army of the Confederate States. His commission dated from June 22, 1862. The only field officer, Smith had served as major of the 11th Regiment, SCV, from September 19, 1861, to May 4, 1862. He was not re-elected at the reorganization in May 1862. According to the *Mercury*, Smith was one of the three best officers displaced by the re-election process at the reorganization.[7] After the 2nd Battalion was disbanded, Smith served as assistant adjutant general to Brigadier General S.R. Gist. He was wounded at the battle of Franklin, Tennessee. Assigned to command the 16th Regiment, SCV, on March 31, 1865, Smith was also given command of the Consolidated 16th and 24th Regiment with the rank of major on April 8 or April 9, 1865.

COMPANIES

Company A was commanded by Edmund Rhett Jr., who was appointed captain on July 23, 1862, with rank from June 22. After the battalion was disbanded, Rhett still held the rank of captain in the Provisional Army of the Confederate States in 1863 and 1864. A surgeon's letter dated May 30, 1864, stated that Rhett had a chronic inflammation of the left lung with adhesion of the lung to the pleura. He also suffered from a peri-rectal abscess.

Company B was commanded by Paul Hamilton Waring, also appointed captain on July 23 with rank from June 22. While serving as a volunteer on the staff of Brigadier General William B. Taliaferro at Battery Wagner on July 15, 1863, Waring was killed by a Federal sharpshooter from a distance of twelve hundred yards.[8]

Company C was commanded by James Lowndes, who was appointed captain on July 23 with rank from June 23.

BRIGADE AFFILIATIONS

The battalion was part of the brigade of Brigadier General W.S. Walker and was stationed in South Carolina during its six-month existence.

MAJOR MOVEMENTS AND ENGAGEMENTS

On July 16, 1862, Company C was ordered into camp at McPhersonville. The battalion was stationed at McPhersonville in Beaufort District from July 16 until September 29, when it was transferred to Fort Johnson on James Island. The battalion remained there throughout November and probably December.[9] The 2nd Battalion Sharpshooters was disbanded on December 28, 1862.

5.

THE 24TH REGIMENT, SOUTH CAROLINA VOLUNTEERS

The 24th Regiment, SCV, was also called Capers's regiment, the 24th South Carolina Sharpshooters and the Gallant 24th.[1] It was raised according to resolutions passed by a special session of the South Carolina legislature in November and December 1861 that authorized the governor to seek volunteer enlistments for service in defense of the state. The Federal invasion of Port Royal in early November 1861 and the subsequent threat to Charleston caused Governor Pickens to issue a call on December 9 for twelve thousand volunteers to enlist for twelve months.[2] The 24th Regiment's first six companies, A to F, were raised under the governor's authority in late 1861 and early 1862.[3] According to an article in the *Mercury* of December 24, the 24th Regiment was in the process of organizing.[4] The regiment's final organization, however, occurred under the authority of an act passed by the Confederate Congress on February 28, 1862.

Two South Carolina Militia officers, Clement Hoffman Stevens, colonel of the 16th Regiment, and Ellison Capers, lieutenant colonel of the 1st Regiment Rifles, jointly raised the 24th Regiment. Governor Pickens appointed Stevens and Capers as colonel and lieutenant colonel, respectively. By January 13, 1862, several companies were receiving instruction at Camp Gist about four miles below Charleston in St. Andrews Parish. Three days later, the count was six companies, designated A to F.[5] It was still six, according to the *Mercury*, on February 20; four more were needed to complete the regiment.[6] The original six companies had enlisted for twelve months' service in December 1861 and January 1862. Governor Pickens and the Executive Council determined in March to allow no more twelve-month enlistments. Furthermore, they proposed to create a full regiment by adding four companies if Stevens's six existing companies would re-enlist for the duration of the war.[7] The companies agreed. Company E responded first, according to Jones, changing its enlistment on March 18, but the record shows that Christian Sigwald, captain of Company A, was recommissioned on the sixteenth, an indication that his company might have been the first to re-enlist.[8] All six had signed up for the duration by March 24, 1862.[9] The creation of the regiment gained approval from Governor Pickens and the Executive Council on April 1; that same day, South Carolina's adjutant and inspector general issued Special Order No. 23 authorizing the regiment's creation. The 24th was briefly designated the 1st Regiment, Infantry, of Recent Acquisition, in early April, and by the fourth, the regiment of 950 men was based on Cole's Island. Though field officers' commissions were dated April 1, the appointments were actually made on April 30, 1862. The last four companies, designated G, H, I and K, mustered in service on April 15 and April 21 for the duration of the war. The date Jones gives for the regiment's organization, April 20, 1862, possibly refers to the date the regiment was finally complete.[10] In December 1862, the South Carolina legislature passed a law revoking the commissions of the three field officers of the 24th Regiment and requiring them to stand for re-election.[11] After several months of confusion, including threats of resignation from both Stevens and Capers, the War Department chose simply to ignore the law; the new elections never took place.[12]

On April 9, 1865, near the end of the war, 221 men of the 24th and 224 of the 16th were merged into a single regiment named the 16th and 24th Consolidated Regiment. Colonel Benjamin Burgh Smith, formerly of the 16th, was given command of the new regiment. Smith was assigned the task of consolidating remnants of companies from both former regiments into five each and merging the resulting ten into a single regimental unit. Thomas C. Morgan and Theodore Gaillard Croft were named lieutenant colonel and major, respectively. The 16th and 24th Consolidated Regiment surrendered with the Army of Tennessee on April 26, 1865, and marched back to South Carolina. Men of the original 16th disbanded at Spartanburg, and those from the 24th disbanded at the companies' individual muster grounds.

FIELD OFFICERS

Clement Hoffman Stevens of Charleston, known as both "Rock" and "the Old Fellow," was the regiment's first colonel.[13] The brother of Peter F. Stevens, colonel of the Holcombe Legion, he was born in Connecticut and was cashier of the Planters and Mechanics Bank in Charleston at the outbreak of the war.[14] C.H. Stevens is also credited with building the Iron Battery at Cummings's Point on the north end of Morris Island in early

1861. While serving as an aide to Brigadier General Barnard E. Bee, he was wounded at First Manassas. Stevens was colonel of the 16th Regiment, South Carolina Militia, until October 6, 1861, when Governor Pickens authorized him to raise a regiment.[15] He raised the 24th Regiment between December 1861 and April 1862. Stevens's appointment as a colonel in state service probably came on January 20, 1862; he was commissioned colonel of the 24th Regiment on April 30, when the regiment was officially authorized, with rank from April 1. Stevens was severely wounded in the arm and breast at Chickamauga on September 20, 1863.[16] Promoted to brigadier general on January 20, 1864, he was assigned to the command of Wilson's Georgia Brigade the same day. During the battle of Peach Tree Creek near Atlanta on July 20, 1864, Stevens suffered a dual calamity: his horse fell on him, and a Minié ball struck him behind the right ear. The ball was extracted, and he seemed to be doing fairly well until the evening of the twenty-fourth, when his condition rapidly deteriorated.[17] Stevens died at dawn on July 25 at the home of LeRoy Napier in Macon, Georgia.[18] He was buried at Charleston's Magnolia Cemetery, but his remains were later moved to St. Paul's Episcopal Church in Pendleton.[19] "He was not only loved by his command, but was looked upon by officers of high position in the army as one of the best generals in the field."[20] He "nobly and irreproachably" fulfilled his duties.[21]

Ellison Capers of Charleston helped Clement Stevens raise the 24th Regiment. They had a family connection by marriage; Capers's sister was married to Stevens's brother.[22] Capers resigned his position as professor at The Citadel on November 25, 1861. He was appointed lieutenant colonel in state service on January 13, 1862, and resigned as lieutenant colonel of the 1st Regiment Rifles, South Carolina Militia, on January 25.[23] Capers was appointed lieutenant colonel of the 24th Regiment in Confederate service on April 30, though his commission actually dated from April 1. He commanded the regiment at Cole's Island from mid-April to mid-May 1862, and it was he who led the first attack on the enemy at James Island on June 3. During the battle of Secessionville on June 16, Colonel Johnson Hagood ordered Capers to investigate why the flanking battery of two 24-pounder cannon at the Clark House was silent. Finding the gunners inexperienced in the operation of the cannon, Capers brought them into action and commanded the battery himself for the remainder of the fight. The battery was renamed Battery Reed after the battle; a small monument honoring Capers marks the spot.

Capers was in charge of the district between the Ashepoo and Combahee Rivers in March 1863. He also led the advance of skirmishers at Wright's farm near Jackson, Mississippi, on May 14, 1863, when he received a painful, though not dangerous, wound in the right leg.[24] He was wounded again, this time a serious injury to the left thigh, at Chickamauga on September 20, 1863.[25] Capers was promoted to colonel on March 16, 1864, with rank from January 20, when Stevens was promoted to brigadier general. Capers commanded the 24th Regiment in Johnston's Georgia campaign and was slightly wounded near Tanner's Ferry, Georgia, on May 16, 1864.[26] He was wounded twice more in 1864: first a slight wound at Peach Tree Creek on July 20 and then a severe injury to the left ankle at Franklin, Tennessee, on November 30.[27] Capers was promoted to brigadier general on March 1, 1865, and commanded Gist's Brigade in North Carolina that year.[28] He was paroled at Greensboro on May 1, 1865. Capers enjoyed a long postwar career as an Episcopal priest and was a popular speaker at many Confederate monument dedications.

Andrew J. Hammond of Hamburg in Edgefield District was the first major of the regiment. His commission was dated April 1, 1862. Hammond raised company I and served as its first captain. Colonel Stevens recognized Hammond for bravery at Secessionville.[29] Hammond tendered his resignation on December 16, 1862, citing poor health. He had been absent from the regiment for several months because of rheumatism that put him on crutches. Colonel Stevens supported Hammond's resignation: "Because of the condition of physical incapacity under which Major Hammond suffers, I believe that acceptance would be for the good of the service."[30] The resignation was accepted on January 2, 1863.

Christian B. Sigwald of Charleston, previously captain of Company A, was promoted to major on January 1, 1863, a date also shown as the second. He "reluctantly accepted the promotion for fear that he could not perform the duties" associated with the office.[31] His concern was probably related to a physical limitation, one that caused him to resign the post only three months later. Sigwald tendered his resignation on March 23, stating initially that he suffered from chronic inflammation of the bladder and prostate and that his wife was also in poor health. In an attempt to clarify the situation and avoid any appearance of inconsistency, he wrote a letter explaining that while serving as colonel of the 16th Regiment, South Carolina Militia, before the war, he had been kicked in the lower abdomen by a horse. He believed the injury was the reason that horseback riding caused him problems.[32] Sigwald's resignation was accepted on April 1, 1863; he was later appointed police chief of Charleston. Krick gives Sigwald's first name as Christopher.[33]

Morgan Thomas Appleby of Colleton was promoted from captain of Company C to major as Sigwald's replacement. The date of Appleby's promotion is not recorded, but he was first shown as major on the two-month muster roll that was completed on April 30, 1863. Elected to a four-year term in the South Carolina Senate representing St. George's Dorchester Parish in October 1862, Appleby resigned his commission on June 11, 1863. Possibly contributing to the resignation was the fact that Appleby had experienced personal conflicts with other officers in the regiment, notably with Lieutenant Colonel Capers, who had upbraided him in front of the men during the battle of Wright's farm on May 14, 1863.[34]

Jesse Stancel Jones of Colleton was promoted from captain of Company E to major on July 12, with rank from June 11, 1863. Jones was severely wounded in the right shoulder at Chickamauga on September 20, 1863.[35] He was promoted to lieutenant colonel on March 25, 1864, with rank from January 20, when Stevens was promoted to brigadier general. Jones was severely wounded in the jaw and neck at Franklin, Tennessee, on November 30, 1864.[36] He died on the night of December 7 in the division hospital at the A.M. Harrison house near Franklin.[37] Ellison Capers wrote, "his loss will be much felt by the regiment and is greatly deplored by his colonel."[38]

David F. Hill of Anderson was promoted to major from captain of Company F on March 28, with rank from January 20, 1864, when Jones was promoted to lieutenant colonel. Shot in the chest three times, Hill was killed at Jonesboro, Georgia, on September 1, 1864, while attempting to rally the 2nd Georgia Battalion.[39] Capers wrote, "A cool, brave man, and a good soldier, Major Hill's loss is deplored by every man and officer of his regiment."[40]

Thomas C. Morgan, captain of Company K, was serving as acting major when he was slightly wounded in the neck about May 17, 1864.[41] He was still acting major on August 22 when he was severely wounded in the neck and face.[42] Whether or not he was actually promoted to major in September 1864 after Hill's death is unclear. The *CSR* lists him as captain on an inspection report dated September 22, 1864, and does not record promotion to major. Jones, on the other hand, states that Morgan was promoted to major of the 24th Regiment in September 1864.[43] Morgan was named lieutenant colonel of the 16th and 24th Consolidated Regiment on April 9, 1865, and paroled at Greensboro on May 1.

COMPANIES

Company A, the Marion Rifles, was composed of men from Charleston.[44] It was formed principally from the officers and men of Christian B. Sigwald's Company, the Marion Rifles, of the 16th Regiment, South Carolina Militia. The Marion Rifles had been organized with men of the Marion fire station on Columbus Street in Charleston, and Sigwald had been elected captain on

November 28, 1860.[45] The company volunteered for Stevens's new regiment on October 16, 1861, and the *Mercury* was able to report on December 24 that Company A was organizing and rapidly filling, adding that it would be an "old fashioned Swamp Fox party."[46] According to the *Mercury*, the men of Company A volunteered for twelve months' state service on Christmas Day, though both the *Charleston Daily Courier* and the *CSR* show December 31 as the original muster date.[47] Both dates could be legitimate; the men probably agreed to muster in on the twenty-fifth and actually did so on the thirty-first. Sigwald was elected captain on the thirty-first; he was recommissioned captain on March 16, 1862, when the company re-enlisted for the duration of the war at the governor's request.[48] The Marion Rifles formed the right flank company of the 24th Regiment.[49]

Sigwald was promoted to major on January 1, 1863, a date also shown as the second. John Henry Steinmeyer Jr. was promoted from second lieutenant to captain on February 23.[50] Steinmeyer managed to survive the war, though his career had its harrowing moments. For example, at three in the morning on May 14, 1863, he was in command of the regiment's skirmishers and posted only three hundred yards from the Federal lines during the engagement at Wright's farm near Jackson, Mississippi, when his group of about fifty men found themselves confronting two enemy regiments. They steadily fell back in the face of overwhelmingly superior numbers until Steinmeyer was wounded and captured, along with sixteen of his men, at about three in the afternoon.[51] He was held with other Confederate prisoners in a temporary jail at the Jackson State Capitol for several days after the battle. When Federal troops evacuated Jackson after a few days, Steinmeyer was paroled and helped organize other recently released Confederate soldiers in Jackson. He was sent to the Paroled Prisoners Camp at Demopolis, Alabama, about May 24 and was released from there on June 5.[52] Steinmeyer had arrived in Charleston by June 17, though still on parole.[53] He returned to the regiment and sustained a slight wound in the left leg at Chickamauga on September 20, 1863. The *Mercury* reported, erroneously, that he was killed in action near Resaca on May 17, 1864. Though not killed, Steinmeyer was severely wounded in the shoulder at Kennesaw, Georgia, on June 25; he was also captured again, this time at Ship's Gap, Georgia, also called both Dick's and Taylor's Ridge, on October 16.[54] Held first at Nashville, he was taken on October 23 to the Military Prison at Louisville, Kentucky. Three days later, Steinmeyer was moved to Johnson's Island, Ohio, and was finally released on June 16, 1865. Ellison Capers wrote that Steinmeyer was one of "my best officers and my excellent friend."[55]

Company B, the Pee Dee Rifles, was composed of men from Marlboro and Marion Districts. Raised in the summer of 1861, it was accepted into the

24th Regiment by Colonel Stevens on December 4.[56] Company B mustered in for twelve months of state service on December 25 and re-enlisted in Confederate service for the duration of the war on March 24, 1862.[57] James Edwin "Ed" Spears, an 1859 graduate of The Citadel, was elected captain on December 4, 1861. After Colonel Stevens wrote on January 12, 1863, that he was "incompetent and unqualified to discharge the duties of his office," Spears resigned without giving a reason on January 27.[58] He served as an enrolling officer for a time after his resignation and, on December 13, 1863, applied for an appointment as a lieutenant in the 1st Regiment, South Carolina Infantry (Regulars). Spears may also have enlisted as a private in Company H of the Hampton Legion on March 1, 1864. He died at home in 1865. First Lieutenant Robert Johnson was promoted to captain in May or June 1863.[59] Johnson was severely wounded in the thigh at Chickamauga; also his right arm was fractured and amputated either at Peach Tree Creek on July 20 or at Atlanta on July 22, 1864.[60] He was furloughed from the hospital on August 4, 1864, and probably never returned to the regiment. According to the *Memory Roll*, Johnson resigned and was replaced by C.D. Easterling, but the *CSR* does not record Johnson's resignation. Easterling held the rank of first lieutenant and was never promoted to captain. He was captured at Marlboro, South Carolina, on March 5, 1865. He was taken to Fort Delaware and was released sometime in June.

Company C, known as Captain M.T. Appleby's Company, was composed of men from St. George and Dorchester in Colleton District.[61] It mustered in service for twelve months at George's Station on January 7, 1862. Morgan Thomas Appleby raised the company and was elected its captain on December 28, 1861. He was promoted to major in 1863, but the exact date of the promotion is not recorded. He was first listed at that rank on the muster roll for the months of March and April 1863, and First Lieutenant William Capers Griffith was promoted to captain in May or June the same year. Griffith commanded the 24th Regiment at the battle of Nashville.[62] He continued to serve until April 1865 but did not command a company in the 16th and 24th Consolidated Regiment.[63]

Company D, the Evans Guard, was composed of men from the Whippy Swamp area of Beaufort District.[64] The Evans Guard was named in honor of the "Hero of Leesburg," General N.G. Evans.[65] Company D men enlisted for twelve months at Camp Gist near Charleston on January 16, 1862, and re-enlisted for the duration of the war in March.[66] According to Jones, another company called the Whippy Swamp Guard formed the nucleus of Company D.[67] Company D, 11th Regiment, SCV, went by that name and was reorganized in March 1862, possibly giving its men an opportunity to re-enlist in Company D of the 24th. Or perhaps men of the two companies served in a common prewar militia unit by that name. William James Gooding, elected captain on December 28, 1861, enlisted along with the men on January 16, 1862.[68] He resigned on November 11, citing poor health, and was replaced by First Lieutenant A.B. Addison in November or December 1862. Gooding later served in the 11th Regiment and was incapacitated by a wound, serving out the rest of the conflict as collector of Confederate war taxes in Beaufort District.[69] Addison also resigned (on June 11, 1863), giving reasons of physical disability and poor general health. Evidently of a different opinion, Colonel Stevens wrote: "for reasons other than physical disability Captain Addison can be of no use to his command."[70] Abram E. Bowers was promoted from first lieutenant to captain on June 11, 1863.[71] He was slightly wounded in the back between May 17 and June 23, 1864.[72] Wounded again at Nashville, Bowers died on December 25, 1864.[73]

Company E, the Colleton Guard, was composed of men from that district.[74] The men enlisted for twelve months on January 16, 1862, while based at Camp Gist near Charleston; they re-enlisted for the duration of the war on March 18, 1862. Jesse S. Jones, elected captain on January 1, 1862, mustered in with the men on the sixteenth. He was promoted to major on June 11, 1863, and was replaced by First Lieutenant Joseph "Joe" K. Risher the same day.[75] Though suffering with chronic rheumatism in the Fairgrounds Hospital in Atlanta in October and November 1864, Risher did return to the regiment.[76] Twice wounded, he surrendered with the company on April 26, 1865, and was paroled on May 1.[77] One card in the *CSR* states that Second Lieutenant John Warren, Risher's brother-in-law, was promoted to captain on June 11, 1863. This is an error—it conflicts with Risher's own promotion, and other cards indicate that Warren was promoted first lieutenant, not captain, on that date. Wounded in the left knee on June 16, 1864, near Atlanta, Warren's leg was amputated, and he died from the wound on July 6, still at the rank of first lieutenant. Warren was probably never captain of Company E.

Company F, Hill's Company, was composed primarily of men from Anderson District, though some came from Abbeville District.[78] Its men gathered near Carswell Baptist Church at Hall Township in Anderson District.[79] Company F men enlisted for twelve months on January 13, 1862, and mustered in Confederate service for the duration of the war on March 28.[80] David F. Hill, elected captain on January 1, mustered in with the men on the thirteenth. Hill suffered a slight chest wound at Chickamauga on September 20, 1863. He was promoted to major on March 28, 1864, with rank from January 20.[81] His replacement, First Lieutenant Samuel W. Sherard, was also awarded captain's rank as of January 20. The *Mercury* records the name as W.S. Shuard.[82] Sherard had been wounded at Jackson, Mississippi, on May 14, 1863, and was still in an Atlanta hospital on the twenty-third.[83] He was also slightly wounded in the breast at Peach Tree Creek on July 20, 1864.[84] Sherard was captured on October 16, 1864, at Ship's Gap, Georgia, also called Dick's Ridge and Taylor's Ridge.[85] Held first at Nashville, he was moved on the twenty-fifth to the Military Prison at Louisville, Kentucky. The next day, Sherard was taken to Johnson's Island, Ohio, and was held until his release on June 16, 1865.[86]

Company G, Pearson's Company, composed of men from Richland District, was one of the four new companies that mustered in the 24th Regiment after March 1862.[87] Company G mustered in for the duration of the war at Camp Johnson (Lightwood Knot Springs) near Columbia on April 15. John H. Pearson, a Columbia lawyer and master in equity for Richland District, had raised the company. Elected captain on March 19, Pearson mustered in with the men on April 15. Though granted a few hours' leave in Charleston on October 21, Pearson overstayed his time and missed the departure of the regiment for Pocotaligo on the twenty-second. He also failed to report to Colonel Stevens when he rejoined the regiment at Pocotaligo and made an unauthorized visit to Charleston when the regiment returned to James Island on October 24. He was court-martialed for these offenses and, on November 12, was found guilty of three charges, including being absent without leave, and was suspended for three months. After the verdict, Pearson requested reassignment to a judicial position in keeping with his training and experience. Military courts for each army corps were in the process of organization at the time.[88] Several letters recommending Pearson for judge advocate, all bearing dates in November 1862, can be found in his file. Revealing in early 1863 that he had suffered from an anal fistula for six or seven months, Pearson tendered his resignation on January 28, citing continuous ill health. The resignation was accepted on February 23. Colonel Stevens wrote that "the interest of the service would be greatly promoted by the acceptance of his resignation."[89] On February 23, First Lieutenant Hilliard D. Hamiter was promoted to captain, replacing Pearson. Hamiter was slightly wounded in the heel at Chickamauga on September 20, 1863.[90] He also suffered a severe wound to the head at Atlanta on July 22, 1864.[91] He was in a hospital in Columbia in August 1864 and on medical leave the next month, but nothing appears in the record after that time.[92]

Company H, Thomas's Company, was composed of men from the Richburg community in Chester District.[93] Another of the four new companies to muster in the 24th Regiment after March 1862, Company H joined up for the duration of the war at Camp Johnson near Columbia on April 15. James Alexander "Alex" Thomas, a veteran of the Mexican War who lost his left arm during the battle of Mexico City on September 13, 1847, raised Company H.[94] Thomas was about thirty-five years old when he was elected captain, probably on March 19, 1862. His friends thought he should resign because of his disability.[95] Thomas might have agreed; in the fall of 1862, he requested a leave of absence, citing important private business that absolutely required his attention and threatening to resign if leave was not granted. Colonel Stevens, sounding as if he were dealing harshly with a disabled veteran, wrote that, while he saw insufficient cause, he would recommend accepting Thomas's resignation "to fill the office with a man who was willing to make the sacrifice that Captain Thomas thinks too great to render his country."[96] The resignation was accepted on October 29.[97] W. Lyle Roddey was promoted from first lieutenant to captain on December 1. The *Mercury* spelled the name as Roddy.[98] Roddey suffered a minor wound to the shoulder at Chickamauga.[99] He was more seriously injured, this time a head wound, on May 28, 1864, at Dalton, Georgia.[100] Roddey was wounded yet again (in the forehead) at Jonesboro, Georgia, on either August 31 or September 1 of the same year. He was captured at Ship's Gap, Georgia, on October 16.[101] Held first at Nashville, he was moved on the twenty-third to the Military Prison at Louisville, Kentucky. After three days, Roddey was taken to Johnson's Island, Ohio, and held until his release on June 16, 1865.[102]

Company I, the Edgefield Light Infantry, was composed of men from that district.[103] It might also have been called the Edgefield Guard.[104] Company I was one of four new companies, all of which mustered in the 24th Regiment after March 1862. Andrew J. Hammond raised the company and was elected its captain on January 25, 1862.[105] Records show that the company was at Lightwood Knot Springs on April 11.[106] It soon moved to Cole's Island, where the men mustered in service for the duration on April 21. Though Hammond was elected in January, his commission was dated March 20. Hammond had served as captain of the Edgefield Hussars, Company A of the Cavalry Battalion, Hampton Legion, since the summer of 1861. When Hammond was appointed major of the 24th Regiment as of April 1, 1862, Lafayette B. Wever was either promoted or elected captain the same day.[107] Often absent from the company because of illness, especially chronic diarrhea, Wever was on medical leave from August 1864 until his return in March 1865. Still not really well, he left again on April 20.[108] He was paroled on May 18 at Augusta, Georgia, as captain of Company I, 24th Regiment. James Adams Tillman, first lieutenant of Company I, was promoted to captain of Company G of the 16th and 24th Consolidated Regiment in April 1865. The *Memory Roll* indicates that he served also as captain of Company I of the 24th Regiment. This is probably incorrect. Tillman was probably never a captain in the 24th Regiment; instead, his first experience as captain was likely in the Consolidated Regiment formed on April 9, 1865. Tillman was wounded four times: in the left arm at Chickamauga; slightly at Mill Creek Gap, Georgia, on May 9, 1864; again in both legs at Calhoun, Georgia, on May 16; and finally at Franklin, Tennessee. He was paroled with the rank of captain on May 1, 1865, at Greensboro. Tillman lived only a year after the war; he died from the effects of his wounds and from illness on May 4, 1866.[109]

Company K, Tompkins's Company, was composed of men from Hamburg in Edgefield District.[110] The last of the four new companies to join the 24th Regiment after March 1862, Company K mustered in service at Lightwood Knot Springs near Columbia on April 15 for the duration of the war. The company joined the regiment at Cole's Island on April 20.[111] Samuel S. Tompkins, who was commissioned captain on April 23, had served as major and volunteer aide-de-camp to Brigadier General M.L. Bonham at the battle of First Manassas. Citing a physical disability, Tompkins resigned on August 14, 1862.[112] Colonel Stevens wrote that Tompkins resigned through no fault of his own.[113] He returned to South Carolina, where he was assigned to the Quartermaster Department and served also as agent for collections of tax-in-kind at Hamburg.[114] The *Mercury*, the *Memory Roll* and the *CSR* all spell his name Tomkins, but he signed official documents Tompkins.[115] First Lieutenant Thomas "Tom" C. Morgan was promoted to captain, but the date does not appear in the *CSR*.[116] Morgan was wounded in the left side of the throat at Chickamauga. While acting major, he was also wounded in the right arm and slightly in the neck at Calhoun Gap, or Tanner's Ferry, Georgia, on May 16, 1864.[117] While still acting major, Morgan suffered a severe wound to the face at Atlanta on July 22, 1864.[118] Whether or not he was actually promoted to major when Hill was killed in September 1864 is unclear. The *CSR* shows him as captain on an inspection report dated September 22 and does not record a promotion to major. Jones, however, wrote that Morgan was promoted to major of the 24th Regiment in September 1864.[119] He did become lieutenant colonel of the 16th and 24th Consolidated Regiment on April 9, 1865, and he was paroled at Greensboro on May 1.

BRIGADE AFFILIATIONS

The 24th Regiment was assigned to the Department of South Carolina, Georgia and Florida from April 1862 to May 1863, with the exception of January and February when it was attached to the Department of

North Carolina.[120] From January 15, 1862, to April 4, 1863, the brigade commanded by Brigadier General A.H. Colquitt comprised the 16th, 24th and 25th Regiments, SCV, the 46th Georgia Regiment, the 7th South Carolina Battalion and Preston's Battery of South Carolina Light Artillery.[121] In June 1862, the 24th was assigned to a temporary brigade called the Advanced Forces, commanded by Johnson Hagood. Other units in the brigade were Hagood's 1st Regiment, SCV, the (11th) Eutaw Battalion, the 46th Georgia Regiment and McEnnery's Louisiana Battalion. States Rights Gist's Brigade, organized May 1863, comprised the 16th and 24th Regiments, the 46th Georgia Regiment, the 8th Georgia Battalion and T.B. Ferguson's Battery of South Carolina Light Artillery, all of which remained with the brigade until the battle of Franklin, Tennessee. It was part of the Army of the Department of Mississippi and Eastern Louisiana from May to September 1863, when it transferred to the Army of Tennessee. Ellison Capers commanded the brigade after the battle of Franklin. On March 31, 1865, it comprised the 16th and 24th Regiments, SCV; the 46th and 65th Georgia Regiments; the 8th Georgia Battalion; and the 2nd Battalion, Georgia Sharpshooters.[122]

MAJOR MOVEMENTS AND ENGAGEMENTS

The first six companies of the 24th Regiment gathered at a camp of instruction near Charleston on January 16, 1862.[123] Company I left Edgefield for Lightwood Knot Springs about seven miles north of Columbia on April 4 and arrived there the next day.[124] Company I was still there on the eleventh but soon moved on to Cole's Island, where the men mustered in service on April 21 for the duration of the war.[125] Companies G, H and K were also at Camp Johnson near Lightwood Knot Springs, where they mustered in for the duration on April 15. Later that month, Companies G, H, I and K were sent to Camp Gist about four miles below Charleston on the main highway to Savannah. On April 16, nine companies, A to I, replaced Hagood's 1st Regiment as the garrison at Battery Island and at Fort Palmetto on Cole's Island on the Stono River. Company K joined the 24th Regiment at Cole's Island on April 20.[126] All but two companies evacuated Cole's Island on May 14 under orders to perform picket duty about two miles from Secessionville on James Island.[127] The remainder of the regiment, consisting of Lieutenant Colonel Capers and one hundred and sixty men from two companies, also evacuated Cole's Island and Battery Island on May 20 while under fire from Federal gunboats.[128] The next day, as sixty men from Company E performed picket duty at Battery

Island, six men were captured.[129] Four companies, A, B, D and E, and the Charleston Battalion saw action on June 3 while trying to salvage three artillery pieces from Chichester's Battery that had bogged down in the marsh at Legare's place on Sol Legare Island.[130] A detail from the regiment skirmished near the Presbyterian Church on James Island on the fifth and seventh. With most of the regiment on picket duty, only companies D, G, I and K were engaged on the right flank of the Confederate lines during the battle of Secessionville on June 16.[131] The regiment moved to Secessionville on July 8 and remained on James Island throughout the summer and autumn, occupied with picket duty, manning artillery batteries and performing construction work on gunboats.[132]

On October 22, the 24th Regiment moved by rail to Pocotaligo but arrived there after the battle was over; the men returned to James Island on the twenty-fourth. Because Federal troops at New Bern, North Carolina, were threatening the Wilmington & Weldon Railroad, the 24th Regiment left Charleston by rail in the early morning hours of December 15 and arrived at Wilmington the next day.[133] Accompanying the 24th were the 25th Regiment, SCV; the 46th Georgia Regiment; and Preston's Battery. The 7th Battalion, the 16th Regiment, Culpeper's Battery and Waties's Battery were also sent to North Carolina then and were based about nine miles from Wilmington where the railroad crossed the North East River near New Hanover City. On December 17, the 24th Regiment and Preston's Battery moved farther up the railroad line. After two months, the men marched to Wilmington and boarded the train for Charleston on February 12, 1863, arriving at The Citadel Green late the next day. The regiment left Charleston, again by rail, for Pocotaligo on February 18 and arrived early the next day. There, the men built batteries, bridges and roads around Pocotaligo.[134] On March 6, Companies F, H and I marched about fourteen miles to the Combahee and Ashepoo Rivers.[135] They bivouacked near Ballouville in Colleton District and provided infantry support as well as more construction work on the batteries there. On the eleventh, Company I was sent to man a battery on the Ashepoo River. Companies F, H and I left Ballouville on April 4, and the rest of the regiment left Pocotaligo the next day; all were back at Secessionville by the sixth or seventh.

Brigadier General S.R. Gist's new brigade was organized in early May 1863. The 24th Regiment left Camp Maloney on May 4 and passed through Charleston on the sixth on its way to Jackson, Mississippi, to relieve the siege of Vicksburg.[136] Following a circuitous route involving both rail and boat, the regiment arrived at Jackson at about six in the evening on May 13. The next morning at three, the men were engaged as skirmishers in a rear guard action at O.P. Wright's farm three miles from Jackson on the Clinton Road.[137] The regiment evacuated Jackson and moved north toward Yazoo City on the fourteenth. It left there for Calhoun Station on the fifteenth, and three days later, it was in line of battle at Cross Lanes. The regiment moved toward Canton on May 19 and on the twentieth was joined there by the 16th Regiment. From this time until the end of the war, the 24th and 16th Regiments served together in Gist's brigade. Their major movements and engagements are discussed below. The brigade bivouacked near Cordt's Pond from May 21 to May 30 and marched to Yazoo City on the thirty-first. Leaving there on June 14, the brigade marched for two days by way of McNamara's Ferry on the Big Black River to Vernon. The men marched toward Vicksburg on July 1 to alleviate some of the pressure there. Vicksburg capitulated on July 4. The 16th and 24th Regiments left Birdsong's Landing on the Big Black River about July 6 and arrived at Jackson on the eighth. From July 9 to July 16, the 16th and 24th Regiments were based at Canton, Mississippi, during the siege of Jackson. The brigade evacuated Jackson on the sixteenth and marched east to Morton, where the men rested in camp for five weeks.

On August 25, the two regiments left Morton by rail and arrived at Tyner's Station near Chattanooga on the thirty-first to join the Army of Tennessee. The 16th Regiment left there by rail on September 4 and arrived at Rome, Georgia, the next day to support the cavalry on the extreme left of the Confederate lines. The men of the 24th Regiment, as well as the 8th Georgia Battalion, Ferguson's Battery and a small part of the 46th Georgia Regiment, boarded a train for Ringgold on September 18. The 16th and most of the 46th Georgia Regiment were left at Rome to wait for a later train. The 16th Regiment remained on detached duty near Rome and was not engaged during the battle of Chickamauga on September 19 or September 20, 1863. The 24th Regiment was delayed at Kingston Station but arrived at Catoosa Station, near Ringgold, in the morning of September 19. The 24th guarded the ammunition wagon train as it marched that night to the battlefield at Chickamauga thirty miles away. The 24th was engaged at Chickamauga on the right of the Confederate lines on the twentieth. The men remained on the battlefield the next morning and marched to Chattanooga later in the day. The 16th Regiment rejoined the brigade on the twenty-third as it marched toward Chattanooga. The 16th and 24th Regiments bivouacked at the foot of Lookout Mountain on the left of the Confederate line during the siege of Chattanooga from September 23 to November 23. Both regiments evacuated their positions on November 23 and marched to the right of the Confederate lines on Missionary Ridge, where they were under fire but only lightly engaged at the north end on the twenty-fifth; they also acted as the rear guard for the corps during the withdrawal on November 26. Companies B, E and K of the 16th Regiment were detailed to support Ferguson's Battery in a rear guard action at Graysville, Georgia, the same day. Most of the men in these companies and three of Ferguson's four cannon were captured during that engagement.[138] On the withdrawal into north Georgia, the two regiments were held in reserve during the rear guard action at Ringgold Gap. Both regiments arrived at Dalton, Georgia, on November 27 and had constructed winter quarters two miles east of Dalton by December 15. On February 11 and February 12 and from February 23 to February 28, the men of the 24th Regiment were in line of battle near Red Clay but were not engaged. Leaving their winter quarters on May 6, 1864, both regiments marched to Mill Creek Gap on Rocky Face Ridge near Dalton. Company I of the 24th Regiment was engaged at Mill Creek Gap in a skirmish on May 9. The men marched that night toward Resaca, but the brigade was held in reserve during the engagement at Resaca on May 10. The 24th Regiment was engaged about halfway between Resaca and Calhoun the next day, and the men of both regiments were able to camp at nearby Gideon's Ford on the Oostenaula River for the next four days. The 16th and 24th Regiments were engaged at McGinnis's Ferry on the Oostenaula River on May 14 but were held in reserve while under shellfire at Resaca on May 15. The 24th Regiment and the 1st Battalion of Georgia Sharpshooters were engaged at Tanners's Ferry near Calhoun on May 16; the 16th Regiment suffered a few casualties while being held in reserve that day. The 16th and 24th were in line of battle on the nineteenth, but they were not engaged near Cassville. The men crossed the Etowah River that night and bivouacked along the Allatoona Road until May 24. Both regiments were present, but not engaged, at New Hope Church on the twenty-fifth; the 24th Regiment suffered a few casualties that day. The regiments established heavy skirmish lines northwest of Marietta after May 25. They skirmished there on June 1 and marched to a reserve position near Gilgal Church on June 4. The men moved on the ninth into a supporting position on Pine Mountain, where they were involved in skirmishes until the eighteenth.[139] Gist's Brigade was ordered to Kennesaw Mountain on June 19. The 16th and 24th endured nearly constant artillery and rifle fire at Kennesaw Mountain for thirteen days beginning June 20. The regiments were engaged at Kennesaw Mountain on June 20, 24 and 27 and remained in line of battle until July 2. They left Kennesaw Mountain on the night of the second and marched to Smyrna Church, five miles south of Marietta. The 16th Regiment was engaged, and the 24th Regiment endured shelling at Smyrna Church on July 3 and 4, and they evacuated on July 5, marching down the Atlanta Road toward the Chattahoochee River.[140] The regiments crossed the river on July 10 and camped nearby until the eighteenth. On July 19, the men occupied a new line just south of Peach Tree Creek, about three miles from Atlanta. The two regiments were engaged at the battle of Peach Tree Creek on July 20 and at the battle of Atlanta on the twenty-second.[141] Neither regiment was engaged at Ezra Church on July 28. They remained in the Atlanta trenches during late July and August 1864. Companies A, B, F, K and I of the 24th Regiment were engaged in severe picket fights on August 5, 6 and 17. The 16th and 24th marched toward Jonesboro on August 30 and arrived there the next day. The 24th Regiment was engaged there the evening of the thirty-first, but the 16th was held in reserve once again. Both regiments were engaged there on September 1. The regiments withdrew to Lovejoy on the night of September 2 and remained in the vicinity until September 19. After a ten-day truce, the men left Jonesboro on the nineteenth, crossed the Chattahoochee River and marched westward toward Palmetto Station, Georgia. The regiments recrossed the river on September 29 and began their march through northern Georgia. The brigade captured a Federal garrison at Dalton on October 13 and destroyed twenty miles of railroad track between Dalton and Tunnel Hill.

As Sherman pursued Hood, the 24th Regiment skirmished in a rear guard action at Ship's Gap, also called Taylor's Ridge, Georgia, on October 16.[142] The regiments reached Gadsden, Alabama, on October 21, marched past Decatur and Florence and crossed over the Tennessee River into Tennessee on November 13.[143] Hood's army reached Spring Hill on the twenty-ninth but failed to take advantage of an opportunity to attack the unprepared Federal forces as those forces passed through that night. Gist's Brigade was engaged in the debacle at Franklin on November 30. On December 2, Hood's army advanced toward Nashville. The two regiments were shelled near Nashville on the fourth, and the men skirmished there on December 5, 7, 8 and 15. On the sixteenth, the Army of Tennessee was routed at Nashville. The army reorganized at Franklin the next day and withdrew to the south. The 24th Regiment skirmished in a rear guard action with Federal cavalry at Rutherford's Creek, about eight miles from Spring Hill, on the nineteenth.[144] The brigade crossed the Tennessee River on the twenty-seventh, and the men arrived at Corinth, Mississippi, on December 31, 1864. The brigade left Corinth on January 10, 1865, and arrived at Tupelo, Mississippi, on the thirteenth. The men rested there until January 24, when the two regiments left for South Carolina by a circuitous route of four hundred and sixty miles by foot, rail and boat. Arriving in South Carolina on February 9, the men crossed the Saluda River on the seventeenth and reached Newberry two days later.

They passed through Unionville on March 2, moved into North Carolina and arrived at Charlotte on the eleventh. From there, the men marched to Smithfield on March 20. The 16th and 24th Regiments were not engaged at Averasboro or Bentonville. The Army of Tennessee bivouacked near Smithfield from April 1 to April 8.[145] The 16th and 24th Regiments were consolidated on April 9 and, as the Consolidated 16th and 24th Regiment, SCV, surrendered with the Army of Tennessee on April 26. The men were paroled on May 1.

6.

The 16th and 24th Regiment, South Carolina Volunteers, Consolidated

The 16th and 24th Regiment, SCV, Consolidated, was created on April 9, 1865, at High Point, North Carolina, from remnants of the 16th and 24th Regiments, SCV. The original 16th contributed 224 men, and 221 came from the 24th. Benjamin Burgh Smith, who was appointed colonel at the consolidation, was ordered to organize a new regiment by condensing the twenty companies of the two regiments into ten. The 16th Regiment was consolidated into Companies A, B, D, E and F and the 24th into Companies C, G, H, I and K.

Field Officers

Benjamin Burgh Smith of Charleston was assistant adjutant general of States Rights Gist's Brigade with the rank of major in 1864. Before then, also at the rank of major, he was the only field officer of the 2nd Battalion of South Carolina Sharpshooters. He was shot through the thigh at the battle of Franklin while commanding the 16th Regiment in the absence of its field officers.[1] When the 16th and 24th Regiments were consolidated on April 9, 1865, Smith was appointed its commander with the rank of colonel. He was paroled with the regiment on May 1, 1865.

Thomas C. Morgan, captain of Company K of the 24th Regiment, had also served as acting major of that regiment. Whether or not he was ever officially promoted to that rank is unclear.[2] Morgan was promoted to lieutenant colonel of the 16th and 24th Consolidated Regiment on April 9, 1865. He was paroled at Greensboro on May 1, 1865.

Theodore Gaillard Croft of Greenville was promoted to major of the Consolidated 16th and 24th Regiment on April 9, 1865. He had been captain of Company C of the 16th Regiment before the consolidation.

COMPANIES

Company A was commanded by G.W. Holtzclaw, previously captain of Company F of the 16th Regiment. It was composed of men who had been in the 16th Regiment.

Company B's commander, C.M. Furman, was previously captain of Company H of the 16th Regiment. It was composed of men who had been in the 16th Regiment.

Company C was commanded by William Allston Gibbes, previously captain of Company D of the 16th Regiment. Company C men came from both the 16th and 24th Regiments.

Company D was commanded by Edward G. Roberts, previously captain of Company I of the 16th Regiment. It was composed of men who had been in the 16th Regiment.

Company E's commander, Richard H. Alexander, served previously as first lieutenant of Company B of the 16th Regiment. He had been wounded at Jonesboro and was present at the surrender. Company E was composed of men who had been in the 16th Regiment.

Company F was commanded by J.L. McCullough, previously first lieutenant of Company E of the 16th Regiment. It was composed of men who had been in the 16th Regiment.

Company G was commanded by James A. Tillman, previously first lieutenant of Company I of the 24th Regiment. It was composed of men who had been in the 24th Regiment.

Company H was commanded by William M. Beckham, previously a lieutenant in Company G of the 24th Regiment. It was composed of men who had been in the 24th Regiment.

Company I's commander, Adrian C. Appleby, served previously as a lieutenant in Company C of the 24th Regiment. His father, Moses T. Appleby, was captain of the company. It was composed of men who had been in the 24th Regiment.

Company K was commanded by C.S. Beaty, previously a lieutenant in Company F of the 24th Regiment. It was composed of men who had been in the 24th Regiment.

MAJOR MOVEMENTS AND ENGAGEMENTS

On April 10, 1865, the new regiment marched for six miles northwest on the Louisburg Road. The next day, the men marched to Raleigh and had reached Chapel Hill by the thirteenth. The regiment moved on to Ruffin's

Mill on the fourteenth; the men crossed both the Haw and Alamance Rivers on the fifteenth. The next day, they marched fifteen miles toward Salisbury and camped near Goldsboro on the seventeenth. Following a short rest, the men drilled between April 20 and April 24 and took up the march again on the twenty-sixth, covering ten miles on the High Point Road. The Army of Tennessee surrendered the same day, and the men, who were paroled on May 1, left on the third for their homes in South Carolina. Those of the original 16th Regiment disbanded at Spartanburg, while men of the 24th marched home as organized companies and disbanded at their original muster grounds.

7.

Independent Infantry Organizations

The Battalion of South Carolina State Cadets, Local Defense Troops

The Battalion of South Carolina State Cadets, Local Defense Troops, was also called John B. White's Battalion; the Local Defense Troops, Charleston; the Boy Battalion; and the Battalion of State Cadets–South Carolina Infantry. It was created on January 28, 1861, by an act of the South Carolina General Assembly.[1] The same act also created the South Carolina Military Academy, a new institution combining The Citadel Academy in Charleston and The Arsenal Academy in Columbia. Made up of companies from both schools, the Battalion of State Cadets was designed to become part of the military organization of the state.[2]

Field Officers

Peter Fayssoux Stevens of Clarendon and Anderson Districts was superintendent of the South Carolina Military Academy in early 1861 and as such commanded the Battalion of South Carolina State Cadets. He also commanded both the Iron Battery and the Point Battery on Morris Island during the bombardment of Fort Sumter in mid-April. Stevens resigned on August 8, 1861, to enter the Episcopal ministry. He was ordained in October.[3] Even so, he responded to the need of his state and accepted an appointment to the post of colonel of the Holcombe Legion on November 21. About a year later, on September 17, 1862, he was slightly wounded at Sharpsburg.[4] Stevens tendered his resignation on September 22, writing, "Impelled by a sense of the imminent danger which threatened South Carolina last fall, I entered the army. Experience has but confirmed my former impressions that a minister of the Gospel is out of place as a military commander. I, therefore, respectfully tender my resignation to take effect on the 30 day of the present month, should God spare my life to that day."[5] The resignation was accepted on October 8, and Stevens entered a career in the Episcopal ministry in South Carolina.[6]

James Benjamin White of Georgetown replaced Stevens as superintendent of the South Carolina Military Academy and commanded the battalion after August 1861. He was promoted from superintendent of The Arsenal to superintendent of The Citadel Academy on August 8, with the rank of major, and he held the position throughout the war. Interestingly enough, this family contributed three brothers, all majors, to the Confederate cause. One, Richard Green White, served as major of the 10th Regiment; the other, William Capers White, served as major of the 7th.

Companies

Company A, the Citadel Cadets, was composed of men from the entire state. Hugh Smith Thompson, professor of belles lettres and ethics and later governor of South Carolina, was captain for the entire war.[7] This company, also called the Battalion of State Cadets (Citadel), was further broken down into two companies, designated A and B. Captain Thompson commanded Company A.[8] G.G. Wells might have commanded Company A, but the *CSR* lists him as second lieutenant of Company B. First Lieutenant Nathaniel Walker Armstrong, professor of mathematics and mechanical philosophy at The Citadel, commanded Company B.[9] He was paroled at Augusta, Georgia, on May 25, 1865. R.F. Lawton might have commanded Company B at some point, but the *CSR* does not list him.

Company B, the Arsenal Cadets, was also composed of men from the entire state. John Peyre Thomas, a professor at The Citadel who held the rank of captain in April 1861, commanded the company. Thomas was in charge of the Blakely cannon during the bombardment of Fort Sumter in April 1861. When Stevens resigned in August 1861, Thomas was promoted to major and transferred to Columbia as superintendent of The Arsenal, a post that included command of the Battalion of Arsenal Cadets. Actually, Thomas commanded three different organizations during the war: the Battalion of Arsenal Cadets from 1861 to 1865, Thomas's Battalion in 1863 and the Regiment of Detailed Men in 1864 and 1865. Company B was also divided into two companies, designated A and B. First Lieutenant John Bellinger Patrick, professor of mathematics at The Arsenal, commanded Company A, while Lieutenant Alfred Junius Norris, professor of belles lettres and history at The Arsenal, and Second Lieutenant Percival S. Norris led Company B. Alfred Norris was captain of Company A, 15th Battalion,

South Carolina Artillery, from June 6, 1861, until he resigned his commission on January 1, 1862. He was paroled at Augusta, Georgia, on May 26, 1865. One card spells his name as Noris. Percival S. Norris was graduated from The Citadel in August 1864 and applied for a commission as lieutenant in the 1st Regiment, South Carolina Regulars (Butler's regiment).

Brigade Affiliations

White's Battalion was part of DeSaussure's 5th Subdivision of Ripley's 1st South Carolina Military District in August and September 1863. By January 31, 1865, the Battalion of State Cadets was in Stephen Elliott's Brigade along with eight companies of the 1st Cavalry Regiment, three of the 1st Artillery Regiment, two of the 2nd Artillery Regiment, Company D of the South Carolina Siege Train and some Georgia units.[10] The Arsenal Cadets were under the command of A.C. Garlington after the evacuation of Columbia on February 17, 1865.

Major Movements and Engagements

As part of South Carolina's response to Major Robert Anderson's moving his garrison from Fort Moultrie to Fort Sumter on December 26, 1860, about fifty cadets from The Citadel were sent to Morris Island on January 1, 1861.[11] They were among the first companies of volunteers on Morris Island, and they constructed and manned Major P.F. Stevens's Battery along with the Vigilant Rifles, the German Riflemen and the Zouave Cadets. Serving as the artillery detachment, the Citadel Cadets fired upon the Union vessel *Star of the West* on January 9, 1861. Only a few were stationed on Sullivan's Island and in Charleston; about seventy remained at The Citadel. The cadets returned to The Citadel on February 4 and were granted a leave of absence the following April. They were not engaged as a corps during the bombardment of Fort Sumter on the twelfth and thirteenth; some, however, served the batteries at White Point Garden, and various individuals participated with other units during the battle.

Officers and cadets from both The Citadel and The Arsenal Academy drilled new recruits in 1861. Superintendent of The Arsenal James B. White and twelve of his cadets drilled new recruits of the Hampton Legion in Columbia that summer.[12] Citadel cadets not only drilled new recruits in Charleston, but were also sent to Anderson to work with Orr's rifles, to Georgetown to work with the 10th Regiment and even to Virginia.[13] On November 2, 1861, the Arsenal Cadets escorted 150 Federal prisoners from the railroad station to the Columbia city jail.[14] When Federal naval and land forces occupied Port Royal on November 7, Citadel Cadets were sent to Wappoo Cut the same day as infantry support for the Washington Artillery to protect Charleston's "back door." They remained for about two weeks. Forty-two Arsenal Cadets were also sent to Charleston on November 9 to assist in its defense, but they returned to Columbia on the twenty-second. About June 3, 1862, Citadel Cadets were sent to Newton's Cut on James Island to help repel the Federal troop landings there.

On June 9, a group of thirty-six Citadel Cadets, eager for action, marched out of The Citadel and formed a company called variously the Cadet Troop, Cadet Company or Cadet Rangers, and mustered in state service in Aiken's regiment, South Carolina Partisan Rangers, also called the 16th Battalion, South Carolina Cavalry. The company became Company F of the 6th Regiment, South Carolina Cavalry, in November. Though the superintendent promptly suspended the students, and the Board of Visitors expelled them, the Association of Graduates received the men as members in good standing after the war. The Citadel Cadets were not engaged during the battle at Secessionville on June 16. On March 18, 1863, the corps was ordered to report to General Beauregard in Charleston in case of an attack, but the record is unclear as to how long they were in the field or even whether or not they were there.[15] The Arsenal Cadets tendered their services for local defense in the early summer of 1863; the offer was accepted. Ordered into active service on July 10, they were sent to Charleston, where they guarded the Commissary and Quartermaster Departments for about six weeks before returning to Columbia on September 1. The Citadel Cadets, who performed similar service in Charleston throughout the summer, were relieved from duty on September 28.[16] In early 1864, Citadel cadets were called out to guard both commissary stores and wharves in Charleston.[17] They were used again on May 23 as pickets near Grimball's Causeway on James Island.[18] Citadel Cadets were also sent to James Island for about a week to guard Federal prisoners captured during the boat assault on Fort Johnson on July 3. About the same time, Arsenal Cadets were called to Charleston to perform guard duty. From July to September, Citadel Cadets performed guard duty in Charleston and occasionally accompanied Federal prisoners to Andersonville.[19] From October 6 to October 12, Arsenal Cadets guarded Federal officers at Camp Sorghum on the Congaree River near Columbia.[20] Citadel Cadets were sent to Orangeburg on November 20, and some cadets also performed guard duty at the prison at Florence. Late November and early December found the cadets from both The Citadel and Arsenal gathered in Charleston awaiting deployment. It came on December 4, when they were sent by rail to Pocotaligo. The battalion was within ten minutes of arriving on the battlefield when the 5th Georgia Regiment gave way, and action ceased for the day.[21] Both companies were engaged in what the *Mercury* called their "baptism of fire" at the battle at the Tullifinny River on December 7, 1864.[22] Though neither was engaged on the eighth, the Cadet Battalion was placed on the left of the Confederate line on December 9. There, it saw limited action but suffered no losses.[23] The Arsenal Cadets were sent back to Columbia after the battle of Tullifinny, but those from The Citadel remained for picket duty and drilled nearby until they were sent to James Island on the twenty-fifth.

Arsenal cadets guarded Federal officers at the insane asylum in Columbia in mid-January.[24] Citadel Cadets saw action at Grimball's Causeway, James Island, on February 10, as did Arsenal Cadets supporting Thomas's Battery stationed near the Congaree River Bridge at the foot of Gervais Street in Columbia on the fifteenth. Arsenal Cadets also patrolled the streets of Columbia the next day and aided in the city's evacuation at about two in the morning on the seventeenth. They marched with A.C. Garlington's Brigade through Winnsboro, Lancaster Court House and Chesterfield to Wadesboro, North Carolina, even though Governor Magrath had said they were not to cross into North Carolina.[25] The governor ordered both the Arsenal Cadets and the South Carolina Militia to return to South Carolina on March 10 because of the threat of a Federal raid.[26] The Arsenal Cadets marched back to Charlotte, where they boarded a train for Chester, South Carolina. From Chester, they marched to Spartanburg, arriving on March 8.[27] Following the governor's orders, J.P. Thomas moved the Arsenal Cadets to Greenville about March 20.

The Citadel Cadets, meanwhile, participated in the retreat from James Island on February 16. They withdrew with Confederate forces from Charleston but did not cross over into North Carolina.[28] On March 20, the Citadel Cadets arrived in Spartanburg, where they went into camp on the Wofford College campus with the Arsenal Cadets. In late March, the Citadel Cadets joined the Arsenal cadets in Greenville. The Citadel Cadets were furloughed for a month in April, but the Arsenal Cadets skirmished with Federal raiders between Greenville and Williamston on May 1 before moving south. They were in camp at Newberry when they were furloughed and disbanded by Governor Magrath on May 9.[29] Though neither company actually surrendered to Federal troops, the Citadel Cadets were included in the parole in compliance with the military convention reached on April 26, 1865, at the Bennett House near Durham, North Carolina.

CUNNINGHAM'S BATTALION

Cunningham's Battalion remains something of a mystery; probably, it was not a South Carolina unit at all. When, or even whether, it existed is still unclear, as is the battalion's state of origin; it might have been a Georgia unit. The *CSR* lists Major John Cunningham as commander of a South Carolina Battalion but gives no details. A Charleston lawyer named John Cuningham served as colonel of the 17th Militia Regiment in 1860 and 1861. He announced his candidacy for colonel of the 3rd Regiment, South Carolina State Troops, in the summer of 1863 but did not win the election.[30] He was, however, elected captain of Company K of that regiment on October 1.[31] By October 1864, this John Cuningham was in poor health.[32] Another John Cunningham, a Savannah merchant during the war, most likely commanded the battalion. Four possible scenarios, any one of which could apply, are discussed here:

The most convincing explanation for Cunningham's Battalion is that it was actually a Georgia reserve unit. In July 1864, Captain John Cunningham commanded three companies of the 1st Georgia Regiment of Reserves, all of which were based in the 3rd Military District of South Carolina.[33] According to the *CSR*, in October 1864, Major John Cunningham commanded a ten-company regiment identified only as the South Carolina Reserves located in the Military District of Georgia and the Fifth Sub-District of South Carolina.[34] This entry was probably the source of the *CSR*'s reference to Cunningham's Battalion as a South Carolina unit. In reality, Cunningham's command was a Georgia, not a South Carolina, Reserve Regiment, and its commander, John Cunningham, was almost certainly the Savannah merchant and not the Charleston lawyer. We know, first, that the Charleston Cuningham was in poor health at the time; we also know that a series of articles he wrote for the *Charleston Daily Courier* in October and November 1864 were signed without the addition of a military rank.[35] Furthermore, no South Carolina reserve battalion in existence in late 1864 was commanded by a John Cunningham, though Major John Cunningham was an officer in the 1st Regiment of Georgia Reserves whose colonel was W.R. Symons.[36] Sifakis states that Cunningham's Battalion surrendered in North Carolina with the Army of Tennessee on April 26, 1865.[37]

Another possible explanation of the confusion begins in February 1863 when General Beauregard called for volunteers to help defend Charleston.[38] The appeal resulted in the creation of two new battalions whose members enlisted specifically "for and during the attack on Charleston."[39] One, commanded by John Peyre Thomas, was raised in Columbia; the other, under an unknown commander, was raised from men already in service but on furlough in South Carolina at the time. Thomas's Battalion was in the field from April 7 to April 15.[40] The other battalion was stationed at Mount Pleasant and was disbanded when the emergency was over about April 15, 1863.[41] The possibility exists that the Charleston John Cuningham commanded the second battalion. Support of this position is derived mostly by process of elimination: The only reserve battalions raised in South Carolina during the entire war were the two put together in March 1863 and those raised in the summer of 1864. The only battalion whose commander is unknown is the second of those raised in 1863. Evidence against Cuningham as commander is supplied by a biographical sketch printed in the *Charleston Daily Courier* in September 1863. The synopsis of Cuningham's wartime career does not credit him with a battalion command.[42]

A third scenario goes back to May 1861, when John Cuningham, the Charlestonian, attempted to raise either a regiment or a legion of ten or eleven companies that would enlist for the duration of the war.[43] The proposed regiment would comprise eight infantry and two rifle companies. The legion would differ from the regiment only in the addition of one battery of flying artillery. The Darlington Guards and other companies in Gregg's six-month regiment offered their services to Cuningham.[44] Robert Meriwether, previously captain of Company H in Gregg's regiment, also raised a company for the regiment in Edgefield District.[45] In August, Cuningham complained bitterly that both Orr's regiment of rifles and Maxcy Gregg's regiment had been accepted for the duration of the war. He felt that the western part of the state was being given preferential treatment.[46] By September 1861, a number of companies were forming for the express purpose of joining Cuningham's regiment.[47] Cuningham gave public notice at that time that he had purchased one thousand Enfield rifles and was proposing to raise and equip a rifle regiment.[48] By November 9, Governor Pickens had authorized Cuningham to raise the rifle regiment, and by the eleventh, five companies had been accepted.[49] In mid-November, the newspaper reported that organization was nearly complete and the regiment would be known as the Calhoun Rifle Regiment.[50] According to the paper, the colonel was to be John Cuningham, Robert Martin was to be lieutenant colonel and the major was yet undetermined.[51] On January 18, 1862, the public was told that Cuningham's regiment was the eighteenth from South Carolina to volunteer for twelve months of service. No other information regarding Cuningham's effort exists; his attempts to raise a regiment or a legion ultimately failed.[52] In any event, his efforts in 1861 were not directed toward creating a battalion of reserves.

The fourth scenario is that Cunningham's South Carolina Battalion never existed, and its inclusion in the *CSR* was simply a mistake.

BROOKS'S BATTALION REGULAR INFANTRY

Brooks's Battalion Regular Infantry was also called Brooks's Battalion of Regulars, the 2nd Foreign Battalion, C.S.A., and The Foreign Battalion. Only its field- and company-grade officers were South Carolinians. The Confederate Congress passed a law allowing all foreign-born soldiers in the Union army held as prisoners of war by the Confederate States of America to take the oath of allegiance to the Confederate government and enlist in the Confederate army.[53] Brooks's Battalion was formed in the fall of 1864 from Federal prisoners who were held at the stockade at Florence and took advantage of the law. Most of the men were from Ireland, Germany and Spain, but other European nations were represented as well. One captain, however, Vincent F. Martin of Company A, wrote that a serious mistake was made when many Americans passing themselves off as Englishmen were erroneously allowed to enlist. When the battalion was organized at Summerville in October 1864, its six hundred men were divided into five companies whose officers were drawn from the 1st Regiment, South Carolina Artillery (Regulars), and the 1st Regiment, South Carolina Infantry (Regulars). J.H. Brooks himself wrote in 1891: "The experiment failed, the men deserting and showing generally no loyalty to the Confederate cause and were returned to prison."[54] The 1st Foreign Battalion, commanded by Lieutenant Colonel Julius G. Tucker, continued to exist after Brooks's Battalion was disbanded.[55]

Field Officers

John Hampden Brooks of Edgefield District commanded the Foreign Battalion. A brother of Congressman Preston S. Brooks, he had served previously as captain of Company H of the 7th Infantry Battalion. He was wounded three times on May 16, 1864, at Drewry's Bluff where most of Company H was lost. General Hagood cited Brooks for conspicuous gallantry at that battle. Because of his courage, experience, military knowledge and judgment, Brooks was appointed commander of the 2nd Foreign Battalion with the rank of lieutenant colonel. After that experiment failed, Brooks briefly commanded the reserve forces in Charleston before returning to his previous post in the 7th Battalion. J.B. Kershaw wrote in 1862: "Captain Brooks is a gentleman of high character and position, highly educated and of fine talent. He has established his character as an accomplished and gallant officer by efficient services in the field in command of a company for the last year."[56]

Major Bryan of General Beauregard's staff, appointed to help with the organization of the battalion, never reported for duty and was never connected with the command.[57]

Companies

Company A was commanded by Vincent F. Martin, a first lieutenant in the 1st Regiment South Carolina Infantry Regulars. Accidentally shot through both legs by a Confederate sentry at Port Royal Ferry while in the Charleston Light Dragoons in 1862, Martin continued to suffer from effects of the wound until the end of the war.[58] He joined the 1st Regiment, South Carolina Infantry Regulars, and returned to command Company C of the 1st Infantry after the Foreign Battalion was disbanded. On sick leave at home when the war ended, Martin did not surrender nor was he discharged.[59] Later he wrote a brief history of the battalion.[60]

Company B was commanded by John C. Minott, a lieutenant in Company G of the 1st Regiment, South Carolina Infantry Regulars. Minott returned to the 1st Infantry after the Foreign Battalion was disbanded. He was wounded by a shell fragment at either Averasboro or Bentonville while in command of Company G.[61]

Company C was commanded by Eldred Simkins, a first lieutenant in the 1st Regiment, South Carolina Artillery (Regulars). Simkins returned to the 1st Artillery after the Foreign Battalion was disbanded and served until the end of the war.

Company D was commanded by David Lewis Wardlaw, an officer in the 1st Regiment, South Carolina Infantry (Regulars). Suffering from the effects of an old wound, Wardlaw did not return to the 1st Infantry after the Foreign Battalion was disbanded.

Company E was commanded by B. Gaillard Pinckney, previously captain of the Carolina Light Infantry in the 1st Regiment Rifles, South Carolina Militia. Pinckney had been left in command of the camp at Summerville when the battalion went to Savannah. When it was disbanded, Pinckney took the remainder of his men back to the prison stockade at Florence.

Major Movements and Engagements

The battalion drilled at Summerville from October 10 until late November 1864. The men were issued tents, clothing and equipment, but were not yet armed. Brooks received permission from General Hardee to participate in the defense of Savannah, which was under threat from Sherman at the time. About November 30, detachments of Companies A, B, C and D were sent to Honey Hill but arrived too late for the battle. Company E was probably left in camp at Summerville.[62] On December 2, the battalion was ordered to Savannah and placed in key outposts in the defensive lines around the city.[63] The men initially behaved very well while under fire near Savannah.[64] On December 16, however, some of them launched a plan to kill all the officers of Brooks's Battalion and desert across the lines to join Sherman's army. Betrayed by an orderly sergeant named Sinner, the plotters were ordered to surrender by the officers of the battalion who were supported by Georgia Reserves. As a result, Brigadier General H.W. Mercer issued orders for four other orderly sergeants and three additional ringleaders to be court-martialed and shot. After the mutiny, most of the remaining men, now considered prisoners of war, worked with the officers on the pontoons near Savannah. The battalion evacuated Savannah at about four in the morning on December 21, the men continuing with their death threats to the officers. So it was that the remnants of Companies A, B, C and D marched to Hardeeville, boarded the train there and returned to the prison stockade at Florence.[65] Company E, which had been left behind at Summerville, had also been sent back to the stockade at Florence on December 18.[66] A few of the men, presumably those considered loyal, were assigned to the 1st Regiment, South Carolina Infantry Regulars, and the 1st Regiment, South Carolina Artillery Regulars. Brooks, who was placed in command of unattached troops in Charleston, soon returned to his original command at his own request. Most of the company officers, in fact, returned to their respective commands from which they had never resigned.[67] Brooks wrote: "My appointment to [the battalion's] command was intended as a compliment to me, and I took it as such, but really, I was never sanguine of the success of the experiment. In a fortress, it might have succeeded, but in the open field it was a hazardous undertaking. If success had been possible, the officers I had were preeminently fitted to achieve it."[68] Tucker's 1st Foreign Battalion remained in service until at least February 14, 1865. Perhaps learning from Brooks's experience, Lieutenant General Hardee ordered Tucker to recruit new men for his battalion only from Irish and French prisoners and to use them only for engineering duty.[69]

8.

The 6th Regiment, South Carolina Cavalry

The 6th Regiment, South Carolina Cavalry, was called by several names, among them Aiken's regiment Mounted Partisan Rangers, 1st Regiment South Carolina Partisan Rangers and the 1st Regiment Partizans.[1] It became a full regiment in a roundabout way: the 16th Battalion, South Carolina Cavalry—also called both the 16th Battalion, South Carolina Partisan Rangers, and the 6th Battalion, South Carolina Cavalry—was organized on July 21, 1862, at Camp Preston near Columbia; its six companies were designated A to F. The men volunteered for the duration of the war at the initial enlistment in July and August.[2] According to the *Mercury*, the Partisan Rangers mustered in the 6th Cavalry Battalion on July 27, an indication that the Rangers had existed as a separate organization before the battalion was created.[3] Company G, the battalion's seventh, was added on August 6, and three previously independent companies were attached on November 1, raising the battalion to regimental strength and to ultimate redesignation as the 6th Regiment, South Carolina Cavalry. Sifakis records the date of organization as January 19, 1863.[4] Most likely, the partisan regiment was organized on November 1, 1862, since the colonel's commission bore that date. In January 1863, the men gave their consent to change the regiment's designation from "partisan" to "regular cavalry (regiment) of the line," a move that probably took place officially on January 19, one day after the 5th Regiment was created.[5]

Field Officers

Hugh Kerr Aiken of Charleston, the regiment's first and only colonel, commanded the 16th Battalion at the rank of lieutenant colonel from

July 21, 1862, until the regiment's creation on November 1, 1862. He was promoted to colonel on March 19, 1863, with rank from November 1, 1862. Aiken was severely wounded at Trevilian Station on June 11, 1864, when a Minié ball struck him near the right collarbone, traveled through the chest and exited near the shoulder blade.[6] He received a sixty-day furlough on August 25.[7] Aiken was killed near Darlington, South Carolina, at Stokes's Bridge, also called Kelly Town and Lynches Creek, on February 24, 1865. He had served as brigade commander from Brigadier General John Dunovant's death on October 1, 1864, until his own, though he was never actually promoted to brigadier general. Aiken was a brother of David Wyatt Aiken, colonel of the 7th Regiment, South Carolina Infantry. Private C.M. Calhoun wrote that Aiken "knew no fear and was ever ready to face danger when he felt duty called him to it."[8] U.R. Brooks called him "one of the bravest and most gallant of the old brigade."[9]

Lovick Pierce Miller of Georgetown was elected lieutenant colonel on December 4, 1862; his commission was dated December 13. When Miller, who had served as major of the 23rd Regiment, South Carolina Infantry, was not re-elected at the reorganization in the spring of 1862, he enlisted as a private in Company G of the 16th Battalion on June 29 and was elected lieutenant colonel when the battalion became the 6th Regiment. When Brigadier General John Dunovant's advance guard was stampeded by a Federal outpost on the night of September 30, 1864, Miller was thrown from his horse and suffered scrapes, bruises and a dislocated finger.[10] According to C.M. Calhoun, he was not very popular among the men partly because of the strict discipline he imposed while managing a camp of dismounted troopers near Richmond in 1864.[11] Calhoun called Miller, in fact, the "cowardly Czar of Butler's brigade" and referred to him derisively as "our courageous lieutenant-colonel."[12] Miller himself wrote in 1908 that he was colonel of the 6th Regiment.[13] Though he did command the regiment when Aiken was acting brigadier general, there is no evidence that he was promoted to colonel. U.R. Brooks called Miller "gallant" and "one of the best disciplinarians in the army."[14]

Thomas Barker Ferguson of Spartanburg District, the regiment's only major, was captain of Company D of the 3rd Regiment, South Carolina Infantry, from April 14, 1861, until the reorganization in May 1862. He had enlisted as a sergeant in the 16th Battalion on May 1, 1862, an act that removed him from consideration when elections were held less than two weeks later, on the thirteenth. Ferguson was promoted to major of the 6th Regiment on January 1, 1863. He suffered a serious wound to the leg during the attack on Kilpatrick's camp near Fayetteville on March 10, 1865. According to C.M. Calhoun, the leg should have been amputated immediately, but Ferguson told the surgeon he would rather die than lose his leg and hired a carriage to take him home instead; he survived the trip but died shortly afterward.[15] Captain A.B. Mulligan of the 5th Regiment called Ferguson "a very clever gentleman."[16] Major Thomas Barker Ferguson should not be confused with the Thomas Barker Ferguson who served as captain of Ferguson's Battery, South Carolina Artillery, and, later, as major of artillery.

COMPANIES

Company A, the Carolina Guerrillas, also called Captain Milton A. Sullivan's Company, was composed of men from Laurens, Greenville, Pickens, Abbeville and Anderson Districts, plus a few from Spartanburg District. Milton Arnold Sullivan commanded when it was Company A in the 16th Battalion and retained command in the 6th Regiment. Sullivan died of pneumonia in Columbia on February 19, 1865.

Company B, the Edgefield Rangers, was also called the Edgefield Partisan Rangers and Captain Lewis Jones's Company.[17] Though composed mostly of men from Edgefield District, the company enrolled a few from Richland, Abbeville, Lexington, Marlboro and Colleton Districts. Lewis Jones, who raised, equipped and mounted the company, also commanded it in both the 16th Battalion and 6th Regiment. The fifty-one-year-old Jones resigned on July 4, 1863, saying he did not wish to leave the service but official business required it. His term as sheriff of Edgefield District was about to expire, he explained, and he needed to settle the business of the sheriff's office and attend to the administration of a large estate. James J. Gregg, who was promoted to captain and replaced Jones on July 4, was wounded in the arm at Trevilian Station on June 11, 1864. Reports differ as to the severity of the wound, but Gregg served until the end of the war.[18] Company B had also been Company B in the 16th Battalion.

Company C was called Captain P.W. Goodwyn's Company. Most of its men came from Abbeville and Fairfield Districts, but a few men were from Spartanburg, Anderson, Orangeburg and Laurens Districts. Peter W. Goodwyn commanded when it was Company C in the 16th Battalion and retained command in the 6th Regiment. He was the company's only captain and was considered a "fine officer."[19] While serving as acting major, Goodwyn was wounded by a shell at Trevilian Station on June 11 or June 12, 1864, but remained on duty.[20] He was wounded again that year at Burgess's Mill on October 27. Goodwyn surrendered along with others of the 6th Regiment at Hillsboro, North Carolina, in April 1865.

Company D was called Captain William M. Hale's Company. Hale, who had commanded when it was Company D in the 16th Battalion, retained command for about two months in the 6th Regiment. He was appointed captain of a company of marines on the steamship *Rattlesnake* on December 15, 1862, and resigned his position in Company D on January 6, 1863. First Lieutenant Robert E. Evans was promoted to captain the same day. Evans was wounded in the right foot by a Minié ball on June 3, 1864, at Crouch's Ford, Virginia. He was furloughed from Jackson Hospital on June 8 for thirty days. Reported as absent without leave since October 30, Evans was dropped from the rolls on December 7, 1864. The record does not show the districts represented in Company D.

Company E, the Laurens Partizans, from Laurens and Spartanburg Districts, was also called Captain James P. Knight's Company.[21] Knight, who commanded when it was Company E in the 16th Battalion, retained command in the 6th Regiment. Ailing since August 8, 1864, he resigned for the good of the service on November 2.[22] W.D. Evins was promoted to captain in late 1864.

Company F was called by many names, among them the Cadet Company, the Cadet Troop, the Cadet Rangers, the Citadel Troop and Captain Moses B. Humphrey's Company.[23] It was formed by thirty-six cadets who marched out of The Citadel, formed a company and mustered in state service on June 9, 1862. They entered Confederate service on July 23 as Company F of the 16th Battalion. Though suspended by the superintendent and expelled by the Board of Visitors, the men were received as members in good standing by the Association of Graduates after the war.[24] The Cadet Rangers, who came from all over the state, became the drill cadre for the 6th Regiment and were often used to instruct both officers and men.[25] Moses Benbow Humphrey, who commanded the company in both battalion and regiment, was wounded in the foot and leg during an engagement near the Haulover Cut on John's Island on February 9, 1864.[26] He also sustained a slight wound to the right leg at Trevilian Station four months later, on June 12.[27] Admitted to C.S.A. General Hospital in Charlottesville on the thirteenth, Humphrey was sent to Columbia on July 5. He must have returned to duty shortly afterward because he suffered a flesh wound in the right ankle or leg in mid-August 1864. He was admitted to Jackson Hospital on August 20 and was awarded a sixty-day furlough on September 23. Humphrey was wounded a fourth time when canister shattered an arm while he and two others charged a Federal cannon during the attack on Kilpatrick's camp at Fayetteville on March 10, 1865. Admitted to Pettigrew General Hospital #13 in Raleigh three days later, Humphrey refused amputation. He was furloughed on March 18 and admitted on the twentieth to C.S.A. General

Hospital #11 in Charlotte, where he again refused amputation. Humphrey died from the effects of the wound in Charlotte.[28] The *CSR* records the date of his death as April 30, 1865; the *Memory Roll* says he died in Charlotte on May 27. Humphrey was a "gallant officer," one who "was gifted with a fine intellect."[29]

Company G was called Captain John R. Miot's Company. Its men were from Richland, Abbeville and Edgefield Districts. Miot commanded when it was Company G of the 16th Battalion and retained command in the 6th Regiment. He got drunk with some company privates in October 1863 and was charged on the twenty-ninth with drunkenness while on duty as well as conduct prejudicial to good order and military discipline. Miot resigned on November 4. E.R. Clinkscales was promoted to captain as his replacement in late 1863 or early 1864. Clinkscales was severely wounded, either in the right leg or left knee, on the Boydton Plank Road on October 27, 1864.[30] He was furloughed from the hospital for thirty days on December 24; whether or not he returned to the company is unknown.

Company H, the Yeadon Rangers, was among the last three companies to be added in November 1862 to bring the 16th Battalion to regimental strength.[31] It may have been part of Aiken's Partizan Rangers before it was attached to the 6th Regiment.[32] John J. Maguire, a native of Ireland, organized the company in the spring of 1862. It probably mustered in service on May 1, the date Maguire himself enlisted in state service.[33] The company, known then as Captain John J. Maguire's Company, mustered in Confederate service for the duration of the war on July 27 in Columbia and probably served as an independent company until November. Apparently the company was sent from Columbia to Adams Run immediately after it mustered in Confederate service. According to the *CSR*, it was stationed at Adams Run in Charleston District on July 27 and was still there when it became part of the 6th Regiment in November 1862. The company, whose men came from Orangeburg, Cheraw, Charleston, Spartanburg, Richland, Greenville, Sumter, Marion, Pickens, Abbeville and Colleton Districts, was named for "R. Yeadon, Esquire," who was probably Richard Yeadon, editor of the *Charleston Mercury*.[34] Maguire, who was sixty-two years old in July 1862, was its only captain. He had served previously as captain of Company G of the 11th Regiment, South Carolina Infantry, but was not re-elected at the reorganization in the spring of 1862. He was shot through the head and killed instantly at Reams Station on August 23, 1864.[35]

Company I, Whitner's Troop, was another of the final three added to the 16th Battalion in November 1862 to complete the 6th Regiment. The *CSR* records that Company I was also stationed at Adams Run in September 1862 and was still there when it mustered in the 6th Regiment two months later. Most of its men were from Marion, Sumter and Darlington Districts, though a few came from Williamsburg, Anderson and Kershaw Districts. Joe N. Whitner Jr., the only captain, was wounded at Reams Station on August 23, 1864, and returned to the company sometime after December 31.[36] He surrendered at Hillsboro, North Carolina.

Company K was the last of those added in November 1862 to round out the 6th Regiment. Most of its men were from Chesterfield District, but some came from Pickens District as well.[37] The men mustered in Confederate service for the duration of the war at Adams Run on November 1, 1862. Minor Jackson Hough, who was commissioned on November 2, was the company's only captain. Never wounded, he served until the end of the war.[38] Some Company K men never surrendered.

BRIGADE AFFILIATIONS

The 6th Regiment was attached to the Department of South Carolina, Georgia and Florida from January 1863 to about May 1864.[39] The 4th, 5th and 6th Regiments were attached on May 28, 1864, to M.C. Butler's Brigade in the Army of Northern Virginia. Later brigade commanders were John Dunovant, W.S. Walker, Evander Law and T.M. Logan. After its return to South Carolina in early 1865, the regiment was attached to Hampton's Cavalry Command until the end of the war.[40]

MAJOR MOVEMENTS AND ENGAGEMENTS

All seven companies of the battalion were stationed at Adams Run in Charleston District when the 16th Battalion evolved into the 6th Regiment about November 1, 1862. During the late summer and early fall, the companies had spent some time at Camp Preston on the Lexington side of the Congaree River near Columbia. Though it seems unlikely that companies already in service on the coast would be sent back to Columbia for the sole purpose of launching a new regiment, the *Edgefield Advertiser* announced on September 24 that eight companies, including the Edgefield Rangers, were in a camp near the Saluda Factory outside Columbia and "have been for some time." Two others were expected to arrive soon.[41] Thus, it would appear that the companies had, in fact, been sent from Adams Run to the capital. Shortly after its organization on November 1, 1862, the 6th Regiment was ordered from Camp Preston back to Adams Run. From then until May 1864, the 6th Regiment was assigned to patrol duty on the coast, primarily along the Charleston & Savannah Railroad from John's Island to Bear Island. In December, Company B was based at Jacksonboro, a small station on the Charleston & Savannah Railroad a few hundred yards south of the railroad bridge over the Edisto River. From there it performed picket duty at Bennett's Point on Bear Island, at Cat Island and at various points along the Edisto River.[42] Company F was stationed at John's Island that month, and the remaining eight companies were at regimental headquarters near Adams Run.[43] Company B remained at Jacksonboro until February 1864, while Company F was at John's Island until April 1, 1864.

Company A was ordered to John's Island in March 1863, and remained there until April 1864. On the last day of March, it was involved in a skirmish on Seabrook Island while under the command of Major John Jenkins of the 3rd Regiment, South Carolina Cavalry. Companies A and F drew picket duty jointly at Haulover Cut on John's Island.[44] Adams Run continued as the base of operations for eight companies of the 6th Regiment until April 1864.[45] Elements of the regiment, including Companies B, D and G, acted as support for the Washington Artillery in an engagement on the South Edisto River near Willtown Bluff on July 10, 1863.[46] The artillery battery engaged an armed Federal steamer, the *John Adams*, and two smaller boats, the transport *Enoch Dean* and the tug *Governor Milton*, and sank the latter.[47] Company F also supported the artillery when it engaged two Federal gunboats, *Marblehead* and *Pawnee*, on December 25, 1863, near Legareville on the Stono River. Companies A and F saw action on John's Island from February 9 to February 12.[48] On the morning of the ninth, Company F's picket post near the bridge over Haulover Cut between Seabrook and John's Islands was captured. That morning, Captain Humphrey led his men in a bold attack against overwhelming numbers, setting the tone for the fighting over the next three days. Company F participated in a delaying action against a superior Federal force on February 9 and February 10, and it harassed Federal forces retreating from John's Island on the eleventh. Company F was engaged again in March while supporting the Washington Artillery on John's Island. Company G was based at Camp Bee near Ashepoo in early March.[49] Three companies were based at St. Andrews Parish, while the other seven were probably still at Adams Run.[50]

The 6th Regiment was ordered to Virginia on March 17, 1864, but didn't leave for another two months.[51] On May 5, not long before they left the state, Brigadier General M.C. Butler reviewed the 6th Regiment and the Hampton Legion Mounted Infantry at the Racecourse in Columbia. Both were bound for Virginia.[52] Company F, and probably other companies as well, left Columbia for Richmond on May 17. About half the regiment traveled by rail while the rest drove the horses overland. Arriving in

Virginia on May 29, the 6th Regiment, along with the 4th and 5th, relieved the 1st and 2nd Cavalry Regiments, which had been ordered back to South Carolina. Unlike the 4th and 5th, the 6th Regiment was not present during the engagement at Haw's Shop on May 28.[53] After that, action came thick and fast; the regiment skirmished almost daily from late May to August 1864. It was engaged at both Totopotomoi and Matadequin Creeks near Cold Harbor on May 30 and skirmished on the evening of June 2 at Bottom's Bridge.[54] Picket duty at White Oak Swamp occupied the next few days until the brigade marched to Mechanicsville on June 8. The 6th Regiment rode with the brigade the next day toward Gordonsville to intercept General P.H. Sheridan. Arriving at Louisa Court House about midday on the tenth, the brigade rested that night at Trevilian Station. The 6th Regiment fought at Louisa Court House during the first day's action near Trevilian Station on June 11, and it fought there again on the twelfth.[55] It pursued Sheridan on June 13, crossed the North Anna River on the fourteenth and continued the pursuit for four days until the command changed direction and headed for White House, Virginia, on June 18. The regiment fought at White House on the Pamunkey River on June 20 and June 21.[56] It saw action again on the twenty-fourth at Nance's Shop, also called Ladd's Store.[57] Crossing to the south side of the James River on June 26, the regiment arrived at Stony Creek Station on the Weldon Railroad south of Petersburg on the twenty-eighth. It fought with Wilson's Raiders at Sappony Church on the railroad about three miles from the station that night and again the next morning. The 6th Regiment was not engaged at Reams Station on June 29.

July brought more picket duty and some skirmishing, though the regiment was actively engaged at Reams Station on July 23 and at Lee's Mills on the thirtieth. July also saw some three to five hundred men of Butler's Brigade, all without horses, formed into three new companies, which became known as the "Dismounted Battalion of Butler's Brigade" or the "Stud Horse Battalion."[58] About August 11, the regiment marched for Culpeper but turned toward Richmond instead on the fifteenth. The next day, it marched through the capital city and on to Deep Bottom. The regiment was engaged at White Tavern on August 16 and August 17and saw action on the Darbytown Road near Riddell's Shop on the eighteenth. Crossing again to the south side of the James on the twenty-first, it moved on to a camp on the Squirrel Level Road about fourteen miles south of Petersburg. The 6th Regiment was engaged at Gravelly Run, also called Monck's Neck Bridge, about two miles west of Reams Station on August 23 and fought again the next day at a spot between the station and Stony Creek.[59] Whether or not it saw action at the station on the twenty-fifth is unclear; according to *Saddle*

Soldiers, the brigade was not engaged, but U.R. Brooks leaves the impression that Dunovant's Brigade was engaged on August 25 at Reams Station.[60] D.S. Freeman confirms its engagement there on the twenty-fourth.[61]

The regiment camped and picketed at various sites along the Boydton Plank Road throughout most of September. About a hundred men of Dunovant's Brigade, including a few from the 6th Regiment, took part in the City Point, or Beef Steak, Raid which occurred over a three-day period from September 14 to September 17. Butler's Division created a diversion by engaging Federal pickets near Burgess's Mill on three successive mornings during the raid. The division fought again near the mill on the nineteenth. Besides several skirmishes along the Vaughn and Squirrel Level Roads from September 27 to September 30, the regiment was also engaged at some point during the month at Wyatt's farm. Some of its companies were held in reserve while others fought during the engagement at the McDowell House on September 29.

The 6th Regiment was part of an engagement at Mrs. Cummings's farm October 1, 1864.[62] It also opposed Grant in an engagement on October 27 on the Boydton Plank Road near Burgess's Mill during Grant's attempt to take the South Side Railroad, his last effort in 1864 to turn Lee's right flank.[63] That fall, the men from the 4th, 5th and 6th Regiments without serviceable horses were sent to Stony Creek, Virginia, on the Weldon Railroad about twenty miles from the brigade's position.

On December 1, a Federal force overran and captured one hundred and twelve of the dismounted men, including twenty-eight from the 6th Regiment, at Stony Creek Depot.[64] The regiment saw action on December 7 at Belfield on the Meherrin River about twenty miles below Stony Creek Station and on the eighth at Hicksford.[65] Only Company B was engaged at Weldon, North Carolina, on December 9. A portion of the 5th and 6th Regiments, without their horses and under the command of Captain McTureous, left Virginia hurriedly in late December. Bound for the South Carolina coast, the detachment was engaged at Heyward's Place near Argyle before the end of the month.[66]

Butler's Division, comprising the 4th, 5th and 6th Regiments and Young's Brigade, was sent back to South Carolina on January 19, 1865, both to help impede Sherman's advance and to procure horses. Once again, the men traveled by rail, and the horses went overland.[67] The regiment skirmished day and night from February 14 to April 13, 1865.[68] Posted on the Lexington side of the Congaree River in mid-February, it clashed with Kilpatrick's cavalry a day or two before Columbia was occupied. Companies B and F helped with evacuation of the city on February 17, and they were the last to leave the city.[69] The regiment skirmished at Killian's Mill north of Columbia on the eighteenth and marched through Winnsboro and Cheraw. It fought at Stokes's Bridge, also called Kellytown and Lynches Creek, on February 24 before crossing the Catawba River into North Carolina at Land's Ford and moving on to Wadesboro. Skirmishes followed at Solomon's Grove on March 9 and Monroe's Crossroads on the tenth.[70] The regiment also participated in the attack on Kilpatrick's camp near Fayetteville on the tenth. Though not engaged at Averasboro on March 16, the regiment skirmished from March 19 to March 22 and was actually engaged at Bentonville on the twentieth and the twenty-first. The regiment marched through Raleigh and Durham to Hillsboro. Calhoun wrote that the entire 6th Regiment left camp for home on the evening before the surrender.[71] The men marched all night and broke up into smaller squads the next morning before disbanding, probably at Charlotte.[72] Company F disbanded but never surrendered. The 6th Regiment was officially included in the surrender of the Army of Tennessee on April 26, 1865.

9.

The 7th Regiment, South Carolina Cavalry

The 7th Regiment, South Carolina Cavalry, was created in March 1864 at Drewry's Bluff, Virginia. Wade Hampton had suggested the creation of a new cavalry regiment for his division the previous November.[1] The nucleus for such a regiment—the five-company battalion of the Holcombe Legion—already existed and was in Virginia; the remaining five companies would be John H. Tucker's and William L. Trenholm's Squadrons of two companies each, plus one from Edward M. Boykin's Squadron of Mounted Riflemen. Thus it was that the 7th Regiment was officially created on March 18, 1864. But the War Department disbanded the regiment on May 29, ordering its colonel, W.P. Shingler, back to his original command of the Holcombe Legion Infantry. The action also left the lieutenant colonel, A.C. Haskell, temporarily without a command and returned the major, Edward M. Boykin, back to the command of his company. The War Department's action was countermanded the same day, however, by Major General Robert Ransom Jr., who ordered Haskell and Boykin to return to the new regiment. By mid-June, President Davis ordered the regiment reorganized. At the same time, he appointed Haskell colonel, I.G. McKissick lieutenant colonel, Boykin major.[2]

Field Officers

William Pinckney Shingler of Berkeley in Orangeburg District was appointed lieutenant colonel of the Holcombe Legion on November 21, 1861, a rank that placed him in command the legion's Cavalry Battalion. He was promoted to colonel of the legion on November 5, 1862, with rank from October 8, when P.F. Stevens resigned. In spite of the new rank, Shingler continued to command the Cavalry Battalion only because the Infantry Battalion was serving under a different command.[3] Shingler was given command of the newly created 7th Regiment in March 1864.[4] The adjutant general changed plans on May 27, ordering Shingler to take command of the Holcombe Legion Infantry Regiment and replacing him with A.C. Haskell as commander of the 7th Cavalry Regiment. When the War Department followed up by disbanding the 7th Regiment two days later, Shingler, on the thirtieth, promptly resigned. Wade Hampton wrote that Shingler resigned rather than assume command of the legion's infantry as ordered. Haskell's view was that the War Department directed Shingler to go to the Western Army as commander of the regiment to which he properly belonged, meaning the Holcombe Legion Infantry.[5] Krick believed Shingler resigned because of a running dispute with Jefferson Davis.[6] There is no evidence that Shingler commanded the infantry component of the Holcombe Legion in late May or early June 1864, only that he resigned about May 30. The *Mercury* reported a few days later that officers of the Cavalry Battalion, Holcombe Legion, "regretted" Shingler's removal.[7]

Alexander "Aleck" Cheves Haskell of Abbeville District and Columbia was appointed the first lieutenant colonel of the 7th Regiment about April 28, 1864, retroactive to the twentieth.[8] With the regiment disbanded on May 29 and Shingler's resignation the next day, Haskell was officially without a command, at least temporarily, but General Ransom ordered his retention. He was appointed colonel when the regiment was reorganized in mid-June. Haskell's rank was confirmed on June 10, effective from April 20. Haskell had been appointed military secretary to Maxcy Gregg, colonel of the 1st Regiment, SCV, on February 2, 1861. He wrote later that he was elected lieutenant of Company I in Colonel Maxcy Gregg's reorganized regiment in August 1861, but actually served as Gregg's chief of staff.[9] On December 31, he was appointed aide-de-camp to Maxcy Gregg, who was at the time a brigadier general. Haskell was also named assistant adjutant general on Gregg's staff with the rank of captain on January 28, with rank from January 18, 1862, a position he held until he was appointed lieutenant colonel of the 7th Regiment in March 1864.

Haskell was wounded in the right shoulder at Fredericksburg on December 13, 1862.[10] Another injury—this time to the left ankle—occurred on May 2, 1863, at Chancellorsville while Haskell was serving as assistant adjutant general to Brigadier General Samuel McGowan.[11] Twenty years would pass before he recovered fully from this wound.[12] He also suffered a severe abdominal wound during a battle on the Old Church Road near Cold Harbor on May 30, 1864, when he and his horse and other accoutrements were struck seven times.[13] This wound, initially thought to be fatal, involved his kidneys and bladder.[14] On the Darbytown Road on

October 7, 1864, Haskell again escaped death but lost his left eye.[15] At Old Church, when the left eyeglass from his binoculars had been shot out, he had set them aside, but then, when he lost his eye, he picked them back up because the binoculars "matched" him again. In spite of all this, Haskell had rejoined the regiment by the end of January 1865.[16] He was paroled with the regiment at Appomattox Court House on April 9.[17] Both Maxcy Gregg and A.P. Hill recommended Haskell for promotion to brigadier general.[18] Hill called him "a most gallant and accomplished officer."[19] Shortly before he died, Gregg requested a promotion for Haskell whom he called a "true friend and a good officer."[20]

Isaac Going McKissick of Union District was appointed the second lieutenant colonel of the 7th Regiment following Haskell's brief tenure at the post. McKissick was unofficially promoted to major and was reassigned to the Infantry Battalion of the Holcombe Legion about March 1864 but refused to leave his cavalry company and remained as captain of the McKissick Rangers. The *CSR* is unclear as to whether McKissick was intended to be the original major of the 7th Cavalry and was simply appointed lieutenant colonel when Haskell was named colonel, or whether he was promoted directly from captain. When the regiment was reorganized in June 1864, McKissick was appointed lieutenant colonel, retroactive to April 20. McKissick had served as captain of Company D of the Cavalry Battalion, Holcombe Legion, which became Company C of the 7th Regiment. McKissick was wounded first at Williamsburg and then suffered a severe thigh injury on the Old Church Road near Cold Harbor on May 30, 1864. Because he wouldn't apply for an honorable discharge, someone else applied for him on February 27, 1865. A note in the *CSR* states that he was honorably retired on March 22, but retirement was revoked four days later, probably because McKissick returned to the regiment. He did apply for disability from the thigh wound about April 1, 1865.[21] While still on crutches, McKissick was paroled with the regiment at Appomattox Court House on April 9, 1865.[22] C.I. Walker, lieutenant colonel of the 10th Regiment, wrote of McKissick: "His lifelong career has been so distinguished as a soldier, a citizen, and a statesman that every comrade…knew well his worth and appreciated the nobility of his character."[23]

Edward Mortimer Boykin of Kershaw District was appointed major of the regiment on April 25, 1864. The commission was not initially confirmed because the regiment was disbanded on May 29, and Boykin was ordered back to his former post as captain of Company K. Ransom's countermanding order of the same day, however, allowed him to remain with the regiment as major, and he was reappointed at the time of the regiment's reorganization in mid-June. The commission was approved on September 27, 1864, with rank from the seventh. Boykin was severely wounded in the thigh on the Old Church Road near Cold Harbor on May 30, 1864.[24] According to the *Memory Roll*, he was appointed lieutenant colonel effective April 1, 1865, as McKissick's replacement. This promotion was never confirmed, however, probably because of McKissick's convoluted record of retirement and disability during that period. Boykin was also struck in the chest by a spent ball near Amelia Springs on April 5, 1865.[25] He was paroled with the regiment at Appomattox Court House on April 9, 1865.[26]

James Longstreet Doby of Kershaw District, captain of Company H, was promoted to major effective April 1, 1865, according to the *Memory Roll*. This promotion, like Boykin's, was never confirmed, and neither promotion is supported by the *CSR*.

COMPANIES

Company A was previously Company A, the Marion Men of Winyah, Captain John H. Tucker's Squadron, South Carolina Cavalry, an independent unit comprising two companies that served along the coast from May 1861 until its attachment to the 7th Regiment when it was created on March 18, 1864. Most of the men were from Georgetown, Williamsburg and Darlington Districts, but a few came from Charleston and Horry Districts. After joining the regiment, Company A of Tucker's Squadron retained its designation, and Company B became Company F. Both joined the regiment in Virginia in early June. Tucker, the former squadron commander, became the first captain of Company A in the 7th Regiment. He was awarded a sixty-day furlough in mid-November, probably because of poor health. His request for a thirty-day extension on December 26 was denied, and he tendered his resignation on January 20, 1865. It was accepted on February 7, and Henry Thomas McDonald was placed in command.[27] A lieutenant in March 1865, Tucker was paroled at Appomattox Court House on April 9 at that rank.[28] One card in the *CSR* states that he held the rank of captain at the end of the war, but another shows his highest rank as lieutenant. More information on Tucker's company and squadron appears under independent cavalry organizations.

Company B, the Rutledge Mounted Riflemen, had been half of an independent squadron called Captain William L. Trenholm's Squadron–the Rutledge Mounted Riflemen and Horse Artillery. It, too, had served along the coast until merging into the 7th Regiment on April 7, 1864. Company A of Trenholm's Squadron became Company B, and Company B became

Company G of the 7th Regiment. Since the squadron left its artillery in South Carolina when it joined the 7th Regiment, the name Rutledge Mounted Riflemen and Horse Artillery had been shortened to Rutledge Mounted Riflemen by the time the unit joined the 7th Regiment in Virginia on May 27. Company B's commander, William Lee Trenholm, expected to become the first lieutenant colonel of the regiment, but the appointment went to A.C. Haskell instead. Trenholm, who was wounded in the thigh at Old Church, Virginia, on May 30, 1864, was promoted to lieutenant colonel on March 6, retroactive to February 25, 1865, and assigned to command the 19th Battalion, South Carolina Cavalry. "He had the reputation of being an excellent officer."[29] Trenholm's successor as captain of Company B was Legare J. Walker.[30] Walker was wounded in the left foot at Old Church, Virginia, on May 30, 1864. He was severely wounded again, this time in the right thigh, and was taken prisoner on April 7, 1865, at Farmville, Virginia. Admitted two days later to the Field (Flying) Hospital of the 24th Corps, Army of the James, he was released on June 15, 1865. More information on the company appears under independent cavalry organizations.

Company C, the McKissick Rangers or McKissick's Rangers, had been Company D of the Cavalry Battalion, Holcombe Legion. The company was composed mostly of men from Union, York, Newberry and Chester Districts, along with a few from Spartanburg and Greenville Districts. The company, raised in Union by Isaac Going McKissick, mustered in service on December 17, 1861.[31] McKissick, who was the only captain in the Holcombe Legion, retained command when the company joined the 7th Regiment in March 1864.[32] Though unofficially promoted to major and reassigned to the legion's Infantry Battalion about that time, McKissick refused to leave his cavalry company. Even so, he was promoted to lieutenant colonel of the 7th Regiment that summer, retroactive to April 20, 1864. His replacement, John W. Palmer, was promoted to captain the same day.[33]

Company D, the Congaree Mounted Guard, was previously Company B of the Cavalry Battalion, Holcombe Legion.[34] Its other names were the Congaree Mounted Riflemen and the Congaree Cavaliers.[35] Though a few men came from Union, York, Chester and Newberry Districts, it was composed mostly of men from Richland, Fairfield, Sumter and Lexington Districts.[36] Second Lieutenant Campbell R. Frost, who was elected captain at the reorganization in May 1862, commanded the company in both the Holcombe Legion and 7th Regiment.[37] Frost was killed on May 30, 1864, at Old Church, Virginia.[38] His replacement, John D. Caldwell, was paroled with the regiment at Appomattox Court House on April 9, 1865.[39] One recently published work names George W. Melton captain of Company D.[40] Though one card in the *CSR* also lists him as captain, Melton signed official documents as first lieutenant, and the index to the 7th Regiment gives first lieutenant as his highest rank.

Company E, the Newberry Rangers, had been Company C in the Holcombe Legion's Cavalry Battalion. It was composed mostly of men from Newberry, Laurens and Edgefield Districts, along with a few from Union District. Raised originally as an independent cavalry company in May 1861, it was first known as the Palmetto Light Dragoons.[41] J. Wash Williams, who was elected captain on May 3, 1862, retained command in the 7th Regiment.[42] Thrown from a horse in early August 1864, Williams suffered injuries to the brain and spinal cord. He was awarded a twenty-five-day leave of absence on August 12 and subsequently received several extensions of the leave. He had been absent without leave since January 16, and when he did not report for duty by February 11, 1865, Colonel Haskell requested that he be dropped from the roll. Haskell added that Williams's conduct in action had been less than satisfactory, probably indicating that he was the captain who, on May 30, 1864, "was removed for leaving the field at the commencement of the engagement."[43] On March 19, Williams asked for restoration to command so he could withdraw honorably because of physical disability. Haskell disapproved the request and ordered him dropped, but General Lee revoked the order and the resignation was accepted effective February 27, 1865.[44] Lieutenant Silas Walker, who commanded the company from February 27 until the close of the war, was paroled with the regiment at Appomattox with the rank of lieutenant.[45]

Company F was previously Company B of the Marion Men of Winyah, Captain John H. Tucker's Squadron, South Carolina Cavalry. The squadron is more fully defined under Company A. Most Company B men were from Georgetown, Williamsburg and Horry Districts, though a few came from Sumter, Marion, Spartanburg and Marlboro Districts. William Lewis Wallace, MD, former commander of Company B of the original squadron, was the only captain of Company F in the 7th Regiment.[46] Wallace suffered from rheumatism and was absent so often in the fall of 1864 that Colonel Haskell said he drank excessively and for that reason treated his men poorly.[47] Wallace commanded a group of fifteen men near Georgetown in early April 1865 and was not paroled at Appomattox Court House.[48] More information on the company appears under independent cavalry organizations.

Company G, the other half of Trenholm's Squadron (see Company B) or the Rutledge Mounted Riflemen, merged into the new 7th Regiment, South Carolina Cavalry, on April 7, 1864, and joined its ranks in Virginia on May 27. J.J. Magee, who had been elected captain on May 23 or May 24, 1863, was wounded at Old Church, Virginia, on May 30, 1864, and died from the wound in a Federal prison in late July.[49] The *CSR* and Kirkland both state that he was killed in action on May 30, 1864.[50] William Henry Jeffers was promoted to captain with rank from May 30.[51] He was paroled with the regiment at Appomattox Court House on April 9, 1865.[52] Most Company G men were from Anderson, Greenville and Pickens Districts, though some came from Fairfield, Clarendon, Colleton, Charleston and Abbeville Districts. More information on the company appears under independent cavalry organizations.

Company H, the Kirkwood Rangers, which had been Company E of the Holcombe Legion's Cavalry Battalion, was also called the Kirkwood Cavalry, the Kirkwood South Carolina Cavalry and the Kirkwoods.[53] It may also have been called the Camden Rangers.[54] Most of its men were from Camden in Kershaw District and from Chesterfield District, along with a few from Darlington, Charleston, Fairfield, Sumter and Richland Districts. James Longstreet Doby, who was elected captain on June 18, 1862, retained command of the company in the 7th Regiment.[55] Doby sustained a flesh wound to the inner thigh near Riddell's Shop on August 15, 1864.[56] He was sent to General Hospital #4 and was given a thirty-day furlough on the twenty-second. Though the *Memory Roll* records that Doby was promoted to major about April 1, 1865, such promotion, if it happened at all, was never confirmed. His name does not appear on the list of those paroled at Appomattox Court House on April 9, 1865.[57]

Company I, the Claremont Cavalry, was previously Company A of the Cavalry Battalion, Holcombe Legion. It was also called the Claremont Troop.[58] Composed mostly of men from Sumter and Clarendon Districts, the company rolls included a few men from Chesterfield District. Robert C. Webb was promoted from first lieutenant to captain on April 20, 1863.[59] Webb, who commanded in both legion and regiment, was killed while leading the company on May 30, 1864, at Old Church, Virginia.[60] His replacement, J. Franklin Bradford, was promoted to captain the same day.[61] Bradford was paroled with the regiment at Appomattox Court House on April 9, 1865.[62]

Company K, the Wateree Mounted Rifles, was also called Boykin's Company Mounted Rifles and the Boykin Rangers.[63] Still another name was Captain E.M. Boykin's Company A, Mounted Squadron of Rifles, SCV. Originally composed mostly of men from Camden in Kershaw District, others from Clarendon, Sumter and Horry Districts and a few from Richland, Greenville and Marion Districts joined later.[64] Company K had previously been Company A of Captain E.M. Boykin's Squadron, Mounted Rifles, which comprised two companies of state troops. First Lieutenant Edward Mortimer Boykin had been elected captain of the company on September 5, 1862. Between October 1863 and January 1864,

Governor M.L. Bonham allowed the squadron's two companies to leave state service and muster in Confederate service.[65] Accordingly, Company A of the squadron was assigned to the 7th Regiment on February 3, 1864, and Boykin was appointed the regiment's first major on April 25. First Lieutenant David St. P. DuBose, who was promoted to captain in May, was wounded in the calf by a rifle ball at Old Church, Virginia, on the thirtieth.[66] DuBose was paroled with the regiment at Appomattox Court House on April 9, 1865.[67] More information on the company appears under independent cavalry organizations.

BRIGADE AFFILIATIONS

The 7th Regiment was attached to Martin W. Gary's Brigade from May 12, 1864, until the surrender at Appomattox. Gary's Brigade comprised the 7th Regiment, South Carolina Cavalry, the Hampton Legion Mounted Infantry, the 24th Regiment, Virginia Cavalry, the 7th Regiment, Georgia Cavalry, and Harkerson's Battery.[68]

MAJOR MOVEMENTS AND ENGAGEMENTS

The 7th Regiment assembled at its headquarters near Drewry's Bluff south of the James River below Richmond in April, May and June 1864.[69] On May 10, Companies C, D, E, H, I and K had been ordered to reconnoiter near the Petersburg Turnpike, their first action as a unit in Virginia. Engaged at Drewry's Bluff on May 16, the regiment returned to Richmond on the twentieth.

Back in South Carolina, Companies B and G, the former Trenholm's Squadron or the Rutledge Mounted Riflemen, left Pocotaligo and Coosawhatchie on April 7, arrived in Virginia on May 15 and joined the regiment about May 27, just as it was moving to the north side of the James River. Eight companies, all except A and F, were engaged as dismounted troops at Old Church on the Old Church Road near Matadequin Creek on May 30.[70] All three field officers and three captains were wounded during the battle, and two captains were killed. The 7th Regiment withdrew to the south side of the Chickahominy River that evening. Companies A and F, the Marion Men of Winyah, joined the regiment in early June. The regiment saw action on the third at Hanover Court House, also called Second Cold Harbor, and was in camp near McCleland's Bridge in early June, though some elements drew picket duty at Salem Church from the tenth to the twelfth.[71] Throughout the summer and fall of 1864, the 7th Regiment served primarily between the Chickahominy and James Rivers. The regiment saw action again at Riddell's Shop on June 13, at Malvern Hill on the fourteenth and skirmished at Nance's Store on the fifteenth and seventeenth.[72] The site of the June 15 skirmish was also called Smith's Store.[73] The regiment was engaged again at Samaria Church, which also appears as St. Mary's Church, on June 24, and Company B fought at the Atling farm near Deep Bottom on July 7.[74] The regiment endured artillery fire daily from the eighth to the fourteenth at a spot north of the James River. Shelled again on the fifteenth and twenty-sixth, it was engaged at Tilghman's Gate on July 27. The men also fought on July 28 at Fisher's farm.

The 7th Regiment supported the artillery firing from Wilcox's Place on August 3 and August 4 and returned to picket duty on the sixth. For three months, from August 1 to November 1, the regiment was incessantly involved in small engagements north of the James River, usually fighting as infantry. It saw action at its camp at Gatewoods and at Fussell's Mill on August 14 and was engaged near Fisher's farm from August 14 to August 18.[75] Those engagements included one at Riddell's Shop on August 15 and at the White Tavern on the Charles City Road on the sixteenth.[76] Company D was detached in August for duty at Taylorsville, about twenty miles north of Richmond. The regiment fought at New Market Heights on September 29 and at Roper's farm on the thirtieth.[77] It skirmished for the next week along the Charles City Road. An encounter with Brigadier General A.V. Kautz's bodyguard on the Darbytown Road on October 7 cost Colonel Haskell his left eye. The regiment skirmished on the Charles City Road on October 13 and fought on the Nine Mile and Williamsburg Roads on the twenty-seventh before the campaign closed near the end of October.

From November to March 1865, the 7th Regiment helped to guard the left flank of the Army of Northern Virginia by performing picket and scout duty north of the James River near Richmond. On March 11, 1865, the regiment moved north of Richmond but returned to the capital on the seventeenth. A fifty-man detachment skirmished at Goochland, about thirty miles above Richmond, on March 11.[78] From March 17 to March 28, the 7th Regiment was stationed about four miles below Richmond between the Williamsburg and Nine Mile Roads.[79] The regiment's baggage was moved from winter quarters into Richmond on April 2, and men of the regiment withdrew from their lines early on the third, riding through a southern Richmond suburb called the Rocketts and into the mob scene that was the city itself. Here, they acted as the rear guard during the evacuation of Richmond. The regiment was the last organized body of Confederate cavalry to leave Richmond, and its men burned Mayo's Bridge behind them.

After camping for the night on the Burkeville Road about eleven miles from Richmond, the regiment crossed the Appomattox River after dark on the fourth and camped a mile farther along. The men skirmished near Amelia Springs and bivouacked there on the night of April 5. Again acting as rear guard, the men skirmished near Burkeville and Farmville on April 6 and near the Farmville Bridge over the Appomattox River on the seventh. After marching through the night of April 7, the advance guard comprising the 7th Regiment, along with the Hampton Legion Mounted Infantry and the 24th Virginia Regiment, arrived at Appomattox Court House on the evening of the eighth. They skirmished to the west of Appomattox Court House shortly after arriving there on the eighth and again the next day.[80] Robert E. Lee tapped Colonel A.C. Haskell for the task of surrendering all the Confederate cavalry, including the 7th Regiment, to Brigadier General Wesley Merritt on April 9, 1865, at Appomattox Court House.[81] Men of the 7th Regiment received their paroles on April 11.

10.

The 15th Battalion, South Carolina Cavalry

Krick lists Council B. Wooten as major of the 15th Battalion, South Carolina Cavalry.[1] Sifakis writes that the battalion was organized in 1862.[2] Even so, the organization does not appear in the *CSR*, nor is it discussed in other documents dealing with South Carolina cavalry battalions and regiments. Still another argument against the existence of a 15th Cavalry Battalion is that numerical designations were not duplicated among South Carolina battalions after the spring of 1862. For example, the 10th, 12th, 14th, 16th, 17th and 19th Battalions were cavalry units; the 11th and 13th Battalions were infantry; and the 15th and 18th Battalions were artillery. For these reasons, it appears unlikely that the 15th Battalion was a South Carolina cavalry organization.

11.

The 19th Battalion, South Carolina Cavalry

The 19th Battalion, South Carolina Cavalry, also called Kirk's Battalion, was organized with five companies on December 20, 1864. It was formed by consolidating two companies of Kirk's Squadron Partisan Rangers, Keitt's Company of Mounted Riflemen, Company B of Boykin's Squadron Mounted Rifles and Captain Sparks's Company, also called the Ripley Rangers. Two more companies, Fair's and A.C. Earle's, were added on February 22, 1865.[1]

Field Officer

William Lee Trenholm was appointed lieutenant colonel in command of the battalion on March 6, 1865, with rank from February 25. Trenholm was previously captain of Company B, 7th Regiment, South Carolina Cavalry. The *CSR* lists him as W.F. Trenholm.

Companies

Company A, called Kirk's Company, South Carolina Partisan Rangers, was previously designated Company A in Kirk's Squadron, Partisan Rangers, an independent cavalry unit. Manning J. Kirk was appointed as its captain on July 11, 1862. It may also have been called the May River Troop. On February 24, 1864, Kirk's Company was separated into two, A and B, and was designated Kirk's Squadron, South Carolina Partisan Rangers. Its men re-enlisted for the duration of the war then.[2] Kirk retained command of both Company A and the two-company squadron, and S.T. Walker was elected captain of Company

B. Company A men were from Beaufort District. On December 20, 1864, Company A became Company A, and Company B became Company C of the 19th Battalion, South Carolina Cavalry. Kirk retained command of Company A in the 19th Battalion. For more information, see independent cavalry organizations.

Company B was an independent company called Captain E.S. Keitt's Company Mounted Riflemen, SCV, from April 30 to December 20, 1864. Its previous designation had been Company M of the 20th Regiment, SCV, from July 17, 1863, to April 30, 1864. Most of its men were from Richland, Newberry, Anderson and Marlboro Districts, though a few men came from Orangeburg, Charleston, Fairfield, Edgefield, Abbeville, Lexington and Spartanburg Districts. Ellison Summerfield Keitt, elected captain on June 10, 1863, commanded the company until the end of the war. It was attached to the 19th Battalion as Company B on December 20, 1864. For more information, see independent cavalry organizations.

Company C was previously Company B, Kirk's Squadron of Partisan Rangers, discussed above with Company A. Company C's captain, S.T. Walker, was elected on March 7, 1864. Most of the men were from Beaufort, Barnwell and Colleton Districts, though a few came from Union and Charleston Districts. Walker retained command when the company became part of the 19th Battalion on December 20, 1864. Walker surrendered at Durham Station, North Carolina. For more information, see independent cavalry organizations.

Company D, Captain J.J. Steele's Company, was previously Company B of E.M. Boykin's Squadron of Mounted Rifles comprising two companies of state troops. The squadron was created about November 5, 1862, when Boykin's Company was expanded to create a new two-company squadron. Boykin's Company became Company A, and W.N.G. Rodgers's Company was designated Company B at that time. Governor Bonham allowed Boykin's Squadron to leave state service and muster in Confederate service sometime in late 1863 or early 1864.[3] Boykin's Squadron transferred to Confederate service in January 1864, but it mustered in for the duration on March 11. Company A became Company K of the 7th Regiment, South Carolina Cavalry, on March 18, and Company B became independent about the same time. Company B, whose men hailed from Georgetown and Williamsburg Districts, requested upon mustering in Confederate service that the company be reorganized, and they elected J.J. Steele captain. The company was stationed in Georgetown District from April to at least October 31, 1864.[4] Steele retained command when the company became Company D of the 19th Battalion, South Carolina Cavalry, in December 1864. For more information, see independent cavalry organizations.

Company E, the Ripley Rangers, was previously an independent company known as Captain A.D. Sparks's Company, South Carolina Cavalry. It was composed primarily of men from Lexington, Marion and Marlboro Districts, along with a few from Sumter, Chesterfield, Darlington, Anderson and Union Districts.[5] Organized as an infantry company on April 3, 1862, it was Company L of the 20th Regiment, SCV, until it was detached on April 30, 1863. It served as an independent cavalry company from that time until it became Company E, 19th Battalion, South Carolina Cavalry, on December 20, 1864. Its captain, Alexander D. Sparks, who was elected on April 3, 1862, retained command through the company's independent phase and the first four days of battalion status.[6] Suffering from illness, Sparks had been absent for thirteen months by January 15, 1864. His disease was pronounced incurable, and a medical board recommended retirement. The secretary of war rejected the recommendation, and Sparks finally resigned because of poor health on December 24, 1864. The resignation was accepted on January 7, 1865, and command of Company E passed to First Lieutenant C.P. Bolton. For more information, see independent cavalry organizations.

Company F, raised as a company of reserves, served in the 8th Battalion, South Carolina Reserves.[7] Its men, who had mustered in Confederate service in November 1864, were ordered on February 22, 1865, to transfer permanently to active service "with the consent of the officers and men." The company was assigned to the 19th Battalion.[8] One source states, probably incorrectly, that the company was raised specifically for service in the 19th Battalion.[9] William Young Fair was its captain.

Captain A.C. Earle's Company, South Carolina Cavalry, was also attached to the 19th Battalion on February 22, 1865, but was never assigned a letter designation.[10] Previously Company B of the 37th Battalion, Virginia Cavalry, it was composed mostly of the men from Anderson and Pickens Districts, along with a few from Greenville District. Earle had resigned on October 13, 1864, four months before the company's reassignment, and he was not replaced. Thus it was that the company had no captain during its brief time in the 19th Battalion. For more information, see independent cavalry organizations.

Brigade Affiliations

The 19th Battalion was attached to the Department of South Carolina, Georgia and Florida in January and February 1865. On January 31, one company, either D or E, was attached to Brigadier General James H. Trapier's Brigade, and the other four companies were attached to the brigade of Colonel A.M. Rhett.[11] In March and April, it was part of Brigadier General T.M. Logan's Brigade, M.C. Butler's Division, Wade Hampton's cavalry corps.[12]

MAJOR MOVEMENTS AND ENGAGEMENTS

The 19th Battalion was stationed on the line between Charleston and Georgetown until Charleston's evacuation in February 1865. From December 26 to December 28, Companies A and C were stationed at Pocotaligo, but Kirk's Squadron departed for Charleston on January 5.[13] Company B was based at Andersonville between Charleston and Georgetown in December 1864 when it joined the 19th Battalion, and Company D was stationed at Battery White near Georgetown at the same time. Companies A and C supported the withdrawal of the Marion Artillery after an engagement with Federal barges at Seewee Bay on February 16, 1865. Company D helped resist Potter's Raid along the Black River in April 1865.[14] The battalion participated in the Carolinas' campaign until the end of the war.

12.

Independent Cavalry Organizations

DeSaussure's Squadron Regular Cavalry, South Carolina Army

DeSaussure's Squadron Regular Cavalry, South Carolina Army, was the cavalry component of the state's Regular Army. It was created under a December 31, 1860 resolution of the Secession Convention authorizing the creation of one or two regiments of regulars, each to consist of enlisted men who would serve for twelve months. The governor would appoint company and field officers, and the Senate would confirm the appointments. With a single exception, every captain Governor Pickens chose for the Regular Army had been either an officer in the Mexican War, or had attended West Point and served as an officer in the United States Army.[1]

The General Assembly passed an act on January 28, 1861, changing the required length of service to three years and the composition of the force to one infantry regiment, one artillery battalion and one squadron of cavalry. The infantry regiment was Richard H. Anderson's 1st Regiment, South Carolina Infantry Regulars; the artillery battalion was Roswell Ripley's 1st Battalion, South Carolina Artillery Regulars; and William Davie DeSaussure's two-company squadron made up the Regular Cavalry component. This mixed force constituted the South Carolina Regular Army. Governor Pickens wrote on May 13 that the cavalry squadron consisting of eighty men was "a fine corps."[2] Some consideration was given at that time to disbanding the cavalry squadron, and its officers were willing to accept that fate if President Jefferson Davis agreed.[3] Governor Pickens, however, recommended to Davis that it would be good for the service if the squadron were retained as either cavalry or infantry.[4] Accordingly, on May 17, Adjutant and Inspector General Samuel Cooper ordered DeSaussure's Squadron to be mustered in Confederate service as infantry.[5] Several considerations prompted this action: J.J. Lucas wrote that the government lacked the funds necessary to mount DeSaussure's Squadron, and DeSaussure himself became restless and resigned, relinquishing command at some point between April and early June 1861.[6] James Jonathan Lucas, who was serving as an aide-de-camp to Governor Pickens at the time, was solicited to take his place.[7] Lucas was appointed squadron commander at the rank of major on June 6, the same day his unit mustered in Confederate service as infantry for three years or for the duration of the war.[8] Lucas's Squadron, referred to as the Dismounted Dragoons, South Carolina Regular Force, awaited orders while based at Sullivan's Island in June.[9] Lucas immediately requested that the secretary of war provide mounts for the squadron and order it to Virginia. The War Department denied the request; instead, by order of General R.H. Anderson, the squadron was converted to heavy artillery. The *Confederate Military History Series* records that Lucas, initially a major of cavalry, had his appointment changed to major of artillery.[10] Major of infantry is not mentioned. So it was that command of DeSaussure's Squadron of Regular Cavalry passed to James J. Lucas about June 6, 1861, and the squadron itself was changed first to infantry and then to artillery with the designation of 15th Battalion, South Carolina Artillery.

Field Officers

William Davie DeSaussure, a Columbia lawyer and legislator who commanded the cavalry squadron at the rank of major, had raised and commanded the Richland Company of the Palmetto Regiment in the Mexican War; he was wounded at Cherubusco.[11] A captain of dragoons in the United States Army, he had also participated in the Utah Expedition before the war. Governor Pickens recommended DeSaussure as captain of the third company of regulars; confirmation by the Senate followed on January 19, 1861. Though the governor was busily recommending officers for the newly created Regular Army at the time, he had not yet designated which officer would serve in which branch, and DeSaussure was confirmed again on January 28 as major of the cavalry battalion.[12] He was also commissioned captain in the Provisional Army of the Confederate States on July 19, with rank from March 16. But, as recorded earlier, DeSaussure had given up command of the battalion before it mustered in Confederate service on June 6. He was elected colonel of the new 15th Regiment, South Carolina Infantry, on September 9, 1861, while retaining his commission as a major in the South Carolina Regular Army.[13] DeSaussure was killed at Gettysburg.[14]

James Jonathan Lucas of Society Hill and Charleston had served as captain of the Palmetto Guards for seven years before the war. On December 31, 1860, he became aide-de-camp to Governor Pickens with the rank of lieutenant colonel. Pickens appointed Lucas major in command of DeSaussure's Squadron on June 6, 1861; he retained command when the squadron was redesignated the 15th Battalion, South Carolina Artillery, probably in the summer of 1861.

Companies

Company A, originally called the 2nd Company, was commanded by Captain John Bordenave Villepique, who eventually attained the rank of brigadier general.[15] Alfred J. Norris commanded Company A after June 6, 1861.

Company B, originally called the 1st Company, was commanded at first by Nathan George Evans.[16] Captain S.R. Ferguson replaced Evans, and Samuel D. Shannon commanded the company after June 6, 1861.[17]

Major Movements and Engagements

DeSaussure's Squadron of Regular Cavalry was present on Sullivan's Island during the bombardment of Fort Sumter in April 1861. The dismounted squadron under the command of J.J. Lucas was still based at Sullivan's Island on July 9. It was redesignated the 15th Battalion, South Carolina Artillery, probably in late June or early July. Battalion headquarters was moved to the Stono fortifications on James Island on July 9, and the two companies, by then an artillery organization, were sent to Fort Pickens on Battery Island. More information on the 15th Battalion, South Carolina Artillery, appears in Chapter 14.

13.

THE 1ST BATTALION/1ST REGIMENT, SOUTH CAROLINA ARTILLERY REGULARS

The 1st Battalion, South Carolina Artillery, raised by the state in early 1861 as part of the South Carolina Regular Army, comprised five companies, A to E. The Secession Convention passed a resolution on December 31, 1860, authorizing the creation of one or two regiments of regulars, each to consist of 640 men willing to serve for twelve months. The governor was to appoint company and field officers whose commissions were to be confirmed by the Senate. The General Assembly passed an act on January 28, 1861, changing both the initial enlistment—to three years—and the composition of the Regular Army—to one infantry regiment, one artillery battalion and one squadron of cavalry. Four to six companies, one of which was to be equipped as a harnessed battery of light or "flying" artillery, would make up the artillery unit.[1] The infantry regiment was Richard H. Anderson's 1st Regiment; South Carolina Infantry Regulars; the artillery battalion was Roswell Ripley's 1st Battalion, South Carolina Artillery; and the cavalry component was W.D. DeSaussure's Squadron, Regular Cavalry.

The artillery battalion, comprising Companies A to E, mustered in Confederate service on May 24, 1861. At that time, the captains of Companies B, C, D and E resigned to accept higher rank in other commands. The five-company battalion grew by two more—F and G—in October and November. The General Assembly authorized the 1st Battalion to become a full regiment in December.[2] After two more companies, H and I, were added in February 1862, the nine-company battalion was officially redesignated the 1st Regiment, South Carolina Artillery, on March 25. It was also known as the 1st Heavy Artillery Regiment and Rhett's regiment. Company K, formed on April 12, brought the regiment to its full complement of ten. P.G.T. Beauregard asked the men to re-enlist on February 8, 1864, and, as with most Confederate organizations at that time, the men re-enlisted with their original commands.[3]

FIELD OFFICERS

Roswell Sabine Ripley, born in Worthington, Ohio, and living in Charleston, served as brevet major in the 2nd Artillery Regiment of the United States Army before the War Between the States. Governor Pickens appointed him lieutenant colonel as a staff officer on January 2, 1861, and as an artillery officer on the twenty-seventh. Ripley commanded the 1st Artillery Battalion until August 15, when he was appointed brigadier general in command of state forces.[4]

William Ransom Calhoun, a native of Pendleton and a graduate of West Point, was promoted from captain of Company A to lieutenant colonel of the 1st Battalion on August 15, 1861, and to colonel when the battalion was upgraded to regimental status on March 25, 1862. The date of his commission is also shown as March 13.[5] A disaffection of long standing that had simmered between Calhoun and Lieutenant Colonel Alfred Moore Rhett would soon boil over. Calhoun was captain of Company A when it was sent to Virginia in August 1861. When he was promoted to command the battalion in August 1861, Calhoun chose to remain with his company in Virginia, a decision that angered several officers, including Rhett, Roswell Ripley and T.M. Wagner.[6] Calhoun returned to South Carolina with his company, probably by January 1, 1862, but exacerbated the problem when he took a July leave because the climate in the Charleston harbor area was incompatible with both his health and the efficient discharge of his duties.[7] Finally, on August 18, Calhoun submitted his resignation as colonel of the 1st Regiment, citing poor health and uncertain prospects of recovery. He remained on leave while awaiting official acceptance.[8] At this point, Rhett challenged Calhoun and, on September 5, he killed him in a duel. According to the *CSR*, the duel took place at the Washington Racecourse near Charleston, but another source places it at the Charleston Oaks Club on the Cooper River north of Magnolia Cemetery.[9]

Thomas Martin Wagner of Christ Church Parish in Mount Pleasant was appointed major of the 1st Battalion on October 14, 1861. He had previously served as captain of Company D. The 1st Battalion's only major, Wagner was promoted to lieutenant colonel of the 1st Regiment on April 18, 1862, with rank from March 25. The date of his commission is also shown as March 13.[10] Wagner suffered severe wounds to the thigh and ankle when a 32-pounder cannon exploded on July 5 at Fort Moultrie.[11] He survived the above-the-knee amputation of his left leg, but he died from his wounds at 11:50 a.m. on July 17.[12] J.C. Pemberton had appointed Wagner chief of ordnance of the Department of South Carolina and Georgia about two months earlier, and at the time of his death, Wagner was directing the construction of a battery on Morris Island. The battery was subsequently named in his memory.[13]

Alfred Moore Rhett from Charleston was promoted to major of the regiment on April 17, with rank from March 25, 1862. His commission is also shown with the date of March 13.[14] Previously captain of Company B of the 1st Battalion, Rhett was promoted to lieutenant colonel on July 17, 1862, the date of Wagner's death. After Rhett killed Calhoun on September 5, 1862, a board of examiners in a court of inquiry at Charleston's Military Hall addressed Rhett's role in the duel. Though condemning the practice of dueling, the court's finding "was not such as to deter General Beauregard from recommending Rhett's promotion to colonel."[15] He was named colonel of the regiment on December 11, retroactive to September 5, 1862. Rhett received a slight wound to the hand on August 23, 1863, when a shell crashed into a room at Fort Sumter where he and other officers were at dinner.[16] Rhett was given command of a brigade in Taliaferro's Division of Hardee's corps during the withdrawal into North Carolina in 1865. He was captured near Averasboro on March 15 when, having mistaken Federal for Confederate cavalry, he rode out in advance of his pickets.[17] He was held first at New Bern, was moved to Hart's Island in New York Harbor on April 10, was sent to Fort Delaware on the sixteenth and was released on July 24. Rhett came from a prominent family—his father was the arch-secessionist Senator Robert Barnwell Rhett, and his brother was Edmond Rhett. Though known as "a magnificent disciplinarian," Rhett was always considered just, and he won the affection and confidence of the men and officers under his command.[18]

Joseph Atkinson Yates of Charleston was promoted to major from captain of Company E on July 17, 1862, when Wagner died. He was promoted to lieutenant colonel on December 10, with rank from September 5, the date Calhoun was killed. Yates commanded the artillery on Morris Island when Federal troops captured its south end on July 10, 1863. He was slightly wounded in the hand at Fort Johnson on July 3, 1864.[19] Yates was paroled at Greensboro on April 28, 1865.

Ormsby Blanding of Sumter was promoted to major from captain of Company C on December 10, 1862, retroactive to September 5, 1862. He was severely wounded in the left arm at Averasboro, North Carolina, on March 16, 1865.[20] Blanding was sent first to the C.S.A. General Hospital #9 in Greensboro, then he was moved to the C.S.A. General Hospital #11 in Charlotte, and on April 12, 1865, he was furloughed. His arm was nearly useless for many years.[21] Though the *Memory Roll* records that Blanding was promoted to colonel, such a promotion would have been unlikely because Colonel Rhett was a prisoner of war, and Lieutenant Colonel Yates was still on active duty. The *CSR* does not confirm the promotion.

COMPANIES

Company A, the Sumter Battery, was called by various names in the 1st Battalion, among them Captain W.R. Calhoun's Battery, the Calhoun Battery, the Calhoun Artillery, the Calhoun Flying Artillery and the Light Battery. After the regiment was created, it was called Preston's Battery and Blake's Battery.[22] Later in the war, it was also referred to as DeLorme's Battery because second lieutenant Thomas M. DeLorme commanded the battery at times.[23] The Sumter Battery was the only light artillery battery in the 1st Battalion/Regiment. Company A served in Virginia from August to December 1861. During that time, a two-gun detachment of Company A called the Star Battery was detailed to serve with the 5th Infantry Regiment. Though the exact origin of Company A's name is unknown, it was probably associated with Revolutionary War General Thomas Sumter, since the men were not from Sumter District, and the name predated the bombardment of Fort Sumter. Most of the men were from Richland, Anderson, Laurens, Union and Kershaw Districts, though a few came from Charleston, Abbeville and Spartanburg Districts. The company mustered in the Provisional Army of the Confederate States on May 18, 1861, at Fort Moultrie. William Ransom Calhoun had been appointed the first captain by January 24, 1861.[24] He was promoted to lieutenant colonel in command of the battalion on August 15, 1861, and he later served as colonel of the regiment. William Campbell Preston Jr. commanded the company in the 1st Battalion but was not promoted from first lieutenant to captain until December 10, 1862, retroactive to August 15, 1861.[25] He retained command when the Sumter Battery became Company A of the 1st Artillery Regiment on March 25, 1862.[26] When Preston was promoted to major of artillery in the Provisional Army of the Confederate States on April 2, 1863, he resigned his commission with the 1st Regiment.[27] Preston, a lieutenant colonel at the time, was killed at Peachtree Creek near Atlanta on July 20, 1864.[28] Francis D. Blake, previously first lieutenant in Company B, was promoted to captain of Company A on July 13, 1863, with rank from April 2. Captured while in command of the picket line at Bentonville, North Carolina, on March 22, 1865, Blake was taken to a prison on Harts Island in New York Harbor on April 10; he was sent to Fort Delaware on the fifteenth and was released on June 17, 1865.

Company B was called the Brooks Flying Artillery. Its captain, James Henry Hallonquist, had been appointed by January 24, 1861, but he resigned in April to accept a promotion to major in the Confederate States Provisional Army.[29] Hallonquist had held the rank of captain in the 4th Company of South Carolina Regulars as early as February 16, 1861, but whether or not he had been assigned to Company B then is unclear.[30] He later served as major and lieutenant colonel of the 2nd Battalion, Alabama Artillery.[31] Alfred Moore Rhett was promoted from first lieutenant to captain on April 18, replacing Hallonquist.[32] Company B men mustered in the Confederate States Provisional Army at Fort Sumter on May 24, 1861. Rhett was promoted to major of the 1st Regiment on April 17, 1862, with rank from March 25. Company B retained its designation when the 1st Regiment was created on March 25, and David George Fleming, a graduate of The Citadel, was appointed captain then. He had served as captain of Company I since January 1, 1862. While on duty at Fort Sumter in August 1863, Fleming was struck by a shell during an 879-shot fusillade hurled at the fort. Remarkably, he was not injured.[33] Three days later, on August 23, Fleming was bruised by the same shell that had slightly injured Rhett when it exploded above the officers' mess at Fort Sumter during a meal.[34] Fleming resigned when he was named colonel of the 22nd Regiment, SCV, on June 2, 1864, and was killed at the Crater on July 30. Julius M. Rhett was promoted to captain of Company B on August 8, 1864, retroactive to June 2. Rhett was a lieutenant in Company B when he was wounded in the foot at Fort Sumter on August 18, 1863. He was injured again at Averasboro, North Carolina, on March 16, 1865, and was admitted to the C.S.A. General Hospital #3 in Greensboro on March 19.[35]

Company C was composed of men from Greenville and Spartanburg Districts. The Senate confirmed George S. James as captain of the 3rd Company of Regulars, on January 19, 1861. He was apparently reappointed on March 29, with rank from the sixteenth. James had served as a first lieutenant in the 4th Artillery Regiment of the United States Army from June 1856 to December 1860. It was James who gave the command on April 12 to fire the first shot on Fort Sumter from the Beach Battery at Fort Johnson. Company C mustered in the Confederate States Provisional Army at Fort Johnson on May 22, but James resigned on July 6.[36] He was elected lieutenant colonel in command of the 3rd Battalion, South Carolina Infantry, on January 31, 1862, and was killed at South Mountain on September 14. Ormsby Blanding, first lieutenant of Company E, was promoted to captain and was moved to Company C as James's replacement on July 6, 1861. He assumed command on July 8 and continued to lead when the company became Company C in the 1st Regiment on March 25, 1862.[37] Blanding was promoted to major on December 10, 1862, with rank from September 5. Charles W. Parker, formerly an officer in Companies D and E and also adjutant of the regiment, was promoted to captain on December 10, effective from July 17, 1862.

Company D's first captain, J. Randolph Hamilton, is listed as captain of the Marine Artillery Company on February 16, 1861.[38] He resigned his commission in April. First Lieutenant Thomas Martin Wagner, who had assisted Hamilton in raising the company, also succeeded him as captain, effective April 2. The men mustered in the Confederate States Provisional Army at Fort Moultrie on May 17. Wagner was appointed the battalion's major on October 14, and Henry S. Farley became the company's third captain. He had been a lieutenant in Company C before transferring to Company D at the same rank on August 6. He was promoted to captain on December 10, 1862, retroactive to October 14, 1861.[39] In February 1862, Farley transferred again, this time to captain of Company H of the 1st Artillery Regiment. Francis "Frank" Huger Harleston became the fourth captain of Company D on December 10, 1862, with rank from January 1.[40] Harleston, both captain of cadets and first honor graduate of the South Carolina Military Academy's Class of 1860, may have commanded the company for a few weeks before the 1st Regiment was created on March 25, 1862; he retained command of Company D when it became Company D of the 1st Regiment. He was slightly wounded by a shell at Fort Sumter on August 20, 1863.[41] Company D completed a tour as the garrison at Fort Sumter on November 21 and then left, but Harleston remained behind at the request of Major Stephen Elliott. At about 4:30 a.m. on the twenty-fourth, as he was inspecting the exterior of the fort's eastern (sea) face, Harleston was struck in both arms and thighs by fragments of a thirty-pound rifled shell and died five hours later.[42] Thus, he became the first Confederate officer killed at Fort Sumter.[43] Harleston's death was felt keenly by all those who knew him. A battery on the north side of James Island near Fort Johnson was named for him, and The Citadel erected a marble tablet in his memory in 1884.[44] McMillan King was promoted to captain on February 11, 1864, effective from November 24, 1863. King was wounded at Bentonville, North Carolina, on March 19, 1865.

Company E's first captain was Stephen Dill Lee, previously a first lieutenant in the 4th Artillery Regiment of the United States Army.[45] He was listed as captain of the 2nd Company, South Carolina Regulars, on February 16, 1861.[46] Promoted out of the regiment by April, Lee eventually became the youngest lieutenant general of the Confederacy. Joseph A. Yates replaced him as captain on May 19, and the company mustered in the Confederate States Provisional Army five days later at Fort Moultrie. Yates retained command when the company became Company E of the 1st Regiment on March 25, 1862.[47] When Yates was promoted to major on July 17, 1862, he was succeeded by J. Ravenel Macbeth, whose December 10 promotion to captain dated from September 5. During the Federal assault on the south end of Morris Island on July 10, 1863, Macbeth suffered both capture and a wound to the head.[48] He was held on Hilton Head Island until October and on the sixth, was taken to Fort Columbus in New York Harbor; on October 9, he was moved to Johnson's Island, Ohio.[49] Because of illness or wounds, or both, he was paroled on October 12, 1864.[50] Macbeth was probably exchanged at Cox's Wharf on the James River on October 15, along with 333 other prisoners of war.[51] He rejoined the company at Savannah on December 9. Macbeth lost an arm, and his entire battery was captured at Averasboro, North Carolina. He was admitted to the C.S.A. General Hospital #3 at Greensboro in April 1865.[52]

Company F was added to the 1st Battalion in October 1861 and was mustered in on the fourteenth at Fort Sumter. John Gadsden King was appointed captain on December 10, 1862, with rank from October 14, 1861.[53] King had served as captain of the Marion Artillery in the 1st Regiment Artillery (Militia). Company F retained its designation when the 1st Regiment was created on March 25, 1862. King was the only captain in both battalion and regiment.

Company G joined the battalion, mustering in the Confederate States Provisional Army on November 1, 1861, at Fort Moultrie. Its men were probably from Charleston. William Henry Peronneau was appointed captain on December 10, 1862, retroactive to October 31, 1861.[54] The only captain in the battalion, he retained command when the company became Company G of the 1st Regiment on March 25, 1862. Peronneau, who suffered from poor vision, retired to the Invalid Corps on November 5, 1864, to avoid losing his sight altogether by remaining on active duty. James Read Pringle was promoted to captain on January 12, 1865, with rank from November 5, 1864. He was paroled at Greensboro.

Company H was added to the 1st Battalion in February 1862, about a month before it became a regiment. Henry S. Farley, a West Point cadet when the war started, was its first captain, having transferred from Company D when Company H was organized. He retained command in the 1st Regiment. Farley resigned on June 22, 1863, and by October 7, he was a captain in the cavalry corps of the Army of Northern Virginia. He commanded the dismounted cavalry corps of the Army of Northern Virginia for about fifteen months in 1864 and early 1865. P.M.B. Young recommended on March 4, 1865, that Farley, then a major, be promoted to colonel. Krick, however, does not list Farley as either a major or a colonel.

Henry Russell Lesesne was promoted to captain of Company H on July 13, 1863, with rank from June 5. Lesesne suffered slight wounds to the head and back at Battery Gregg on August 18, 1863.[55] He was killed at Averasboro on March 16, 1865. Brigadier General William B. Taliaferro wrote in April that Lesesne was "one of our best officers."[56] First Lieutenant Edward Lowndes was promoted to captain on April 4, but the promotion was never officially approved.

Company I also was added in February 1862, and it retained the designation when the regiment was officially created a month later. David G. Fleming was appointed its captain on December 10, 1862, with rank from January 1, 1862. He was appointed captain of Company B in March 1862, when the battalion became a regiment, and he probably never commanded Company I in the 1st Regiment. John C. Mitchel Jr., previously both a second lieutenant in Company B and a first lieutenant in Company C, was promoted to captain of Company I. The *CSR* says he was appointed captain on April 17, 1862, effective from various dates, among them February 25, March 25 and March 26, 1862. The *CSR* also notes that he was appointed captain on December 10, 1862, with rank from March 25. An unpublished source records that his promotion to captain was effective on March 13, 1862.[57] Mitchel replaced Stephen Elliott as commander of Fort Sumter on May 4, 1864, and he remained there until his death on July 20.[58] At about one that afternoon, while standing at the lookout sentinel on the rampart of the southwest angle and observing the effects of artillery fire, Mitchel was struck below the left hip by fragments of a mortar shell. He died at 4:45 p.m.[59] Captain John Johnson, engineer in charge of the fort, described Mitchel as "an accomplished officer and a high-toned gentleman."[60] Only four days earlier, Brigadier General Roswell Ripley had recommended Mitchel for promotion to major, writing that he "commands the respect and commendation of every officer with whom he has been associated."[61] Charles Inglesby, previously an officer in four companies—D, E, G and I—was promoted to captain on August 8, 1864, with rank from July 20. Paroled at Greensboro on May 1, 1865, he wrote a historical sketch of the regiment.

Company K, made up of men from Fairfield, Lancaster, Union, Spartanburg and Anderson Districts, was added to the 1st Regiment on April 12, 1862. Julius A. Sitgreaves was appointed captain on April 17, 1862, effective from March 13.[62] He suffered from poor health and tried to be reassigned to a more congenial climate, but his attempt failed, and he resigned on June 5, 1863. On September 6, his health apparently improved, he wrote to the secretary of war to ask for a new appointment. Alfred S. Gaillard was appointed captain of Company K on July 13, 1863, retroactive to June 22. He was slightly wounded at Fort Sumter on August 20, 1863.[63] Gaillard was wounded again, this time in the back, and was taken prisoner at Bentonville, North Carolina, on March 19, 1865. He was released on June 13 after treatment at the United States Army General Hospital at New Bern. John L. Black, colonel of the 1st Cavalry Regiment, described Gaillard as "a most excellent officer, and accomplished gentleman."[64] Black also wrote, incorrectly, that he was killed at Bentonville.

Brigade Affiliations

The 1st Battalion, South Carolina Artillery, was in R.G.M. Dunovant's Brigade in early 1861. It served in the Department of South Carolina from August to November 1861 and in the various subdivisions and military districts of the Department of South Carolina, Georgia and Florida from November 1861 to late 1864.[65] In February 1863, the *Mercury* reported that Company A was attached to Colquitt's Brigade along with several infantry units, among them the 46th Georgia Regiment, the 7th South Carolina Battalion and the 16th, 24th and 25th Regiments, SCV.[66] Seven companies of the regiment were attached to Roswell Ripley's Brigade in late November 1864, and the other three were attached to Taliaferro's Brigade.[67] A.M. Rhett's Brigade had been formed on December 28, 1864, by combining the 1st Regiment, South Carolina Artillery (Regulars); the 2nd Regiment, South Carolina Artillery; and the 1st Regiment, South Carolina Infantry (Regulars).[68] Seven companies of the 1st Artillery Regiment were attached to Rhett's Brigade on January 31, 1865; the rest were in Stephen Elliott's Brigade, along with the Battalion of State Cadets, eight companies of the 1st Cavalry Regiment, two from the 2nd Artillery Regiment, Company D of the South Carolina Siege Train and some Georgia units.[69] By the end of March, Rhett's Brigade comprised the original South Carolina Regular Army–1st Regiment, South Carolina Artillery (Regulars); the 1st Regiment, South Carolina Infantry (Regulars); and J.J. Lucas's 15th Battalion, South Carolina Artillery.[70] William Butler was placed in command of the brigade after Rhett was captured on March 15.[71] Companies of the 1st Regiment often served detached.

Major Movements and Engagements

The entire 1st Battalion, except for Company A, served in the Charleston area throughout its fourteen-month existence. Company B was sent to Fort

Moultrie to replace the Washington Artillery about January 28, 1861.[72] In late January, Company A moved from the Cannonsboro Arsenal to the seashore.[73] During the bombardment of Fort Sumter in April, the battalion's companies were scattered around Charleston Harbor. Company A occupied Fort Moultrie's Oblique Battery. Company B occupied the Sumter Battery at Fort Moultrie, both Mortar Battery #1 and the Enfilade Battery on Sullivan's Island and the Mount Pleasant Battery.[74] Company C occupied the two mortar batteries—Beach and Hill—at Fort Johnson on James Island; one of these, the right-hand mortar at Beach, is famous for firing the first shot over Fort Sumter on April 12, 1861. Company D occupied Fort Moultrie, the Dahlgren Battery and the Floating Battery on Sullivan's Island from March to October 1861.

Two companies—A and D—were ordered to occupy Fort Sumter after the surrender on April 13, and the fort became the battalion's headquarters then.[75] Three months later, on July 4, Company A left Fort Sumter for Charleston.[76] It was converted to a six-gun light artillery battery and left for Virginia on July 30.[77] Attached to D.R. Jones's Brigade, it served in the Manassas area until the end of the year. During the time Company A spent in Virginia, a two-gun detachment known as the Star Battery served with the 5th Infantry Regiment. Company A was never actively engaged in Virginia and returned to Charleston on January 1, 1862.[78]

Company B was sent to Fort Sumter in May 1861 and remained there until September 1863. Company C left Fort Johnson on May 29 for Fort Pickens on Battery Island along the Stono River, arriving there the next day and remaining for a couple of months with Company H of the 1st Regiment, South Carolina Infantry Regulars. Company C was sent to Fort Sumter on July 9.

Company D was stationed at Fort Moultrie from March to October 1861 and at Fort Sumter from January 1862 to June 1863. Company E was at Fort Moultrie from May to October 1861 and at Castle Pinckney from January to April 1862. Company F was stationed at Fort Sumter for two years, from September 1861 to August 1863, while Company G, which was based at Fort Moultrie until October 31, 1861, was sent to Fort Sumter from January 1862 to April 1863. Companies H and I remained at Fort Sumter from February until April or May 1862.

On March 25, 1862, the 1st Battalion was redesignated the 1st Regiment, South Carolina Artillery Regulars. The regiment was assigned, with few exceptions, to the various forts and batteries in and around the Charleston area from March 1862 until Confederate forces evacuated the city in February 1865. Its companies usually served alone or in detachments of several companies. The regiment never served as a single unit until after the evacuation.

Company A, the regiment's light battery stationed on James Island in June 1862, was engaged at Rivers's Causeway on June 3 and at Grimball's plantation on the tenth.[79] Company B served at Fort Sumter from May 1861 to September 1863, and Company D served at the fort from April 1861 to June 1863. Meanwhile, Company E served at Castle Pinckney for three months from January to April 1862. Company C, based at Church Flats in May 1862, was sent to Battery Beauregard on Sullivan's Island on May 8 and to Fort Sumter on the twenty-second. It was send to Fort Pemberton on James Island on June 7 or June 8. Later, on June 17, it was stationed at James Island Creek on the "western lines" of James Island. During June, six companies—B, D, E, F, G and H—were based at various sites in Charleston Harbor, while Companies I and K were stationed at Sullivan's Island. Company E was based at Fort Sumter for nearly a year, from May 1862 to April 1863, while Company F was assigned to the fort from September 1861 to August 1863. Company G was stationed there from January 1862 to April 1863. Company H served at Castle Pinckney from May 1862 to April 1863 and at Fort Sumter in May and June 1863. Company I took its turn at Fort Sumter from February 17 until it was moved to Battery Beauregard on Sullivan's Island on May 21, 1862. Company K also served at Battery Beauregard from April 30, 1862, to June 1863.

Though some references record the regiment's involvement at the battle of Secessionville on June 16, 1862, it saw no action there. The confusion is best explained by the fact that, for a time in June, Thomas Lamar's new 2nd Artillery Regiment, which did participate in the battle, was also called the 1st Artillery Regiment.

Company C was sent to Fort Johnson on James Island on September 5, 1862, and to Fort Sumter the next day, remaining there until April 1863. Company A was stationed at Fort Johnson in September and October 1862, while Company H was at Castle Pinckney, and Companies I and K were at Battery Beauregard.[80]

In December 1862, Federal troops at New Bern, North Carolina, threatened the Wilmington & Weldon Railroad.[81] Troops that were moved up in response to the threat included Company A of the 1st Artillery Regiment, Companies B and C of the 3rd Artillery Battalion, the 7th Infantry Battalion and three infantry regiments—the 16th, 24th and 25th—and the 46th Georgia Regiment.[82] Company A left Charleston by rail for Wilmington at two in the morning on December 15. Arriving the next day, the men were at the Northeast River on the eighteenth. The company left North Carolina on February 15, 1863, bound for Pocotaligo, where it remained until April.

On January 30, 1863, Companies D, F and I were engaged as sharpshooters during the capture of the USS *Isaac P. Smith* on the Stono

River.[83] In early 1863, Companies B, C, D, E, F, G and I garrisoned Fort Sumter, while Company K was stationed at Battery Beauregard and Company H at Castle Pinckney and Fort Ripley. Seven companies—B, C, D, E, F, G and I—were engaged when Federal ironclads attacked the fort on April 7.[84] Company K, stationed at Battery Beauregard then, missed the action. Company A returned to Secessionville in May 1863, and Company G was based at Castle Pinckney from May to October 1863. Elements of the 1st Regiment, including Company I, were sent to the Inlet Batteries at the south end of Morris Island on May 27, 1863; they were joined on June 10 by Company E. Captain John Mitchel had supervised the construction of these batteries until they were completed about June 1.

Company C was sent to Battery Gregg at Cummings's Point on Morris Island in May 1863. For four weeks beginning on June 12, the Inlet Batteries were engaged with Federal troops on Folly Island. During June, five companies were at Fort Sumter, one was at Cummings's Point, two were at the "New Batteries" on the south end of Morris Island, one was at Castle Pinckney and one was at Fort Ripley.[85]

Companies E and I, along with a detachment from Company H, were engaged on July 10 on the southern end of Morris Island; Company E lost all its records that day,[86] and each company lost some of its men to capture.[87] Another section of Company H was stationed at Battery Gregg on the north end of the island during the battle. Companies E, H and I also saw action during the assault on Battery Wagner on July 11, and Company I fought there again on the twelfth and thirteenth.[88] Fighting continued at Wagner for Companies E and I on July 18, while Company H was engaged at Battery Gregg the same day. The men of Company A also served two field howitzers during the July 18 engagement at Battery Wagner. The next day, Company G was moved from Castle Pinckney to Morris Island.[89] It probably moved to Sullivan's Island on the twenty-third, but it had been sent back to Morris Island by July 31.[90] Company A was back at James Island, and five others were at Fort Sumter by the thirtieth.[91] Company D was at Morris Island on July 30.[92]

Company K was sent to Battery Bee on Sullivan's Island in July 1863, and a detachment was moved to Battery Wagner on August 12. Company C was engaged daily at Battery Gregg from July 25 to August 5, 1863.[93] Company C was sent to Fort Sumter on August 5 and was engaged there until the twenty-sixth. On August 5, Company H went to Morris Island, where it remained until at least the fifteenth.[94] Company C was sent to Fort Johnson on August 26 and remained there until December. Company F was also ordered to Fort Johnson on the twenty-sixth. Companies C, E and H suffered casualties on Morris Island during the period from August 1 to August 20. Companies D and H garrisoned Battery Ramsay in August, and Company I was at Fort Sumter from August 17 to August 21.[95] As the garrison at Battery Wagner, Company E saw action on August 17. Elements of the 1st Regiment were also based near Secessionville about the same time.

Most of the companies of the 1st Regiment served as the garrison at Fort Sumter at various times during the first great bombardment, which lasted from August 17 to September 2, 1863. They were gradually evacuated: Company K, for example, was sent from Sumter to Sullivan's Island on August 21.[96] A detachment of Company K was at Morris Island from August 21 to August 26.[97] Companies C and F left Fort Sumter on August 24, and several others evacuated Fort Sumter on the night of August 25.[98] Company D left the fort and returned to Charleston on the night of August 28.[99] Companies A, C, F and I were at James Island on the thirty-first, Companies H and K were at Sullivan's Island, Company D was probably at Charleston and Companies B, E and G were still at Fort Sumter.[100] Companies E and G left that day, and only Company B remained at the fort as September began. The 1st Regiment was officially relieved at Fort Sumter on September 3; Company B, the last of the 1st Regiment to leave the Fort, did so on September 4.

The 1st Regiment, though not actually based at Fort Sumter, was engaged during both the Federal ironclad attack on September 8 and the assault on September 12. Company B was stationed at Fort Johnson from September 5, 1863, to February 14, 1864. Companies D, E and H were at Battery Ramsay in Charleston on September 20, 1863, Company G was at Castle Pinckney and Fort Ripley, Company K was at Sullivan's Island and Companies A, B, C, F and I were stationed at James Island.[101] Company E remained at Battery Ramsay until the following February. Company H was at Battery Ramsay from September 1863 until it moved to Castle Pinckney November 3, 1863. Company I, stationed at Fort Johnson on James Island from September to December 1863, was under almost continuous fire. Company F was based at Battery Wampler on James Island from September 1863 to April 1864. Company K was at Battery Ramsay from September 25 until it was sent to Fort Sumter to October 5.

Four companies were at Fort Sumter, Charleston and Castle Pinckney on November 1, 1863, while Companies B, C, F and H were stationed at the eastern division of James Island serving as heavy artillery. One section of Company A was also there as light artillery, while the other was based at the western division in the same capacity.[102] A rotational system for garrison duty at Fort Sumter was put in place about this time: Company G was sent to Fort Sumter on November 3 to relieve Company K the next day when K was sent to Battery Waring.[103] Company D relieved Company G at Fort Sumter on November 12, and G was ordered to Battery Waring.[104] Company D was probably engaged during the boat attack at Fort Sumter on the night of November 19 and was on rotational service there until February 1864.

Company G rotated back to Fort Sumter in early December and was relieved on the tenth.[105] Company K was sent to Fort Sumter the same day.[106] It suffered casualties when the magazine exploded at 9:30 a.m. on December 11 and was relieved by Company D on the twenty-eighth.[107] Company K was at Battery Ramsay in late December. Four companies were at Fort Sumter, Charleston and Castle Pinckney on December 31, five at James Island and one—Company D—at Fort Sumter.[108]

On January 31, 1864, five companies were stationed at Charleston, Fort Sumter and Castle Pinckney, while four, including Company A, were at James Island.[109] Company G was at Battery Harrison near Fort Johnson from January to December 1864. Company I, which was at Battery Ramsay in January and February, was sent to Fort Sumter on March 21 and stayed there until it was relieved by Company F on April 5.[110] Company K was sent to Fort Johnson on February 15 and remained there until December. Company C was sent to Battery Ramsay on February 15 and was at Fort Sumter from March 6 until it returned to the battery on the twenty-first.[111] Company B began a series of moves on February 2 that took it first to Battery Ramsay, then on to Fort Sumter on the twenty-first and back to Ramsay on March 6. It was then sent to Battery Waring on March 17 and back to Fort Sumter to relieve Company F on the twenty-sixth.[112] In March and April 1864, Company D was based in Charleston; from May to August it was at Battery Marion on Sullivan's Island. Similarly, Company E was based at Fort Ripley in March and April, and from May to October, it was at Fort Johnson. Company I was sent to the Charleston City Batteries about April 26.

On April 30, 1864, six companies were based at Charleston, Fort Sumter and Sullivan's Island; four, including Company A, were stationed on James Island.[113] By May 6, five—C, D, E, H and I—were at Castle Pinckney, Fort Ripley and Charleston; Company B was at Fort Sumter, and the other four were probably at James Island.[114] Company C was ordered to Fort Sumter on May 5 and was sent to serve the Blakely Battery in Charleston on the twenty-seventh. It was based at Battery Marion on Sullivan's Island from June 3 to November 25. Company F was stationed at Castle Pinckney from May to December 1864. Company B was sent to Battery Bee on Sullivan's Island in May or June and returned to Battery Pringle on James Island on July 2. Company H was sent to Battery Bee in May and was ordered to Sullivan's Island in December 1864. Lieutenant DeLorme's section of

Company A under the command of Major Manigault was engaged at Rivers's Causeway, also called Johnson's Point, on James Island on July 2. It lost two of its Napoleon guns that day.[115] Companies G, K and part of E saw action during the boat assault on Fort Johnson on July 3 while they were at nearby Battery Simkins. The same three companies were also engaged at Simkins during the second boat assault on July 10.[116] Companies B and D were engaged at the Stono Batteries during the attack on Battery Pringle from July 4 to July 9. Most companies of the 1st Regiment were ordered back to Sullivan's Island on July 14.[117] By the end of the month, six companies were at Charleston and its northern defenses, while four, including Company A, were at James Island.[118]

Company A was sent to Mount Pleasant on August 6; it moved on December 11 to Pocotaligo, and it returned to Mount Pleasant on the nineteenth. Meanwhile, a detachment of Company I was sent to Battery Ramsay on August 21.[119]

On October 31, six companies were at Sullivan's Island, Charleston and Castle Pinckney, while three were at James Island.[120] Company E was sent to Battery Wampler on James Island in November. Company I was ordered to Battery Marshall on Sullivan's Island that month. Company E was sent on December 3 to serve the fixed battery on the Louisville Road about three miles from Savannah and was engaged there on the tenth. Company E evacuated Savannah on December 19 and returned to Fort Johnson on the twenty-second.[121]

The 1st Regiment, which converted to infantry in February 1865, was part of the Confederate forces who evacuated Charleston. Rhett's Brigade, of which the regiment was a part, acted as the rear guard during the withdrawal into North Carolina in February and March 1865. The regiment was engaged on the east bank of the Pee Dee River during the withdrawal from Cheraw in March.[122] It also saw action at Averasboro on March 15 and March 16 and at Bentonville on the nineteenth. The regiment surrendered with the Army of Tennessee at Durham Station, North Carolina, on April 26, 1865. Its numbers had thinned greatly in only two months. The regiment's rolls, which had shown forty-five officers and more than a thousand men in February 1865, showed only eleven officers and one hundred and twenty-five men at the end.

14.

The 15th Battalion, South Carolina Artillery

The 15th Battalion, South Carolina Artillery, was also called Lucas's Battalion, South Carolina Heavy Artillery; the 15th Heavy Artillery Battalion; and the Dismounted Dragoons. Composed of regular troops of the South Carolina Army, it evolved somewhat circuitously from a squadron of cavalry into an artillery battalion. DeSaussure's Squadron was the cavalry component of the South Carolina Regular Army, which was created by the Secession Convention on December 31, 1860, and modified by the legislature on January 28, 1861. William Davie DeSaussure of Columbia, appointed major by the governor on January 28, 1861, was its first commander.[1] On May 17, Adjutant and Inspector General Samuel Cooper ordered the squadron mustered in Confederate service as infantry.[2] J.J. Lucas wrote that the government lacked the funds needed to mount the squadron, and DeSaussure grew restless and resigned.[3] He gave up command sometime between April and early June, whereupon James Jonathan Lucas, who was serving as an aide to Governor Pickens, was solicited to take over.[4] Lucas was appointed to command the squadron on June 6, 1861.[5] Though known as Major J.J. Lucas's Squadron Cavalry, it mustered in Confederate service as infantry on June 6 for three years or for the duration of the war. The two companies mustered in as "dismounted dragoons" and were based at Sullivan's Island awaiting orders at the time.[6] The name stuck; Lucas's men became known as the Dismounted Dragoons, South Carolina Regular Force.[7] Lucas, to no avail, submitted a request that the secretary of war provide mounts and order the squadron to Virginia. Instead, Brigadier General R.H. Anderson ordered the squadron converted to heavy artillery. The *Confederate Military History Series* records that though Lucas was initially a major of cavalry, his appointment was changed to major of artillery.[8] No reference to Lucas as major of infantry appears.

So it was that command of DeSaussure's Squadron of Regular Cavalry passed to Lucas in June 1861, and the identity of the squadron itself was changed first to infantry and then to artillery with the ultimate designation of 15th Battalion, South Carolina Artillery, later Heavy Artillery. The battalion initially comprised two companies. Another under Captain Frederick Childs was added as Company C about November 15, 1862. For a brief period in June 1863, the Gist Guard, Mathewes's Battery and Company B of the German Artillery were also part of the 15th Battalion.[9]

FIELD OFFICER

James Jonathan Lucas of Society Hill and Charleston was captain of the Palmetto Guards for seven years before the war. He became an aide to Governor Pickens with the rank of lieutenant colonel on December 31, 1860 and was appointed major of cavalry on June 6, 1861.[10] Lucas commanded the fortifications along the Stono River, including Fort Pemberton, known as the "back door to Charleston," until the city's evacuation in February 1865. Lucas was wounded twice: the first a slight wound at Averasboro and the next a more severe one from a musket ball in the right side at Bentonville. He was recuperating at the Officers' Hospital at Raleigh when the surrender came.[11] The only field officer in the 15th Battalion, Lucas survived the war.

COMPANIES

Company A, reorganized on June 6, 1861, was probably composed of some men from Chester District. It had served in DeSaussure's Squadron, South Carolina Cavalry Regulars, until June 1861. Alfred Junius Norris, who assumed command of Company A about June 6, resigned on January 1, 1862. Norris had been a member of General Samuel McGowan's staff, and after the resignation, he became professor of history and belles letters at The Arsenal Academy in Columbia, where he stayed until February 1865. Two days after resigning, Norris was replaced by John Hilary Gary, brother of Brigadier General Martin W. Gary and brother-in-law of Brigadier General N.G. Evans.[12] Gary had served as captain of the short-lived company called the South Carolina College Cadets in the spring of 1861. At Battery Wagner on August 12, 1863, Gary was struck behind the ear by a shell splinter. It impacted so severely it caused delirium.[13] Five days later, at 8:20 a.m. on August 17, he died from the wound.[14] Roswell Ripley remembered Gary as "a gallant and accomplished young officer of high promise."[15] A battery near Mount Pleasant was named posthumously for him. First Lieutenant E.B. Colhoun from Company B was transferred to Company A and was promoted to captain on August 17. He was paroled with the battalion in North Carolina in 1865. Though several cards in the *CSR* spell the name Calhoun, his signature reads Colhoun. Another memorable member of Company A was First Sergeant Samuel A. Tynes, who was mortally wounded at Battery Wagner on July 20, 1863, and for whom a battery along the Stono River on James Island was named.

Company B was also reorganized on June 6, 1861, from men who had served in DeSaussure's Squadron. The same day, Governor Pickens appointed Samuel D. Shannon as captain, but he resigned four months later, on October 10. T.S. Fayssoux, a first lieutenant in Company A, was promoted to captain of Company B on December 10, but he, too, resigned after only ten days. The company's third captain, Robert Pringle, lasted somewhat longer—from December 20 until he was killed in action at Battery Wagner on August 21, 1863.[16] A battery at Dill's plantation on James Island near the Stono River was named in Pringle's memory.[17] Mary Boykin Chesnut incorrectly records the name as Charles Alston Pringle.[18] First Lieutenant J. Guignard Richardson of Company A transferred to Company B as its captain on August 21. Richardson was wounded and captured at Averasboro, North Carolina.

Company C was called Captain Childs's Company, South Carolina Artillery, and had earlier been known as Captain Winder's Company, Artillery. It was formed by consolidating the companies of Frederick L. Childs and Stephen D. Lee. Stephen D. Lee's Battery, South Carolina Artillery, also called Captain Lee's Company, Artillery, mustered in service about May 12, 1861. It had been raised in Baltimore as a regular battery in the Confederate army, and from May 12, 1861 to July 18, 1862, it was an independent company under Lee's command.[19] About a hundred men strong at first, its numbers had been greatly reduced by desertion before the battery was merged into the 15th Battalion. Lee's Battery served at Cole's Island from May 1861 to early 1862. Childs's Company was similar; Charles S. Winder had raised it as battery of regular artillery in Baltimore with about a hundred men in early 1861, but it, too, had been severely depleted by desertion.[20] When Winder was promoted to major of artillery in the Regular Army on March 16, 1861, Frederick L. Childs took over command of the battery, which assumed Childs's name. It left Baltimore; Childs and sixty-four of his men arrived in Charleston about March 25, 1861.[21] Mustering in service on the twenty-fifth, the battery was sent immediately to Castle Pinckney.[22] It also served at the Charleston Arsenal before joining the 15th Battalion.

Lee was promoted to colonel of artillery, and his battery was consolidated, probably unofficially, with Childs's Battery on July 18, 1862, to create a new independent artillery battery. Childs's Consolidated Battery remained independent until November 15, 1862, about the time Lucas applied to add it to his battalion. The two were ordered officially consolidated, and the new company was attached to Lucas's Battalion as Company C on November 15, 1862.[23] Childs apparently left the company then and eventually rose to the rank of lieutenant colonel in the 2nd Battalion, North Carolina Local Defense Troops.[24] Theodore Brevard Hayne, appointed captain by the secretary of war on November 7, was assigned to command Company C on the twenty-third.[25] He was paroled at Greensboro on April 28, 1865.[26]

Brigade Affiliations

From its creation until early 1865, the 15th Battalion served in several subdivisions and military districts of the Department of South Carolina, Georgia and Florida. On November 20, 1864, it was attached to Brigadier General William Taliaferro's Brigade.[27] Shortly thereafter, on December 28, it moved to Colonel Edward C. Anderson's Brigade along with the 18th Artillery Battalion and others, including George L. Buist's four-battery battalion comprising Gilchrist's, Mathewes's, Mulches's and Johnson's Batteries and some Georgia units.[28] On January 31, 1865, the 15th Battalion was not attached to a brigade.[29] About then, the battalion was converted to infantry and became part of Elliott's Brigade.[30] By the end of March, however, the battalion was united with the other elements of the original South Carolina Regular Army, the 1st Regiment Infantry and the 1st Regiment Artillery, in A.M. Rhett's Brigade.[31] William Butler assumed command of the brigade after Rhett was captured on March 15.[32]

Major Movements and Engagements

The 15th Battalion was stationed in the Department of South Carolina, Georgia and Florida for the entire war except for the final withdrawal into North Carolina. Companies A and B were stationed at Sullivan's Island from May to July 9 or July 10, 1861. Its headquarters was established at the Stono fortifications on James Island on the ninth, and the companies were sent to Fort Pickens on Battery Island. The two-company battalion moved to Fort Palmetto on Cole's Island later that month, and by mid-November, it was back at Fort Pickens.[33] Along with the 24th Volunteer Regiment, the battalion was the garrison on Cole's Island from September 1861 until the island's evacuation on May 8, 1862. On May 10, it was sent to Fort Pemberton on James Island, where it saw action with Federal gunboats on the Stono River on May 30.

Though headquartered at Fort Pemberton until August 1864, the battalion's companies were more scattered in 1863 and 1864 than during the battalion's first year. Company A, for example, was sent to Fort Waddy on October 2, 1862, and to Battery Means from November to the following February. It was ordered back to Fort Pemberton from March to October 1863, except for a period of service at Battery Wagner in mid-August.[34] Company B, on the other hand, remained at Fort Pemberton for more than a year, from May 1862 to July 1863. Company C, which joined the battalion in November 1862, was also at Fort Pemberton until July 1863. As the garrison of Fort Pemberton, all three were engaged during the capture of the *Isaac P. Smith* on January 30, 1863.[35] Companies A and C fought at or near Grimball's farm on James Island that day. The battalion was still at Fort Pemberton in June 1863.[36]

The battalion remained at James Island in July and August, its companies alternating for service at Battery Wagner.[37] Ordered to Wagner on July 19, Company A was engaged there for four straight days before returning to Fort Pemberton on the twenty-third.[38] It was also at Wagner for a week—from August 10 to August 17.[39] Company B came under heavy enemy fire at Battery Wagner from July 23 to July 27 and from August 16 to August 22.[40] Company C had its turn under fire at Wagner from July 27 to August 1 and from August 20 to August 25.[41] Elements of the battalion were also engaged at Battery Gregg on August 24.

From September to early November 1863, companies of the 15th Battalion were serving as heavy artillery and were dispersed on the Stono River side of James Island.[42] Company A was at Battery Ramsay in Charleston in November and December 1863.[43] Captain Colhoun and forty men from Company A were at Fort Sumter from January 25 to February 8, 1864.[44] Companies B and C remained on James Island during that time.[45] From March 28 to December 1864, Company A was based at Battery Pringle along the Stono River on James Island.

After its service at Battery Wagner, Company B was sent first to Fort Pemberton and then to Battery Tynes, where it served for nearly a year, from October 4, 1863, to August 1864. It was based at the newly built Battery Trenholm along the Stono River on John's Island from October 21 to late December 1864.[46] Company C was sent from Battery Wagner to Battery Pringle on James Island in September 1863; its men remained there until March 28, 1864, when it was ordered to Battery Ramsay in Charleston.[47]

Company C went to Battery Pringle on July 2, 1864. A detachment of the battalion at Fort Sumter was relieved on July 7.[48] Company C was sent to Fort Pemberton in August; from October 16 to December 1864, it was based at Battery Tynes, where the battalion's headquarters was located from September to December 1864.[49] Companies B and C formed part of the garrison at the Stono Batteries on James Island in July 1864; both were engaged in the attack on Batteries Pringle and Tynes from July 8 to July 9, 1864.[50] While stationed at the batteries, both were engaged for ten days in July with the monitors *Lehigh* and *Montauk*, the gunboats *Pawnee*, *McDonough* and *Racer* and a mortar boat.[51] The battalion remained on James Island until its evacuation on February 17 and February 18, 1865.

The 15th Battalion was converted to infantry in early 1865. Rhett's Brigade, to which the 15th Battalion belonged, acted as the rear guard during the withdrawal into North Carolina in February and March. The battalion was engaged at Averasboro on March 15 and March 16, and at Bentonville. The 15th Battalion surrendered with the Army of Tennessee on April 26, 1865.

15.

Independent Artillery Organizations

Stephen D. Lee's Battery–South Carolina Artillery

Stephen D. Lee's Battery–South Carolina Artillery was also called Captain Lee's Company, Artillery. This company of regulars, which mustered in service about May 12, 1861, as an independent company, was commanded by Stephen D. Lee from May 12, 1861, to July 18, 1862.

Lee served in a detached capacity for the existence of his battery, which was raised in Baltimore as a regular battery in the Confederate army.[1] Originally made up of about a hundred men, its numbers had been greatly reduced by desertion before the battery was merged into the 15th Battalion.

Lee's Battery was stationed at Castle Pinckney until May 30, 1861, when it was ordered to Fort Palmetto on Cole's Island. The men remained there until early 1862. Lee was promoted to colonel of artillery that year, and on July 18, his battery was consolidated, probably unofficially, with Charles Winder's (Childs's) Battery as a new independent artillery battery. Childs's Battery remained independent until November 15, 1862, when it was officially consolidated with Lee's and designated Company C of Lucas's 15th Battalion.[2]

16.

THE REGIMENTS OF RESERVES (NINETY DAYS), 1862–1863

The Confederate Conscription Act of April 16, 1862, claimed for active duty all white males between eighteen and thirty-five years of age and caused a significant depletion within the ranks of the militia system.[1] A second conscription law passed on September 27, 1862, further depleted them because it allowed the president to call up men between the ages of thirty-five and forty-five for three years, unless the war ended sooner.[2] These acts took "all the material of armies between the ages mentioned, from the control of the state."[3] The Executive Council wrote, "To meet this new condition of things, it becomes necessary that the State shall adopt further measures to organize its forces and provide for its defence."[4] Soon after the Conscription Act of April 16 passed, the Executive Council decided to separate the men affected from the militia, organize them into companies and regiments and hold them in reserve for the defense of the state or other service at the discretion of the governor.[5]

Consequently, on April 23, 1862, the Executive Council passed resolutions creating two corps of state reserves.[6] The 1st Corps was composed of thirty-five- to fifty-year-old men conscripted from within the existing militia regiments and battalions.[7] They were held for active service as needed anywhere in the state and were to be used as the occasion dictated. They were also subject to patrol and police duty until they were called into active service.[8] Men of the 1st Corps were allowed to elect their own lieutenants and captains. Colonels, lieutenant colonels and majors, on the other hand, were to be appointed by the governor and Executive Council.[9] When not in active service, the men of the 1st Corps of Reserves were to perform patrol duty under the command of officers of the 2nd Corps.[10] By August 30, 1862, elections for company-grade officers had been held, and the 1st Corps, consisting of about eight thousand men, was fully organized into ten regiments, called "Regiments of Reserves."

Each regiment was assigned a numerical designation, two through eleven.[11] To avoid confusion with the 1st Regiment, Charleston Reserves, which was organized the previous October, none was designated the "1st Regiment." The Executive Council's resolution creating the Reserve Corps did not originally apply to the 1st Regiment of Charleston Reserves.[12] By August 22, however, the Charleston Regiment had been officially designated the 1st Regiment of the 1st Corps of Reserves.[13] This modification gave the 1st Corps a total of eleven regiments.

By early October 1862, Governor Pickens had reviewed nine of the ten new reserve regiments.[14] When Federal troops landed at Coosawhatchie later that month, the governor and Executive Council recommended to President Davis that the 1st Corps of Reserves be called into active service.[15] On October 25, Secretary of War G.W. Randolph notified James Chesnut that the Confederate government would accept the 2nd, 3rd, 8th and 11th Regiments of Reserves for local service and would disband the remaining seven. Randolph also indicated that he would accept men over forty for service in the reserve regiments and would place those between thirty-five and forty, as well as conscripts from the seven disbanded regiments, in existing South Carolina units. The 2nd, 3rd, 8th and 11th Regiments of Reserves—about three thousand men—were expected to be in camp in about twenty days.[16] The Executive Council rejected Randolph's proposal on a technicality.[17]

On November 4, the secretary again recommended calling up four reserve regiments. The same day, the Executive Council issued a resolution ordering the 2nd, 3rd, 8th and 11th to report to General Beauregard in Charleston for ninety days of Confederate service.[18] On the fifth, the council recommended calling into active service the 5th, 6th, 7th and 9th Reserve Regiments; the secretary of war agreed.[19] Though President Davis preferred to accept eight regiments for three years or for the duration of the war, he was willing to go along with the ninety-day stipulation.[20] The president modified the plan on November 11 and accepted the eight regiments into service.[21] On the eighteenth, eight of the ten new regiments of the 1st Corps went into Confederate service for ninety days of state defense. These were the 2nd, 3rd, 5th, 6th, 7th, 8th, 9th and 11th. Four were ordered to report first to Lightwood Knot Springs north of Columbia before traveling to Charleston.[22] The 4th and 10th Regiments were disbanded on November 7 because of disaffection among the men.[23]

The Secession Convention expired by its own ordinance on December 12, 1862; the next day, the General Assembly declared many decisions of the Executive Council invalid.[24] It revoked, for example, the council's order to disband the 4th and 10th Regiments of Reserves. A few days later, on

December 18, the General Assembly passed an act forbidding any reserve regiment to serve more than ninety days. It also determined to replace council-appointed field officers and required that new elections be held on January 1, 1863.[25] Beauregard objected to the new law since the regiments were at the time "in the face of the enemy," and Governor M.L. Bonham requested and received permission to appeal the law. Only a few companies held new elections, and even those results were never seriously considered.[26] At the end of ninety days, on February 10, 1863, the 1st Corps reserve regiments were disbanded.[27] The thirty-five- to forty-year-old men of the corps, however (those previously exempt from active service because of their age), were now required by the second conscription law to enter active service. On February 18, 1863, Governor Bonham ordered the 1st, 4th and 10th Regiments of Reserves back into the field and the remainder held in reserve in anticipation of an immediate Federal assault on Charleston.[28] The governor suspended his order on March 9, and the reserves remained at home.[29]

FIRST REGIMENT CHARLESTON RESERVES, SOUTH CAROLINA MILITIA

The 1st Regiment Charleston Reserves, South Carolina Militia, was raised from volunteers in early 1861. Three companies of previously organized home guards added a fourth company in mid-April, legally forming a battalion of four hundred men, who elected a major to command them.[30] By October 11, five new companies had been added, enlarging the unit to regimental strength; the men soon elected a colonel.[31] The regiment carried between seven hundred and twelve hundred and fifty men on its rolls, including a number of prominent South Carolinians.[32] Many were the "exempt respectability" of Charleston, gray-haired gentlemen over forty-five as well as those otherwise exempt from active military duty. Some were also in the 16th Regiment, South Carolina Militia.[33] A corporal in the 16th, West Point graduate William C. Heyward, had served as colonel of the 11th Regiment, SCV, in 1861 and early 1862 but had failed to be re-elected at the reorganization in May. Heyward was a good officer and one of many lost to the service through the re-election process. He died from exposure on September 1, 1863.[34]

In December 1861, a bill was proposed in the legislature to make this regiment part of the 4th Brigade of South Carolina Militia.[35] The determination was made, however, that though the companies had been legally organized, the regiment itself had not. The bill failed to pass, and the legislature dissolved the regiment in December 1861.[36] It was allowed to reform in January as part of the militia system with the same name, same officers and same company organization.[37] The *Mercury* lists nine companies—eight musket and one rifle—in January 1862.[38] A tenth was added later that year, and by August, the regiment was attached to the 4th Brigade, South Carolina Militia, whose men came from the same area.[39]

The Secession Convention passed a resolution on February 7, 1862, ordering all white male inhabitants of Charleston between the ages of sixteen and eighteen and from forty-five to sixty to report to the regiment for duty unless otherwise exempt or enrolled in another organization.[40] The Executive Council modified this order in August, resolving that all male residents of Charleston between the ages of thirty-five and fifty must enroll in the regiment and those between sixteen and eighteen and fifty and sixty-five must enroll in the 2nd Corps of Reserves. By the twenty-second, the adjutant and inspector general had designated the Charleston Regiment of Reserves as the 1st Regiment of the 1st Corps of Reserves.[41] This addition gave the 1st Corps eleven regiments. According to the *CSR*, the regiment was in the service of the Confederate States only when called out by the commanding general of the Department of South Carolina and Georgia.

Field Officers

Francis M. Robertson, previously captain of the 4th Company, was elected major of the battalion in August 1861.[42] When the regiment was organized in early October, Robertson was elected its colonel.[43] He apparently resigned his commission by February 1862.

Alexander Henry Brown, elected major on October 15, was either promoted or elected lieutenant colonel two days later.[44] Brown was promoted to colonel in February 1862 to fill the position left vacant by Robertson's resignation.[45] Brown also served as assistant provost marshal and provost marshal for Charleston in May and June 1862.

B.G. Heriot, elected major on October 17, had apparently resigned his commission by mid-December.[46]

C.W. Graves was elected major by December 11, 1861, replacing Heriot.[47] He resigned in February 1862.

Robert N. Gourdin became lieutenant colonel on February 17, 1862, when Brown was promoted to colonel.

J.W.A. Wardlaw was elected major on February 17, 1862.[48] He also served as major in the 1st Regiment Charleston Guard.

Companies

Company A, the Hibernian Guard, was also called Company #1. It was formed as a reserve company from older members of the Irish Volunteers on December 31, 1860, and was commanded by Thomas Ryan from early 1861 to at least October.[49] John F. O'Neill, formerly a lieutenant in Company H, was captain of Company A from December 19 to December 24, 1861.

Company B, the Charleston Home Guard, also called Company #2, was commanded by George S. Hacker from June 5 to at least November 1862.[50]

Company C, the Pickens Rifles, also known as Company #3, was the right flank company.[51] James H. Taylor commanded the company twice: in December 1861 and from June 5 to at least November 1862.[52]

Company D, also called Company #4, was commanded by John C. Martin after September 3, 1861.[53] Francis M. Robertson had commanded the company earlier in 1861.

Company E, also called Reserve Guard #5, was commanded by Henry D. Lesesne.

Company F, also called Company #6, was commanded by T.W. Holwell.

Company G, also called Company #7, was commanded first by John E. Bowers and later by W.W. Sale.[54]

Company H, also called Company #8, was organized on September 25, 1861, and was commanded by John Dougherty.[55]

The Pickens Rifles, bearing the same name as Company C but probably a distinct unit, was attached to the regiment as its ninth company in the fall of 1861. It was assigned neither a number nor a letter designation. It was commanded by S.K. McDonald before August 1861 and by L.H. Charbonnier afterward.[56] This company is discussed in more detail elsewhere under Captain L.H. Charbonnier's Company, South Carolina Militia, in Volume I and under the 1st Regiment Rifles, South Carolina Militia, in this volume.

There was no Company I, but there was an unorthodox use of the letter J to designate the company commanded by M.D. Porter. Though the *Mercury* does not mention a Company J, the *CSR* notes that Company J was called into service by Major General Robertson on June 7, 1862.[57] The *Charleston Daily Courier* called it Company I.[58]

Company K, the tenth, was added in late 1862 and was commanded by a Captain Henry.[59]

Major Movements and Engagements

After the great fire in Charleston in December 1861, the regiment helped guard the devastated city.[60] When it was called up for duty on January 5, 1862, about 150 of the 1,250 men responded. The regiment was placed on provost duty in Charleston when regular troops left to take the field at James Island in early June. Garrisoned at the Charleston Arsenal from June 5 to August 21, the regiment also guarded the city's communications and jail.

THE 2ND REGIMENT RESERVES

The 2nd Regiment South Carolina Reserves, (Ninety Days) 1862–1863, was one of ten new regiments in the 1st Corps of Reserves. Its men came from the same geographic boundaries as those of the 4th Division, South Carolina Militia.[61]

Field Officers

Ellerbe Boggan Crawford Cash of Chesterfield District was colonel of the 2nd Reserve Regiment. Cash had been colonel of the 8th Regiment, SCV, but was not re-elected at the reorganization in May 1862.

William H. Evans of Darlington was lieutenant colonel of the 2nd Regiment.[62] He had served previously as captain of Company F, 8th Regiment, SCV.

J.B. Chandler of Williamsburg District was major of the 2nd Regiment.[63]

Companies

The regiment had ten companies, designated A to K, but the *CSR* lists no company rolls.

Company A, probably from Lexington District, was commanded by a Captain Evans.[64]

Company B was commanded by a Captain Ellerbe.

Company C was commanded by a Captain Williamson.

Company D, from Williamsburg and Georgetown Districts, was commanded by Samuel D. McGill.[65]

Company E was commanded by a Captain Dunbar.

Company F was commanded by a Captain Rouse.

Company G was commanded by a Captain McGillbery.

Company H was commanded by a Captain Philips.

Company I was commanded by a Captain Larimore.
Company K's commander is unknown.

Brigade Affiliations

The regiment was assigned to the Department of South Carolina, Georgia and Florida for its entire ninety-day existence.[66]

Major Movements and Engagements

On August 5, 1862, the Executive Council authorized Colonel E.B.C. Cash to raise a permanent volunteer corps of artillery from men of the 2nd Regiment of Reserves to man the guns at Stone's Landing. This corps was apparently never organized.[67] The 2nd Regiment, in camp on August 1, 1862, was sent to Florence on the twelfth and to Camp Marion three days later.[68] The 2nd Regiment spent September and part of October at Fort Finger on the Pee Dee River. Later in October, it was transferred to Georgetown; it was stationed there on the seventeenth, having arrived without arms or ammunition. At that time, Brigadier General Trapier wrote of the 2nd Regiment: "It is questionable whether they can be rendered efficient in that time [90 days], even if well armed and equipped. At present they are literally worth nothing at all."[69] The regiment was based at Camp Chesnut near Georgetown in December.[70] The men guarded ordnance, commissary and quartermaster stores at Georgetown.[71] The 2nd Regiment was disbanded at Georgetown on February 3, 1863.[72]

THE 3RD REGIMENT RESERVES

The 3rd Regiment Reserves (Ninety Days), 1862–1863, was one of the ten new reserve regiments in the 1st Corps of Reserves. It was also called the "Old Guard of the Mountains."[73] Seven companies were from Greenville District; three came from the 5th Regiment, South Carolina Militia, in eastern Pickens District.[74] The 3rd Regiment was organized about the same time as the other reserve regiments, but it mustered in service a few months later. On August 22, 1862, the *Camden Confederate* listed nine of the new regiments of reserves, but omitted the 3rd.[75] Other newspapers mentioned the existence of the 3rd Regiment in August.[76] The 3rd Regiment mustered in service on November 13, 1862, at Greenville with nine hundred men.[77]

Field Officers

Charles James Elford, a forty-two-year-old Greenville lawyer, was colonel of the 16th Regiment, SCV, until the reorganization. He was not re-elected on April 29, 1862. Elford applied for a position as the commander of a camp of instruction or an enrolling officer in September. He was commissioned colonel of the 3rd Regiment of Reserves in November 1862.

E.P. Jones was nominated by the Executive Council for the position of lieutenant colonel in late August 1862 but refused to accept it.[78]

Stanley Stephen Crittenden was lieutenant colonel of the 3rd Regiment.[79] A first lieutenant in Company G of the 4th Regiment, SCV, in 1861 and early 1862, Crittenden was also first lieutenant of Company B, 13th Battalion. He was wounded by a Minié ball in the left breast at Seven Pines while serving as adjutant of the 4th Regiment. While Crittenden was recovering, Governor Pickens appointed him lieutenant colonel of the 3rd Regiment of Reserves.[80] After the regiment's ninety-day service expired in February 1863, Crittenden returned to the 13th Battalion as a private. By that time the battalion had become Company I, Hampton Legion Mounted Infantry.[81]

Daniel Grice of Pickens was major of the regiment.[82] He probably served later as captain of Company F, probably in the 1st Battalion Reserves, in 1864 and 1865.[83]

Companies

Company A from Greenville District was commanded by John Charles.

Company B, also from Greenville District, was commanded by Thomas B. Roberts. The first captain of Company A of the 16th Regiment, SCV, he was not re-elected at the reorganization. In July 1863, Roberts was elected colonel of the 1st Regiment, South Carolina State Troops.

Company C from Greenville District was commanded by W.R. Berry.

Company D from Greenville District was commanded by Davis W. Hodges. Hodges was previously captain of Company H, 16th Regiment.

Company E, another Greenville District company, was commanded by William B. Green.

Company F, commanded by William H. Goodlett, was from Greenville District. Goodlett commanded another company, known as Goodlett's Home Guards, in 1864 and 1865.

Company G, probably also from Greenville District, was commanded by Joel Farmer.

Company H, probably from eastern Pickens District, was commanded by William M. Jones.[84]

Company I, also probably from eastern Pickens District, was commanded by W.E. Welborn.[85]

Company K, probably another eastern Pickens District company, was commanded by Henry C. Briggs.[86]

Brigade Affiliations

The 3rd Regiment Reserves, part of the 1st Corps of Reserves, was assigned to the Department of South Carolina, Georgia and Florida throughout its ninety-day existence.

Major Movements and Engagements

On November 13 and November 14, the regiment passed through Columbia en route to Charleston.[87] It arrived there on the twenty-eighth with about seven hundred men and went into camp along the Charleston & Savannah Railroad for about three days.[88] The regiment moved next to Pocotaligo and set up camp about a mile from Pocotaligo Station.[89] It was based at Pocotaligo during its ninety-day existence. From November 13 to at least December 31, the field and staff officers were based near Pocotaligo at Camp Goldsmith, which probably took its name from the regiment's quartermaster. When the 3rd Regiment was disbanded in early February 1863, the thirty-five- to forty-year-old men were required to enter active service; the rest left for home, arriving at Greenville on February 14.[90]

THE 4TH REGIMENT RESERVES

The 4th Regiment Reserves (Ninety Days), 1862–1863, was one of ten new regiments of the 1st Corps of Reserves. Most of its men came from companies raised in Anderson District. Others lived within the limits of the 2nd Militia Regiment of Pickens District, and some were from a militia company based in Abbeville District near its border with Anderson District.[91] Governor Pickens and the Executive Council passed a resolution on November 7, 1862, disbanding the 4th Regiment and voiding all commissions issued to its officers, a move attributed to "disaffection among the men."[92] Thus the 4th Regiment was not among the eight reserve regiments called up for duty in November 1862.

Field Officers

J.B.E. Sloan of Anderson, previously colonel of the 4th Regiment, SCV, was colonel of the regiment by late August 1862.[93] He tendered his resignation about October 24, 1862.[94]

R.A. Maxwell of Anderson was the regiment's lieutenant colonel.[95]

J.W. Norris of Pickens served as major of the regiment.[96]

Companies

T.E. Wood commanded Company I, from Spartanburg.

T.H. Russell, captain of one of the regiment's companies, was court-martialed for disobedience of orders and mutiny in October 1862.[97] He served in 1863 as a captain in Thomas's Battalion.

THE 5TH REGIMENT RESERVES

The 5th Regiment Reserves (Ninety Days), 1862–1863, was also part of the 1st Corps of Reserves. Its men were mostly from Abbeville District, though some were 1st Corps reservists from the 7th and 9th Militia Regiments from Edgefield District.[98] The 5th Regiment served from November 5, 1862, to February 15, 1863.[99]

Field Officers

Thomas Glascock Bacon of Edgefield was appointed colonel on August 15, 1862.[100] Previously colonel of the 7th Regiment, SCV, he was not re-elected at the reorganization in the spring of 1862. In ill health, Bacon was often absent from the regiment.

James "Jim" Benjamin Griffin of Edgefield was appointed lieutenant colonel on August 15, 1862.[101] Previously lieutenant colonel of the Hampton Legion, Griffin was elected colonel of the legion in August 1862 but declined that position in favor of the one in the 5th Regiment Reserves. When the legislature ordered January 1, 1863 elections for field officers in the Regiments of Reserves, Bacon wrote that while his own re-election was assured, he stood to lose Griffin, whom he considered an able and efficient officer, unless General Beauregard intervened. Beauregard's response was, "What is all this?"[102] Whatever the reason, the General Assembly revoked the order, and new elections were not held. Griffin later served as colonel of the 1st Regiment, South Carolina Junior Reserves.

Edward E. Noble of Abbeville was appointed major of the regiment on August 15, 1862.[103]

Companies

Company A, commanded by Benjamin Zachary Herndon, enlisted at Abbeville. He served later as lieutenant colonel of the 3rd Regiment, Junior Reserves.

Company B, from Chester, was commanded by William A. Lomax, who resigned on November 29, 1862. First Lieutenant Lewis C. Parks became brevet captain the same day.

Company C, commanded by John B. Holmes, enlisted at Hamburg in Edgefield District.

Company D was commanded by Toliver Hearn.

Company E was commanded by Jefferson "Jeff" P. Nixon, a veteran of the Mexican War.[104] Francis "Frank" W. Burt might also have commanded the company.[105]

Company F was commanded by John F. Talbert, who had commanded a company called the Jefferson Nullifiers in early 1861.

Company G, commanded by James M. White, enlisted at Abbeville.

Company H also enlisted at Abbeville. Captain W.K. Bradley was its commander until his resignation on November 28, 1862. First Lieutenant James S. Robinson was promoted to captain the same day.

Company I, commanded by John W. Hearst, enlisted at Abbeville. According to a sketch in *Cyclopedia of Eminent and Representative Men of the Carolinas*, Columbus Lafayette Hollingsworth was captain of this company. Hollingsworth was actually captain of Company I of the 2nd Regiment, South Carolina Militia; there is no record in the *CSR* that he ever served as captain of Company I of the 5th Regiment Reserves.[106]

Company K, which enlisted at Edgefield, was from the lower battalion of the 7th Regiment, South Carolina Militia. J.A. Bland was its first captain.[107] Benjamin W. Bettis also commanded the company.

Brigade Affiliations

The 5th Regiment, South Carolina Reserves, served in the Department of South Carolina, Georgia and Florida for its ninety-day existence.

Major Movements and Engagements

On October 8, 1862, the *Edgefield Advertiser* reported that the Edgefield District companies from the 7th and 9th Regiments, South Carolina Militia, were scheduled to assemble soon at Liberty Hill.[108] More than a month later, the entire regiment was ordered to report to Summerville during the period from November 17 to November 26.[109] It was in Charleston on the twenty-sixth and moved on to Jacksonboro the next day.[110] A veteran of the regiment, however, wrote that the men stayed at the Old American Hotel on King Street in Charleston for about two weeks before moving to Jacksonboro.[111] By December 3, the regiment had been received into service for ninety days, dating from November 4.[112] The 5th Regiment, mustering about 490 men, was stationed at Camp Griffin near Jacksonboro in Colleton District until February 15, 1863.[113]

THE 6TH REGIMENT RESERVES

The 6th Regiment Reserves (Ninety Days), 1862–1863, was composed of men from York, Chester and Fairfield Districts.[114] Though the governor and Executive Council appointed the regiment's field officers on August 19, the companies did not muster in service until November 18, 1862.

Field Officers

Andrew Jackson Secrest of Chester, previously lieutenant colonel of the 6th Regiment, SCV, was appointed colonel of the 6th Regiment Reserves on August 19, 1862. When he was not re-elected at the reorganization of the 6th Regiment, SCV, in the spring of 1862, Secrest enlisted as a private in the 4th (13th) Battalion before being appointed to command the 6th Reserves. He later served as a private in Company B of the 4th Regiment, South Carolina Cavalry.

James Nelson Shedd of Fairfield District was appointed lieutenant colonel on August 19, 1862. Before the reorganization, Shedd had served as captain of Company D of the 6th Regiment, SCV, but he was not re-elected in May 1862. Shedd then served for ninety days with the 6th Reserves and later, as both captain and major, in the 22nd Regiment, SCV.

Daniel Williams of York was appointed major of the 6th Regiment on August 19, 1862.[115] He later served as major of the 1st Battalion of South Carolina Reserves.

Companies

Company A, from Chester, mustered in service on November 18, 1862, with Robert Boyd as its captain.

Company B, also from Chester, mustered in service on November 18, 1862; Captain Thomas Wilks, also shown as Wilkes, commanded.

Company C was from Chester and also mustered in service on November 18, 1862. Captain F.P. Ingram commanded the company.

Company D was from the Town Beat and Briar Patch Beat of the 34th Regiment, South Carolina Militia, from York District.[116] Its commander was Captain J.T. Lowry. This company is not listed in the *CSR*, probably because its men refused to report for duty. It appears that the company protested the governor's authority to appoint the regiment's field officers, and the men reported for duty at Columbia only symbolically "through Captain Lowry."[117] Lowry later served as captain of Company B, 5th Regiment, South Carolina State Troops, in late 1863 and early 1864.

Company E, from York, mustered in service on November 18, 1862, with Harvey H. Drennan as its captain.

Company F from Fairfield District, commanded by Captain John McLurkin, mustered in service on November 18, 1862. McLurkin served as captain of Company H, 4th Regiment, South Carolina State Troops, in late 1863 and early 1864.

Company G, from York District, mustered in service on November 18, 1862, with William J. Bowen as its commander. He served as captain of Company K, 5th Regiment, South Carolina State Troops, in late 1863 and early 1864.

Company H from Ridgeway in Fairfield District, commanded by Robert R. Rosborough, mustered in service on November 18, 1862.

Company I, also from Fairfield District, mustered in service on November 18, 1862. It was commanded by Captain O.R. Thompson.

Brigade Affiliations

The 6th Regiment, South Carolina Reserves, served in the Department of South Carolina, Georgia and Florida for its ninety-day existence.

Major Movements and Engagements

Governor Pickens ordered the 6th Regiment into Camp Hampton near Columbia on November 18, 1862. It left camp on December 15 under orders from General Beauregard and reported to Brigadier General Walker at Pocotaligo. The regiment was stationed at nearby Camp Walker until February 16, 1863.

THE 7TH REGIMENT RESERVES

The 7th Regiment Reserves (Ninety Days), 1862–1863, was one of ten that comprised the 1st Corps of Reserves. Its men came primarily from the 35th, 36th and 37th Regiments, South Carolina Militia, from Union and Spartanburg Districts, though three companies were from York District.[118] Field officers were commissioned by the governor on August 19, 1862. The twelve companies of the 7th Regiment were called up for active duty and accepted for ninety days of service on November 5, 1862, and the men actually mustered in at Columbia on the twentieth. The 7th Regiment was disbanded about February 17, 1863.

Field Officers

William Blackburn Wilson of York, a lawyer and signee of the South Carolina Ordinance of Secession, was commissioned colonel of the 7th Regiment on August 19, 1862.[119] Wilson was captain of Company F of the 17th Regiment, SCV, before the reorganization and served later as acting brigadier general. At the end of the war, he was adjutant of the 3rd Military District of South Carolina.[120]

J.B. Tolleson of Spartanburg District was commissioned lieutenant colonel on August 19, 1862.[121]

William Sartor McJunkin of Union was commissioned major on August 19, 1862.[122] He had served previously as captain of Company B, 18th Regiment, SCV.

Companies

Company A, from Spartanburg District, was commanded by Joel Ballenger.[123] He later served as captain of Company G, 5th Regiment, South Carolina State Troops, in 1863 and 1864.

Company B, the Rocky Creek Troop, was commanded by John M. Caldwell.[124]

Company C was commanded by J.E. Cleary.

Company D was commanded by W.M. Grisham.

Company E's commander, Charles W. Scott, had served as captain of Company E of the 5th Regiment, SCV, from October 9, 1861, until the reorganization in the spring of 1862.

Company F, from York District, was commanded by Robert A. Black.

Company G was commanded by J.J. McDowell.

Company H, from Spartanburg District, was commanded by John McCulloch.

Company I, from York District, was commanded by J.S. Dawson.

Company K's commander, William G. Hughes Sr., served as captain of Company M, 5th Regiment, South Carolina State Troops, in late 1863 and early 1864.

Company L was commanded by J.H. Vandike, who resigned on January 15, 1863. His replacement, First Lieutenant T. Wesley Wyatt, commanded the company but was not promoted to captain.

Company M was commanded by Clough H. Maybry.

J.L. McMakin served as captain of a company from York District; its letter designation is unknown.[125]

Brigade Affiliations

The 7th Regiment, South Carolina Reserves, was attached to the Department of South Carolina, Georgia and Florida for its entire existence.

Major Movements and Engagements

The regiment was scheduled for review at Gaffney's Old Field near Limestone Springs in early October 1862, but for some reason the review never took place.[126] After being called up for service on November 5, the regiment was stationed at the fairgrounds in Columbia from November 20 to December 12.[127] The next day, the men were sent to Mount Pleasant. They remained there until the regiment was disbanded on February 17, 1863.

THE 8TH REGIMENT RESERVES

The 8th Regiment, South Carolina Reserves, (Ninety Days), 1862–1863, was another in the 1st Corps of Reserves. It was originally called the "Pet Lambs" and had become known as the "Bloody Eighth" by January 1863.[128] Since the regiment's service record shows no engagements, it is probably safe to say that the latter was a term of derision. Men of the 8th Regiment had come from companies of the 5th Brigade, South Carolina Militia, from Lancaster, Kershaw, Clarendon, Sumter and Richland Districts.[129] The 8th was one of the four reserve regiments called up for service in or near Charleston in early November 1862.[130] Its enlistment date was November 4, and the regiment was mustered out on February 3, 1863.[131]

Field Officers

James H. Witherspoon of Lancaster District was appointed colonel of the 8th Regiment. An order from the General Assembly to hold elections for field officers on January 1, 1863, was only partially obeyed by the regiment; three companies voted while the others refused to open the polls. The compliant companies re-elected Witherspoon as colonel.[132] He became colonel of the 4th Regiment of South Carolina State Troops in August 1863.

William M. Shannon of Kershaw District, lieutenant colonel by appointment, was rejected by the three companies voting in the January 1863 election in favor of Captain F.M. Mellett. Shannon was able to retain his post when the General Assembly voided the entire election process in mid-January.[133] In February 1864, Shannon resigned his position as state agent for furnishing labor for projects along the coast and accepted the presidency of the Branch Bank of the State at Camden.[134]

Thomas Taylor of Richland District, who had been appointed major, was also rejected at the January election in favor of Captain J.H. McKnight.[135] Taylor managed to hold on when the elections were deemed invalid by the General Assembly.[136]

Companies

Company records are sketchy, and only a few letter designations have been preserved.

Captain John W. Dargan's Company, designated Company F, was from Sumter District.[137]

Edmund Davis from Columbia was captain of Company H.[138]

Captain W.H. Casson's Company, designated Company I, was the Headquarters Company.[139]

Captain F.M. Mellett's Company was from the 3rd, 6th and 7th Beats of the 20th Regiment, South Carolina Militia, in Sumter District.[140] Mellett also served as both captain of Company I and lieutenant colonel in the 4th Regiment, South Carolina State Troops, in late 1863 and early 1864.

Captain H.W. Campbell's Company was from the Upper Battalion of the 21st Regiment, South Carolina Militia, from Lancaster District. It was organized on August 1, 1862.[141]

Captain John Nelson Sowell's Company was from the Lower Battalion of the 21st Regiment, South Carolina Militia, from Lancaster District. It was organized on August 1, 1862.[142] Sowell was captain of Company B, 4th Regiment, South Carolina State Troops, in late 1863 and early 1864.

Columbus Cureton Haile commanded a company from Kershaw District. Haile had been captain of Company G of the 2nd Regiment, SCV, until May 1862. He also served as captain of Company C in the 4th Regiment, South Carolina State Troops, in late 1863 and early 1864.

James H. McKnight commanded a company from Clarendon District. He was captain of Company D, 4th Regiment, South Carolina State Troops, in late 1863 and early 1864.

Thomas R. Brown commanded a company from the 23rd Regiment, South Carolina Militia, in Richland District. He also served as captain of Company G, 4th Regiment, South Carolina State Troops, in late 1863 and early 1864 and as lieutenant colonel of the 5th Battalion Reserves in 1864 and 1865.

A Captain Skinner commanded one company; J.L. Shaw and a Captain Bell commanded two others.[143]

Brigade Affiliations

The 8th Regiment, South Carolina Reserves, was attached to the Department of South Carolina, Georgia and Florida for its entire existence.

Major Movements and Engagements

The 8th Regiment was ordered to Camp Hampton on the South Carolina Railroad about four miles below Columbia on November 19, 1862.[144] Reviewed there on November 21, it remained for drill and instruction.[145] The regiment left Camp Hampton by rail for Charleston on December 9 and arrived at two in the morning on the tenth. Later the same day, the regiment departed, again by rail, for Kingstree. After four days, the regiment marched on to Georgetown, arriving on the seventeenth with about 450 men.[146] It settled in at Camp Chesnut about a mile west of Georgetown and slightly north of Sampit Creek.[147] On February 11, 1863, the *Lancaster Ledger* reported that the 8th Regiment had disbanded "last week."[148]

THE 9TH REGIMENT RESERVES

The 9th Regiment Reserves, (Ninety Days), 1862–1863, was among the ten in the 1st Corps of Reserves. Its men were from the upcountry: Laurens District was represented, as well as the 45th Regiment, South Carolina Militia, from Union and Spartanburg Districts, and the 38th Regiment, South Carolina

Militia, from Newberry District.[149] The 9th Regiment was called up for active duty on November 5, 1862.[150] It was disbanded about February 17, 1863.

Field Officers

James Henderson Williams of Newberry was appointed colonel of the 9th Regiment. He had served as colonel of the 3rd Regiment, SCV, from February 6, 1861, until he resigned at the reorganization on May 14, 1862. Next, Williams accepted command of the 9th Regiment Reserves. From August 1863 to early February 1864, he commanded the 5th Regiment of South Carolina State Troops. Finally, Williams served as major and lieutenant colonel of the 4th Battalion, South Carolina Reserves, from April 1864 until the close of the war.

Anthony Cook Fuller of Laurens was appointed lieutenant colonel of the 9th Regiment.[151]

John W. Arnold of Laurens was appointed major of the 9th Regiment.

Companies

Company A, commanded by James Hudgens, was from Laurens District.[152]

Company B, commanded by W.J.M. Jones, was also from Laurens District. Jones also served as captain of Company D, 5th Regiment, South Carolina State Troops, in 1863 and 1864 and as captain of Company D, 4th Battalion, South Carolina Reserves, in 1864 and 1865.

Company C, commanded by William Stewart, was from Laurens District.

Company D, commanded by B.S. Jones, was from Laurens District.

Company E, commanded by G.F. Mosely, was from Laurens District.

Company F was from Newberry District. Its first captain, Josiah Stewart, resigned on December 1, 1862, because of a physical disability.[153] His replacement, Private A.K. Tribble, was elected captain about December 1, 1862, and served until February 14, 1863.

Company G was commanded by B.H. Martin, whose name might have been Mathis.[154]

Company H was commanded by Jesse Campbell.

Company I, commanded by Benjamin Wofford, was from Spartanburg District.

Company K, the Yemassee Volunteers from Hardeeville in Beaufort District, was commanded by J.R. Fuller.[155]

Brigade Affiliations

The 9th Regiment, South Carolina Reserves, was attached to the Department of South Carolina, Georgia and Florida for its entire existence.

Major Movements and Engagements

Companies A, B and D of the 9th Regiment were stationed at Camp Means near Charleston from November 17, 1862, to February 14, 1863. Companies C, E, F, G, H and I were stationed at the Charleston Racecourse then. The regiment was disbanded on February 17, 1863.

THE 10TH REGIMENT RESERVES

The 10th Regiment Reserves (Ninety Days), 1862–1863, was for a time part of the 1st Corps of Reserves. Its men came from the 10th Regiment, South Carolina Militia, of Edgefield District; the 39th Regiment, South Carolina Militia, of Newberry and Lexington Districts; the 14th Regiment, South Carolina Militia, of Orangeburg District; and the 15th Regiment, South Carolina Militia, of Lexington and Orangeburg Districts.[156] On November 7, 1862, Governor Pickens and the Executive Council passed a resolution disbanding the 4th and 10th Reserve Regiments and vacating all officers' commissions. Dissatisfaction among the men prompted this move.[157] Thus, the 10th Regiment was not among the eight reserve regiments called up for duty in November 1862.

Field Officers

James M. Baxter of Newberry was appointed colonel of the 10th Reserve Regiment.[158] Previously lieutenant colonel of the 3rd Regiment, SCV, Baxter had not been re-elected at the reorganization.

A.G. Salley of Orangeburg was appointed lieutenant colonel of the regiment.[159]

J.G. Wolfe of Lexington was appointed major of the regiment.[160]

THE 11TH REGIMENT RESERVES

The 11th Regiment Reserves (Ninety Days), 1862–1863, was one of ten, numerically designated two through eleven, making up the 1st Corps of South Carolina Reserves.[161] Its men were from the 11th (Barnwell), 12th

(Beaufort), 13th (Colleton), 14th (Orangeburg) and 43rd (Barnwell) South Carolina Militia Regiments.[162] The 11th Regiment served from November 11, 1862, to February 16, 1863.[163]

Field Officers

John J. Ryan was appointed colonel of the 11th Regiment.[164]

William F. Hutson was appointed lieutenant colonel of the regiment.

James L. Davis of Barnwell was appointed major of the regiment.[165]

Companies

Company A, from Barnwell, was commanded by Joseph Stallings.[166]

Company B was commanded by W.H. Dyches.

Company C was commanded by J.E. Kitching.

Company D, from Colleton, was commanded by Richard B. Black, who died from congestion of the brain at Pocotaligo on December 22, 1862.[167]

Company E was commanded by Jacob E. Free.

Company F was commanded by S.P. Kitching. Its men were from Barnwell and Beaufort Districts.[168]

Company G was commanded by D.S. Tyler. Its men enlisted at Orangeburg.

Company H was commanded by Lewis Dantzler. Its men enlisted at Orangeburg.

Company I, commanded by E.S. Riley, was made up of men from Colleton District.[169]

Company K was commanded by O.P. Williams. Its men enlisted at Walterboro in Colleton District.

Company L was commanded by C.S. Kirkland. Its men were from Barnwell and Beaufort Districts.[170]

Brigade Affiliations

The 11th Regiment, South Carolina Reserves, was attached to the Department of South Carolina, Georgia and Florida for its entire existence.

Major Movements and Engagements

The 11th Regiment arrived at Pocotaligo on November 19, 1862, and spent its ninety-day enlistment at nearby Camp Ida.[171]

17.

The Regiments of South Carolina State Troops (Six Months), 1863–1864

Federal assaults along the South Carolina coast were anticipated during the summer of 1863. Consequently on June 6 and again on July 31, President Davis called on the governor to provide 5,384 volunteers for local defense and special service.[1] Governor Bonham responded on June 16, ordering the militia to honor Davis's request.[2] The Confederate president's authority was based on two acts passed by the Congress. One passed on August 21, 1861, was entitled "An act to provide for local defense and special service"; the other, passed on October 13, 1862, was "An act to authorize the formation of volunteer companies for local defense."[3] The first authorized the president to accept volunteers in whatever capacity and for any duration he might determine for defense of exposed places or other special service.[4] Under this act, volunteers would be mustered in Confederate service, and, under the original plan, the president would appoint field officers. Men would be between forty and forty-five years old and would serve within the state for six months.[5] If the quota of 5,384 men was not met by volunteers, then the governor would institute a draft of men between forty and fifty. Sixteen- and seventeen-year-old militiamen were not liable to be drafted. Militia regiments were ordered to assemble at their muster grounds on July 7 to organize new companies either by accepting volunteers or, if necessary, by conscription.[6] Each company was expected to carry 64 to 125 privates on its roster, and each regiment would comprise ten companies.[7] Company-grade officers were elected in early July.[8] On the twenty-third, President Davis agreed to allow the men to elect their own field officers on the grounds that all were volunteers; he ordered July 31 elections for all five regiments.[9] Davis also required that the regiments be ready for service immediately afterward. The presidential call-up resulted in five new regiments totaling about 5,000 volunteers known collectively as the South Carolina State Troops (Six Months). It was understood that the troops were raised for local defense and special service, especially the defense of Charleston.[10] The new regiments, numbered one through five, were ready for service on August 1, 1863, but were not called to active duty until September 4 or September 5.[11] General Beauregard sent one regiment to Pocotaligo and the other four to Charleston.[12]

The six-month term of enlistment was originally supposed to date from September 5. Governor Bonham argued successfully in December that the term should date from August 1.[13] Even so, the debate continued over the exact date the term of service should end. Men in the ranks felt it should be January 31, while the authorities held out for February 1. Many men left their posts in late January; finally, General Samuel Cooper declared that the five regiments of South Carolina State Troops were mustered out of service on February 1, 1864.[14] Based on the conscript law passed on February 17, 1864, men between forty and forty-five years were not mustered out and were conscripted into the service instead.[15]

THE 1ST REGIMENT, SOUTH CAROLINA STATE TROOPS

The 1st Regiment, South Carolina State Troops, also called Roberts's regiment, was organized in early July 1863 with about one thousand men but was not called into service until September 4.[16] Militia regiments contributing to its formation were from the following districts: the 1st from Greenville, the 3rd from Greenville (two companies), the 2nd and 5th from Pickens, the 4th and 42nd from Anderson, the 6th and 8th from Abbeville and the 9th from Edgefield.[17] The 1st Regiment was mustered out of service on February 3, 1864.[18]

Field Officers

Thomas B. Roberts of Greenville was the regiment's only colonel. Previously captain of Company A, 16th Regiment, SCV, he was not re-elected at the reorganization in 1862. He had also served as captain of Company B, 3rd Regiment Reserves in late 1862 and early 1863.

W. Ludlow Hodges of Abbeville was lieutenant colonel of the 1st Regiment. He has served as captain of Company B, 7th Regiment from May 1861 to May 1862, but was not re-elected at the reorganization.

William Elbert Welborn of Anderson was major of the 1st Regiment.

R.L. Burn of Greenville was adjutant and possibly also held the rank of major. Burn resigned on January 29, 1864. A young man, he preferred active service in the field.

Companies

Company A came from the 42nd Militia Regiment of Anderson District. Thomas H. Russell was its captain. He had served previously as a captain in Thomas's Battalion and was a captain in one of the regiments of Junior Reserves in late 1864 and 1865. Company A consisted of detailed men and boys stationed at Tunnel Hill in that part of Pickens District now in Oconee County. Its primary purpose was to arrest deserters and those who overstayed their furloughs. According to the *Memory Roll*, the company was created under the authority of a "General Morriman," possibly meaning Colonel Perriman, and reported to Major B.B. McCreery at his headquarters in Anderson. It was disbanded at Tunnel Hill. Captain James "Jim" A. Long commanded a company that might have been Company A in the 1st Regiment.

Company B was commanded by Bennett C. Jones, who died of disease in Easley on March 15, 1864.[19]

Company C, from the 4th Regiment, South Carolina Militia, of Anderson District, was commanded by Captain B.F. Duncan. The *Confederate Veteran* states that Company C of the South Carolina State Troops under "Major" Duncan was assembled at Florence and later was part of the "2nd Regiment," probably indicating the 2nd Battalion, South Carolina Reserves.[20]

Company D was commanded by Francis W. Buist.

Company E was commanded by Robert O. Tribble.

Company F, from Abbeville, was commanded by Robert C. Sharp. It was organized at Lomax's, and Sharp was elected on July 8, 1863.[21]

Company G was commanded by M.T. Fowler.

Company H was commanded by Captain W.A. Beacham. It was raised from the 1st Regiment, South Carolina Militia, of Greenville District.[22] Edward Powell might also have commanded the company.[23]

Company I, from Abbeville, was commanded by John W. Hearst, MD. It was organized at Morrow's Old Field, and Hearst was elected on July 8, 1863.[24] According to the *Memory Roll*, John White commanded Company I, which refused as a company to enter Confederate service. White's name does not appear in the *CSR*.

Company K was commanded by Samuel McKittrick.

Brigade Affiliations

The 1st Regiment, South Carolina State Troops, was attached to the Department of South Carolina, Georgia and Florida for its six-month existence.[25]

Major Movements and Engagements

On September 11, 1863, the 1st Regiment was ordered to rendezvous at the railroad the next day and to move by rail to Charleston.[26] Upon its arrival, the regiment reported to Fort Ripley.[27] It remained in the Charleston area until it was disbanded in early February 1864.[28] Company I and probably other companies as well served as the provost guard for the city during their time in Charleston. When the great fire of December 25, 1863, swept through the city, Company I was ordered out at 2:30 a.m. and put in charge of the fire engine "Vigilante." It worked until the fire was extinguished. The 1st Regiment was never involved in a skirmish or battle.

THE 2ND REGIMENT, SOUTH CAROLINA STATE TROOPS

The companies of the 2nd Regiment of South Carolina State Troops were organized on July 7, 1863. They came from militia regiments in the following districts: the 7th and 10th of Edgefield, the 11th and 43rd of Barnwell, the 12th of Beaufort, the 13th of Colleton, the 14th of Orangeburg, the 15th of Orangeburg and Lexington (two companies) and the 39th of Newberry and Lexington.[29] The regiment held elections for field officers on July 31 and was organized the next day, at least on paper, for six months' duty.[30] It was called into service on September 4 or September 5 with about 1,035 men and entered the field about September 12.[31]

Field Officers

William Fort of Lexington was elected colonel on July 31, 1863. He was absent in October while attending the legislature. Fort would be court-martialed before he was mustered out of service.[32]

George A. Lewie was elected lieutenant colonel on July 31, 1863. He may have commanded one of the companies before being elected lieutenant colonel.

Walter Quattlebaum of Lexington District was elected major on July 31, 1863. In 1864 and 1865, he served as captain of Company C, 6th Battalion Reserves.

Companies

Company A, from the 15th Regiment, South Carolina Militia, of Orangeburg and Lexington Districts, was commanded by Edward Kinsler.[33] Kinsler had previously served as captain of Company H, 20th Regiment, SCV.

Company B, from Edgefield District, was commanded by George D. Huiett.

Company C was commanded by D.L. Dantzler, who was elected captain on July 7, 1863. Made up of men from Orangeburg District, it was formed from Dantzler's Company #1 of Orangeburg's 14th Regiment, South Carolina Militia.

Company D, commanded by James H. Buckner, was composed of men from Beaufort District.

Company E, from Barnwell District, was commanded by John M. Brabham.

Company F, commanded by George H. Chapman, was formed from Chapman's Company of the 39th Regiment, South Carolina Militia, on July 7, 1863. Its men were from Newberry and Lexington Districts.

Company G was commanded by Thomas Bennet Tyler, who was elected captain on July 7, 1863. It was formed from the 15th Regiment, South Carolina Militia, of Orangeburg and Lexington Districts.

Company H, commanded by Robert Black, was from Walterboro in Colleton District and was formed from the 13th Regiment, South Carolina Militia.

Company I, from Edgefield District, was commanded by James Carroll Brooks, brother of John Hampden Brooks and father of U.R. Brooks.[34]

Company K was commanded by S.S. Wise, who was elected captain on July 7, 1863. Its men were from Barnwell District and were organized from Wise's Company of the 11th Regiment, South Carolina Militia. W.L. Cave might also have served as captain.[35]

Brigade Affiliations

The 2nd Regiment was assigned to the Department of South Carolina, Georgia and Florida for its six-month existence.[36]

Major Movements and Engagements

On September 9, 1863, the regiment was ordered to rendezvous the next day and move by rail to Pocotaligo in Beaufort District.[37] Stationed at Pocotaligo until early October, it had moved to McPhersonville in Beaufort District by the third. The regiment left McPhersonville about October 31 for Pocotaligo. The men remained there until February 2, 1864.[38] Company D was on detached duty in late 1863 and early 1864.[39] Based at Hardeeville, it served at the Savannah River trestle in November and December and at Purysburg from December 31, 1863, to January 31, 1864. The 2nd Regiment was mustered out of service on February 2, 1864.[40]

THE 3RD REGIMENT, SOUTH CAROLINA STATE TROOPS

The 3rd Regiment, South Carolina State Troops, also called the 3rd State Troops (Six Months) and the 3rd South Carolina State Troops, was formed from militia regiments in the following districts: the 16th, 17th and 19th of Charleston, the 18th of Summerville in Charleston, the 31st of Williamsburg and Georgetown, the 32nd of Marion and the 33rd of Horry.[41] Its companies were raised in early July 1863 and mustered in Confederate service for six months, effective from August 1. Elections for field officers were ordered held on July 31, but the 3rd Regiment was unable to organize at that time because none of its officer candidates polled sufficient votes to warrant a commission.[42] In an interesting turnaround, company officers were elected on October 1, and elections for field officers followed on the twelfth.[43] Because they were below minimum strength, Companies F, G, H, I and K were disbanded in December. By the end of 1863, the 3rd Regiment had "ceased to be in Confederate service."[44] Its remaining four or five companies mustered out of service on January 31 and February 1, 1864.

Field Officers

John E. Carew was elected colonel on October 12, 1863. Carew had served as captain of the Brooks Guards in January 1861.[45]

R.A. Rouse, captain of Company C until October 12, 1863, was elected lieutenant colonel.

J.J. Anderson, who had enlisted as a private in Company A on September 7, was elected major on October 12, 1863.

N. Gustavus Rich was elected colonel, probably on July 31, 1863, but the election was nullified.[46]

Companies

Company A, from Williamsburg, was commanded by William H. Johnson, who was elected captain on July 7, 1863. In late 1864 and 1865, he commanded Company E of the 7th Battalion Reserves.

Company B, from Marion Court House, was commanded by James Dupre, who was elected captain on July 7, 1863.

Company C, also from Marion Court House, was initially commanded by R.A. Rouse, who was elected captain on July 7, 1863. When Rouse was elected lieutenant colonel in October, he was replaced by First Lieutenant Thomas L. James on November 4.

Company D, from Conwayboro in Horry District, was commanded by A.H. Johnson. Z.J. Drake of Marlboro might also have commanded the company.

Company E, from Charleston, was commanded by E.M. Barnwell.[47] It was probably raised from the ranks of the 18th Regiment, South Carolina Militia.

Company F, also from Charleston, was commanded by David Riker.[48]

Company G, from Charleston, was commanded by John G. Martin.[49]

Company H, another Charleston company, was commanded by W.M. Pelot.[50]

Company I, from Lancaster District, was commanded by James Dixon Caskey. Caskey had served as captain of Company I, 17th Regiment, SCV, but was not re-elected at the reorganization in 1862. Caskey later served as captain of Company I, 3rd Regiment, Junior Reserves. When Company I, State Troops, was organized on July 7, 1863, it failed to secure enough volunteers in the forty to forty-five age group and resorted to drafting men between forty and fifty years of age.[51]

Company K, from Charleston, was commanded by John Cuningham.[52] Previously colonel of the 17th Regiment, South Carolina Militia, Cuningham had also offered as a candidate for colonel of the 3rd Regiment, South Carolina State Troops.

Brigade Affiliations

The 3rd Regiment was attached to the Department of South Carolina, Georgia and Florida for its entire six-month existence.[53]

Major Movements and Engagements

Only five companies of the 3rd Regiment had been organized by September 4, 1863. Part of the reason for this shortfall was that the 16th Regiment, South Carolina Militia, was on active duty and had not been able to organize its quota of "six-months troops."[54] On September 6, the 3rd Regiment was ordered to report to Georgetown immediately.[55] Some of its companies had been stationed at nearby Camp Witherspoon since August 1 and would remain there until February 1, 1864. The post was named for the commander of the 4th Regiment, South Carolina State Troops. Three companies of the 3rd—A, B and D—had reported at camp on August 1, and Company C arrived on September 23. These four companies remained at Georgetown until late January 1864 under the command of Lieutenant Colonel Rouse.[56] The remaining six companies, E to K, were based at

Summerville in November and December 1863. Companies F to K were disbanded in December 1863; the fate of Company E is unknown. One company was based at Camp DeSaussure in Summerville from July 10 to September 26, 1863. The *Mercury* implied that this company mustered out of service on September 26.[57] This company, raised from the 18th Militia Regiment, might have been Company E. One company was still based at Summerville in January 1864.[58] On January 10, one company, consisting of Colonel Carew, his staff and about twelve men, mustered out of service, probably at Summerville.[59] One of the four at Georgetown mustered out on January 31. The three remaining companies at Georgetown "deserted" on January 31, claiming their six-month enlistment had expired.[60]

THE 4TH REGIMENT, SOUTH CAROLINA STATE TROOPS

The 4th Regiment State Troops was also called the 4th State Troops and the 4th Regiment, South Carolina Militia.[61] Its companies were organized on July 7, 1863, and field officers were elected on the thirty-first. Ordered to assemble in Kingstree on September 3, companies of the 4th Regiment, totaling 1,045 men, mustered in service the next day.[62] The regiment was organized from existing militia regiments in the following districts: the 20th from Sumter, the 21st from Lancaster, the 22nd from Kershaw, the 23rd from Richland (two companies), the 44th from Clarendon, the 24th and 25th from Fairfield (one company each), the 27th from Chester, the 28th from Chesterfield, the 29th from Darlington and the 30th from Marlboro.[63] The 4th Regiment was disbanded on February 1, 1864.

Field Officers

James H. Witherspoon of Lancaster District was elected colonel of the regiment on July 31, 1863. He was unopposed in the election.[64] Witherspoon had served as colonel of the 8th Regiment Reserves in late 1862 and early 1863. Though in poor health, he was elected to the Confederate Congress in October 1863.[65]

F.M. Mellett of Sumter was captain of Company I when he was elected lieutenant colonel on July 31. He defeated three opponents: Captain A.J. Green of Company A, J.W. Harrington of Marlboro District and William Perry Gill, captain of Company L.[66] Mellett was known as a "favorite with the troops."[67]

John C. Evans of Chesterfield District was captain of Company K when he was elected major on July 31; his opponents were T.J. Ancrum of Kershaw District and James H. McKnight of Company D.[68] Evans was considered a "good officer."[69]

Companies

Company A was raised from Beat Companies 1, 2 and 4 in the Upper Battalion of the 23rd Regiment, South Carolina Militia, from Richland District.[70] It was commanded by Allen Jones Green, previously lieutenant colonel of the 23rd Regiment, SCV. On September 15, 1863, Green was promoted to major in the Provisional Army of the Confederate States and appointed to the conscript bureau. S. David Friday was promoted from first lieutenant to captain, replacing Green as captain on September 20.

Company B, from Lancaster Court House, was commanded by John Nelson Sowell, who was elected on July 7, 1863.[71] Sowell had served previously as a captain in the 8th Regiment Reserves.

Company C from Kershaw District was raised from the 22nd Regiment, South Carolina Militia.[72] Its commander was Columbus Cureton Haile, also elected on July 7. Captain of Company G of the 2nd Regiment, SCV, until May 1862, Haile also served as captain of a company in the 8th Regiment Reserves in late 1862 and early 1863. After his term in the 4th Regiment, Haile enlisted in the 23rd Regiment, SCV, as a private. Elected lieutenant of his company, he was captured at Five Forks in April 1865 and was released in June.[73] Captains Sowell of Company B and Haile of Company C requested permission to raise a company from the 4th Regiment to elevate the 7th Battalion, South Carolina Infantry, to regimental strength. Apparently this plan never materialized since the 7th remained a battalion until the end of the war.

Company D, from Clarendon District, was commanded by James H. McKnight, elected captain on July 7, 1863.[74] McKnight had served as captain in the 8th Regiment Reserves in late 1862 and early 1863.

Company E's commander, David G. Wood, was elected captain on July 7, 1863. The company was formed from Captain Wood's Company of Darlington's 29th Regiment, South Carolina Militia.

Company F was commanded by Nelson M. Gibson, who was elected captain on July 7, 1863. It was formed the same day from Gibson's Company of Marlboro's 30th Militia Regiment.

Company G was commanded by Thomas R. Brown, who was elected captain on July 7, 1863. It was organized in Columbia from Brown's Company of the Lower Battalion of Richland District's 23rd Militia Regiment on July 14.[75] Brown had served as captain in the 8th Regiment

Reserves in late 1862 and early 1863. He later served as lieutenant colonel of the 5th Battalion, South Carolina Reserves, in 1864 and 1865.

Company H's commander, John McLurkin, was elected captain on July 7, 1863. McLurkin had served as captain of Company F, 6th Regiment Reserves, in late 1862 and early 1863. Company H was formed from McLurkin's Company of Fairfield District's 24th and from Captain Fawcett's Company of the district's 25th Militia Regiments.[76] McLurkin's Company was also called the Chester Cavalry. McLurkin was captain of Company B, 3rd Battalion, South Carolina Reserves, in late 1864 and 1865.

Company I's commander, F.M. Mellett, was elected captain on July 7, 1863. The company was formed from Mellett's Company of Sumter District's 20th Regiment, South Carolina Militia. Mellett had served as captain in the 8th Regiment Reserves in late 1862 and early 1863. He was elected lieutenant colonel on July 31, 1863, and First Lieutenant Thomas D. Gerald was promoted to captain the same day. Gerald also served as captain of Company B, 5th Battalion, South Carolina Reserves, later in 1864.

Company K was commanded by John C. Evans, who was elected captain on July 7, 1863. Organized on the same day, the company was formed from Evans's Company of Chesterfield District's 28th Regiment, South Carolina Militia.[77] Evans was elected major on July 31, and First Lieutenant Samuel D. Timmons replaced him as captain the same day.

Brigade Affiliations

The 4th Regiment, South Carolina State Troops, was attached to the Department of South Carolina, Georgia and Florida during its six-month existence.[78]

Major Movements and Engagements

On August 24, 1863, the 4th Regiment, South Carolina State Troops, was ordered to rendezvous at Kingstree on September 3, march to Georgetown and report to Brigadier General James H. Trapier.[79] Its companies assembled on the Northwestern Railroad at Kingstree as ordered and probably marched toward Georgetown the same day. Colonel Witherspoon was appointed commandant of a post west of Winyah Bay, about three miles from Georgetown, on the eighth.[80] It was known thereafter as Camp Witherspoon. Most, if not all, the companies served in the vicinity of Georgetown from early September 1863 to late January 1864.[81] During September and October, the regiment was assigned light duty, light drill and guard duty in the Georgetown area.[82] Company B served at Battery

White overlooking Winyah Bay from September 1863 to January 1864. A large portion of the 4th Regiment, claiming their enlistment had expired on January 31, went home.[83]

THE 5TH REGIMENT, SOUTH CAROLINA STATE TROOPS

The 5th Regiment South Carolina State Troops was also called the 5th Regiment of State Troops and the 5th Regiment, South Carolina Militia.[84] Its captains were elected on July 7, 1863, and the regiment's twelve companies were fully organized by mid-August. The regiment assembled for duty on September 11, 1863, in Charleston. It was created from existing militia regiments in the following districts: the 34th and 46th from York, the 35th from Union, the 36th (two companies) and the 37th from Spartanburg, the 38th from Newberry, the 40th and 41st from Laurens, the 45th from Union and Spartanburg and the 26th from Chester.[85]

Field Officers

James Henderson Williams of Newberry had served as colonel of the 3rd Regiment, SCV, but was not re-elected at the reorganization in May 1862. The fifty-year-old Williams was also colonel of the 9th Regiment of South Carolina Reserves in late 1862 and early 1863 before he commanded the 5th Regiment, South Carolina State Troops, in late 1863 and early 1864. Finally, he was lieutenant colonel of the 4th Battalion of Reserves from April 1864 until the close of the war. Williams was also a member of the legislature in December 1863.[86]

John A. Bradley of Chester was a private in Company A when he was elected lieutenant colonel of the 5th Regiment on July 31, 1863. He was considered "an estimable man, and an excellent officer."[87]

Lucian P. Sadler of York was elected major of the 5th Regiment on July 31, 1863. Sadler had served as captain of Company F, 17th Regiment, SCV, from December 1861 to April 1862.

Companies

Company A, from Chester District, was commanded by John Hardin, who, in late 1864 and 1865, served as captain of Company E, 3rd Battalion, South Carolina Reserves.

Company B, the left flanking company, was from York District.[88] Its commander was John T. Lowry.[89] Company B organized on July 7, 1863, at

Smith's Old Field in York District and was made up of men from the 34th Militia Regiment.[90] Lowry had served as captain of Company D, 6th Regiment Reserves, in late 1862 and early 1863. He was also captain of Company D, 3rd Battalion, South Carolina Reserves, in late 1864 and 1865.

Company C was from Newberry District, and its first captain was probably Ben Mathis. By October 28, 1863, however, Thomas H. Crooks was captain of the company.[91]

Company D was from Laurens District. Its men, who enlisted at Boyd's Old Field, were commanded by W.J.M. Jones, who had served as captain of Company B, 9th Regiment, South Carolina Reserves, in late 1862 and early 1863; he was captain of Company D, 4th Battalion Reserves later in 1864.

Company E, from Spartanburg District, was commanded by Oliver H. Moss. Moss had raised a company for the 3rd Regiment, SCV, but apparently it did not go into service.

Company F was also from Spartanburg District. Its men enlisted at Bomar's Old Field on August 1, 1863, under the command of Samuel M. Snoddy. He served as captain of Company C, 1st Battalion, South Carolina Reserves, in 1864 and 1865.

Company G, from Spartanburg District, was commanded by Joel Ballenger. Captain of Company A of the 7th Regiment, South Carolina Reserves, in late 1862 and early 1863, Ballenger was major of the 1st Battalion, South Carolina Reserves, in late 1864.

Company H was from Spartanburg and Union Districts. Commanded by J.W. Bobo, its men were assembled at Newman's Old Field.

Company I, from Laurens District, was commanded by W.W. Sloan.

Company K, from York District, was commanded by William J. Bowen. Though Bowen never reported for duty, his company did.[92] He had served as captain of Company G, 6th Regiment Reserves, in late 1862 and early 1863. Z.D. Smith might also have commanded this company.[93]

Company L, from Chester District, was commanded by William Perry Gill, who lost the election for lieutenant colonel of the 4th Regiment, South Carolina State Troops. In late 1864 and 1865, he served as major of the 3rd Battalion Reserves.

Company M, from Union District, was commanded by William G. Hughes Sr. He had served as captain of Company K, 7th Regiment Reserves, in late 1862 and early 1863.

Brigade Affiliations

The 5th Regiment was assigned to the Department of South Carolina, Georgia and Florida.[94]

Major Movements and Engagements

The 5th Regiment was called up for active duty on September 4, 1863, with a roster showing 1,096 men.[95] It was ordered to rendezvous at nearby railroad stations on September 11, move by rail to Charleston and report to General Ripley.[96] Moving rapidly, the regiment was able to assemble for duty in Charleston on the eleventh.[97] The men spent the rest of September and October in the city.[98] In response to a Federal raid at Warm Springs, North Carolina, that threatened the upstate of South Carolina, the 5th Regiment left Charleston by rail on October 30 and arrived in Greenville on November 1.[99] Three days later, the regiment marched four miles north of town to Camp Bonham, which was located near the stone house. While the regiment was based near Greenville, Williams also commanded E.M. Boykin's Squadron of South Carolina Cavalry. The regiment left Camp Bonham on November 19, marched to Greenville and traveled by rail to Branchville, arriving on the twentieth. The men set up camp there the next day.[100] On November 22, the regiment marched about a mile and a half from Branchville on the road to New Bridge over the Edisto River and set up Camp Williams, named to honor its colonel.[101] The regiment left the camp on the twenty-sixth to stand guard at Raysor's Bridge, also on the Edisto River. Companies K and L had been detached two days earlier and sent about thirty miles downstream to Four Hole Swamp, arriving on the twenty-sixth.[102] On January 27, 1864, Company B was sent to guard the Post at Summerville, which was on the railroad about a mile and a half from town.[103] Company K remained about six miles west of Ridgeville, serving in the vicinity until February 5, when it returned to Branchville. The remainder of the regiment continued to serve near Raysor's Bridge until they, too, moved back to Branchville, where the regiment was disbanded on the fifth. The men went home immediately.[104]

1. John Gore Dunovant, a Chester native, had served in the United States Army before the war and as major and colonel in the 1st Regiment Infantry (Regulars) in 1861 and 1862. Found guilty of drunkenness and dismissed from the service in November 1862, he was given command of the 5th Regiment, South Carolina Cavalry, in July 1863 and promoted to brigadier general in August 1864. Dunovant was killed in October 1864 in Virginia. *Courtesy Chester County Historical Society.*

2. Thomas Abraham Huguenin was major of the 1st Regiment, South Carolina Infantry (Regulars). Huguenin graduated from The Citadel in 1859 and remained there as a mathematics professor. He replaced John Mitchel as commander of Fort Sumter in July 1864. Slightly wounded on four occasions, Huguenin was paroled at Greensboro. *Courtesy The State Printing Company.*

3. Ellison Capers was a professor at The Citadel, lieutenant colonel of the 1st Regiment Rifles, South Carolina Militia, colonel of the 24th Regiment and brigadier general. Wounded five times, Capers enjoyed a long postwar career as an Episcopal priest and was a popular speaker at many Confederate monument dedications. *Courtesy The Citadel Archives & Museum.*

4. Thomas Martin Wagner was major and lieutenant colonel in the 1st Regiment, South Carolina Artillery (Regulars). Severely wounded when cannon exploded in July 1862 at Fort Moultrie, he survived amputation of the left leg but soon died from his wounds. A battery on Morris Island under construction was named in his memory. *Courtesy South Caroliniana Library, University of South Carolina, Columbia.*

5. James Benjamin White was promoted from superintendent of The Arsenal to superintendent of The Citadel Academy on August 8, 1861, with the rank of major and held the position throughout the war. Interestingly enough, his family contributed three brothers, all majors, to the Confederate cause. In addition to James Benjamin, Richard Green White served as major of the 10th Regiment and William Capers White, of the 7th. *Courtesy The Citadel Archives & Museum.*

6. Hugh Smith Thompson, professor of belles lettres and ethics and later governor of South Carolina, was captain of Company A, The Citadel Cadets, for the entire war. *Courtesy The Citadel Archives & Museum.*

7. Nathaniel Walker Armstrong was professor of mathematics and mechanical philosophy at The Citadel and commander of Company B, The Citadel Cadets. *Courtesy The Citadel Archives & Museum.*

8. Stanley Stephen Crittenden was wounded in the left breast at Seven Pines while serving as adjutant of the 4th Regiment. While recovering, he served as lieutenant colonel of the 3rd Regiment Reserves in late 1862 and early 1863 before returning to the 13th Battalion, which by that time had become Company I, Hampton Legion Mounted Infantry. *Courtesy Greenville County Historical Society.*

9. Alfred Moore Rhett from Charleston served as a captain, major, lieutenant colonel and colonel in the 1st Regiment, South Carolina Artillery (Regulars). Then-Lieutenant Colonel Rhett killed his colonel, William Ransom Calhoun, in a duel in September 1862, but was soon promoted to fill Calhoun's spot. Captured near Averasboro in March 1865, he was released in July. *Courtesy South Caroliniana Library, University of South Carolina, Columbia.*

10. Moses Benbow Humphrey was a Citadel cadet who left the institution with thirty-six others in June 1862 to form Company F, 6th Regiment, South Carolina Cavalry, and he became its captain. He died from the effects of his fourth wound just before the end of the war. *Courtesy The Citadel Archives & Museum.*

11. John Hilary Gary was captain of the short-lived South Carolina College Cadets in early 1861. As captain of Company A, 15th Battalion, South Carolina Artillery, he was mortally wounded at Battery Wagner in August 1863. A battery near Mount Pleasant was named posthumously for him. *Courtesy Oakley Park and The South Carolina Confederate Relic Room and Museum, Columbia.*

12. John Henry Steinmeyer Jr. was captain of the Marion Rifles, Company A, 24th Regiment. Wounded and captured in May 1863 at Wright's Farm near Jackson, Mississippi, he was soon paroled and returned to the regiment. He was captured again, this time at Ship's Gap, Georgia, in October 1864 and released from Johnson's Island, Ohio, in June. *Courtesy Old Darlington District Chapter SCGS and The War Between the States Museum.*

13. Alexander Cheves Haskell had been a staff officer under Generals Gregg and McGowan until he was appointed colonel of the 7th Regiment, South Carolina Cavalry, in March 1864. He suffered numerous serious wounds, including the loss of his left eye in October 1864. Haskell rejoined the regiment by the end of January 1865 and was paroled at Appomattox. He enjoyed a long and successful postwar career. *From* Cyclopedia of Eminent and Representative Men of the Carolinas.

14. Francis Huger Harleston was captain of Company D, 1st Regiment, South Carolina Artillery (Regulars). He held the dual honors of captain of cadets and first honor graduate of the South Carolina Military Academy's Class of 1860. He was struck by shell fragments and killed in November 1863 at Fort Sumter. A battery on the north side of James Island near Fort Johnson was named for him, and The Citadel erected a marble tablet in his memory in 1884. *Courtesy The State Printing Company.*

15. John C. Mitchel Jr. was captain of Company I, 1st Regiment, South Carolina Artillery (Regulars). He replaced Stephen Elliott as commander of Fort Sumter in May 1864 and was killed there by a mortar shell in July. *Courtesy The State Printing Company.*

16. *Above left:* Giles J. Patterson was captain of Company A, 3rd Regiment Junior Reserves in 1864 and 1865. He was active in local and state politics after the war. *From* Cyclopedia of Eminent and Representative Men of the Carolinas.

17. *Above right:* William Ashmead Courtenay was elected captain of the Meagher Guards, a company of Charleston Irishmen in the 1st Regiment Rifles, South Carolina Militia, in January 1862. He later served as captain of Company #6, a combination of the Jasper Greens of the 17th Regiment and the Emerald Light Infantry of the 1st Regiment. *From* Cyclopedia of Eminent and Representative Men of the Carolinas.

18. John Luther Branch was a graduate of The Citadel, colonel of the 1st Regiment Rifles, South Carolina Militia, and an engineer at Battery Wagner. *Courtesy The Citadel Archives & Museum.*

18.

THE BATTALIONS OF SOUTH CAROLINA RESERVES (1864–1865)

The official name of the Confederate conscript law passed on February 17, 1864, was "An act to organize forces to serve during the war."[1] Adjutant General Samuel Cooper implemented the new law on March 1.[2] Its terms declared that all white male citizens of the Confederate States between the ages of seventeen and fifty were liable for service within their respective states for the duration of the war.[3] Those between eighteen and forty-five were to remain in their current organizations. Seventeen-year-olds, along with men from forty-five to fifty, were required to form a reserve corps, elect their own field and company officers and organize themselves into companies and battalions or regiments as their numbers might dictate.[4] Within thirty days of March 15, men were required either to enroll in an existing local defense company or to organize a new company. "Those between seventeen and eighteen and between forty-five and fifty were organized and commanded by Brigadier General [James] Chesnut under an appointment by President Davis; some were called into active service at Charleston, of course, at Confederate expense."[5] Camps of instruction were established and provisions made for exemptions.[6] Eight new battalions, designated the 1st to 8th Battalions, South Carolina Reserves, were created under this law; later, they were known as the Battalions of Senior Reserves to distinguish them from the Regiments of Junior Reserves. Veterans applying for pensions in the 1920s called them, simply, "reserves."

Several newspapers weighed in on the subject: the *Yorkville Enquirer* reported in late March that the new battalions would not be called into active service "unless a greater emergency occurs."[7] In early April, the *Daily South Carolinian* reported that all eligible men were to enroll before April 16; the papers also reiterated that the purpose of the new battalions was to serve as a "reserve for state defense" within the boundaries of the state.[8] In addition, the *Yorkville Enquirer* reported on June 15 that the eight new battalions had been organized.[9]

General Chesnut ordered each battalion to elect a major as its commander on June 24.[10] He also issued an order on July 13 calling the reserve battalions to active duty "at once" because of the need for infantry support of artillery batteries on both John's Island and James Island.[11] By July 20, several reserve battalions were in the field.[12] The battalions continued to muster in state service throughout the summer; on October 31, they entered Confederate service.[13] Some were disbanded shortly before the end of the war, while others were merged into nonreserve South Carolina regiments on April 9, 1865.

THE 1ST BATTALION SOUTH CAROLINA RESERVES

The 1st Infantry Battalion Reserves, also called Williams's Battalion, was organized in the summer of 1864 with seven companies.[14] It was in service by July 31.

Field Officers

Daniel Williams was elected major of the 1st Battalion on June 24, 1864.[15] He had been succeeded by Joel Ballenger by December 26.[16] Ballenger had served as captain of Company A of the 7th Regiment, South Carolina Reserves, in late 1862 and early 1863 and as captain of Company G, 5th Regiment, South Carolina State Troops, in late 1863 and early 1864.

Companies

Company A, from the part of Spartanburg District that is now in Cherokee County, was commanded by Daniel H. Smith.[17]

Company B, from Anderson and Greenville Districts, was commanded by Edward Powell.

Company C, from Spartanburg District, was commanded by Samuel M. Snoddy.[18] Snoddy served previously as captain of Company F, 5th Regiment, South Carolina State Troops, in 1863 and early 1864.

Company D, from Spartanburg District, was commanded by William Forrester.[19] James L. McCormick may also have commanded the company.

Company F's commander might have been D.J. Grice, whose company in one of the state's reserve units, also F, saw action on December 7, 1864, at the Tullifinny River but suffered no casualties.[20] This is most likely Daniel Grice of Pickens, who was major of the 3rd Regiment Reserves in 1862 and 1863. Pension records show Daniel Grice to be captain of Company D, 1st Regiment Junior Reserves.

One company in the 1st Battalion was commanded by a Captain Jones.[21]

Brigade Affiliations

The 1st Battalion, South Carolina Reserves, was attached to the Department of South Carolina, Georgia and Florida from the summer of 1864 to February 1865. During that time, it was attached to Ripley's Brigade, to Taliaferro's Brigade in December 1864, to Chesnut's Brigade in December 1864 and January 1865 and to Mercer's Brigade in January 1865.[22] From January 31 to April 10, 1865, the 1st, along with the 2nd, 6th and 7th Battalions was also attached to Brigadier General Albert G. Blanchard's Brigade.[23]

Major Movements and Engagements

Most of the companies of the battalion were stationed initially in and around Charleston. By July 31, 1864, the 1st Battalion was based in the 1st Military District, which included Sullivan's Island, Long Island and Christ Church Parish.[24] Men of Company A were assigned chiefly to guard prison camps in Charleston, Florence and Columbia. Lieutenant John McCarley's company was on guard duty at the Confederate Military Prison in Columbia in October.[25] By November 20, the battalion was based at the Post of Columbia.[26] Apparently two companies were based in Columbia under Lieutenant McCarley, and the other five were also in Columbia, possibly performing separate duty under the command of Captain Edward Powell.[27] During the skirmishes near the Tullifinny River on December 7 and December 9, the 1st Battalion guarded the Confederate left flank, but was probably not engaged otherwise.[28] By December 26, it had occupied the Bee's Creek works near Coosawhatchie.[29] It was at Grahamville on the twenty-eighth.[30] Company A was stationed in Columbia when Charleston was evacuated in February 1865, but some of the other companies were engaged there during the evacuation. The battalion participated in the withdrawal through South Carolina in February 1865 and was probably engaged at Florence on March 5. It withdrew into North Carolina that month. According to Sifakis, the battalion was engaged at Bentonville.[31] Leave was granted in mid-March to every man in the battalion who could find a horse and join the active cavalry. Most of the young men left to seek suitable mounts. About half were successful; they served as scouts until the end of the war in lower South Carolina with Ferguson's Brigade of Wheeler's Cavalry. The other half, who remained infantrymen, were stationed at Newberry at the close of the war.[32] On April 9 at Smithfield, North Carolina, the 1st, 2nd, 6th and 7th Battalions, South Carolina Reserves, were consolidated with several first-line South Carolina units—the 3rd Battalion, 2nd, 3rd, 7th, 8th, 15th and 20th Regiments—to form the (New) 2nd, 3rd and 7th Regiments, SCV.

THE 2ND BATTALION SOUTH CAROLINA RESERVES

The 2nd Battalion, from Anderson and Pickens Districts, was also called Barnette's Mounted Infantry. It was called into state service as early as May 1864 and into Confederate service on October 31.[33]

Field Officers

Major D.J. Barnette of Anderson commanded the 2nd Battalion Reserves.[34]

Companies

Company A was commanded by Jesse McGee.

Company B, from Anderson District, was commanded by Ira Williams.[35]

Company C was called the Spartan Rangers, the Spartanburg Rangers and the Spartan Rangers Independent Cavalry–Reserves.[36] Though most of its men were from Spartanburg District, a few came from Union, Colleton, Greenville, Charleston and Pickens Districts. The commander was William Terrell Wilkins, who had served previously in Company G, 7th Regiment Reserves, and in Company F, 5th Regiment, South Carolina State Troops. The company, organized when reserves were called out in 1864, was composed almost entirely of self-equipped seventeen-year-old boys and forty-five-year-old men.[37] It served as a detachment of mounted reserves and operated independently for most of its existence. After a few weeks of training in Greenville District, the men were ordered to the coast, where they served nearly until the close of the war. Company C was attached at one time to the 1st Regiment, South Carolina Cavalry. It was in a number of engagements from the Savannah to the Pee Dee River, notably Adams Run, Honey Hill and Moncks Corner. The company disbanded in North Carolina at the end of the war.[38] The *CSR* incorrectly lists the Spartan Rangers on the roster of the 2nd Battalion, South Carolina Cavalry Reserves, as Company L of the 3rd Regiment, South Carolina Cavalry.

Company D, commanded by R.M. Willis, was from Barnwell District.[39]

Company E, commanded by Benjamin F. Dickson, was from Anderson District.[40] It was composed of men between forty-five and fifty years old. The company mustered in at Anderson on April 16, 1864, and served in the field for the last six months of the war.[41] There appears to be some confusion between this company and Company C of the 1st Regiment, South Carolina State Troops. The latter was raised from the 4th Militia Regiment of Anderson District and was commanded by Captain B.F. Duncan, a name that could be a corruption of Dickson. The *Confederate Veteran* reported that Company C of the South Carolina State Troops under "Major" Duncan was assembled at Florence and later became part of the "2nd Regiment," probably indicating the 2nd Battalion, South Carolina Reserves.[42]

Company F was commanded by John S. McWhorter from Pickens District. Pension records also list McWhorter's Company as A of the 1st Battalion and J.R. Bowden as captain of Company F of the 2nd Battalion. Bowden's company, also from Pickens District, was called up for service in July 1864 and was composed of seventeen-year-old boys. It was sent to both Sandy Springs in Anderson District and Tunnel Hill in Pickens District. The company was ordered next to Columbia to guard Federal prisoners. It moved to Charlotte as Sherman approached Columbia and on to Salisbury, where the prisoners were exchanged. It was ordered back to Charlotte, where the men drew picket duty and skirmished with Sherman's troops. The company marched from Charlotte to Newberry and on to Greenville. It was disbanded there in May 1865.[43] Bowden was previously captain of Company I, 3rd Battalion, South Carolina Artillery.

Company G, commanded by John C. Martin, was from Abbeville District.[44]

Company H, commanded by James Doran Kay, was from Pickens District.[45] It was also called Captain Kay's Detachment, South Carolina Mounted Reserves, and the Palmetto Mounted Infantry.[46] Kay organized a company of independent cavalry scouts from Anderson and Pendleton on August 16, 1864, at Sandy Springs in Anderson District.[47] Kay's Company was listed in the *CSR* in several ways: as both Troop H and Company H of the 1st Battalion, State Reserves; as Company H of the 2nd Battalion, South Carolina Reserves; and as Company F of the 2nd Battalion, South Carolina Reserves. One source records it incorrectly as Company D.[48] Kay's Company served independently from the 2nd Battalion in late 1864 and 1865.

W.R. Jones might have commanded an Anderson District company in the 2nd Battalion.

Brigade Affiliations

The 2nd Battalion, South Carolina Reserves, was attached to the Department of South Carolina, Georgia and Florida from the summer of 1864 to February 1865. It was attached to Taliaferro's Brigade in December 1864, to Chesnut's Brigade in December 1864 and January 1865 and to Mercer's Brigade in January 1865.[49] From January 31 to April 10, 1865, the 1st, 2nd, 6th and 7th Battalions, South Carolina Reserves, were attached to Brigadier General Albert G. Blanchard's Brigade.[50]

Major Movements and Engagements

Captain Kay's Company served independently from the 2nd Battalion.[51] It moved from Sandy Springs in Anderson District to the coast, where its men served as coast guards until the end of the war.[52] On November 22, 1864, General Chesnut ordered the company to Grahamville. The men arrived on December 7 but left the same day for Coosawhatchie. Kay's Company was near the Coosawhatchie River on December 26.[53] It acted as an independent company in Blanchard's Brigade on March 31, 1865, but its fate beyond date time is unknown.[54]

The *Official Records* does not list the 2nd Battalion along with other reserve battalions on October 31, 1864.[55] It was probably on active duty then, possibly serving near Savannah.[56] Captain Martin's Company G, and probably the rest of the battalion as well, guarded Federal officers in Columbia.[57] On December 26, 1864, the 2nd Battalion was at the Dawson's Bluff works on the Coosawhatchie River.[58] By the twenty-eighth, it was at Grahamville.[59] Company E, and probably the entire battalion, withdrew into North Carolina as part of McLaws's Division in 1865. On April 9 at Smithfield, the 1st, 2nd, 6th and 7th Battalions, South Carolina Reserves, were consolidated with several first-line South Carolina units—the 3rd Battalion, 2nd, 3rd, 7th, 8th, 15th and 20th Regiments—to form the (New) 2nd, 3rd and 7th Regiments, SCV.

THE 3RD BATTALION SOUTH CAROLINA RESERVES

The 3rd Battalion, South Carolina Reserves, mustered in state service on September 15 and in Confederate service on October 31, 1864.

Field Officers

William Perry Gill of Chester District was elected major of the 3rd Battalion on June 24, 1864.[60] He had served as captain of Company L, 5th Regiment, South Carolina State Troops, in 1863 and early 1864.

Companies

Company A, from Union Court House in Union District, was commanded by John W. Sanders.

Company B, from Fairfield District, was commanded by John McLurkin. McLurkin was Captain of Company F, 6th Regiment, South Carolina Reserves, in late 1862 and early 1863, and he also served as captain of Company H, 4th Regiment, South Carolina State Troops, in 1863 and early 1864.

Company C, from Yorkville in York District, was commanded by Milton A. Currence.[61] It was raised from the 46th Regiment, South Carolina Militia, and enrolled on April 15, 1864.

Company D, also from Yorkville, was also formed on April 15, 1864. It was raised from the 34th Militia Regiment, and John T. Lowry had been elected captain by April 20.[62] He served as captain of Company D, 6th Regiment Reserves in late 1862 and early 1863 and as captain of Company B, 5th Regiment, South Carolina State Troops, in 1863 and early 1864. The first election was nullified for some reason, and when a new vote was taken on June 4, the men elected First Lieutenant William Lawson Brown captain.[63]

Company E, from Chester in Chester District, was commanded by John Hardin.[64] Hardin had served as captain of Company A, 5th Regiment, South Carolina State Troops, in late 1863 and early 1864.

Brigade Affiliations

The 3rd Battalion Reserves, along with the 4th, 5th and 8th Reserve Battalions, made up a brigade commanded by Brigadier General James Chesnut from December 1864 to March 1865. On March 25, the four battalions were ordered to join Blanchard's Brigade, which comprised the 1st, 2nd, 6th and 7th Reserve Battalions.[65] This order, however, had not been carried out by March 31.[66]

Major Movements and Engagements

Several of the reserve battalions were already on duty by July 20, 1864, and the 3rd had been ordered to "be in readiness."[67] On September 15, companies of the 3rd Battalion went into camp and mustered in service.[68] That day the battalion left by rail for Hamburg via Columbia.[69] The men reached their destination on September 17 and set up camp in the woods on Schultz's Hill opposite Augusta, Georgia.[70] Soon afterward, the battalion moved a short distance to Camp Meriwether and remained there for about three weeks of training.[71] On October 1, it was ordered to leave for Florence the next day.[72] The 3rd and 6th Battalions left Hamburg by rail on October 2 and arrived at Florence at four in the morning on the third.[73] The *CSR* states, incorrectly, that the battalion was in Florence as early as September 15. The 3rd performed guard duty at the Confederate Military Stockade in Florence until at least February 3, 1865.[74] During that time, the battalion also made regular trips to Wilmington, escorting Federal prisoners slated for exchange.[75] The battalion left Florence on January 11 but had returned by the twenty-seventh; it remained there until early February.[76] Companies of the battalion also served at Augusta and Savannah in Georgia; at Hamburg, Charleston and Port Royal in South Carolina; and at Wilmington, Salisbury and Raleigh in North Carolina. The battalion was in Wilmington, in fact, when that city was captured. In mid-March 1865, Company D was guarding prisoners on the train as it withdrew with the rest of the battalion from Wilmington toward Goldsboro.[77]

In March 1865, the battalion was assigned to General Chesnut's Brigade in the Department of South Carolina, Georgia and Florida. On the sixteenth, Chesnut ordered four reserve battalions—the 3rd, 4th, 5th and 8th—to assemble at their rendezvous sites to receive a fifteen-day furlough and then to reassemble afterward. The furlough was given to allow the men time to procure horses.[78]

On April 9 at Smithfield, the 1st, 2nd, 6th and 7th Battalions, South Carolina Reserves, were consolidated with several first-line South Carolina units—the 3rd Battalion, 2nd, 3rd, 7th, 15th and 20th Regiments—to form the (New) 2nd, 3rd and 7th Regiments, SCV. The 3rd Battalion was not included in this consolidation and was paroled at Chester in April or May 1865.[79]

THE 4TH BATTALION SOUTH CAROLINA RESERVES

The 4th Battalion, South Carolina Reserves, mustered in state service on April 16 and in Confederate service on October 31, 1864. Its men were from Abbeville, Laurens and Newberry Districts.[80]

Field Officers

James Henderson Williams of Newberry was elected major of the battalion in July 1864. He was promoted to lieutenant colonel in command of the battalion, probably on October 31. Williams had served as colonel of the 3rd Regiment, SCV, until the reorganization. Afterward, he served as colonel of the 9th Reserve Regiment for ninety days in late 1862 and early 1863 and as colonel of the 5th Regiment, South Carolina State Troops, from August 1863 to February 1864. Williams resigned as lieutenant colonel of the 4th Battalion in 1865.[81]

John W. Ferguson of Laurens was major of the 4th Battalion and was its commander after Williams resigned.[82] Ferguson, a teacher by profession, had served previously in Company F, 3rd Regiment, SCV.

Companies

Company A, commanded by William H. Holman, was organized on March 12, 1864.[83] It was composed of seventeen- and eighteen-year-olds from Prosperity, then called Frog Level, in Newberry District, who mustered in service as volunteers in April 1864. Some died of yellow fever contracted on the South Carolina coast.

Company B, from Abbeville District, was commanded by Milton "Milt" W. Coleman.

Company C, from Newberry District, was commanded by John F. Sims. It was organized near Columbia in July 1864.[84]

Company D, from Laurens District, was commanded by W.J.M. "Mat" Jones.[85] He had been captain of Company B, 9th Regiment, South Carolina Reserves, in late 1862 and early 1863 and captain of Company D, 5th Regiment, South Carolina State Troops, in late 1863 and early 1864. Jones had also served as captain of Company Raiborn in the 3rd Regiment, SCV, when that regiment was in state service in early 1861.[86]

Company E, from Laurens District, was commanded by Elijah "Lige" M. Cooper.

Company F, from Abbeville District, was commanded by Wesley Robertson. Previously a private in Company B, Robertson transferred to Company F on November 1, 1864.

Brigade Affiliations

The 4th Battalion Reserves was brigaded with the 3rd, 5th and 8th Battalions, South Carolina Reserves, under the command of Brigadier General James Chesnut from December 1864 to March 1865. On March 25, the 3rd, 4th, 5th and 8th Reserve Battalions were ordered to join Blanchard's Brigade, which at the time comprised the 1st, 2nd, 6th and 7th Reserve Battalions.[87] By March 31, however, that order had not been carried out.[88]

Major Movements and Engagements

Most of the information about the 4th Battalion comes from a discussion of Company A in the *Memory Roll* and a few sketches in *Recollections and Reminiscences.* A newspaper records that Holman's Company arrived in Charleston on July 11, 1864, to help in the defense of the city.[89] Apparently the companies of the 4th Battalion did not always serve together as a single unit; some who guarded Federal officers at the city jail in Charleston in July 1864 might still have been there as late as November.[90] According to the *CSR*, Company A served in Florence from August 3 until the end of 1864.[91] Though the prison camp there opened in September, Company A possibly served in some other capacity from early August until the camp was ready. Company B was stationed at the prison camp in Florence in September and October, and Companies D and E were there in November and December. The entire battalion was at Florence from mid-October for at least a month.[92] Company C had been transferred by December 1 to guard Federal prisoners at the asylum in Columbia and remained there until February 14, 1865.[93] The *Memory Roll* records that the 4th Battalion was the main prison guard at Florence up to the surrender. When the Florence stockade closed in February 1865, the 4th Battalion probably withdrew into North Carolina with Hardee's army. Men of the 4th Battalion served as prison guards at both Wilmington and Goldsboro in 1865.[94] On February 14, Company C was sent with prisoners to Charlotte. It remained there for about six weeks, moved on to Chester for another two weeks and finally moved to Newberry.

In March 1865, the battalion was assigned to Brigadier General James Chesnut's Brigade in the Department of South Carolina, Georgia and Florida. On the sixteenth, Chesnut ordered his four reserve battalions—the 3rd, 4th, 5th and 8th—to assemble at their rendezvous sites, receive a fifteen-day furlough and reassemble afterward. This furlough was to allow the men time to procure horses.[95] The 4th Battalion, South Carolina Reserves, was disbanded at Newberry after its officers learned that Johnston had surrendered.[96] On April 9 at Smithfield, the 1st, 2nd, 6th and 7th Battalions, South Carolina Reserves, were consolidated with several first-line South Carolina units—the 3rd Battalion, 2nd, 3rd, 7th, 8th, 15th and 20th Regiments—to form the (New) 2nd, 3rd and 7th Regiments, SCV. The 4th Battalion, South Carolina Reserves, was a not part of this consolidation.

THE 5TH BATTALION SOUTH CAROLINA RESERVES

The 5th Battalion, South Carolina Reserves, also called Brown's Battalion, mustered in state service on September 15 and in Confederate service on October 31, 1864. The 5th Battalion was from Lancaster, Kershaw, Clarendon, Sumter, Richland and Chesterfield Districts.[97]

Field Officers

Thomas R. Brown commanded the battalion initially with the rank of major; by November 20, 1864, he held the rank of lieutenant colonel.[98] He had served as captain of Company G, 4th Regiment, South Carolina State Troops, in 1863 and 1864.

Companies

Company A, from Richland District, was commanded by William H. Miller. Its men enlisted at Columbia.

Company B, from Sumter District, was commanded by Thomas D. Gerald, who had served as captain of Company I, 4th Regiment, South Carolina State Troops, in 1863 and early 1864. Company B was organized on April 16, 1864.[99] E.A. Brown also commanded the company.

Company C, from Chesterfield District, enlisted at Cheraw. It was commanded by James P. Harrall.

Company D, from Kershaw District, was commanded by John Thompson. Its men enlisted at Camden.

Company E, from Lancaster District, was organized on April 16, 1864, and James Small was elected captain the same day. Its men enlisted at Lancaster Court House.

Company F, from Clarendon District, was commanded by William Francis Butler. Its men enlisted at Manning.[100]

Brigade Affiliations

The 5th Battalion, South Carolina Reserves, was brigaded with the 3rd, 4th and 8th Battalions, South Carolina Reserves, under the command of Brigadier General James Chesnut from December 1864 to March 1865. On March 25, the 3rd, 4th, 5th and 8th were ordered to join Blanchard's Brigade, which at the time comprised the 1st, 2nd, 6th and 7th Reserve Battalions.[101] By March 31, the order had not been carried out.[102]

Major Movements and Engagements

Company E rendezvoused at Camden on September 15, 1864, and left by train for Charleston the next day.[103] Men of the 5th Battalion served as prison guards at Florence from September 15 to December 31, 1864.[104] When Charleston was evacuated, some members of the battalion escorted prisoners from Florence to Wilmington, Goldsboro and Raleigh before returning to Wilmington to exchange them.[105] Other men of the battalion stayed behind in Florence to guard sick prisoners and to serve as pickets, bridge guards and messengers.[106] In March 1865, the battalion was in Brigadier General James Chesnut's Brigade in the Department of South Carolina, Georgia and Florida. On the sixteenth, Chesnut ordered his four reserve battalions—the 3rd, 4th, 5th and 8th—to assemble at their rendezvous sites for fifteen-day furloughs and reassemble afterward. The furlough was given to allow the men time to procure horses.[107] According to a sketch in *Recollections and Reminiscences*, the battalion was disbanded in March 1865 while it was attached to Chesnut's Brigade.[108] At least part of the 5th Battalion reassembled. About fifty of its men under Brown's command were engaged at Dingle's Mill near Sumter on April 9, and it also saw action on the extreme left of the Confederate line at the skirmish near Boykin's Mill on April 18.

Company C was paroled at Camden, but the fate of the remaining five companies is not documented. The 5th was not part of the consolidation on April 9 when the 1st, 2nd, 6th and 7th Battalions, South Carolina Reserves, were merged with several first-line South Carolina units—the 3rd Battalion, 2nd, 3rd, 7th, 8th, 15th and 20th Regiments—to form the (New) 2nd, 3rd and 7th Regiments, SCV.

The 6th Battalion South Carolina Reserves

The 6th Battalion, South Carolina Reserves, also called Meriwether's Battalion, mustered in state service with seven companies in September and in Confederate service on October 31, 1864. It was made up of men from Lexington, Edgefield and Orangeburg Districts.[109]

Field Officers

Robert Meriwether was elected major on June 24, 1864.[110] He had been elected captain of one of the battalion's companies, probably either D or E, and defeated Captain Quattlebaum of Company C in the election for major. Meriwether had also been captain of Company H in Maxcy Gregg's

1st Regiment, SCV (Six Months), from January to July 1861, and had served in the 5th Regiment, South Carolina State Troops, as well. His name was spelled in a variety of ways, including Merriwether and Merriweather, but Meriwether is correct.[111]

Companies

Company A, from Orangeburg District, was commanded by Samuel E. Moorer.

Company B, from Lexington District, was commanded by Nathaniel "Nat" Harmon.

Company C, from Lexington and Edgefield Districts, was commanded by Walter Quattlebaum.[112] He had served as major of the 2nd Regiment, South Carolina State Troops, in 1863 and 1864. His first name also appears as William.[113] The company was organized about April 24, 1864, from the 9th Regiment, South Carolina Militia.[114]

Company D, formed from the 10th Militia Regiment in the eastern half of Edgefield District, was organized at Richardsonville about September 2, 1864.[115] Ira Cromley, who had served as captain of Company D of the 19th Regiment, SCV, until May 1862, was its captain.

Company E, which had been part of the 9th Regiment, South Carolina Militia, in Edgefield District, was commanded by G.D. Mims.[116]

Company G, from Newberry District, was commanded by J.C. Williams.

Captain L.S. Johnson raised a company in April 1864 from the 7th Regiment, South Carolina Militia, in Edgefield District.[117] The fate of Johnson's company is unclear.

Captain Tom Jones raised a company in April 1864 from the 10th Militia Regiment in Edgefield District.[118] Pension records show that it belonged to the 6th Battalion and was designated Company B.

Brigade Affiliations

The 6th Battalion, South Carolina Reserves, was attached to the Department of South Carolina, Georgia and Florida from the summer of 1864 to February 1865. During that time, it was attached to Ripley's Brigade, to Taliaferro's Brigade in December 1864, to Chesnut's Brigade in December 1864 and January 1865 and to Mercer's Brigade in January 1865.[119] From January 31 to April 10, 1865, it, along with the 1st, 2nd and 7th Reserve battalions, was attached to Brigadier General Albert G. Blanchard's Brigade.[120]

Major Movements and Engagements

The 6th Battalion was ordered to rendezvous at Orangeburg on July 25, 1864.[121] It is unclear whether the battalion operated as a single unit over the next six weeks. Company D, and probably also the other companies, left their muster grounds on September 9, traveled by rail via Columbia to Hamburg in Edgefield District and camped at Shultz's Hill across the river from Augusta before moving on to nearby Camp Meriwether.[122] The 6th and 3rd Battalions left Hamburg by rail on October 2 and arrived at Florence at four in the morning on the third.[123] The battalion guarded Federal prisoners in the stockade at Florence until early November.[124] In early October, a detail of the 6th Battalion was sent to guard Federal prisoners on their way to Charleston for exchange.[125] Still at Florence on November 20, the battalion was sent to Augusta, Georgia, about November 21.[126] It remained for about two weeks before leaving for Charleston. The battalion arrived at Honey Hill at midnight on November 30 after the battle there had ended. It skirmished at Combahee Ferry in early December 1864, and by the twenty-sixth, it was stationed at the Bee's Creek works near Coosawhatchie.[127] Two days later, the battalion was at Grahamville.[128] It withdrew from the line of the Charleston to Savannah Railroad just as Sherman began his march through South Carolina, and it passed through Cheraw on its march into North Carolina. The 6th Battalion was not engaged at Averasboro on March 16, but it did see action at Bentonville.[129] After that battle, the 6th Battalion marched to Smithfield, where, on April 9, it, along with the 1st, 2nd and 7th Battalions, South Carolina Reserves, was consolidated with several first-line South Carolina units—the 3rd Battalion, 2nd, 3rd, 7th, 8th, 15th and 20th Regiments—to form the (New) 2nd, 3rd and 7th Regiments, SCV. At that time, the 6th Battalion ceased to exist. The older men were sent home, and the younger ones were attached to other units.[130] Some continued to serve until the Army of Tennessee surrendered on April 26, 1865.

THE 7TH BATTALION SOUTH CAROLINA RESERVES

The 7th Battalion, South Carolina Reserves, was also called Ward's Battalion. The men were from Georgetown, Marion, Williamsburg, Horry, Marlboro and Darlington Districts.

Field Officers

James Washington Ward of Darlington commanded the battalion with the rank of major. He had served previously as a lieutenant in Company E of the 8th Regiment, SCV. Ward commanded the battalion until it was consolidated on April 9, 1865.[131] Captain Richard D.F. Rollins of Darlington also commanded the battalion from time to time when Ward was absent.[132]

Companies

Company A, from Williamsburg and Darlington Districts, was commanded by Richard "Dick" D.F. Rollins, who had served previously as major of the 9th Battalion, South Carolina Infantry. John N. Phillips may also have commanded Company A.

Company B, from Horry District, was commanded by Philip D. Anderson, also shown as B.G. Anderson.

Company C, from Marlboro District, was commanded by Nick H. McIntosh.

Company D, from Marion District, was commanded by William H. Crawford.[133]

Company E was commanded by William H. Johnson. Some pension records show Johnson's company as I. Its men were from the area that is now Florence County, which was created in 1888 from four districts: Marion, Darlington, Clarendon and Williamsburg. Johnson had commanded Company A of the 3rd Regiment, South Carolina State Troops, in 1863 and 1864.

Company F, from Georgetown District, was commanded by Lemuel A. Grier.

P.A. Brunson is shown in pension records as captain of a Florence company in the 7th Battalion.

Brigade Affiliations

The 7th Battalion, South Carolina Reserves, was attached to the Department of South Carolina, Georgia and Florida from the summer of 1864 to February 1865. It was attached to Trapier's Brigade as late as January 31, 1865.[134] From the end of January until April 10, the 1st, 2nd, 6th and 7th Battalions, South Carolina Reserves, were attached to Brigadier General Albert G. Blanchard's Brigade.[135]

Major Movements and Engagements

The 7th Battalion was stationed at the Post of Florence where its men served as prison guards at the stockade from October to early December 1864.[136] Later in December, the 7th was based at Georgetown. It was sent to the Hardee House near Savannah on the eighteenth before falling back to Jacksonboro near Charleston.[137] In late December 1864 or early January 1865, a detail of eighteen men from the 7th Battalion was sent with Federal prisoners to Wilmington.[138] Sifakis records that the 7th was engaged at Bentonville.[139] On April 9 at Smithfield, the 7th, along with the 1st, 2nd and 6th Reserve Battalions, was consolidated with several first-line state units—the 3rd Battalion, 2nd, 3rd, 7th, 8th, 15th and 20th Regiments—to form the (New) 2nd, 3rd and 7th Regiments, SCV. The 7th Battalion combined with the 2nd and 20th Regiments to become the (New) or Consolidated, 2nd Regiment, SCV, at that time

THE 8TH BATTALION SOUTH CAROLINA RESERVES

The 8th Battalion, South Carolina Reserves, also called Stallings's Battalion, mustered in state service on July 15 and in Confederate service on October 31, 1864. Its men were from Charleston, Colleton, Barnwell and Orangeburg Districts.[140]

Field Officers

S.H. Stallings of Barnwell commanded the battalion with the rank of major until he died of disease in Charleston on October 12, 1864.[141]

William H. Bartless Sr. of Charleston, who replaced Stallings as commander in October 1864, was not promoted to major. Captain of Company A, he died of typhoid fever at the General Hospital in Columbia on March 27, 1865.[142] Bartless's son was captain of Company H of the 25th Regiment, SCV.

William W. Hutto, previously captain of Company C, commanded the battalion after Bartless died. It is unknown if he actually received a promotion to the rank of major.

Companies

Company A, from Charleston, was commanded by William H. Bartless Sr. He enlisted at Charleston on June 21, 1864, for the duration of the war. A.E. Parker may have commanded the company after Bartless became acting major.

Company B, the Confederate Reserve Corps of Colleton District, was commanded by Henry W. Fishburne. He enlisted at Walterboro for the duration of the war on April 16, 1864. Company B reported for duty on July 15, 1864.

Company C, from Barnwell and Beaufort Districts, was commanded by William W. Hutto. Its men enlisted at Barnwell Court House.[143] Clark C. Cooper was promoted to captain after Hutto became major.

William Young Fair was captain of a company in the 8th Battalion.[144] Its letter designation was probably G. The record shows that its men mustered in Confederate service in November 1864. On February 22, 1865, they were ordered to transfer permanently to active service "with the consent of the officers and men" and were assigned to the 19th Battalion, South Carolina Cavalry.[145]

Abe Jones might have commanded a company in the 8th Battalion.

Brigade Affiliations

The 8th Battalion Reserves was attached to the Department of South Carolina, Georgia and Florida.[146] It was brigaded with the 3rd, 4th and 5th Reserve Battalions and was commanded by Brigadier General James Chesnut from December 1864 to March 1865. On March 25, all four reserve battalions were ordered to join Blanchard's Brigade, which, at the time, comprised the 1st, 2nd, 6th and 7th Battalions, South Carolina Reserves.[147] By March 31, however, the order had not been carried out.[148]

Major Movements and Engagements

From July 15 to August 31, 1864, Company B was stationed at Battery Wilkes. Between August 31 and December 31, Companies A and C spent some time guarding Federal prisoners at Camp Asylum in Columbia; records show that the three-company battalion was at Sullivan's Island and Christ Church Parish on October 31.[149] Although a list of the organization of troops for November 20 shows no 8th Battalion, the omission is probably an oversight.[150] On December 26, the battalion was on the Coosawhatchie Road near Honey Hill, and by the twenty-eighth, it was at Grahamville.[151] The battalion withdrew into North Carolina in February 1865, and in March, it was part of Chesnut's Brigade in the Department of South Carolina, Georgia and Florida. On the sixteenth, Chesnut ordered his four reserve battalions—the 3rd, 4th, 5th and 8th—to assemble at their rendezvous sites to begin a fifteen-day furlough and to reassemble afterward. The furlough was to give the men time to procure horses.[152] On April 9, at

Smithfield, the 1st, 2nd, 6th and 7th Reserve Battalions were consolidated with several first-line South Carolina units—the 3rd Battalion, 2nd, 3rd, 7th, 8th, 15th and 20th Regiments—to form the (New) 2nd, 3rd and 7th Regiments SCV. The 8th Battalion was not part of the consolidation, and pension records indicate that it was dissolved at Charlotte on April 26, 1865.

19.

The Regiments of Junior Reserves, South Carolina State Troops

In August and early September 1864, South Carolina made all white males between the ages of sixteen and sixty liable for service in the state militia.[1] The state also called on each militia regiment to contribute one company toward the creation of four new regiments. These, designated the 1st, 2nd, 3rd and 4th Regiments, Junior Reserves, South Carolina State Troops, were also called Regiments of South Carolina Militia and Regiments of South Carolina State Troops.[2] Veterans applying for pensions in the 1920s called them simply "militia" or "state troops." Some even referred to them as "battalions of state troops."[3] Not to be confused with the 1st, 2nd, 3rd and 4th Regiments, South Carolina Militia, that existed before and during the war, Junior Reserves regiments were made up of sixteen-year-olds and some men as old as sixty. Prior to call-up, militia units served as home guards and performed other local duties.[4] All militia regiments were ordered to rendezvous on September 12, 1864, to raise a company of Junior Reserves from each.[5]

Following is a list of militia regiments and brigades, along with their commanders and rendezvous sites, affected by the September 1864 order:

1st Brigade—the 1st, 2nd, 3rd, 4th, 5th and 42nd Regiments gathered at Belton in Anderson District under the command of Lieutenant Colonel J.W. Harrison.

2nd Brigade—the 6th, 7th, 8th, 9th and 10th Regiments met at the Ninety Six Depot under the command of Lieutenant Colonel William P. Butler.

3rd Brigade—the 11th, 12th, 13th, 14th, 15th and 43rd Regiments massed at Branchville under the command of Lieutenant Colonel A.P. Aldrich.

4th Brigade—the 16th, 17th, 18th and 19th Regiments rendezvoused at Charleston under the command of Lieutenant Colonel Wilmot G. DeSaussure.

5th Brigade—the 20th, 21st, 22nd, 23rd and 44th Regiments gathered at Camden under the command of Lieutenant Colonel A.H. Boykin.

6th Brigade—the 24th, 25th, 26th and 27th Regiments massed at Winnsboro under the command of Lieutenant Colonel C.F. Hampton.

7th Brigade—the 28th, 29th and 30th Regiments were scheduled for organization at a later date.[6]

8th Brigade— the 31st, 32nd and 33rd Regiments were also to be organized at a later date.[7]

9th Brigade—the 34th, 35th, 36th, 37th and 46th Regiments met at Union Court House under the command of Lieutenant Colonel R.G. McGaw.

10th Brigade—the 38th, 39th, 40th, 41st and 45th Regiments massed at Newberry Court House under the command of Lieutenant Colonel W.D. Simpson.

After the organization in September, the men returned home for a time but reassembled at Hamburg in late November. Apparently companies of Junior Reserves were not placed together in regiments based on their previous brigade status in the militia. On February 25, 1865, Governor Magrath ordered all militiamen between sixteen and seventeen to assemble in Spartanburg by April 1 ready to defend the state. He also ordered The Citadel and Arsenal cadets to command a camp of instruction there.[8] By early April, all four regiments had been disbanded.[9] The older men were allowed to go home, but the "boys" were required to remain in service as "State Troops, First Class Militia."[10] In early April, about seven hundred sixteen-year-olds were busy drilling while being held for state service at Spartanburg.[11] On April 3, the order came to reorganize immediately and report to Captain J.P. Thomas at Greenville. The move did not take place, however, and the State Troops, First Class Militia, was either furloughed or disbanded on April 8. Because these regiments were in state service, Confederate records on them do not exist. The best sources are contemporary newspapers, the *Recollections and Reminiscences* series and pension application records.

THE 1ST REGIMENT, JUNIOR RESERVES, SOUTH CAROLINA STATE TROOPS

The 1st Regiment, Junior Reserves, was also called the 1st Regiment, South Carolina State Troops.[12] Most of its men were from Anderson and Laurens Districts. When the Junior Reserve regiments were ordered to rendezvous at various locations throughout the state on September 12, 1864, the sixteen-year-olds of the 1st Regiment reported to Camden the next day, elected company officers and returned home as ordered.[13] Field officers were elected on December 27.[14] The *Edgefield Advertiser* reported on December 28 that the 1st Regiment had recently been organized.[15]

Field Officers

Colonel James Benjamin Griffin, the first major of the Hampton Legion, was elected colonel of the 1st Regiment on December 27, 1864.[16] Promoted to lieutenant colonel of the Hampton Legion in July 1861, he had been elected its colonel in August 1862, but he declined the position. Griffin had also served as lieutenant colonel of the 5th Regiment Reserves (Ninety Days) in 1862 and 1863.

Benjamin Zachariah Herndon was elected lieutenant colonel of the regiment, also on December 27, 1864.[17] He had served previously as captain of Company A, 5th Regiment Reserves, in 1862 and 1863.

S.P. Dikes, whose name also appears as S.A. Dike, was elected major of the regiment on December 27, 1864.[18]

William Preston Thompson, captain of Company K, may have served as major of the regiment at one time.

Companies

Company A, from Greenville, was probably commanded by David R. Anderson. He may have commanded Company A of the 1st Battalion Senior Reserves instead. Pension records also show that W.H. Harrison commanded Company A.

Company B, from Anderson District, was commanded by Captain John W. Bramlett. He had served as captain of Company D of the 18th Regiment earlier in the war.

Company C was commanded by William F. Prescott of Edgefield District. He was captain of Company I, 7th Regiment, SCV, until the spring of 1862.

Company D, from Pickens District, was commanded by Daniel Grice. A D.J. Grice is also shown in the pension records as captain of Company F, 1st Battalion Senior Reserves.

Company E, from Edgefield, was commanded by John P. Mickler.

Company F was commanded by M.W. Watson.

Company G was commanded by Robert J. Robinson, who had raised it from students at Wellington Academy in Calhoun Falls, Abbeville District.[19] Organized at Calhoun Falls and mustered in service at Hamburg on December 1, 1864, its men traveled by rail to Grahamville and followed the regiment into North Carolina.

Company H was from the old 4th Regiment, South Carolina Militia, in Anderson District. Professor Thomas H. Hall, a graduate of West Point, commanded the company, which consisted of about one hundred men between the ages of sixteen and sixty.[20] B.Z. Herndon might have commanded this company before he was elected lieutenant colonel. Hall had commanded a company called the Spartan Rangers in 1861.

Company I, from Colleton District, may have been commanded by John R.P. Fox, who had commanded Company I of the 1st Regiment, South Carolina Cavalry, until January 1865.

Company K, from Anderson, was commanded by William Preston Thompson, who may have also served as major. This company is also listed as E.

One company was commanded by a Captain Bruns.

Brigade Affiliations

The 1st Regiment was attached to Chesnut's Brigade in December 1864 and January 1865. In January and early February 1865, it was part of Rhett's Brigade with the 1st Regiment, South Carolina Artillery (Regulars); the 1st Regiment, South Carolina Infantry (Regulars); the 19th Battalion, South Carolina Cavalry; the 19th Regiment, South Carolina Militia; Parker's Battery; and some Georgia units.[21] Artemas Darby Goodwyn commanded a brigade comprising the 1st, 2nd, 3rd and 4th Regiments of Militia (Junior Reserves). It is unclear exactly when the 1st Regiment was part of that brigade, but it was probably from mid-February to April 1865.[22]

Major Movements and Engagements

Men of the 1st Regiment reported to Camden on September 13, 1864, elected company officers and left for home as ordered.[23] All the Junior Reserves reassembled at Hamburg on November 26 and formed themselves into four regiments. The 1st left Hamburg on December 2 by rail for Grahamville via Charleston, camped at the Old Depot on Line Street and had arrived at Coosawhatchie by the ninth.[24] The men were sent to Honey Hill but missed the battle there by a full ten days. In December, when the regiment was stationed at the trestle over the Tullifinny River near Hardeeville, it was shelled by Federal gunboats.[25] The regiment was stationed next at Grahamville, two miles from the Charleston & Savannah Railroad, where it guarded the lines near the railroad.[26] One company moved to a battery along the railroad. The regiment was in the works at the

Tullifinny River by December 26, and by the twenty-eighth, it had reached Coosawhatchie.[27]

Junior Reserve regiments performed guard and picket duty along the Charleston & Savannah Railroad, serving at Adams Run and Green Pond for about a month in early 1865. In early February, they were sent to James Island. Measles struck in mid-February, decimating the 1st Regiment and leaving only about one hundred men fit for active duty.[28] At that time, the 1st was based at James Island.[29] At the same time, Goodwyn's Brigade evacuated Charleston and marched to Moncks Corner, where the men boarded a train for Cheraw; the 1st Regiment arrived on February 27.[30] After about a week of picket duty, the brigade moved into North Carolina.

On February 25, Governor Magrath asked General Beauregard to send Goodwyn's Militia Brigade and the Citadel Cadets back to South Carolina to deal with an expected Federal raid on the upstate of South Carolina.[31] On March 11, the brigade broke camp and marched back to South Carolina.[32] Moving through Charlotte to Chester in late March or early April, the brigade reached Spartanburg, where the men were granted furloughs of about two weeks and instructed to reassemble at certain locations afterward. Most went either to Columbia or to their homes. Colonel Griffin was at home in Edgefield for about a week on April 19.[33] Before the furlough expired, however, the Army of Northern Virginia had surrendered, and the four regiments were not reassembled.[34]

THE 2ND REGIMENT, JUNIOR RESERVES, SOUTH CAROLINA STATE TROOPS

The 2nd Regiment, Junior Reserves, was also called the 2nd Regiment, South Carolina State Troops.[35] Its men came from Greenville, Edgefield, Lexington, Marion, Barnwell and Pickens Districts. Following orders to rendezvous on September 12, 1864, the sixteen-year-olds of the 2nd Regiment organized themselves into companies and went home.[36] Field officers were elected on December 27.[37]

Field Officers

The *Daily Southern Guardian* listed field officers for the 2nd Regiment on December 31, 1864, but did not include a colonel, supporting the fact that its veterans applying for pensions in the 1920s called it the 2nd Battalion, State Troops.[38]

W.H. Duncan was elected lieutenant colonel of the regiment on December 27, 1864.[39]

David "Dave" H. Rice was elected major of the regiment on December 27, 1864.[40] He commanded Company G before being elected major.

Companies

Company A was commanded by William G. Muller, MD. He might have served as major at sometime. William M. Shuler, MD, previously lieutenant colonel of the 11th Regiment, may also have commanded the company.

Company B, also called the Saluda Company, was from Edgefield District and was commanded by Captain Washington Hodges Timmerman, MD.[41] One sketch states that Timmerman's Company was actually Company H.[42] Timmerman had served previously as captain of Company K of the 19th Regiment, SCV. Numerous other pension applications list John L. Bozard as captain of Company B.

Company C, organized in September 1864 at Marion Court House, was commanded by William J. Davis.[43]

Company D, from Barnwell District, was commanded by Captain Robert M. Willis.[44]

Company F, commanded by Captain Daniel J. Avinger, was composed of men from Orangeburg and Lexington Districts, though some were from Barnwell, Colleton, Edgefield and Richland Districts.[45] Though the record is unclear as to Company F's regiment, it almost certainly belongs to the 2nd. One survivor, W.G. Albergotti, wrote a brief history of Avinger's Company, saying it was raised in the summer of 1864 and was composed of sixteen-year-old boys, placing it definitely in one of the Junior Reserve regiments. Pension records confirm these facts. He added, however, that the company was designated Company F of the 2nd Battalion, South Carolina State Troops—a statement commonly repeated in pension records—and was in a battalion led by A.D. Goodwyn as colonel, W.H. Duncan as lieutenant colonel and a major named Muller. The problem is there was no such unit as the 2nd Battalion, South Carolina State Troops, and there was no regiment of Junior Reserves with the slate of field officers Albergotti names. The author included more intriguing details: first, that the company mustered in (at either Batesburg, Hamburg, or Bamberg) in July 1864, after which its men were promptly sent home; secondly, that the field officers were of mature years and had already retired from Confederate service for various reasons, mostly disability.[46] Finally, a different source confirms that Avinger's Company was disbanded at Spartanburg in April 1865.[47] These accounts appear to confirm that

Avinger's Company was in either the 2nd or 3rd Regiment, Junior Reserves, though most likely the 2nd.

Company G, from Lexington District, was commanded by David "Dave" H. Rice until he was elected major in December 1864. Rice had commanded Company H, 17th Regiment, SCV, until the reorganization in 1862. S.C. Lamotte probably succeeded Rice as captain. Josiah Howell might have also commanded the company.[48]

Company H, from Barnwell District, might have been commanded by George H. Kirkland. Pension records also show him as commander of Company D of the 3rd Regiment, probably a reference to his earlier command of Company D, 3rd Regiment, South Carolina Cavalry.

Company I, from Pickens District, was commanded by Columbus Lafayette Hollingsworth.[49] Pension records indicate Hollingsworth's Company was I of the 1st Regiment Junior Reserves and that it was composed of sixteen-year-old boys from Claremont Academy located in what is now Oconee County. Hollingsworth, its principal, was honorably discharged on December 8, 1864.[50]

Company K, from Greenville District, was commanded by Tom Hunt.[51]

Captains J.C. Cary, Thomas H. Russell and Daniel Lester all commanded companies of sixteen-year-old boys from the Oconee area of Pickens District. These companies might have been attached to the 2nd Regiment, Junior Reserves.[52] Russell had served previously as captain of Company A, 1st Regiment, South Carolina State Troops, in 1863 and 1864. Russell's company, described as a home guard company, served in late 1864 and 1865 and was disbanded at Walhalla.

Joseph D. Allen of Bamberg commanded a company of Junior Reserves, probably in the 2nd Regiment.

Brigade Affiliations

Artemas Darby Goodwyn commanded a brigade comprising the 1st, 2nd, 3rd and 4th Regiments of Militia, Junior Reserves.[53] In January and February 1865, the 2nd, 3rd and 4th Regiments were under Goodwyn's command in B.H. Robertson's Brigade.[54]

Major Movements and Engagements

Men of the 2nd Regiment reported to their rendezvous point, elected their company officers about September 13, 1864, and returned home as ordered.[55] Company D mustered in service in August and spent about three days at Bamberg before it was dismissed. All Junior Reserve companies reassembled at Hamburg on November 26 and formed into four regiments; the 2nd remained at Hamburg for about two weeks.[56] Companies C and D, perhaps even the entire regiment, were sent to Grahamville through Columbia and Charleston. The men made camp at Honey Hill, about five miles from Grahamville.[57] Company D, and likely the rest of the regiment as well, arrived at Honey Hill shortly after the battle there ended, though the 2nd did engage some skirmishers.[58] It was also on the field at Tullifinny River but probably not engaged in the action from December 7 to December 9.[59] After about two weeks at Honey Hill, Company C was ordered to Coosawhatchie, where it guarded the Charleston & Savannah Railroad and engaged in several more skirmishes.[60] The 2nd, 3rd and 4th Regiments were ordered to the vicinity of Green Pond and Adams Run on December 20 and remained in the area until February 1865.[61] Company C spent the three winter months at Tullifinny Creek engaged in picket duty along the railroad.[62] The regiment was back at Honey Hill on December 26 and at Grahamville two days later.[63] The three regiments were also sent to James Island in early February.

Goodwyn's Brigade evacuated Charleston in mid-February and marched to Moncks Corner, where the men boarded a train for Cheraw. After performing a week of picket duty, the brigade moved into North Carolina. The 2nd Regiment was ordered to Laurinburg for a few days. On February 25, Governor Magrath asked General Beauregard to send Goodwyn's Brigade and the Citadel Cadets back to South Carolina in anticipation of a Federal raid on the upstate.[64] The brigade left its camp on March 11 and marched back toward South Carolina.[65] It moved through Charlotte to Chester in late March or early April and on to Spartanburg, where the 2nd Regiment was furloughed and ordered to reassemble at Orangeburg in two weeks.[66] Most of the men left for home. But before the furlough expired, the Army of Northern Virginia surrendered, and the four regiments did not reassemble.[67]

The 3rd Regiment, Junior Reserves, South Carolina State Troops

The 3rd Regiment, Junior Reserves, was also called the 3rd Regiment, South Carolina State Troops.[68] Ordered to rendezvous on September 12, 1864, the sixteen-year-olds of the 3rd Regiment organized into companies and left for home.[69] According to the *Mercury*, field officers were elected on December 6.[70] The companies of the 3rd Regiment were from Chesterfield, Darlington, Marlboro, Horry, Marion, Sumter, Clarendon, Williamsburg, Richland and Georgetown Districts.

Field Officers

Artemas "Artie" Darby Goodwyn commanded the 3rd Regiment, Junior Reserves, with the rank of colonel.[71] The *Confederate Military History Series* says Goodwyn became colonel of the regiment about seven months before the war ended, but, according to the *Mercury*, he was elected on December 6, 1864.[72] Goodwyn was previously lieutenant colonel of the 2nd Regiment, SCV. A wound forced his resignation from that command on June 3, 1863, and although he was still suffering from its effects, he raised a company of boys called the Bonham Guards, which became Company K of the 3rd Regiment, Junior Reserves. As senior colonel in the four Junior Reserve regiments, Goodwyn commanded the brigade, which was named for him.

J.W. Harrington of Marlboro was elected lieutenant colonel on December 6, 1864.[73] He commanded the brigade in Goodwyn's absence.

J.J. McIver of Darlington was elected major on December 10, 1864.[74]

Henry Graham Hartzog, captain Company G, was promoted to major at some time.[75]

Companies

Company A, from Chester, was commanded by Giles J. Patterson. Pension records also show his first name as Jiles and that he may have commanded Company E instead. George Washington Oswald, previously major of the 1st Regiment Mounted Militia, commanded a Colleton District company recorded in pension records as both A of the 3rd Regiment and B of the 1st Regiment. A Captain McLeakin may have also commanded the company.[76]

Company B, from Clarendon District, was commanded by Daniel Judson Bradham, who had served as a second lieutenant in Company I of the 23rd Regiment until he lost an arm at Second Manassas and resigned on January 29, 1863.

Company C was commanded by Kulton Carver.[77]

Company D, from Bennettsville in Marlboro District, mustered in service in September 1864.[78] Captain Z.J. Drake commanded the company.

Company E from Sumter District was commanded by John S. Bradley. Albert Blakeney commanded a Chesterfield company that is designated E in some pension records.

Company F, from Kingstree in Williamsburg District, was commanded by Captain H.B. McKnight.

Company G was commanded by Captain Henry Graham Hartzog of Bamberg, who was later promoted to major of the regiment.[79] Edward E. Evans commanded a company that was from Marlboro District and was organized in Darlington.[80] His company is listed as both E and G in pension records.

Company H, from Fairfield District, was commanded by Captain Charles Broom. Some pension records show Broom's Company as F.

Company I, from Lancaster District, was commanded by James Dixon Caskey, previously captain of Company I, 3rd Regiment, South Carolina State Troops. His widow stated in her pension application that Caskey commanded Company B.

Company K, from Columbia in Richland District, was raised by A.D. Goodwyn in August 1864. It was called the Bonham Guards in honor of Governor Milledge L. Bonham.[81] When Goodwyn was elected colonel of the 3rd Regiment, a soldier named Pooser became captain of the Bonham Guards. When he was detailed for other duty, sixteen-year-old Lawrence Walter Taylor was made captain and served until the end of the war.[82]

One company was from Newberry, one was from Spartanburg and one was from Kershaw District.

Brigade Affiliations

As its senior colonel, A.D. Goodwyn commanded the brigade bearing his name. In January and February 1865, the 2nd, 3rd and 4th Regiments, still under Goodwyn's command, were part of B.H. Robertson's Brigade.[83]

Major Movements and Engagements

The men of the 3rd Regiment reported to their rendezvous point, elected company officers about September 13, 1864, and returned to their homes as directed.[84] About November 26, the companies were sent to a camp in Hamburg, Edgefield District, for instruction.[85] After about two weeks of training, the 3rd moved with the other regiments to Grahamville through Columbia and Charleston. The 2nd and 3rd were ordered to Honey Hill, where the battle of November 30 had been fought, and remained in the area for two to three weeks.[86] The 3rd Regiment, like the 2nd, might also have skirmished in the vicinity of Honey Hill.

Over the next two months, the regiment served at Adams Run, Green Pond, Coosawhatchie, Pocotaligo and other points as guards and pickets along the Charleston & Savannah Railroad. The 2nd, 3rd and 4th Regiments were ordered to the vicinity of Green Pond and Adams Run on December 20.[87] On December 26, the 3rd Regiment was at Honey Hill, and on the twenty-eighth, it was at Grahamville.[88] In early February 1865, the 3rd was ordered to James Island, where the 1st and 2nd Regiments were already stationed, to serve as the rear guard during the evacuation of James Island. Goodwyn's Brigade evacuated Charleston in mid-February and marched to Moncks Corner, where the men boarded a train for Cheraw. Following about a week of picket duty in Cheraw, the brigade marched into North Carolina, though at the border, the 3rd Regiment's officers debated among themselves whether they should disband rather than enter another state. In the end, they elected to enter North Carolina with the brigade.[89] The regiment went with Hardee's corps as it, too, retreated into North Carolina. The 3rd Regiment escorted six hundred Federal prisoners from Fayetteville to Raleigh, where the prisoners were paroled. From Raleigh, the 3rd was detached to Durham and ordered to guard the Central North Carolina Railroad.

On February 25, Governor Magrath asked General Beauregard to send Goodwyn's Brigade of South Carolina Militia and the Citadel Cadets back to South Carolina in expectation of a Federal raid on the upstate.[90] On March 1, the brigade left its camp and marched back toward South Carolina.[91] It moved through Charlotte to Chester in late March or early April and on to Spartanburg, where the men were furloughed for about two weeks and instructed to reassemble at certain locations afterward. Most went to their homes. Before the furlough expired, however, the Army of Northern Virginia surrendered, and the four regiments did not reassemble.[92]

THE 4TH REGIMENT, JUNIOR RESERVES, SOUTH CAROLINA STATE TROOPS

The 4th Regiment, Junior Reserves, was also called the 4th Regiment, South Carolina State Troops.[93] Its companies were from Anderson, York and Union Districts. Following orders to rendezvous on September 12, 1864, the sixteen-year-olds of the 4th Regiment were organized into companies and sent home.[94] Field officers were elected about December 27.[95]

Field Officers

Robert B. Ligon of Laurens District was elected colonel of the regiment. He had served previously as captain of Company B, 3rd Battalion, SCV. He probably commanded Company C prior to taking command of the regiment.

John Robert Spearman of Newberry District was elected lieutenant colonel. He was captain of Company D prior to the election to lieutenant colonel. This is probably the same John R. Spearman who was captain of Company C, Holcombe Legion Cavalry Battalion, in early 1862.

J.W. Ferguson was elected major.

Companies

Company A, from Union District, was commanded by Thomas S. Wright.[96]

Company B, the Union Laddies, also from Union District, was commanded by Dan A. Townsend.[97] Townsend might have commanded the regiment at one time.

Company C, from York District, might have been commanded by Adolphus Eugene Hutchison, though whether he led Company C, G or H is unclear from the record. Hutchison had served previously as captain of Company J, 5th Regiment, SCV.[98] Some pension records show that John Cook and a Captain Patrick commanded the company.

Company D was commanded by John Robert Spearman of Newberry District until he was elected lieutenant colonel. J.A. "Guss" Kibler of Lexington District probably succeeded Spearman as captain.

Company E was probably from what is now Cherokee County and was commanded by John S. Ezell. His name is also spelled Easel and Eazell.[99] R.M. Cash may also have commanded the company.

Company F, from Laurens District, was commanded by George F. Anderson. Some pension applications list Anderson's Company as C, and others show W.C. Irby as captain of F. Additional pension records show that the captain was M.C. Cox, though others indicate that Cox commanded Company H, 4th State Troops; Company F, 3rd State Troops; and Company B, 5th Battalion Reserves.

Company G, from York District, was commanded by George H. Chapman.

Company H, from Newberry District, was commanded by Roscius F. Atwood and William Boyd. Atwood's name is shown as Attaway in many pension applications.

Company K, probably from Spartanburg District, was commanded by Robert McClure. Some pension records show that he commanded Company G.

Company I was commanded by Thomas E. Wood, MD. John Blair Hunter, MD, may have also commanded the company.[100]

Brigade Affiliations

The 4th Regiment, South Carolina Militia, or Junior Reserves, State Troops, was assigned to the brigade of Artemas D. Goodwyn, known as Goodwyn's Brigade. In December 1864 and January 1865, Goodwyn's command served in Chesnut's Brigade. In January and February 1865, the 2nd, 3rd and 4th Regiments, still under Goodwyn's command, were assigned to B.H. Robertson's Brigade.[101]

Major Movements and Engagements

Men of the 4th Regiment reported to their rendezvous point as ordered in mid-September 1864 and elected company officers, after which they were sent home.[102] The regiment reassembled for training at Hamburg in Edgefield District in late November or early December. After about two weeks, it moved with the other regiments to Grahamville through Columbia and Charleston. The 2nd, 3rd and 4th were ordered to the vicinity of Green Pond and Adams Run on December 20, 1864, and remained in the area until February 1865.[103] Records show that the 4th was at Honey Hill on December 26 and two days later was at Grahamville.[104] In early February 1865, the regiments were sent to James Island. Goodwyn's Brigade evacuated Charleston in mid-February and marched to Moncks Corner to board a train for Cheraw. Following about a week of picket duty, the brigade moved into North Carolina.

On February 25, Governor Magrath asked General Beauregard to send Goodwyn's Brigade and the Citadel Cadets back to South Carolina to deal with an expected Federal raid on the upstate.[105] The brigade left its camp on March 11 and headed back toward South Carolina.[106] It moved through Charlotte to Chester in late March or early April and on to Spartanburg, where the men were furloughed for two weeks and instructed to reassemble at certain locations afterward. Most set out for their homes. Before the furlough expired, however, the Army of Northern Virginia surrendered, and the four reserve regiments did not reassemble.[107]

20.

The Regiments of South Carolina Militia

It was the South Carolina Militia and the South Carolina Regular Army that held the line around Charleston Harbor and along the coast during the first few months of 1861 until additional battalions and regiments of volunteers could be raised and prepared for duty. The militia infantry is discussed first, followed by cavalry and artillery.

Infantry Units

The infantry component of the South Carolina Militia was organized into regiments and brigades. Following is a list of each numbered regiment and its district: 1st—Greenville, 2nd—Pickens, 3rd—Greenville, 4th—Anderson, 5th—Pickens, 6th—Abbeville, 7th—Edgefield, 8th—Abbeville, 9th—Edgefield, 10th—Edgefield, 11th—Barnwell, 12th—Beaufort, 13th—Colleton, 14th—Orangeburg, 15th—Orangeburg and Lexington, 16th and 17th—Charleston, 18th and 19th—Charleston (Summerville), 20th—Sumter, 21st– Lancaster, 22nd—Kershaw District, 23rd—Richland, 24th and 25th—Fairfield, 26th and 27th—Chester, 28th—Chesterfield, 29th—Darlington, 30th—Marlboro, 31st—Williamsburg and Georgetown, 32nd—Marion, 33rd—Horry, 34th—York, 35th—Union, 36th and 37th—Spartanburg, 38th—Newberry, 39th—Newberry and Lexington, 40th and 41st—Laurens, 42nd—Anderson, 43rd—Barnwell, 44th—Clarendon, 45th—Union and Spartanburg and 46th—York.

The 1st Regiment Rifles, South Carolina Militia

The 1st Regiment Rifles, South Carolina Militia, was also called Branch's Rifle Regiment; the 1st Regiment Rifles, Militia; the Militia Regiment of

Rifles; and the 1st Regiment South Carolina Rifles. It comprised all volunteer companies and assembled in Charleston in December 1860.[1]

Field Officers

James Johnston Pettigrew, a Charleston lawyer, was elected colonel of the regiment on December 5, 1860.[2] He left the post, enlisted as a private (along with other members of the Washington Light Infantry) in Company A of the Hampton Legion and went with that company to Virginia in June 1861.[3] Pettigrew did not resign the colonelcy of the 1st Regiment Rifles until August 21, 1861. Sometime during that summer, he became colonel of a North Carolina regiment and was promoted to brigadier general with rank from February 26, 1862. Pettigrew was mortally wounded on July 14, 1863, at Falling Waters, Maryland.

John Luther Branch, a graduate of The Citadel, was elected lieutenant colonel of the regiment on December 5, 1860.[4] He advanced to colonel on August 21, 1861, when Pettigrew resigned.[5] Branch, too, left the regiment at some indeterminate date and later enlisted as a private in Confederate service. Because of poor health, he hired a substitute and began to manufacture tallow candles. On December 29, 1862, Branch applied to Governor Pickens for a new position. Since he later served as an engineer at Battery Wagner, it is reasonable to surmise that the governor honored his request

Ellison Capers was elected major on December 5, 1860.[6] He was promoted to lieutenant colonel on August 21, 1861, when Branch became colonel.[7] Capers began to assist C.H. Stevens in raising the 24th Regiment, SCV, in late September or early October. Capers was appointed to the rank of lieutenant colonel of the 24th Regiment in state service on January 13, 1862, and resigned as lieutenant colonel of the 1st Regiment Rifles on January 25. His commission as lieutenant colonel in Confederate service dated from April 1, 1862.

C.S. Gadsden was elected major on September 9, 1861, to replace Capers.[8]

Companies

Though each of the eleven companies of the regiment had popular names, there is no evidence that they were assigned alphabetic designations from the beginning. According to the *Mercury*, the companies received numeric designations in February 1862.

The Washington Light Infantry was a Charleston militia company organized in July 1807 in anticipation of further conflict with Great

Britain. It was popularly known as The Washingtons.[9] One contingent, the Washington Light Infantry Volunteers, left the regiment to become Company A of the Hampton Legion in June 1861, whereupon Captain Charles H. Simonton expanded the size of the militia company. By August, it was large enough to be divided into two companies, one, designated A, under the command of Simonton and the other, B, led by Captain Edward W. Lloyd.[10] Both companies enlisted later that year in the 11th Battalion, South Carolina Infantry, which later merged into the 25th Regiment, SCV. Simonton commanded Company A until he was elected lieutenant colonel of the 11th Battalion on April 30, 1862. Lloyd retained command of Company B in both the 11th Battalion and 25th Regiment.

On November 11, 1861, the remaining men of the Washington Light Infantry militia company elected B.M. Lee as their captain, replacing the two who left to join the 11th Battalion.[11] Lee's company was called the Washington Light Infantry, Company C.[12] After the war, the Washington Light Infantry Charitable Association erected several impressive monuments honoring its fallen comrades.

The Carolina Light Infantry was organized in 1858 and was incorporated by the General Assembly on January 28, 1861.[13] B. Gaillard Pinckney was captain as early as February 1860.[14] In August 1861, this company was part of the 1st Battalion of the Regiment of Rifles.[15] A group of its men, calling themselves the Carolina Light Infantry Volunteers, enlisted as Company L of Maxcy Gregg's reorganized 1st Regiment, SCV, on August 6.

The Meagher Guards, a company of Charleston Irishmen, existed as early as October 1860; Edward McCrady Jr. was elected captain.[16] On June 7, 1861, he was elected captain of another company of Charleston Irishmen, the Irish Volunteers, this one attached to the 17th Regiment, South Carolina Militia, which contributed most of the men of Company K in Maxcy Gregg's regiment. The Meagher Guards was named in honor of the Irish patriot Thomas Francis Meagher, who had been banished from Ireland and exiled to Tasmania but who managed to escape to New York instead.[17] Unfortunately for the Charlestonians, Meagher himself raised a Zouave company for the 69th Regiment, New York Militia, in 1861. Unwilling to have their company bear the name of a potential foe, the Charlestonians changed their name to the Emerald Light Infantry in May.[18] Michael E. Rooney was elected captain on August 23, replacing McCrady.[19] William Ashmead Courtenay was elected captain of the militia company in January 1862.[20]

The Chichester Zouaves was also called the Charleston Zouave Cadets, the Zouave Cadets and Captain C.E. Chichester's Company.[21] It was organized in August 1860.[22] Peter Fayssoux Stevens was elected captain on December 20, and the company offered its services to the governor the same day.[23] The governor responded with an order to assemble on January 1, 1861.[24] Stevens resigned on March 22 and was named colonel of the Holcombe Legion on November 21, 1861. First Lieutenant Charles E. Chichester was promoted to captain, replacing Stevens in March. Late in 1861, some men left to join Company H of the Hampton Legion; several officers and a number of men also served later in the Gist Guard, South Carolina Heavy Artillery, under Captain Chichester. The original company was dissolved in late January 1862.

The Moultrie Guard, or Guards, also called Captain B.W. Palmer's Company, was a prewar organization that existed as early as 1776.[25] Its captain, Barnwell W. Palmer, served later as a lieutenant in Company E of the Charleston Battalion and also as captain of Company A of the 27th Regiment, SCV. The company was in Confederate service from August 29 to September 7, 1861; it was part of the 1st Battalion of the Regiment of Rifles in August.[26] Palmer's Moultrie Guards was slated to join the Holcombe Legion in February 1862, but for some reason this never happened.[27]

The German Riflemen, another early unit, was organized in 1840.[28] Jacob Small was elected its captain on October 16, 1861.[29]

The Palmetto Riflemen, organized in 1858, was commanded by Alexander Melchers.[30] All of its men were Germans.[31]

The Jamison (or Jamieson) Riflemen was organized about February 1861.[32] It was part of the 1st Battalion of the Regiment of Rifles in August.[33] T.Y. Simons was elected captain on September 24 and again on November 25, 1861.[34]

The Sarsfield Light Infantry, another company of Charleston Irishmen, was organized on August 14, 1861.[35] Its captain was William N. Heyward.[36]

The Beauregard Light Infantry, organized in late July or early August 1861, was commanded by Peter B. LaLane.[37]

The Pickens Rifles was listed by the *Mercury* as part of the regiment in October 1861, though not in January 1862.[38] For further discussion of the Pickens Rifles, see the 1st Regiment Charleston Reserves in this volume.

On February 24, 1862, the 1st Regiment Rifles, Militia and the 17th Regiment, South Carolina Militia, were combined, and officers were elected. The following companies were created at that time and were assigned numeric designations.[39]

Company #1 was a combination of the Calhoun Guards, 17th Regiment, and the Moultrie Guards and the Carolina Light Infantry of the 1st Regiment. Its captain, F.T. Miles, became captain of Company E of the 1st (Charleston) Infantry Battalion in February 1862.

Company #2, called Captain Ramsay's Company, was commanded by David Ramsay. He became captain of Company F of the 1st (Charleston) Infantry Battalion in February 1862.

Company #3 was a combination of the Jamison Rifles of the 1st Regiment and the Brooks Guards of the 17th. Its captain, Thomas Y. Simons, became captain of Company B of the 1st (Charleston) Infantry Battalion in February 1862.

Company #4 was a combination of the Carolina Light Infantry of the 1st Regiment, the Phoenix Rifles and the Sumter Guards of the 17th Regiment and a company called Beat #6. Its captain, Henry C. King, became captain of Company D of the 1st (Charleston) Infantry Battalion in February 1862.

Company #5 was a combination of the Charleston Riflemen and the Cadet Riflemen—both of the 17th Regiment. Its captain, Julius A. Blake, became captain of Company A of the 1st (Charleston) Infantry Battalion in February 1862.

Company #6 was a combination of the Jasper Greens of the 17th Regiment and the Emerald Light Infantry of the 1st. Its captain was William A. Courtenay.

Company #7 was a combination of the Sarsfield Light Infantry of the 1st Regiment and the Montgomery Guard of the 17th. Its captain was W.N. Heyward.

Company #8 was the Irish Volunteers commanded by Edward McGrath. McGrath became captain of Company C of the 1st (Charleston) Infantry Battalion in February 1862.

Companies 9, 10, 11 and 12 filled out the regiment.[40]

Brigade Affiliations

This regiment was part of the 4th Brigade, 2nd Division, South Carolina Militia. The 4th Brigade consisted of two infantry regiments—the 1st Regiment Rifles and the 17th Regiment—though J.P. Thomas wrote that the 16th, 18th and 19th were attached as well.[41] The 4th Brigade also contained one artillery regiment—the 1st Artillery Regiment Militia—and three cavalry troops—the Charleston Light Dragoons, the German Hussars and the Rutledge Mounted Riflemen. Finally, four volunteer fire department companies—the Vigilant Rifles, the Phoenix Rifles, the Aetna Rifles and the Marion Rifles—were also on its roster. The Vigilant Rifles, formed in November 1860, was commanded by Captain Samuel Y. Tupper. Known later as Tupper's Company, it was attached to the 1st Regiment, South Carolina Militia Artillery.

Major Movements and Engagements

The Washington Light Infantry received what was probably the first military order given to Southern troops during the war when, on November 7, 1860, the governor ordered it to take possession of and guard the United States Arsenal in Cannonsboro, which held large military stores, including twenty-two thousand muskets. The Washington Light Infantry took possession about November 12 and remained until December 31, when it was relieved by the Union Light Infantry.[42] On December 27, portions of the Washington Light Infantry, the Meagher Guards and the Carolina Light Infantry were transferred to the garrisons at Fort Moultrie and Castle Pinckney. Thus began the movements of the 4th Brigade, South Carolina Militia, which, early in 1861, placed certain of its elements in positions to defend forts and islands in and around Charleston Harbor until the state's volunteer troops could be brought into service. By December 29, thirty members of the Washington Light Infantry had been moved from Castle Pinckney to Morris Island, leaving behind a garrison of more than a hundred men, including about sixty from the Washington Light Infantry, thirty-five Carolina Light Infantry men, thirty-five from the Meagher Guards and thirty artillerymen to protect Castle Pinckney.[43] The Washington Light Infantry was transferred to Morris Island in January 1861, leaving a detachment at Fort Moultrie.[44] The Zouave Cadets, the German Riflemen and the Vigilant Rifles also moved to Morris Island on January 1 to provide picket and construction services. These units were also infantry support for the Citadel Cadets who manned the artillery at Stevens's Battery during the incident with the *Star of the West* on January 9.[45] The Zouave Cadets left on January 15 and returned to Charleston.

The Moultrie Guard was ordered to Fort Johnson on James Island on January 18.[46] The Washington Light Infantry returned to the city on February 18, and the Meagher Guards also returned in mid-February after seven weeks at Castle Pinckney and Morris Island.[47] Eight companies were sent by steamer to Secessionville on February 26, and the regiment moved on March 8 to Moultrieville on Sullivan's Island, where it remained until April 10. The Carolina Light Infantry and the Meagher Guards were transferred to Sullivan's Island along with the regiment on March 8.[48]

The regiment was divided between the eastern end of Sullivan's Island and Castle Pinckney during the bombardment of Fort Sumter on April 12 and April 13. The Washington Light Infantry occupied Fort William Washington on Sullivan's Island but was not engaged during the bombardment.[49] The Zouave Cadets was based at "Myrtles" on Sullivan's Island from April 10 until it returned to the city on the twentieth.[50] On the evening of April 19, Colonel Jenkins's 5th Regiment, SCV, replaced the 1st Regiment Rifles, which returned to Charleston.

The regiment drilled at the Citadel Square and might have spent the summer of 1861 on Sullivan's Island. It was called out on September 12 to escort Federal prisoners captured at the battle of First Manassas to Castle Pinckney, a duty that lasted until October 20. From September 12 to September 20, the Zouave Cadets guarded Federal prisoners of war in the Charleston Jail. They also garrisoned Castle Pinckney from September 20 until sometime in October. By mid-December, the regiment was stationed at Rockville on Wadmalaw Island, where it was fired upon by Federal gunboats.[51]

Having been on duty continuously since November 9, 1860, the regiment was recalled to Charleston on February 6, 1862, to reorganize for twelve months of Confederate service under an act passed by the General Assembly on December 7, 1861.[52] It was ordered to reassemble on February 19 to reorganize into companies for Confederate service; any company with insufficient numbers would disband.[53] The Moultrie Guard re-enlisted for twelve months on February 12, 1862, with the intention of joining the Holcombe Legion, which was being raised at the time.[54] That plan failed, however, and the captain, B.W. Palmer, went on to command Company A of the 27th Regiment, SCV. The Zouave Cadets disbanded on February 12; most of its members enlisted in other companies. The *Mercury* reported on February 17 that eight of the regiment's companies were recruiting. They were: Washington Light Infantry Companies A and B, the Moultrie Guard, the Jamison Rifles, the Carolina Light Infantry, the Emerald Light Infantry, the Zouave Cadets and the Sarsfield Light Infantry. The three German companies of Charleston were also in the process of consolidating into one at that time.[55] The Sarsfield Light Infantry and the Emerald Light Infantry joined the Charleston Battalion on February 22, 1862, to become part of Company A.[56] On February 24, the regiment elected to combine the remnants of the 1st Regiment Rifles with the 17th Militia Regiment.[57]

THE 1ST REGIMENT, SOUTH CAROLINA MILITIA

The 1st Regiment, South Carolina Militia, was from Greenville District. Its two battalions were the Saluda Battalion, which mustered in service at Bates's Old Field, and the Tyger Battalion, which mustered at Bomar's Old Field.[58] Company H of the 22nd Regiment, SCV, which was organized on December 31, 1861, was composed of men from this regiment.

G.P. Pool was colonel of the regiment in January 1861.[59] W.P. Pool was elected major in March 1863.[60] W.H. Goodlett was colonel in July 1863.[61]

In July 1863, the beats, or companies, included Piney Mountain, Shockley's, Montgomery's, Bomar's, Macon's, Hodges's, Marietta and Potts's Cove. R.J. Smith commanded the Piney Mountain Company in March 1863, W.A. Beacham led Montgomery's Company and Stephen Powell commanded the Wood's Store Company.[62] Company A was commanded by James Anderson, and Company K was commanded by William Preston Thompson. Jefferson Barton was captain of a company in December 1861, and a Captain Jenkins commanded Company A.[63]

The 2nd Regiment, South Carolina Militia

The 2nd Regiment, South Carolina Militia, was from Pickens District. Daniel A. Ledbetter was colonel of this regiment before he became captain of Company A, Orr's rifles. Duncan was the lieutenant colonel.

The 3rd Regiment, South Carolina Militia

The 3rd Regiment, South Carolina Militia, was from Greenville District. In early January 1861, T.L. Bozeman was colonel.[64] The 1st Battalion met at Yeargin's Old Field, and the 2nd Battalion met at Moore's Old Field.[65]

The 4th Regiment, South Carolina Militia

The 4th Regiment, South Carolina Militia, was from Anderson District. C.S. Mattison was its colonel in early January 1861.[66] He later served as both lieutenant colonel of the 4th Regiment, SCV, and major of the 13th Battalion, SCV. G.F. Mosley was elected colonel about January 11, 1862.[67]

The 5th Regiment, South Carolina Militia

The 5th Regiment, South Carolina Militia, was from Pickens District. Joseph Massengale was elected colonel in January 1862. At the same time, L.N. Robbins was elected major of the Upper Battalion and H.C. Briggs was elected major of the Lower Battalion.[68] The only known captains were Olliver F. Smith of Beat Company #3 and William T. King of Beat

Company #4. Both Smith's and King's Companies were in the regiment's 1st Battalion.

The Pickensville Silver Greys was a Pickens District home guard company.[69] It was attached to the 1st Battalion of the 5th Regiment in June 1861.[70] Its captain was John Arial Sr.[71]

THE 6TH REGIMENT, SOUTH CAROLINA MILITIA

The 6th Regiment was from Abbeville District.

THE 7TH REGIMENT, SOUTH CAROLINA MILITIA

The Edgefield Riflemen, created by the General Assembly on January 28, 1861, was attached to the 7th Regiment, South Carolina Militia.[72] Whether this company is related to the Edgefield Rifles, Company C of Maxcy Gregg's six-month regiment, is unclear from the record.

Officers of the 7th Regiment, elected about February 19, 1862, were: Colonel David L. Shaw; major of the Upper Battalion Wilson L. Coleman; and major of the Lower Battalion John C. McDonald.[73] Coleman had served as captain of Company F, 7th Regiment, SCV, in May 1861.

In February 1863, beats of the 7th Regiment, South Carolina Militia, were: Hatcher's, Holsonback's, Horn's Creek, Turkey Creek, Graniteville, Haw Gap, Beech Island and Hamburg.[74]

Colonel John Bland commanded the regiment in January 1865. All its men between the ages of sixteen and sixty-five who were not already in service were ordered to rendezvous at Aiken on January 21, 1865.[75]

THE 8TH REGIMENT, SOUTH CAROLINA MILITIA

The 8th Regiment was from Abbeville District.

THE 9TH REGIMENT, SOUTH CAROLINA MILITIA

The 9th Regiment, South Carolina Militia, was from Edgefield District. Its colonel, J.W. Tompkins, resigned in March 1860.[76] Mat Moss, major prior to March 1860, was elected colonel in his place.[77] S.B. Blocker was elected colonel to replace Moss in March 1861.[78] B.M. Talbert was captain of the

Upper Battalion, and W.F. Prescott was captain of the Lower Battalion. In January 1862, G. Cheatham was elected colonel, J.A. Talbert was elected major of the Upper Battalion and R.D. Brunson was elected major of the Lower Battalion.[79] Beats were Rocky Road, Red Hill, Collins, Dantonsville, White House, Rehoboth, Longmires and Pleasant Lane.[80]

THE 10TH REGIMENT, SOUTH CAROLINA MILITIA

The 10th Regiment, South Carolina Militia, also called the Saluda Regiment, was composed of men from Edgefield District. A.B. Dean, its colonel, resigned in March 1860, and Lieutenant Colonel T.L. Smith was elected in his place.[81] At some point, J.L. Davis was lieutenant colonel in command, and G.D. Huiet was colonel of the regiment in July 1863.[82]

Beats were Briar Patch, Clover Spring, Joe Mays's, Videtto Spring, Huiet's, Rhinehart's, Mine Creek and Watery Branch.[83]

THE 11TH REGIMENT, SOUTH CAROLINA MILITIA

The 11th Regiment, South Carolina Militia, was from Barnwell District. In early February 1862, the men elected R.B. Wilson as colonel, J.L. Davis as major of the 1st Battalion and Gaines Ashley as major of the 2nd Battalion.[84] Captain S.S. Wise commanded one of its companies. Company K of the 2nd Regiment, South Carolina State Troops, was formed from the 11th Regiment.

THE 12TH REGIMENT, SOUTH CAROLINA MILITIA

The 12th Regiment, South Carolina Militia, was composed of men from Beaufort District.[85] John A. Tison of Beaufort was colonel, and a brother, Perry Hamilton Tison of Beaufort, was one of its majors.

THE 13TH REGIMENT, SOUTH CAROLINA MILITIA

The 13th Regiment, South Carolina Militia, was composed of men from Colleton District.

The Colleton Rifle Corps was commanded by Captain Robert Campbell. According to the *Mercury*, the Colleton Rifle Company had disbanded by

September 1862.[86] The rifle corps and the rifle company were probably the same company.

The St. Paul's Rifles, created by the General Assembly on January 28, 1861, was attached to the Lower Battalion of the 13th Regiment.[87]

The Palmetto Volunteers, a rifle company created by the General Assembly on January 28, 1861, was attached to the Independent Battalion of the 13th Regiment, South Carolina Militia.[88]

THE 14TH REGIMENT, SOUTH CAROLINA MILITIA

The 14th Regiment, South Carolina Militia, was composed of men from Orangeburg District. D.R. Barton was its colonel. Captain D.L. Dantzler's Company of the 14th Regiment formed Company C of the 2nd Regiment, South Carolina Sate Troops, in September 1863. The 14th was attached to Brigadier General John K. Jackson's Brigade in January 1865 along with the 1st Foreign Battalion, the Inglis Artillery and Captain Alfred J. Frederick's Company, South Carolina Militia.[89]

THE 15TH REGIMENT, SOUTH CAROLINA MILITIA

The 15th Regiment, South Carolina Militia, was composed of men from Orangeburg and Lexington Districts. Its colonel was D.J. Rumff, also shown as Rumph. He was captured either at Chesterfield on February 28 or Darlington on March 16, 1865, was taken to New Bern, North Carolina, on April 3 and was sent to Old Capitol Prison in Washington the same day. He was moved to Johnson's Island, Ohio, on the ninth and was released on July 25. J.H. Hydrick was major. Captain Bennett Tyler's company became Company G, 2nd Regiment, South Carolina State Troops. In addition, Company A of the 2nd Regiment, South Carolina State Troops, was formed from the 15th Regiment. These two companies were mustered in Confederate service for six months of local defense duty on August 1, 1863. The Lexington Rifle Company, also created by the General Assembly on January 28, 1861, was attached to the 15th Regiment, South Carolina Militia.[90]

THE 16TH REGIMENT, SOUTH CAROLINA MILITIA

The 16th Regiment, South Carolina Militia, was called the "Old Men's Regiment" by the *Mercury* because it was made up chiefly of Charleston's older men.[91] In July 1861, an inspection branded the regiment as a "farce" because, except for Captain Sigwald's Company, it had no uniforms, no weapons and no equipment.[92] Thus the 16th was viewed as the "laughingstock of the populace in contrast with the uniformed and volunteer regiments of the city" until C.H. Stevens took command in the summer of 1861.[93] Under his leadership, the regiment soon took shape and assumed a military bearing. The 16th provided a company to the 3rd Regiment, South Carolina State Troops, in 1863.

Field Officers

Robert A. Young, elected lieutenant colonel in July 1860, was elected colonel in September.[94] He served at that rank until at least December.

Clement Hoffman Stevens was colonel in command from just after the battle of First Manassas until he took command of the 24th Regiment in the winter of 1862.

S.C. DePass, a native of Camden, was lieutenant colonel in late 1861.[95] He was elected colonel on January 11, 1862.[96]

Jno. A. Bowie was elected major of the 2nd Battalion on September 27, 1861.[97] He was elected major of the 1st Battalion on January 11, 1862.[98]

Edward Emerick Sell was elected major of the 2nd Battalion on January 11, 1862.[99] He had served previously as lieutenant in Pendergast's Company.

Edward Magrath, elected colonel of the regiment on February 27, 1863, commanded the regiment until it was disbanded in September.[100]

William Whaley was elected lieutenant colonel on February 27, 1863.[101]

A.O. Andrews was elected major on February 27, 1863.[102]

Companies

Eight beats and two flanking companies made up the regiment.[103]

Eason's Company, Beat #1, was commanded by Fred W. Eason. First Lieutenant N. Sherhammer was elected captain on January 11, 1862.[104] On February 27, 1863, H. Slawson Jr. was elected captain.[105]

Triest's Company, Beat #2, was commanded by M. Triest in January 1862.[106] M. Brewton Pringle was elected captain on June 3, 1860, and W.R. Brailsford was elected on February 27, 1863.[107]

Robinson's Company, Beat #3, was commanded by S.A. Robinson. S.D. Kirk was elected captain on January 11, 1862.[108] On February 27, 1863, B.G. Happoldt was elected captain.[109]

Bancroft's Company, Beat #4, was commanded by J.W. Bancroft Jr., who resigned on November 18, 1861. D. Barrow was elected captain in January 1862.[110] On February 27, 1863, E.H. Locke was elected captain.[111]

Pendergast's Company, Beat #5, was commanded by Edward Pendergast.[112] He was re-elected on February 27, 1863.[113]

Steinmeyer's Company, Beat #6, was commanded by J.H. Steinmeyer Jr., who was elected captain on June 13, 1860.[114] On December 31, 1861, he became second lieutenant in Company A of the 24th Regiment, SCV, and later rose to the rank of captain. H.P. Fuegas was elected captain in January 1862.[115] J.H. Taylor was elected captain on February 27, 1863.[116]

Lawrence's Company, Beat #7, was commanded by E.P. Lawrence. William Ashton was elected captain in January 1862.[117] George S. Hacker was elected captain on February 27, 1863.[118]

Stile's Company, Beat #8, was commanded by C.W. Stiles.

The Jackson Guard, the left flanking company, was organized on April 24, 1861.[119] H.C. Burr was its first captain.[120] William H. Jones commanded the company after Burr.[121] Second Lieutenant J.M. Edwards was elected captain on January 11, 1862.[122]

The Marion Rifles was the right flanking company.[123] Its captain, Christian B. Sigwald, was elected on November 28, 1860.[124] Most of this company's men served later in Company A of the 24th Regiment, SCV. On April 24, 1861, the *Mercury* reported that the Marion Rifles had returned to the city after four months of duty at Fort Palmetto in the Stono Inlet. While attached to the 16th Regiment, this company built Fort Marion.[125]

According to the *Memory Roll*, Professor L.H. Charbonnier's Company, the Pickens Rifles or Pickens Guards, was detailed to the 16th Regiment as the right flanking company.[126] This was probably in November 1861, when the Pickens Rifles relieved the Jackson Guard at Regimental Headquarters, Camp Ripley.[127] The Jackson Guard was then posted to the Charleston Racecourse.

The *Mercury* printed a list of the current captains in January 1865: Edward P. Milliken commanded Company A, James T. Wellsman commanded Company B, W. Alston Pringle commanded Company C, John Dougherty commanded Company D and Peter B. LaLane commanded Company E.[128]

Brigade Affiliations

The 16th Regiment, South Carolina Militia, was part of the 4th Militia Brigade. The brigade's other components in July 1861 were the 17th, 18th, 19th, the 1st Regiment Rifles and the 1st Regiment Artillery.[129] By October, the 18th and 19th Regiments had been removed.[130]

Major Movements and Engagements

Companies 1 to 8, along with Sigwald's Company and the Jackson Guard, were based at Camp Charleston from November 9 to December 12, 1861, while in Confederate service. The regiment was disbanded on September 26, 1863, but later was apparently reorganized.[131]

THE 17TH REGIMENT, SOUTH CAROLINA MILITIA

The 17th Regiment, South Carolina Militia, also called the Charleston Regiment, was a heavy infantry unit composed of men between the ages of forty-five and sixty, all of them from Charleston. It was attached to the 4th Brigade, South Carolina Militia, which was organized on December 20, 1860.[132]

Field Officers

Richard DeTreville was elected colonel of the regiment on July 8, 1861.[133] An 1823 West Point graduate, he served first as a second lieutenant in the United States Army but resigned on April 30, 1825. DeTreville applied for promotion to brigadier general in April 1862 but was unsuccessful. He also served as colonel of the 1st Regiment, South Carolina Reserves.

John Cuningham, a Charleston lawyer who served as colonel of the 17th Regiment in late 1860 and early 1861, attempted unsuccessfully to raise a legion in 1861. He was also slated to become colonel of the Calhoun Rifle Regiment in November 1861, but the fate of this regiment is unknown.[134] He commanded Company K of the 3rd Regiment, South Carolina State Troops, in late 1863 and early 1864. Another man named John Cunningham, a purveyor from Savannah, commanded the 1st Regiment of Georgia Reserves in late 1864 and 1865.

William Pinckney Shingler served as lieutenant colonel of the 17th Militia before he was appointed lieutenant colonel of the Holcombe Legion on November 21, 1861.

James Jonathan Lucas was major of the 2nd Battalion of the 17th Regiment in 1860. He resigned on December 25 to become aide-de-camp to Governor Francis Pickens.[135] Lucas later served as major of the 15th Battalion, South Carolina Artillery.

Peter Charles Gaillard was elected lieutenant colonel on July 8, 1861.[136] Though the *Mercury* reported he had been elected colonel of the regiment in early September 1861, it corrected the rank to lieutenant colonel a month later.[137] Gaillard became major of the Charleston Battalion in April 1862 and colonel of the 27th Regiment, SCV, in October 1863.

Joseph Johnson Jr., captain of the Charleston Riflemen, was elected major on July 8, 1861, but declined to accept the position.[138]

John M. Harleston was major of the 17th Regiment in October 1861.[139]

Companies

The Charleston Riflemen was commanded by Joseph Johnson Jr. until he was elected major in July 1861.[140] The company was organized in 1806.[141] Julius A. Blake was elected captain on August 7, 1861.[142] Many members of the company enlisted in Company A of the 1st (Charleston) Battalion in February 1862.

The Irish Volunteers, composed of Irish Charlestonians, was organized in 1783.[143] It offered its services to South Carolina on September 16, 1860. Edward Magrath was captain in January 1861.[144] The company was part of the 17th Regiment in April 1861.[145] At a meeting of the Irish Volunteers on July 1, 1861, John Mitchel Jr. was elected captain of a new company, the "second company of Irish Volunteers of McCrady's Battalion."[146] Called the Magrath Rangers, it listed sixty-four men on the rolls, twenty-two fewer than it needed to muster in Confederate service.[147] Later in July, the Rangers and a new Charleston company called the Dixie Guards merged to join Maxcy Gregg's newly reorganized 1st Regiment, SCV. H.E. Young was captain of the Dixie Rangers, which had been accepted into Gregg's regiment if the company should reach full strength.[148] The Dixie Rangers never joined Gregg's regiment under that name, but it is possible that the Dixie Rangers and Dixie Guards was the same unit and merged with the Magrath Rangers to join Gregg's reorganized regiment under the name of the Irish Volunteers. Young is not listed as a captain in the *CSR*, and Mitchel was appointed as an officer in the 1st Battalion, South Carolina Artillery (Regulars). Still, the Irish Volunteers furnished two companies for Confederate service: Company K of Gregg's 1st (six-month) Regiment and Company C of the 1st (Charleston) Battalion, which later became Company H of the 27th Regiment.

The Cadet Rifles or Riflemen was organized in 1820.[149] E.M. Whiting was its captain in early 1860. William S. Elliott was elected captain about May 1860 and was still serving in early 1862.[150] Elliott died of disease sometime during the war.[151] The company was part of the 17th Regiment in April 1861.[152]

The Montgomery Guard or Guards was also composed of Irish Charlestonians.[153] James Conner was captain in early 1860.[154] The company was part of the 17th Regiment in April 1861.[155] A man named Brownfield was elected captain on September 2, 1861.[156] Though the company became part of the Charleston Battalion in February 1862, it did not retain its identity.

The Union Light Infantry, organized in 1812, was part of the 17th Regiment in April 1861.[157] David Ramsay was captain in the summer of 1861.[158] Many of its men mustered in Company F of the 1st (Charleston) Battalion in February 1862.

The German Fusiliers, organized in May 1775, was the oldest volunteer corps in South Carolina at the outbreak of the war. In 1834, it divided into two companies—the German Fusiliers and the Mounted German Fusiliers. The Fusiliers participated in the Seminole War in 1836, and certain individuals represented the company in the Palmetto Regiment during the Mexican War. Many of its members also volunteered in 1861 with other German Charlestonians to become Company H in the Hampton Legion. The militia company served with the 17th Regiment in and around Charleston Harbor in 1861. When the call for militia companies to enroll in Confederate service came in February 1862, many of the older fusiliers enlisted in home guard companies. The rest, too few to organize a company, were consolidated with members of the Union Light Infantry to form Company F of the Charleston Battalion.[159] Samuel Lord Jr. was captain of the German Fusiliers when it was part of the 17th Regiment.[160]

The Palmetto Guard, organized on June 28, 1851, was commanded by Thomas W. Middleton in 1860.[161] George Barnwell Cuthbert was elected captain on March 13, 1861.[162] After the bombardment of Fort Sumter, the Palmetto Guard was divided into two companies. About May 1, half its men volunteered to go to Virginia with Captain Cuthbert; they left about May 8 to become Company I of the 2nd Regiment, SCV.[163] The other half remained in Charleston under the command of Ensign George Lamb Buist, who was elected captain that summer.[164] Most of the men who remained behind mustered in an artillery battery known as the Buist Light Artillery, designated Company A, 18th Battalion, South Carolina Artillery, also called the South Carolina Siege Train.[165]

The Sumter Guards, also called the Gamecocks, reorganized twice in 1860, first in October and again in November.[166] The company was part of the 17th Regiment in April 1861.[167] John Russell was elected captain in January 1861 but resigned on May 8.[168] Henry C. King was elected in his place on the twentieth.[169] Many of the Sumter Guards became Company D of the 1st (Charleston) Battalion in February 1862.

The Highland Guards was attached to the regiment in April 1861 according to J.P. Thomas, but this information is not corroborated in the *Mercury*.[170]

The Emmet Volunteers, commanded by P. Grace, is not listed as part of the regiment in late April 1861.[171] Some may have joined the Irish Volunteers in Company K of Gregg's 1st Regiment, SCV, in late July 1861.[172]

The Calhoun Guards, or Guard, commanded by John B. Fraser in January 1861, was part of the 17th Regiment in April.[173] C.D. Barksdale was elected captain on June 5, 1861.[174] A.V. Dawson was elected captain on October 5, 1861.[175] Many of the Calhoun Guards became Company E of the 1st (Charleston) Battalion in February 1862.

The South Carolina College Cadets, commanded by E. Dawkins Rogers, was on duty in Charleston with the 17th Regiment from November 8 to December 10, 1862.

The Phoenix Rifles, or Riflemen, a company commanded by Peter Charles Gaillard on April 23, 1861, was part of the 17th Regiment that month.[176] Gaillard was elected lieutenant colonel of the regiment in July 1861, and Lewis F. Robertson was in command of the company in January 1862.[177]

The Richardson Guard, composed of members of the Palmetto Fire Company, was commanded by Captain J. Symons.[178] Organized at the time the state seceded, it was part of the 17th Regiment, South Carolina Militia.[179] The first captain of the Richardson Guard was John M. Pundt.[180] Its men named the company for D.F. Richardson, whom they elected captain on March 1, 1861.[181] The *Mercury* reported in late April that the Richardson Guard had been detached from the 17th Regiment and attached to Maxcy Gregg's 1st Regiment, SCV, as the right company.[182] Richardson resigned when the company volunteered for service with Gregg's regiment in Virginia about April 23, and Charles H. Axson was elected captain in his place.[183]

The Brooks Guards, or Brooks Home Guards, was organized on January 9, 1861, with John E. Carew as captain.[184] It was stationed on Morris Island until after the bombardment of Fort Sumter in April, and though it was part of the 17th Regiment as late as January 1862, it never again saw active duty. Most of its members were employed on the railroads during the war.[185] When Carew became ill, Andrew Burnet Rhett was elected captain on April 30, 1861.[186] A volunteer detachment, the Brooks Guard Volunteers, elected Rhett captain on May 8 and called for additional volunteers to serve in Virginia.[187] This unit left on May 12 and became Company K, 2nd Regiment, SCV. Another Rhett—Edmund—was elected captain of the militia company in September.[188]

The Jasper Greens, organized in mid-September 1861 by Charleston Irishmen, was attached to the 17th Regiment.[189] Its captain, M.P. O'Conner, was elected that month.[190] Thought the company became part of the Charleston Battalion in February 1862, it lost its identity in the process.

Brigade Affiliations

The 17th Regiment, South Carolina Militia, was attached to the 4th Brigade, South Carolina Militia.

Major Movements and Engagements

On December 27, 1860, the 17th Regiment, South Carolina Militia, was ordered to occupy the Charleston Arsenal.[191] The Union Light Infantry surrounded The Arsenal for three days and received its surrender on December 30.[192] The company then remained at The Arsenal to guard the site. The Palmetto Guard and the Calhoun Riflemen had alternated shifts with the Irish Volunteers and the German Fusiliers in guarding The Arsenal in late December.[193] The Charleston Riflemen garrisoned Fort Johnson in December 1860, and by January 11, the Palmetto Guard and the Irish Volunteers were moved to Morris Island.[194] The Montgomery Guards moved to Morris Island on the nineteenth to relieve the Vigilant Rifles, another 4th Brigade company raised from one of Charleston's volunteer fire departments. The Calhoun Guard, and probably also the Charleston Riflemen, was sent to garrison the Cannonsboro Arsenal in early February, and the Palmetto Guard was sent to the seashore in mid-March.[195]

Relieved of duty at the Cannonsboro Arsenal in mid-March, the Charleston Riflemen was sent to Battery Island in the Stono River on April 6 and remained there during the bombardment of Fort Sumter from April 12 to April 13.[196] The troops were relieved about April 27.[197] During the action at Fort Sumter, 15 Sumter Guards were at the Trapier Battery on Morris Island, and the Palmetto Guard was divided between the Iron Battery at Cummings's Point and the Point Battery, both also on Morris Island.[198] The rest of the Sumter Guard was at Stevens's (or the Iron) Battery.[199] Altogether, the 17th Regiment counted 418 men on Morris Island on April 11.[200] Elements of the Palmetto Guard occupied Fort Sumter after the battle.[201] The remainder of the regiment was based on Morris Island between Gadberry and Vinegar Hill in late April.[202] The 17th was relieved from duty on April 29 and returned to Charleston two days later.[203]

In September, the right wing of the regiment comprised the Cadet Riflemen, the Irish Volunteers, the Union Light Infantry, the Montgomery Guard and the Calhoun Guard.[204] The left wing was made up of the Charleston Riflemen, the German Fusiliers, the Palmetto Guard, the Phoenix Riflemen and the Sumter Guard.[205] The Palmetto Guard was sent to Coosawhatchie in the fall. According to the *Mercury*, the regiment was in

Confederate service in late September 1861 and at Rockville on Wadmalaw Island in late December.[206] The Palmetto Guard was stationed at Pocotaligo from February 7 to February 28. Under the terms of an act of the General Assembly passed on December 7, 1861, the regiment, had been recalled to Charleston for reorganization into a twelve-month volunteer regiment.[207] When the regiment returned to Charleston on February 6, 1862, it had been on duty continuously since November 9, 1860, with three months of active service.[208]

The *Mercury* reported in February that three Charleston militia regiments—the 16th, 17th and the 1st Regiment Rifles—would reorganize for twelve months of Confederate service dating from February 19.[209] Individual companies began to recruit in earnest. The Palmetto Guard, already in the field serving as artillery, re-enlisted for three years or for the duration of the war in April 1862. The Union Light Infantry, the Charleston Riflemen, the Sumter Guard, the Jasper Greens and the Cadet Riflemen were also recruiting as new artillery companies.[210] The three German infantry companies from Charleston chose to unite into a single corps. By late February, the Union Light Infantry, the Irish Volunteers, the Montgomery Guard and the Jasper Greens had chosen to join the newly created Charleston Battalion.[211] Eventually, the Charleston Riflemen, the Sumter Guard and the Calhoun Guard also joined the Charleston Battalion. The Montgomery Guard and the Jasper Greens, however, did not retain their identity in the Charleston Battalion. An election held on February 24, 1862, combined the remnants of the 17th Regiment with the 1st Regiment Rifles.[212]

THE 18TH REGIMENT, SOUTH CAROLINA MILITIA

The 18th Regiment, South Carolina Militia, composed of men from Charleston District, was "called into requisition" in December 1861. The regiment raised from its own ranks a company for the 3rd Regiment, South Carolina State Troops, in 1863.

Field Officers

Colonel Mellard and Lieutenant Colonel Moorer commanded the regiment in October 1861.[213]

Thomas D. Ledbetter was elected colonel on November 11, 1862. He had served as major of the Lower Battalion in 1860.[214]

D.C. Rhame was elected major of the Lower Battalion on November 11, 1862.

J.S. Murray was elected major of the Upper Battalion on November 11, 1862.[215]

John Edward Carew was elected colonel on April 4, 1863.[216] In January 1861, Carew had served as captain of the Brooks Home Guards, a company in the 17th Militia Regiment. He commanded the 3rd Regiment, South Carolina State Troops, for a time in 1863 and was elected sheriff of Charleston District in August 1863.[217] Carew commanded the 18th Regiment from April 1863 to at least January 1865.[218]

A.F. Browning, elected lieutenant colonel on April 4, 1863, took a leave of absence on July 14, 1864.

Alfred Shuler was elected major on April 4, 1863.[219] According to the *CSR*, however, Shuler was elected major on July 21 after having served as a private in Company D for ten days and as orderly sergeant for only one.

Companies

Company A was commanded by Robert May.[220]

Company B was probably commanded by a captain named Rumph.[221]

Company C, from St. George's Parish, was commanded by William M. Shuler, MD.[222]

Company D was commanded by John A. Varn.

Company E, the Dorchester Company, was commanded by Thomas Limehouse.[223] He was elected captain on November 30, 1862.[224]

Company F was probably commanded by John W. Hutto.

The Goose Creek Company was commanded by Captain D.C. Rhame in December 1861.[225] Carston William Vose also commanded the Goose Creek Company, probably after Rhame was elected major.

Brigade Affiliations

The regiment was part of the 5th Subdivision, 1st Military District in August and September 1863.

Major Movements and Engagements

The Goose Creek Company was on duty at Rantowles Bridge in December 1861.[226] The regiment was on duty in Charleston from late August to mid-September 1863.[227] It was disbanded on September 29, 1863.[228] The 18th Regiment, under the command of Colonel John Carew, was listed on the organization of troops for January 31, 1865.[229]

THE 19TH REGIMENT, SOUTH CAROLINA MILITIA

The 19th Regiment, South Carolina Militia, composed of men from Charleston, was called into requisition about December 1861. T.S. Marion was its colonel in early 1863.[230] Peter P. Bonneau was colonel from June 1863 until at least May 1864.[231] Julius T. Porcher was major of the Upper Battalion in 1861.[232] He served later as lieutenant colonel of the 10th Regiment. G. Manigault commanded Company A.

The regiment's headquarters was at Mount Pleasant in June 1863.[233] It was ordered to rendezvous at Bonneau's place on May 22, 1864.[234] The 19th Regiment was attached to A.M. Rhett's Brigade in late March 1865, along with the 1st Regiment, South Carolina Artillery; the 1st Regiment, South Carolina Infantry; the 19th Battalion, South Carolina Cavalry; the 1st Regiment, South Carolina Militia; Parker's Battery; and some Georgia units.[235]

THE 20TH REGIMENT, SOUTH CAROLINA MILITIA

The 20th Regiment, South Carolina Militia, was composed of men from Sumter. John B. Moore was its colonel in December 1861.[236] Jonathan Smythe Richardson, captain of Company D of the 2nd Regiment, SCV, in the spring of 1861, was elected major of the Western Battalion on May 9, 1861.[237] F.M. Mellett, captain of one of the regiment's companies, raised Company I, 4th Regiment, South Carolina State Troops, on August 1, 1863. Colonel George Washington Lee commanded the regiment in 1865.[238] The 20th Militia was ordered into active service on April 4, 1865, and about eighty of its men were engaged at Dingle's Mill near Sumter on the ninth.[239] W.B. Murray's Company was active in 1864 and 1865.

THE 21ST REGIMENT, SOUTH CAROLINA MILITIA

The 21st Regiment, South Carolina Militia, was composed of men from Lancaster District. James H. Witherspoon was elected its colonel on January 11, 1862.[240] Robert I. Gardner was elected major of the Lower Battalion. The election for major of the Upper Battalion ended in a tie between William Stevens and John J. Craig.[241] It appears that Craig finally assumed the position. On February 20, 1863, Captain John B. Cousart was elected major of the Upper Battalion, and Captain James D. McIlwain was elected major of the Lower Battalion.[242]

In September 1861, the beats were:[243]

Caskey's Beat #1—Captain James H. Kirk
Indian Land Beat #2—Captain J.W. Wolfe
Funderburk's Beat #3—Captain W.P. Plyler
Nesbit's Beat #4—Captain A.S. Nesbit, succeeded by Captain Joseph Rodgers
Lancasterville Beat #5—Captain H.R. Price, succeeded by Captain John B. Cousart
Gardner's Beat—Captain Robert I. Gardner
Belk's Beat—Captain J.M. Belk
Tank's Beat—Captain W.A. Bell
Stover's Beat—Captain T.G. Bell
Belair Beat—Captain James Miller
Witherspoon's Beat—captain unknown

In May 1862, the beats were:[244]

Upper Battalion Beat #1—Lieutenant Porter
  Beat #2—Lieutenant Wolfe
  Beat #3—Captain Plyler
  Beat #4—Captain Rodgers
  Beat #5—Captain Cousart
Lower Battalion Beat #1—Captain Phifer
  Beat #2—Captain Sowell
  Beat #3—Captain Bell
  Beat #4—Captain Magill

THE 22ND REGIMENT, SOUTH CAROLINA MILITIA

The 22nd Regiment, South Carolina Militia, was composed of men from Kershaw District. On January 11, 1862, Burrell Jones was elected colonel, William Dixon was elected lieutenant colonel and W.A. Ancrum was elected major.[245] Ancrum died later that year. In February 1863, Jones was still colonel, and William Dixon was still lieutenant colonel; but A.M. Kennedy, previously captain of Beat #2, had replaced Ancrum as major.[246] In July 1862, the 22nd Regiment, South Carolina Militia, raised a company, which became Company C of the 4th Regiment, South Carolina State Troops.[247]

On October 19, 1861, A.M. Kennedy was elected captain of Beat #2, and E. Parker was elected captain of Beat #1 at Cureton's Mills on the twenty-sixth.[248] By January 1862, W.E. Hughson (or Hugheson) was captain of Beat #2.[249]

In early February 1863, beats and their captains were:[250]

Beat #1—Lewis J. Patterson
Beat #2—John Thompson
Beat #3—R.R. Williams
Beat #4—John B. Mickle
Beat #5—W.E. Hughson
Beat #6—William Cato
Beat #7—S.B. Hall
Beat #8—John J. Nelson

THE 23RD REGIMENT, SOUTH CAROLINA MILITIA,

The 23rd Regiment, South Carolina Militia, was composed of men from Richland District. In 1860 its colonel was a man named Lorick and its major was a man named Wood.[251] At an election held on February 27, 1863, A.R. Taylor was elected colonel, C.R. Bryce was elected major of the Upper Battalion and Nathaniel Bynum was elected major of the Lower Battalion.[252] Thomas R. Brown was captain of a company in the 23rd that later became Company G, 4th Regiment, South Carolina State Troops, on August 1, 1863.

THE 24TH REGIMENT, SOUTH CAROLINA MILITIA

The 24th Regiment, South Carolina Militia, was composed of men from Fairfield District and was commanded by John McLurkin. One of its companies, Captain Barber's Chester Cavalry, enlisted at Fairfield. A comparison of the rolls shows that most of Barber's men served as part of Company H of the 4th Regiment, South Carolina State Troops, which mustered in Confederate service for local defense for six months from August 1, 1863, to February 1, 1864.

THE 25TH REGIMENT SOUTH CAROLINA MILITIA

The 25th Regiment, South Carolina Militia, was composed of men from Winnsboro in Fairfield District. Its colonel was C.W. Faucett. Some members of the 25th served as part of the 4th Regiment, South Carolina State Troops, which mustered in Confederate service for local defense from August 1, 1863, to February 1, 1864.

THE 26TH REGIMENT, SOUTH CAROLINA MILITIA

The Calhoun Guards, a "Volunteer Company of Light Infantry" from Chester District, and the Chester Rifles were created by the General Assembly on January 28, 1861, and were attached to the 26th Regiment.[253] The Calhoun Guards later mustered in the 6th Regiment, SCV, where it was designated Company A.

THE 27TH REGIMENT, SOUTH CAROLINA MILITIA

The 27th Regiment, South Carolina Militia, was composed of men from Chester District.

THE 28TH REGIMENT, SOUTH CAROLINA MILITIA

The 28th Regiment, South Carolina Militia, was composed of men from Chesterfield District. John C. Evans was captain of a company organized on July 7, 1863, at Chesterfield Court House that formed Company K of the 4th Regiment, South Carolina State Troops, on August 1, 1863.

THE 29TH REGIMENT, SOUTH CAROLINA MILITIA

The 29th Regiment, South Carolina Militia, called the Darlington Regiment, was composed of men from Darlington District.[254] The General Assembly created the Hartsville Light Infantry on January 28, 1861, and attached it to the Upper Battalion.[255] J.E. Wingate was elected colonel on January 11, 1862.[256] J.B. Nettles was elected major of the Upper Battalion, and J.S. Burch was elected major of the Lower Battalion on the same date.[257] David G. Wood was captain of one of the regiment's companies. This regiment formed Company E of the 4th Regiment, South Carolina State Troops, in August 1863.

THE 30TH REGIMENT, SOUTH CAROLINA MILITIA

The 30th Regiment, South Carolina Militia, was composed of men from Marlboro District. Nelson M. Gibson was captain of one of its companies.

THE 31ST REGIMENT, SOUTH CAROLINA MILITIA

The 31st Regiment, South Carolina Militia, was composed of men from Williamsburg and Georgetown Districts. As early as November 1860, some of the men from this regiment formed a company under John G. Pressley.[258] This company was the start of several more: the first two arising from Pressley's first company were the Wee Nee Volunteers, Company F of Maxcy Gregg's six-month regiment and Company E of the 10th Regiment, SCV. W.H. Whitfield was colonel of the 31st Regiment in May 1861.[259]

THE 32ND REGIMENT, SOUTH CAROLINA MILITIA

The 32nd Regiment, South Carolina Militia, was composed of men from Marion District. W.J. Cook was elected colonel on January 11, 1862.[260] A man named Peques was elected major of the Upper Battalion, and a man named Covington was elected major of the Lower Battalion on the same date.[261] D. McD. McLeod was elected colonel on February 4, 1863, even though he was on active duty as major of the 8th Regiment, SCV, at the time. W.J. Davis was captain of one of the regiment's companies. The 31st formed Company F of the 4th Regiment, South Carolina State Troops, in August 1863.

In July 1862, the captains were:[262]
Clough H. Mabry—Company #1
J.H. Vandyke—Company #2
J.J. McDowell—Company #3
William M. Grisham—Company #4

THE 33RD REGIMENT, SOUTH CAROLINA MILITIA

The 33rd Regiment, South Carolina Militia, was composed of men from Horry District.[263] It might have been attached to Harlee's Legion, South Carolina Militia, in late 1861. Elections for field officers were held on October 5, 1861.[264] Charles Allston Jr. was colonel of the regiment, and W.C. White was one of its majors.

The *Official Records* lists the following five companies as of April 3, 1861:[265]

The Waccamaw Light Artillery under Captain Daggett served as a coast guard from North Island to Murray's (Murrell's) Inlet.

The Watchesaw Riflemen under Captain Ward was stationed at Murray's (Murrell's) Inlet.[266]

The Carolina Greys patrolled from Murray's (Murrell's) Inlet to the redoubt at Little River on the North Carolina state line. The company was commanded by Captain T.W. Beaty in May 1861 and by Captain T.F. Gillespie in June.[267]

The All Saints Riflemen under Captain Litchfield was based at the redoubt called Fort Randall on Little River at the North Carolina state line.[268]

A Captain Johnson commanded a company based at the redoubt on the Santee River.

The *Horry Dispatch* lists the following nine companies and their commanders on October 3, 1861:[269]

Wachitaw Rifles was commanded by Captain Nesbit.

Bull Creek Rangers was commanded by Captain Samuel Smart.[270] Smart later commanded Company A of the 9th Battalion, South Carolina Infantry.

All Saints Rifles was commanded by Captain Bessant.

Conwayboro Palmetto Guards was commanded by Captain Malloy.

Cool Springs Home Guard was commanded by Captain Mishoe.

Blantons Cross Roads Volunteers was commanded by Captain Powell.

Floyd Guerillas was commanded by Captain Grainger.

Waccamaw Guerillas was commanded by Captain Todd.

Dog Bluff Home Guards was commanded by Captain Best.

THE 34TH REGIMENT, SOUTH CAROLINA MILITIA

The 34th Regiment, South Carolina Militia, was composed of men from York District. Major G.R. Burris was elected colonel in October 1861.[271] The regiment was reorganized, and new company officers were elected on August 20, 1864.[272] Captain John G. Enloe was elected colonel the following month, on September 16, 1864.[273]

THE 35TH REGIMENT, SOUTH CAROLINA MILITIA

The 35th Regiment, South Carolina Militia, was composed of men from Union District. In February 1862, James U. Goss was colonel, William Gowings was major of the Upper Battalion and Robert Knight was major of the Lower Battalion.[274]

THE 36TH REGIMENT, SOUTH CAROLINA MILITIA

The 36th Regiment, South Carolina Militia, was composed of men from Spartanburg District. Lieutenant Colonel William Bishop was elected colonel on October 10, 1861.[275] George Washington Hamilton Legg was elected colonel on December 28, 1862.[276] Legg had served as lieutenant colonel of the 5th Regiment, SCV, until the reorganization in the spring of 1862. On February 21, 1863, S.M. Snoddy was elected colonel, and Noah White and A.C. Bomar were elected as the two majors.[277]

Companies were the Morgan Rifles, the Spartanburg Light Infantry, Kendrick's Company, Boiling Springs Beat #1, the Johnson Volunteers, Buck Creek Beat #2, May's Old Field Beat, Cashville Beat, Lawson's Fork Volunteers, Pacolet Volunteers, Concord Beat and Hall's Beat #3.[278]

THE 37TH REGIMENT, SOUTH CAROLINA MILITIA

The 37th Regiment, South Carolina Militia, was composed of men from Spartanburg District. In early 1862, Rufus Poole was its colonel.[279]

THE 38TH REGIMENT, SOUTH CAROLINA MILITIA

The 38th Regiment, South Carolina Militia, was composed of men from Newberry District.

THE 39TH REGIMENT, SOUTH CAROLINA MILITIA

The 39th Regiment, South Carolina Militia, was composed of men from Newberry and Lexington Districts. Robert Clayton Maffett, colonel at the outbreak of the war, was elected captain of Company C of the 3rd Regiment, SCV, in April 1861. G.H. Chapman was captain of a company in the 39th Regiment. Two companies came from the 39th: Company C, 3rd Regiment, SCV, under Captain Maffett, and the Rhett Guards, under Captain Whitfield Walker, which became Company L in Maxcy Gregg's (six-month) 1st Regiment, SCV. After Gregg's regiment was reorganized, Walker's Company became Company B.

THE 40TH REGIMENT, SOUTH CAROLINA MILITIA

The 40th Regiment, South Carolina Militia, was composed of men from Laurens District.

THE 41ST REGIMENT, SOUTH CAROLINA MILITIA

The 41st Regiment, South Carolina Militia, was composed of men from Laurens District.

THE 42ND REGIMENT, SOUTH CAROLINA MILITIA

The 42nd Regiment, South Carolina Militia, was composed of men from Anderson District. James Long, its colonel, became captain of Company D, 4th Regiment, SCV, on April 14, 1861.

THE 43RD REGIMENT, SOUTH CAROLINA MILITIA

The 43rd Regiment was from Barnwell District.

THE 44TH REGIMENT, SOUTH CAROLINA MILITIA

The 44th Regiment, South Carolina Militia, composed of men from Clarendon District, was commanded by Colonel John O. Brock in 1862 and Colonel Thomas H. Connors in 1865.[280] About forty men of the 44th were engaged at Dingle's Mill on April 9, 1865, and elements of the regiment also saw action at Boykin's Mill on the eighteenth under Captain Conner.[281]

THE 45TH REGIMENT, SOUTH CAROLINA MILITIA

The 45th Regiment, South Carolina Militia, was composed of men from Union and Spartanburg Districts. S.M. Lanford was elected major of the Upper Battalion on February 23, 1861.[282]

THE 46TH REGIMENT, SOUTH CAROLINA MILITIA

The 46th Regiment, South Carolina Militia, was composed of men from York District. G.E.M. Steele was elected major of the Upper Battalion in October 1860.[283] J.H. Stewart was elected major of the "North" Battalion in early May 1861.[284]

CAVALRY UNITS

THE 1ST REGIMENT, SOUTH CAROLINA MOUNTED MILITIA

The 1st Regiment, South Carolina Mounted Militia, also called Martin's regiment, was raised in the fall of 1861 under a resolution of the South Carolina Convention dated January 1, 1861.[285] In February 1862, William E. Martin wrote that some, though not all, of its companies were formed under the resolution of 1861.[286] The regiment's term of service was scheduled to expire ten days after the next session of the General Assembly.[287] Brought together and called into Confederate service at Pocotaligo in early November 1861, the regiment was created just before the bombardment of Port Royal on the seventh.[288] At the same time, Brigadier General Roswell Ripley authorized Martin to raise additional companies.[289] The regiment was in the field from November 1861 until late January or early February 1862.[290] Its men, all of whom were mounted, were from Charleston, Beaufort, Colleton and Georgetown Districts. Though numerous, the companies were small—only 576 men were on the rolls as of December 27.[291] When the companies were disbanded in early 1862, Martin attempted, unsuccessfully, to raise a new regiment with companies of the 1st Mounted Militia as its nucleus. In late January 1862, the Secession Convention and the Executive Council passed a resolution requiring cavalry companies to be formed into squadrons, but Martin was allowed to recruit an entire regiment of cavalry. The Secession Convention also gave him extended time to muster in the troops. Eight companies were in camp with Martin at Pocotaligo by February 6, and he was in the process of recruiting two more to complete the regiment.[292] When he failed to fill the quota, the companies were either disbanded or turned into independent cavalry companies.

Field Officers

William Edward Martin was elected colonel of the regiment on September 14, 1861.[293] He had been captain of a company called the Charleston Mounted Guard in April and May 1861.[294]

Charles Jones Colcock was elected lieutenant colonel about October 2, 1861.[295] In May 1862, he was elected lieutenant colonel of the 2nd Battalion, Cavalry Reserves, which was also called the 8th Battalion, South Carolina Cavalry. When the 8th Battalion merged into the 3rd Regiment, South Carolina Cavalry, in August 1862, Colcock became colonel of that regiment.

Paul Pritchard was elected major about October 2, 1861.[296]

George Washington Oswald, commander of the Grey Riders of St. Bartholomew Parish, was also elected major about October 2, 1861.[297] He commanded a company, probably in the 3rd Regiment Junior Reserves, in 1864 and 1865.

Companies

The Dorchester Guerillas was also called A.C. Anderson's Company.[298] Its commander, A.C. Anderson, enlisted on November 8, 1861.

The Hardeeville Guerillas was also called John S. Blakewood's Company. Organized in June 1861, its men were from Purysburg and Hardeeville in Beaufort District.[299] Captain John S. Blakewood, who mustered in service along with the men on November 2, died of measles on January 5, 1862.[300] Some members of the company later served with the Calhoun Minute Men of the 8th Battalion, South Carolina Cavalry, and after that, served in Company E of the 3rd Regiment, South Carolina Cavalry.

The Parish Mounted Rangers was also called the Parish Rangers and Captain John Christopher's Company.[301] Its men, from St. James, Goose Creek Parish, in Charleston District, elected John Christopher captain on June 26, 1861.[302] The company mustered in service about November 10 but was relieved of duty on February 13, 1862, by special order from headquarters of the Department of South Carolina, Georgia and Florida.

The Marion Troop was also called Captain Earnest's Company.[303] John B. Earnest was its captain, and the men were from Colleton District.[304] A company of the same name from St. John's Berkeley was commanded by Captain Thomas W. Easterling in July 1861.[305] R.J. Jeffords defeated Easterling in the election for major of the 6th/17th Battalion, South Carolina Cavalry, in April 1862—see 1st Regiment, South Carolina Militia. The *Mercury* reported on two companies—the Marion Rangers and the Marion Scouts—in October 1861. Whether or not either was connected to this company is unclear.[306] Some of the men later served in Company A of the 6th/17th Cavalry Battalion and, later still, in Company D of the 5th Regiment, South Carolina Cavalry.

The Palmetto Rangers was also called Captain H.D. Evans's Company.[307] Its men were from Barnwell District.[308] Hansford D. Evans, who commanded the company, enlisted at Williston on November 16, 1861, when the company was organized. The Palmetto Rangers was soon stationed at Pocotaligo.[309] The company served in the 1st Regiment Mounted Militia from November 16, 1861, to February 7, 1862. Since the men were not allowed to spend their unexpired term in Confederate service, the company probably disbanded at that time.[310] The Palmetto Rangers was one of the eight companies willing to serve if Colonel Martin could raise a new regiment.[311] Some of its men may have served later in Company C, also called Company B, of the 10th Battalion, South Carolina Cavalry.

The St. Helena Mounted Rifles, also called the St. Helena Volunteer Mounted Riflemen and Captain O.P. Fripp's Company, existed as early as September 19, 1861.[312] William Oliver Perry Fripp, who enlisted on November 4 at St. Helena Island in Beaufort District, commanded the small company. Its men mustered in Confederate service the same day for twelve months of local service as vedettes on St. Helena Island. John Peyre Thomas wrote that St. Helena's planters, a mere handful of about thirty men who paid for their own equipment, arms, uniforms, accoutrements and horses, made up the company.[313] During the battle of Port Royal on November 7, the men stood ready with their slaves, boats and flats at Fort Beauregard at Bay Point on Hunting Island and evacuated R.G.M. Dunovant's 12th Regiment after the defeat there. Members of the company lost everything they owned on St. Helena Island after that battle. While based at Pocotaligo Station on January 4, 1862, the St. Helena Mounted Rifles were mustered out of service "by reason of the insufficiency of the members to enable it to hold its rank as a company."[314] The men scattered, most becoming attached to other commands.

The Salkehatchie Guerillas was also called Captain Green's Company and the Saltketcher Guerillas.[315] W. Glenn Green was captain, and the men were from Colleton District.[316]

Heyward's Company, from Charleston District, was commanded by William E. Martin in April 1861 when the company was called the Charleston Mounted Guard.[317] Martin retained command until at least September.[318] Captain George Cuthbert Heyward took over no later than January 1862, but more likely in September 1861, when Martin was elected colonel of the regiment. Some members subsequently served in C.J. Colcock's Company, which was organized on February 26, 1862, and mustered in for the duration of the war on March 12. They became the Ashley Dragoons in the 8th Battalion, South Carolina Cavalry, in May, and in August, they became Company H of the 3rd Regiment, South Carolina Cavalry. This company should not be confused with D.B. Heyward's Company, the Marion Men of Combahee.

The Savannah River Guards was also called T.H. Johnson's Company. Its men were from Barnwell District.[319] Thomas H. Johnson, who enlisted with the men on November 9, 1861, commanded the company. After the 1st Regiment, South Carolina Mounted Militia, disbanded in late January 1862, most of the guards re-enlisted for Confederate service on the twenty-seventh, choosing Johnson's independent cavalry company. The Savannah River Guards was one of those companies willing to serve if Colonel Martin raised a new regiment in early February.[320] The men re-enlisted for the duration of the war on April 2, 1862; in May, the Savannah River Guards joined the 8th Battalion, South Carolina Cavalry, as Company F, and in August, it became Company K, 3rd Regiment, South Carolina Cavalry. A.B. Estes was promoted to captain in the 8th Battalion after Johnson became major.

The May River Troop from Beaufort District was also called M.J. Kirk's Company. It may have been the same as the Bluffton Troop commanded by J.W.R. Pope.[321] Manning J. Kirk, who enlisted at Hardeeville on November 2, 1861, commanded the company, which mustered in service the same day and out again on January 31, 1862. It was another of the eight companies willing to serve if Martin had been successful in raising a new regiment.[322] Some of its men subsequently served in the Ashley Dragoons of the 8th Battalion and in Company H of the 3rd Regiment, South Carolina Cavalry. Some, including Captain Kirk, enlisted in Kirk's Company, South Carolina Partisan Rangers, on July 11, 1862, and subsequently served in Company A of the 19th Battalion, South Carolina Cavalry

The Calhoun Minute Men was also called A.M. Martin's Company. Another, this one called the Red Oak Rangers and also commanded by Captain Martin, was part of the regiment in January 1861. It was probably the same company.[323] The Calhoun Minute Men existed as early as December 10, 1860.[324] Its men, from the upper part of St. Peter's Parish in Beaufort District, mustered in service on November 15, 1861; Alfred Maner Martin, who enlisted the same day, was its commander. This company, too, was willing to serve if Colonel Martin's new regiment had materialized in February 1862.[325] Instead, it mustered out of service on February 15 from its base along the May River. The majority of the men re-enlisted on March 30 for the duration as an independent company called, simply, Captain Martin's Company. It mustered in the 8th Battalion, South Carolina Cavalry, in May 1862 and became Company E, 3rd Regiment, South Carolina Cavalry, in August.

The St. Paul Rangers, also called E.B. Scott's Company, was made up of men from Colleton District.[326] Scott, who enlisted on November 21, 1861, was its commander.[327] The company mustered in service the same day and out again on February 6, 1862.

The Beaufort District Guerillas, also called J.H. Screven's Company, mustered in service on September 7, 1861. It was probably also called the Coosawhatchie Guerillas.[328] John H. Screven, who enlisted at Coosawhatchie the same day, was its commander. The company was organized on July 12, 1861, as a mounted rifle corps for home and coast defense within the limits of the Eutaw Beat of the 12th Regiment, South Carolina Militia, in Beaufort District.[329] The company mustered out of service on January 9, 1862.

The St. Peter's Guards was commanded by Henry C. Smart. Its men, from St. Peter's Parish in Beaufort District, mustered in service on November 5, 1861, at Hardeeville.[330] They mustered out of the 1st Mounted Regiment on January 31, 1862. Many re-enlisted on April 4, 1862, for the duration of the war as an independent company called Captain Smart's Company, South Carolina Cavalry. In August 1862, it became Company F, 3rd Regiment, South Carolina Cavalry. A typical pattern followed by many companies that had served in the disbanded 1st Regiment, South Carolina Mounted Militia, was to re-enlist in the 8th (2nd) Battalion in May and in the 3rd Regiment in August 1862. The St. Peter's Guards, however, served in the 3rd Regiment but was never attached to the 8th Battalion.

The Beech Hill Rangers, also called Wheeler G. Smith's Company, was made up of men from Colleton District. It mustered in service on November 12, 1861, at Pocotaligo.[331] The company, which mustered out on January 31, 1862, near Bluffton, was another of those willing to serve if Colonel Martin's new regiment had materialized.[332] Some of its men enlisted in Company D, 17th Battalion, which became Company C, 5th Regiment, South Carolina Cavalry, in April 1862, while others chose Company A of the 17th Battalion, which became Company D of the 5th Cavalry Regiment.

The Etiwan Rangers was commanded by Keating Simons Sr.[333] Since most of its members were overseers and were paid only if called out, this Charleston company was raised for special service from January 31 to February 4, 1862, at Heyward's Landing on James Island.[334]

The South Carolina Rangers, a company of Charleston men commanded by Robert Josiah Jeffords, existed as early as November 6, 1860. The men re-enlisted in June 1861 as local defense troops serving in the militia.[335] The company probably entered state service on November 6, 1861.[336] After the regiment disbanded in early February 1862, most of the Rangers re-enlisted on the seventeenth for twelve months of Confederate service. Initially an independent company, within a few weeks it had become Company A of the 6th (later the 17th) Battalion, South Carolina Cavalry, and in January 1863, it became Company D, 5th Regiment, South Carolina Cavalry.[337]

The Marion Men of Combahee was raised in December 1860 by the first captain, Dr. W.L. Henderson. Its men were mostly from Colleton District, with a few from the part of Beaufort District that is now Hampton County. In the summer of 1861, Governor Pickens retained the company in South Carolina as a coast guard.[338] Henderson, along with six others anxious for immediate service in Virginia, volunteered to muster with the Beaufort District Troop in the Hampton Legion.[339] His departure having prompted a new election for captain of the company, the men elected Daniel Blake Heyward on July 7, 1861. Henderson became the second sergeant of the Beaufort District Troop.[340] The company was called into service in November 1861 in Martin's regiment and would willingly have served if he had been successful in raising a new regiment a few months later.[341] The company was reorganized on March 19, 1862, its men enlisting unconditionally for the duration of the war.[342] In May 1862, it became Company B of the 8th Battalion, and in August it became Company A of the 3rd Regiment, South Carolina Cavalry.

The Palmetto Hussars, commanded by A. Smith Barnwell, was made up of men from Beaufort District.[343]

The Bluffton Troop, commanded by J.W.R. Pope, may have been another name for the May River Troop.

The St. Paul Home Guard, or St. Paul Mounted Men, was commanded by Hawkins C. King.[344] His middle initial might have been S. Its men, from St. Paul's Parish in Colleton District, entered service on November 27, 1861, and served as mounted guards at the Edisto Ferry.[345]

The Colleton Rangers was commanded by Captain Archibald Lawrence Campbell. Many of its men re-enlisted for the duration of the war as an independent company on March 26, 1862. The company mustered in the 8th Battalion in May and in August became Company B of the 3rd Regiment, South Carolina Cavalry.

The Grey Riders of St. Bartholomew Parish, also called the Colleton Grey Riders, was from St. Bartholomew District.[346] George Washington Oswald commanded the company in October 1861 and was elected major that month. Four months earlier, in June, he had commanded a company called the Walterboro Home Guard. Oswald was later promoted to major of the 1st Regiment Mounted Militia.[347] The relationship of these two companies is unclear. Probably, the Walterboro Home Guard simply evolved into the Grey Riders, though the fate of the Riders is also murky. Possibly it was disbanded when Oswald became major. Some Grey Riders served in the South Carolina Rangers in the same regiment.[348]

William F. Percival's Company, also called the Pickens Rangers, was from Aiken in Barnwell District. It was one of the eight willing to serve if Martin had been able to raise a new regiment in February 1862.[349] Percival's Company mustered in service on November 15, 1861, and was disbanded in late February 1862.[350] Percival raised a new company in 1864.

The Allendale Mounted Guard under the command of Captain William M. Bostick was probably in the 1st Regiment, Mounted Militia.[351] Bostick raised the company in Beaufort and Barnwell Districts not long before it was ordered to Pocotaligo on November 8, 1861. It was part of the coastal defenses until it was disbanded in February 1862. Though the company reorganized for twelve months in February, its eventual fate is unknown.[352] Bostick's Company was one of the eight remaining in camp with Colonel Martin in February 1862 as he worked to recruit a new regiment.[353]

Brigade Affiliations

Martin's regiment served in Drayton's Brigade.

Major Movements and Engagements

Martin's regiment was called into service in early November 1861 to prepare for the anticipated invasion at Port Royal. Most of its companies served at or near Port Royal Ferry for their entire existence, performing picket duty in the area until they were disbanded. Some served elsewhere along the coast. The Beaufort Guerrillas was at Bay Point Island on November 7, 1861.[354] The Calhoun Minute Men was based on the South May River from November 15 to February 15, 1862.[355] The Hardeeville Guerrillas was stationed at Bluffton from November 2 to January 31, and the Dorchester Guerillas were at James Island and Stallsville from November 8 to January 8. The Parish Mounted Rangers served at St. James Goose Creek from November 10 to January 6 before moving to the fortifications on the Charleston neck until February 13, 1862. The Marion Troop was stationed at Camp Colcock from November 10 to January 7, and the St. Helena Mounted Rifles was at Port Royal Ferry from November 4 to January 4. Though the latter was engaged at the battle of Port Royal, it is unclear as to whether other companies of Martin's regiment saw action there. At least one company, the South Carolina Rangers, was stationed at Green Pond in November and December 1861.[356]

The regiment was based near Port Royal in mid-December.[357] A detachment of forty-two men, possibly Percival's Company, was engaged at Port Royal Ferry on January 1, 1862, but, acting primarily as pickets and vedettes, the unit suffered no casualties.[358] The regiment served at Bluffton along the Combahee, Ashepoo and Edisto Rivers, and in the Charleston area during its service.

Many companies of Martin's regiment mustered out of service on January 31, 1862, while at Camp Hartstene in the 5th Military District; some, however, mustered out as late as mid-February. Later the same month, the *Mercury* announced that eight companies of the 1st Mounted Militia Regiment were in camp at Pocotaligo preparing to muster in a new regiment.[359] This announcement refers to the regiment that Colonel Martin attempted to build around a nucleus of existing units from his old command. He failed partly because he was unable to increase the size of the small independent companies to fulfill the requirements of a cavalry regiment.[360] After the 1st Regiment Mounted Militia was disbanded and Martin's plan failed to materialize, two companies dissolved, leaving their men to enlist individually in other units. Other companies remained relatively intact and joined other commands as a group. Four companies joined the 8th (2nd) Cavalry Battalion, and one joined the 17th Battalion. Though the fate of one—Bostick's Company—is unknown, the record accounts for what happened to seven others: D.B. Heyward's, T.H. Johnson's, M.J. Kirk's and A.M. Martin's Companies entered the 8th Battalion, and Smith's Company joined the 17th Battalion; Percival's disbanded, and Evans's probably followed the same course.

THE 3RD REGIMENT, SOUTH CAROLINA CAVALRY, MILITIA

The 3rd Regiment, South Carolina Cavalry, Militia, was commanded by Colonel Joseph Hargrove Morgan, MD, in 1860.[361] In 1861, he served as a private in S.D. Lee's Battery and was slightly wounded in the hand.[362] Morgan later commanded the 14th Battalion and became major in the 5th Regiment, South Carolina Cavalry, on January 18, 1863. The regiment was from Lexington, Orangeburg and Barnwell Districts.

THE 4TH REGIMENT, SOUTH CAROLINA CAVALRY, MILITIA

The 4th Regiment, South Carolina Cavalry, Militia, existed as early as December 1860.

Field Officers

Colonel C.S. Edwards commanded the regiment. W.B. Ryan served as lieutenant colonel, and a man named Farr was major.[363]

Companies

Company C, the Beaufort District Troop or Beaufort Troop and also called Captain John H. Howard's Company, served as volunteers from November 4, 1861, to March 27, 1862. Most of its members enlisted for the duration on March 27 and became Company D (later Company C) in the 3rd Regiment, South Carolina Cavalry. The troop was composed mostly of Beaufort District men, though a few came from Barnwell District, and even Texas was represented. This company is not the same as Company B of the 2nd Regiment, South Carolina Cavalry, though the names were the same. Sixty-one-year-old John H. Howard was its only captain in the 4th Regiment, South Carolina Militia.[364]

John E. Tobin was captain of a squadron of mounted men called the Hammond Huzzars, or Hussars.[365] William Stokes took command of these men from Orangeburg, Beaufort, Colleton and Barnwell Districts sometime in 1861. The company was stationed at Pineville in September, at Walterboro in November and at Bluffton in December 1861. Sent to Camp Hampton near Columbia on January 15, 1862, the Hussars mustered in Confederate service as part of the new 2nd (3rd) Battalion on the nineteenth. Apparently the company changed its name to the Evans Light Dragoons then, probably because only some of its men enlisted in the battalion. Stokes retained command after the Hussars/Dragoons became Company D of the 2nd (3rd) Battalion, a designation the company kept until the reorganization, when it was changed to Company C of the 3rd Battalion. When the 3rd Battalion was itself redesignated the 10th Battalion in September 1862, the company retained its designation as Company C. The Evans Light Dragoons became Company G of the 4th Regiment, South Carolina Cavalry, in December 1862. John E. Tobin had tried to raise a company called the Barnwell District Troop in August 1861, but the fate of this company is unknown.[366] The Hammond Hussars should not be confused with an Edgefield cavalry company commanded by Captain A.J. Hammond.[367]

Other companies were the Charleston Light Dragoons, the German Hussars, the McDonald Troop, the Marion Troop, the Palmetto Troop, the Wassamassaw Troop and the Combahee Troop. The Combahee Troop may have been the same as the Combahee Rangers commanded by Captain T.J. Allen and accepted for police duty and other state service by the Executive Council on May 26, 1862.[368] Some of these troops served later in various cavalry units. The Charleston Light Dragoons eventually served in the 4th Regiment, South Carolina Cavalry, and the German Hussars served with the 3rd Regiment. The Marion Troop, Beaufort Troop and probably Combahee Troop served in the 1st Regiment, Mounted Militia. The Palmetto Troop might have merged into Company G of the 4th Regiment; the Hammond Hussars became Company C of the 10th Battalion, and the Wassamassaw Troop probably became Company D of the 2nd Regiment. The fate of the McDonald Troop is unknown.

The 4th Regiment, South Carolina Militia, was called out for active duty on November 20, 1861, and served on the South Carolina coast at Bluffton.[369]

THE 10TH REGIMENT, SOUTH CAROLINA CAVALRY, MILITIA

The 10th Regiment, South Carolina Cavalry, Militia was commanded by Colonel J.S. Johnson.

ARTILLERY UNITS

THE 1ST REGIMENT ARTILLERY, SOUTH CAROLINA MILITIA

The 1st Regiment Artillery, South Carolina Militia, was also called the 1st South Carolina Militia Artillery.[370] It was attached to the 4th (Charleston) Brigade, South Carolina Militia, commanded by a Charlestonian, Brigadier General James Simons, from 1858 to July 10, 1861. W.G. DeSaussure assumed command of the 4th Brigade in August 1861. According to the *CSR*, many men of the 1st Regiment enlisted in Confederate service in mid-September 1861, and a number of artillery companies from the 1st Regiment re-enlisted between February and June 1862. The regiment remained in service until it was finally disbanded on September 26, 1863, and its eligible men mustered in other commands.[371]

Field Officers

E.H. Locke was elected colonel of the 1st Artillery Regiment on February 18, 1860. He either retained the rank or was re-elected in April 1861, but he resigned in mid-July.[372] Locke may have served again as lieutenant colonel in February 1862.

Wilmot Gibbs DeSaussure of Charleston, lieutenant colonel of the regiment in mid-November 1860, was re-elected in April 1861.[373] He commanded the artillery on Morris Island during the bombardment of Fort Sumter that month and was either promoted or elected colonel of the regiment in July 1861 when Locke resigned.[374] DeSaussure was elected brigadier general of the South Carolina Militia and commander of the 4th Brigade in late August 1861.[375]

John Andreas Wagener, a German immigrant who settled in Charleston, was major of the regiment in mid-November 1860. Wagener had been captain of Charleston's German Artillery from 1847 to 1859, when it was divided into a battalion of two companies under Wagener's command at the rank of major. He either retained the rank or was re-elected major of the 1st Regiment in April 1861.[376] Wagener was probably promoted to lieutenant colonel on July 24, 1861, when DeSaussure replaced Locke as colonel.[377] On September 5, 1861, he was elected colonel of the 1st Militia Artillery Regiment, replacing DeSaussure.[378] Wagener supervised the construction of Fort Walker at Port Royal. He was wounded while commanding the batteries there during the battle on November 7, 1861. Wagener was promoted to brigadier general of militia in 1863 or 1864.[379]

Clelam K. Huger Sr. was elected major of the regiment in April 1861, thus giving the regiment two majors, Huger and Wagener, at the same time.[380] It was typical at the time for South Carolina Militia regiments to have both a senior and a junior major simultaneously. In the 1st Artillery Regiment, one of the two probably commanded the artillery component and the other the infantry and cavalry companies. Huger had been captain of the Rutledge Mounted Riflemen before his election to major. He was elected lieutenant colonel about September 5, 1861, soon after DeSaussure's promotion to brigadier general.[381] Huger was promoted to major in the Confederate States Provisional Army on June 4, 1862, was assigned as an assistant ordnance officer on October 13, 1863, and became chief of ordnance on September 14, 1864. He held a number of positions as an artillery officer in the Department of South Carolina, Georgia and Florida. On March 27, 1865, Huger still held the rank of major as chief of ordnance in Hardee's corps. His son, Clelam K. Huger Jr., a second lieutenant in Company E of the 1st Regiment, South Carolina Artillery (Regulars), died of heart disease on February 26, 1864.

Arthur M. Huger, previously captain of the Marion Artillery, was elected major of the regiment about September 5, 1861.[382] He surrendered at Greensboro in April 1865.

Companies

The *CSR* lists three companies: Company A, commanded by Jacob Small, Company B and Company C, commanded by W.S. Henery. The latter was probably the Washington Artillery. The *Mercury*, however, consistently listed five artillery companies, one infantry company and one cavalry troop attached to the 1st Regiment Artillery, South Carolina Militia, though it never assigned letter designations.[383]

Company B of the German Artillery was also called both Harms's Company, 1st Regiment South Carolina Militia Artillery, and the German Flying Artillery.[384] It had been organized by a group of young Germans in 1841 to join General Sam Houston in Texas.[385] Houston was elected president of Texas, and hostilities there ended before the German Artillery could complete its preparations. Once organized, it became part of the 1st Regiment Artillery, South Carolina Militia. Years later, in 1859, the German Artillery expanded into a battalion made up of Company A and Company B. A group of German Artillery men volunteered for Confederate service, mustering in on August 22, 1861, for five years as the German Volunteers of Charleston. Shortly thereafter, this group became Company B, Hampton Legion Artillery Battalion. Meanwhile, many of the men remained in the militia battalion. Company B of the German Artillery Battalion, South Carolina Militia, was commanded by Captain Henry Harms from 1859 until his resignation on June 5, 1862.[386] The exact date of Company B's enlistment in Confederate service is unclear. The *Confederate Military History Series* records that the German Artillery Company B enlisted on February 12, 1862, and John P. Thomas adds that this enlistment was for the duration of the war.[387] According to the *CSR*, however, Harms's Company mustered in on April 1 for twelve months while stationed at Fort Chapman on the Ashepoo River. Accounts in the *Mercury* differ in several respects. It says, for instance, that about June 5, 1862, most of the men of Company B, the German Artillery Battalion, enlisted in Confederate service as Captain Franz Melchers's Company, South Carolina Artillery (discussed under independent artillery organizations).[388] Melchers's Company subsequently became Company B, German Artillery, SCV, made up mostly of men from Charleston, along with some from Aiken in Barnwell District and a few from Darlington and Georgetown Districts.

Company A of the German Artillery Battalion was also called Didrich Werner's Company, 1st Regiment South Carolina Militia Artillery. Carsten Norhden was elected captain of the company on August 17, 1860.[389] He died at his home in Charleston on August 23, 1861, from an illness contracted after exposure on Morris Island.[390] Didrich Werner, who succeeded Norhden as captain, was wounded in the mouth at the battle of Port Royal on November 7, 1861.[391] According to John P. Thomas, Company A enlisted in Confederate service on February 12, 1862.[392] The record also shows that the company mustered in as Captain Didrich Werner's Company, South Carolina Light Artillery, in June 1862. Following Werner's resignation on March 24, 1863, Captain F.W. Wagener commanded the company; Wagener's Company was later designated Company A, German Artillery, SCV. Most of its men came from Charleston, but some were from Aiken in Barnwell District and from Anderson, Pickens, Lexington and Orangeburg Districts.

The Marion Artillery was later called Captain Edward L. Parker's Company, 1st South Carolina Militia Artillery. Originally composed of Charlestonians, this company was created in 1843.[393] When it was reorganized on September 9, 1861, some men from Georgetown and Kershaw Districts were added, and a few came from Greenville, Richland, Clarendon, Sumter, Abbeville and Pickens Districts. John Gadsden King was the first captain in 1860 and 1861.[394] He resigned in mid-July 1861, not long before receiving an appointment as captain of Company F, 1st Regiment, South Carolina Artillery (Regulars), in October.[395] Arthur M. Huger was elected captain as King's successor in July.[396] When he was elected major of the regiment about September 5, Edward L. Parker was either promoted or elected captain on September 9. The men re-enlisted that month for the duration of the war.[397] A comparison of rolls shows that on June 6, 1862, the majority of members of the Marion Artillery subsequently mustered into Confederate service for the duration of the war as an independent artillery organization known as Captain Edward L. Parker's Company, Marion Artillery, SCV.

The Lafayette Artillery was commanded by Captain J.J. Pope Jr. as early as April 1860.[398] The company had been organized in April 1812 as the Artillery Francais.[399] Originally, most of the men were from Charleston, though later some from Beaufort and York Districts were added. The company, which enlisted in service about September 17, 1861, served as heavy artillery from December 1860 to December 1861, when it converted to light artillery. During February 1862, the company was reorganizing under Captain Pope in preparation for re-enlisting for the duration of the war.[400] The men, however, unanimously elected First Lieutenant John T. Kanapaux, and not Pope, as their captain on February 26, 1862.[401] A comparison of the rolls shows that a number of members of this company subsequently served in Captain John T. Kanapaux's Company, the Lafayette Light Artillery, which mustered in Confederate service for three years on March 13, 1862.[402]

The Washington Artillery of Charleston was organized in 1844 and served in the Palmetto Regiment during the Mexican War.[403] It was part of the 1st Regiment Artillery, South Carolina Militia, when the regiment was called to active duty on December 27, 1860. Designated Company C in the 1st Militia Regiment, it was commanded by Captain George H. Walter as early as July 6, 1860. When Virginia seceded from the Union, eighteen Washington Artillery Militia men volunteered for service and became the nucleus of the Washington Artillery Volunteers, which in turn became Battery A of the Hampton Legion in May 1861.[404] After the eighteen volunteers left for the Hampton Legion, the original Washington Artillery Militia continued to exist as a light artillery battery in the 1st Regiment, South Carolina Artillery Militia.[405] This battery mustered in service on February 20, 1862, for three years or for the duration of the war as Captain Walter's Company, South Carolina Light Artillery, which was also called the Washington Artillery.[406] Two companies thus arose from the ranks of the Washington Artillery Militia for Confederate service. The original members of the Washington Artillery Militia were from Charleston, while the rest of Captain Walter's Company came from Barnwell, Georgetown, Colleton, Winnsboro and Orangeburg Districts and from Augusta, Georgia. After Walter's Company left the regiment, the Washington Artillery apparently continued to exist as a militia company under the command of Captain William S. Henery.

The Vigilant Fire Engine Company formed the Vigilant Rifles, or Vigilant Light Infantry, in November 1860.[407] The men elected Samuel Y. Tupper as their captain. One of several Charleston fire companies in the 4th Brigade, the Vigilant Rifles was attached to the 1st Artillery Regiment of the 4th Brigade sometime after April 1861. The *Mercury* does not include it in the 1st Artillery Regiment in March and April 1861.[408] In October 1861 and January 1862, the *Mercury* places the Vigilant Rifles as part of the 1st Regiment.[409] The company mustered out of service in early 1862. Captain Tupper later commanded a company in the 1st Regiment Charleston Guards and other units as well.

The Rutledge Mounted Riflemen, South Carolina Militia, organized at Charleston on November 9, 1860, was commanded by Captain Clelam K. Huger.[410] The company was attached to the 4th Militia Brigade, which was organized on December 20, 1860. Ordered to Fort Johnson on the day the *Star of the West* was fired upon, the company was later stationed at Wappoo Cut. It mustered in state service in April 1861 and served with the 1st

Artillery Regiment, South Carolina Militia.[411] Huger was elected major in April, and W.L. Trenholm succeeded him as captain when Brigadier General Ripley called the company into Confederate service on September 9.[412] Ripley attached the company to the 1st Artillery Regiment, South Carolina Militia, at that time.[413] Part of the company was stationed at Morris Island and part at Sullivan's Island in late September.[414] By October 22, however, the entire company was at Sullivan's Island.[415] The *Mercury* reported in mid-January 1862 that the company had been relieved of duty based on an 1841 South Carolina militia law.[416] According to the *Memory Roll*, the company was mustered out of service on December 2, 1861, and remained unorganized for nearly three months. Actually, the men remained on duty without pay and worked to recruit enough men to form a new company under Captain Trenholm.[417] The *Mercury* reported that the company was on duty with the 1st Artillery Regiment, Militia, as late as February 17.[418] During January and early February 1862, Trenholm himself recruited many original members of the Rutledge Mounted Riflemen, South Carolina Militia, into a new company called the Rutledge Mounted Riflemen, which mustered in Confederate service for twelve months on February 22, 1862. For further discussion, refer to independent cavalry organizations.

Brigade Affiliations

The 1st Regiment Artillery, South Carolina Militia, was attached to the 4th (Charleston) Brigade, South Carolina Militia. On September 20, 1863, the regiment was attached to DeSaussure's Brigade, South Carolina Militia, along with Magrath's Charleston Guard; the 18th Regiment, South Carolina Militia; and the Cadet Battalion.[419]

Major Movements and Engagements

On November 15, 1860, Colonel Locke offered the services of the 1st Regiment to Governor Pickens. In addition to full preparation as an artillery regiment, the force had been fully equipped and regularly drilled to serve as heavy infantry.[420] Four of its companies occupied Fort Moultrie on December 27, 1860, the day after Major Anderson evacuated it for the more defendable Fort Sumter.[421] The German Artillery, Company A, occupied Castle Pinckney on December 27, but was relieved by February 20, 1861.[422] Company B of the German Artillery, the Marion Artillery and the Lafayette Artillery, which had been sent to Fort Moultrie on December 27, were relieved in early January 1861.[423] The Marion Artillery was sent to Castle Pinckney. The Washington Artillery, which participated in the firing on the *Star of the West*, remained at Fort Moultrie until January 27.[424] The German Artillery, Company B, was sent to the lighthouse on Morris Island on January 11.[425] The Lafayette Artillery was ordered to Fort Palmetto on Cole's Island at the Stono Inlet in early February.[426] The Marion Artillery was transferred about the same time to Fort Johnson on James Island.[427] The Washington Artillery was sent to Cummings's Point on February 11.[428] The Washington Artillery left Cummings's Point in mid-March after four weeks of continuous duty and was replaced by the Marion Artillery.[429]

During the bombardment of Fort Sumter, the Marion Artillery was on Morris Island at the Trapier Battery to the rear of the Cummings's Point Batteries. From there, it participated in the engagement.[430] Both the German Artillery Company B and the Washington Artillery were stationed at Fort Washington on the eastern end of Sullivan's Island during the engagement.[431] The German Artillery Company A was not engaged because it was based on Morris Island at one of the Channel Batteries.[432] The Lafayette Artillery was not engaged either because it was occupied with garrison duty at Fort Palmetto on Cole's Island.[433] The Vigilant Rifles were based at the "Five-gun Battery" on Sullivan's Island east of the Curlew ground.[434] The German Artillery Company B, along with a detachment of the Washington Artillery, returned to Charleston on April 23, and at least part of the Washington Artillery was sent to Fort Pickens soon afterward.[435] The Lafayette Artillery returned on the twenty-fifth after serving for almost three months at Fort Palmetto.[436] The Vigilant Rifles left Sullivan's Island for Charleston on April 22 and was attached to the 1st Artillery Regiment shortly afterward.[437] Elements of the Washington Artillery returned from Fort Pickens on Battery Island about the twenty-seventh, and the rest of the battery returned to Charleston on May 1.[438] The Rutledge Mounted Riflemen was attached to the regiment at sometime during late April.[439] Both the Marion Artillery and the German Artillery Company A returned to Charleston from Morris Island on May 1.[440] The Washington Artillery was stationed at Bull Island from July 18 to August 6, 1861. On September 17, the Vigilant Rifles was ordered to Fort Pickens, and the Lafayette Artillery was ordered to Cole's Island.[441] The Marion Artillery was stationed at Fort Beauregard and at the battery at the breech inlet on Sullivan's Island from September 9 to October 31.[442]

Companies A and B of the German Artillery left Charleston on October 11 for Fort Walker on Hilton Head Island; both were engaged there during the battle of Port Royal on November 7.[443] The Lafayette Artillery returned from Cole's Island on October 31. The German Artillery Company B, and possibly Company A as well, was stationed at Chapman's Fort on the Ashepoo River in December and along the Combahee River at

James Island and at Fort Glover in early 1862. The Washington Artillery performed picket duty from the Edisto to the Ashepoo in late 1861. It was not engaged while stationed at Wappoo Cut near Charleston for two weeks in November. One section of the Washington Artillery saw action at Toogoodoo Creek in late December 1861.[444] The Lafayette Artillery, sent back to Fort Pickens on the Stono River on November 19, returned to Charleston on February 16, 1862.[445] In mid-February 1862, the five artillery companies and the Rutledge Mounted Riflemen were on duty, and the Vigilant Rifles were recruiting.[446]

One section of the Washington Artillery and the Marion Artillery were engaged on the Edisto River on March 29.[447] The Vigilant Rifles re-enlisted for twelve months on February 18, and the Rutledge Mounted Riflemen followed suit three days later.[448] Both German Artillery companies definitely enlisted in Confederate service in early 1862, though some dispute as to specific dates exists. The Washington Artillery's muster date was February 20, and the Lafayette's was March 13. The Marion Artillery mustered in Confederate service on June 6, 1862. The regiment, sorely depleted in numbers after the spring of 1862, continued to serve as infantry in the city of Charleston and was on duty there in August and September 1863.[449] The regiment was disbanded on September 26, 1863.[450]

Appendix 1.

Infantry Companies with Unknown Regimental or Battalion Affiliations

1. The Southern Guards was a company of Wofford College students organized on February 22, 1860. According to one source, the captain was Talliaferro Simpson; another source names T.B. Anderson.[1] Anderson is not listed in the CSR, probably because the company was never in Confederate service.
2. The Charleston Guard, commanded by Captain Myer Jacobs, was composed of alarm men and those otherwise exempted from service.[2] Myer is not listed in the CSR, probably because the company was never in Confederate service.
3. The Snow Hill Guards was a company from Newberry District.[3]
4. The Magrath Guard, a company of Irishmen probably from Charleston, was commanded by a Captain Farrelly.[4] Henry S. Farley was captain of Companies D and H of the 1st Regiment, South Carolina Artillery Regulars, but no Captain Farrelly appears in the CSR.
5. The Hudson Street Guard, a company of "armed juveniles," probably took its name from Hudson Street in Charleston.[5]
6. The Gasper Guards was a company of boys, probably of school age, commanded by Master Algernon Alston.[6] Alston is not listed in the CSR.
7. The Southern Boys was a company commanded by Captain Sam Thomas.[7] Thomas is not listed in the CSR.
8. The University Riflemen, from Greenville, was made up of Furman University students. It existed in January 1861, and it may have become the Brooks Troop, Company B of the Hampton Legion.[8]
9. The Marion Men was commanded by Captain G.B. Lartigue.[9] In July 1861, the *Mercury* announced that Lartigue was unable to complete the organization of the company.[10] He is not listed as a captain in the CSR.
10. The Sumter Cadets was a company of "juveniles."[11]

11. The Hope Guard, a Charleston company, was probably raised from the Hope Fire Engine Company.[12] Company H of the 13th Regiment, SCV, was a Lexington District company also known as the Hope Guards.
12. The Confederate Guards was a home guard company from Williston in Barnwell District.[13]
13. The Citizen Guards was a Chesterfield District company commanded by a Captain Tawh.[14] Tawh is not listed as a captain in the CSR.
14. The Home Guard of Union District was commanded by Captain F. Scaife.[15] This was probably Ferdinand D. Scaife who, in November 1861, became captain of Company A of the 18th Regiment, SCV, and later became its lieutenant colonel.
15. The Carolina Greys was a Charleston company commanded by Captain F. Marion Ronan.[16] Ronan was a lieutenant in the 16th Regiment, South Carolina Militia, but the record is unclear on whether or not the Carolina Greys was a company in that regiment.
16. Captain William Greene was attempting to raise the Manigault Guards in Georgetown in late December 1861.[17] The result of that effort is unknown.
17. Captains O'Connell, Stewart and Pulliam were from Pickens District.[18]
18. The Keitt Guard was commanded by Captain H. Smith Bass.[19] Bass is not listed in the CSR.
19. John W. Carr, a private in the St. George's Volunteers, served later in the 18th Regiment, SCV.[20] Carr was disabled in December 1861. He is not listed in the CSR.
20. Captain Samuel Y. Tupper commanded a "force" of exempt men and others who provided auxiliary services to the army in the defense of Charleston in June 1864.[21] Tupper had been captain of the Vigilant Rifles, part of the 4th Brigade, South Carolina Militia, in 1861. Later that year, he served in the 1st Regiment, S.C. Artillery Militia. Tupper enlisted on July 11, 1863, as captain of Company H of the 1st Regiment, Charleston Guard, South Carolina. An order dated May 29, 1864, authorized him to raise a company of volunteers from those citizens exempt from immediate military duty for service at batteries in Charleston. Another order, this one dated September 23, detached Tupper for duty as an agent of the state commissioners assisting in the removal of noncombatants from Charleston.
21. Captain James K. Mackett of the 1st Battalion was exchanged on October 15, 1864. He was not listed in the CSR.
22. The Foreign Legion was organized on January 18, 1865, to maintain good order in Charleston. It was commanded by Captain Nicholas Scherhammer, previously captain of Beat #1 of the 16th Regiment, South Carolina Militia.[22]

23. Captain W.R. Holmes commanded the Burke Sharpshooters.[23] Holmes is not listed in the CSR.
24. A company of boys called the Davis Guards was raised at the military school in Anderson. The boys were taught by Major B.F. Sloan and Captain Joseph Adams, who probably commanded the company.[24]
25. James Long was captain of Company A of Perryman's Battalion. Either the company or battalion was from Pickens District and was named the Mountain Rangers, but the battalion cannot be definitely identified. The Mountain Rangers served from July 1864 to May 1865 and was disbanded at Greenville. Another captain in this company was George A. Rankin. Pension records show that Long's Company was designated D of the 1st or 8th Reserves in May 1864, or possibly A or B of the 1st Regiment, South Carolina State Troops. Possibly the same James Long was captain of both Company D, 4th Regiment, SCV, and Company A, 13th Battalion, SCV, in 1862 and was colonel of the 42nd Regiment, Militia.
26. Two companies of "Old Men's Home Guards" from the Oconee section of Pickens District were commanded by Captains C.F. Seeba and E.P. Verner.[25]
27. Gregg Light Infantry, probably a militia company in Columbia in 1863, was commanded by William J. Taylor.[26]
28. The Mountain Guards, men exempt from military service, was raised on January 5, 1861, to protect homes and families and quell insurrection.[27] It was commanded by Captain J.J. Quinn. Another company, G of the 18th Regiment, SCV, may have had the same name.
29. The Bethel Guards, a company of exempt men, was organized about January 17, 1861, to protect homes and families in an emergency.[28] Its captain was J.J. Wilson. Thomas and Silverman wrote that the Bethel Guards was Company B of the 5th Regiment, SCV.[29]
30. The Walhalla Riflemen was a Pickens District company in January 1861. Captain __ Hershel may have commanded the company at first, but Jonathan M. Hencken was captain in June 1861.[30] Although the men desired to muster in Orr's Rifles that month, there is no record of the company either there or in Moore's (2nd) Rifles.
31. A company of exempt men was organized in January 1861 in the northwest part of York District; it was commanded by Captain John B. Mintz.[31]
32. A company of exempt men was organized in January 1861 in the Kings Mountain part of York District; its commander was Captain M.R. Bird.[32]

33. The Bull Swamp Guards, organized in Orangeburg District in January 1861, was commanded by Captain L.W. Dash.[33]
34. The Broad River Light Infantry was organized in February 1861 and was commanded by Captain John S. Crosby.[34]
35. The Rich Hill Guards existed in February 1861.[35]
36. The Home Guards of Yorkville, organized in April 1861, was commanded by Captain Asbury Coward.[36]
37. In May 1861, Captain John B. Jackson organized a new company in York.[37]
38. The Carolina Home Guards was raised in February 1861 by W.T. Field and R.C. Clayton. It was probably from Pickens District.[38]
39. The Mountain Creek Home Guards, organized on May 4, 1861, at Kirksey's Cross Roads in Edgefield District, was commanded by W.H. Holloway.[39] Holloway raised another company in the summer of 1861, which became part of Company G, Gregg's 1st Regiment, SCV.
40. A company of Home Guards, organized in Edgefield District on June 1, 1861, was commanded by G.D. Huiet.[40]
41. The Pleasant Lane Home Guards, organized in Edgefield District in June 1861, was commanded by Luke Culbreath.[41]
42. The Greenville Riflemen was organized in June 1861 from an artillery company unable to procure a battery of field artillery.[42] Whether or not this company was related to Company M of Maxcy Gregg's regiment is unknown.
43. A cavalry company of the Home Guards of Edgefield District was organized in June 1861; its captain was Lewis Jones.[43]
44. A company called the Confederate Stars was organized in Columbia in July 1861. Its members were boys who were five to thirteen years old.[44]
45. The Lanham Guards, organized in August 1861, was commanded by T.W. Lanham.[45]
46. The Dean Guards was a mounted infantry company organized in the Pine Grove section of Edgefield District in July 1863 for domestic defense. Theodore Dean was its captain.[46]
47. The Chichester Guards, organized in July 1864 for local defense in Edgefield District, was commanded by E.J. Dawson. It consisted of about fifty managers and operatives at Bath Paper Mills and Southern Porcelain Company and was named in honor of the owner of the Bath Paper Mills.[47]
48. A Home Defense Company, organized on March 16, 1865, in Edgefield, was commanded by E.H. Youngblood. It was made up of about seventy men, most of them either exempt from service or in the 2nd Class militia.[48]

49. The Golden's Creek Company, organized on June 1, 1861, for home defense, was commanded by William Hunter.[49] This company was probably from the Golden's Creek area northeast of Columbia.
50. The Pendleton Home Guard, organized in June 1861, was commanded by F.A. Hoke.[50]
51. The Anderson's Mills Home Guard, commanded by A.G. Field, was organized in July 1861.[51]
52. The Village Creek Home Guard, organized in July 1861, was commanded by Patterson Orr. Members were required to be older than twelve.[52]
53. The Mile Creek Home Guard, commanded by Levi N. Robins, was organized in July 1861.[53]
54. The Claremont Vigilance and Military Volunteer Committee elected Major John C. Miller as president in July 1861.[54]
55. The Snow Creek Vigilant Committee elected J.A. Elrod as president in July 1861.[55]
56. The Pumpkin Town Home Guard was organized in July 1861; G.W. Keith was its captain. It was also called the Mountain Rangers.[56]
57. The Battleground Home Guard, organized at Gill's Creek in May 1861, was commanded by Dr. D.A. Belk.[57]
58. The Independent Blair Guards, a home guard company organized in the lower part of Lancaster District in May 1862, was commanded by T.R. Clyburn.[58]
59. A Home Guard company commanded by John D. Andrews was organized in Lancaster District in May 1862.[59]
60. The Pleasant Hill Guard, organized in May 1861, was commanded by J.E. Rutledge.[60]
61. The Wild Cat Vigilant Company, commanded by J. Funderburk, was organized in May 1861.[61]
62. A Home Guard Company was organized in Lancaster District in May 1861; W.W. Baskin was its captain.[62]
63. The Lynches Creek Home Guards was organized in September 1861 in the lower part of Lancaster District; its commander was the Reverend N. Faile.[63]
64. The Greenville Home Guard was organized in January 1861. C.J. Elford was its captain.[64]
65. A Home Guard Company of Mounted Riflemen, also called the Greenville Home Guards–State Troops, was organized on July 1, 1863, in Greenville District. T.S. Arthur was its captain.[65] In its sole engagement, it forced General I.N. Palmer's Federal raiding column, which was in pursuit of President Davis, from its direct route.

66. A Home Guard Company of Infantry, organized in Greenville District on July 1, 1863, was commanded by G.E. Elford.[66]
67. The Hanging Rock Home Guards was organized in April 1862 in Lancaster District.[67]
68. The Brooks Boys, named for Preston Brooks, was organized in February 1861 from the Upper Battalion of the 2nd Regiment, South Carolina Militia, from Pickens District. Warren R. Marshall was its captain.[68]
69. The Anderson Home Guard, organized in February 1861, was commanded by a Captain Cox.[69]
70. W.P. McKellar was captain of a Greenwood company in September 1861.[70]
71. Captain Alfred J. Frederick commanded a company of South Carolina Militia in January 1865.[71]
72. The Home Guard of Charleston was commanded by Captain G.S. Hacker in May 1861.[72]
73. The City Guard of Charleston was a three-company battalion commanded by Captain H.S. Bass in May 1861.[73]
74. The Palmetto Reserve Guards #6 elected T.W. Holwell as captain on August 25, 1861. This company was composed of harbor pilots, shipmasters and others exempt from military duty.[74]
75. The Yeadon Blues was raised by G.E. Steedman in the summer of 1862 and named in honor of Richard Yeadon, senior editor of the *Charleston Daily Courier*. It was also called the "boys from Aiken."[75] G.E. Steedman's name does not appear in the CSR as captain or lieutenant of any company.
76. The Georgetown Reserves was commanded by Captain David Henry Smith.[76]
77. Willis Wilkinson Shackelford was captain of the Georgetown Home Guard.[77]
78. Captain J.H. Simons's Company, South Carolina Infantry, was commanded by J. Hume Simons. It enlisted in Confederate service for the duration of the war on May 14, 1862, at Charleston; Simons was elected at about the same time. The term of service dated from April 15. It might have been called the Miles Grenadiers.[78]
79. The Chesterfield Eagles, commanded by Neill F. Graham, was probably raised in Chesterfield for special state defense. Graham was captain of Company E of the 9th Battalion, but whether or not the two companies were the same is unclear.
80. The St. Paul's Home Guards was stationed at Adams Run and was charged with local defense. The St. Paul's Rifles, probably the same company, took over garrison duty from the Calhoun Artillery when

it was disbanded in June 1861. A Captain Smith commanded the St. Paul's Rifles.[79]

81. Captain Dougherty's Reserve Corps was commanded by Captain John Dougherty.
82. The Edgefield Reserves, commanded by Captain Joseph Abney, volunteered for twelve months of state service. Upon its organization, the company, in early December 1861, requested service with other Edgefield Companies; whether that request was honored is unknown. A company called the Edgefield Riflemen, however, commanded by Joseph Abney, became Company A of the 22nd Regiment at its organization in May 1862.
83. The Walhalla State Guards from Pickens District was commanded by Captain James O'Connell. See Company D, 22nd Regiment, SCV.
84. The Signal Corps was commanded by Captain Joseph Manigault and Captain C.G. Memminger.
85. The Port Royal Guards was commanded by Lieutenant Randolph Peyton.[80]
86. The Independent Men of Waxhaws, a militia company from Lancaster, was commanded by R.M. Sims.[81]
87. William Shivers commanded the Rebel Guards, a local defense company.[82]
88. Captain H.A. Shaw commanded an Edgefield District company that existed as early as April 1864. It served as a ferry guard at Vienna, South Carolina, before moving to Waynesboro, Georgia, to observe Sherman's troops. It was sent next to Beaufort and then served along the courier line between Augusta and Columbia until February 1865. The company was discharged at Trenton, South Carolina, in April 1865.
89. E.J. Dennis commanded a company of scouts in Charleston District in 1865.
90. Peter Sudduth, or Suddeth, was captain of a company of home guards, also described as a company of reserves, raised in 1864 from Spartanburg and Greenville Districts. The men performed bridge duty and were discharged at Columbia in April 1865.
91. The "Boy Cavalry" was in the 2nd Reserves and was commanded by B.B. McCoy.
92. In late 1864 and 1865, a Captain McMurphy commanded a home guard company of sixteen-year-olds from the part of Beaufort District that is now Hampton County.
93. John Lovell, or Lowell, commanded a home guard company of sixteen-year-olds from Horry District in late 1864 and 1865.

94. E.H. Peeples commanded a company of "old men" in one of the reserve organizations in late 1864 and 1865.
95. George Camp commanded an independent company organized at New Prospect. It performed patrol duty for three to four months.

Appendix 2

Cavalry Organizations with Unknown Regimental or Battalion Affiliations

1. The Horry Hussars from northern Horry District are not mentioned in the CSR.
2. Patterson's Rangers is mentioned in *Saddle Soldiers* as one of the few active cavalry organizations left to guard the South Carolina coast in March 1864, when most of the other organizations were transferred to Virginia. The possibility exists, however, that it was neither a South Carolina unit nor part of a militia or reserve force.[1] No Captain Patterson appears in either the CSR for South Carolina cavalry units or the *Official Records* for March 1864.
3. The Spartan Rangers, commanded by Captain Thomas Hall, was in the process of organizing in January 1861.[2] It may have failed to organize completely, or, instead, it could have been a militia unit since Hall's name does not appear in the CSR. Alternatively, the company may have been the predecessor of Company L, 3rd Regiment, South Carolina Cavalry. A company called the Seneca Rangers, commanded by Captain Thomas Hall, existed in early 1861.[3] It volunteered for service in the 4th Militia Regiment on January 3, 1861.[4] Whether or not the Spartan Rangers and the Seneca Rangers were the same company remains unclear.
4. A Home Guard of Cavalry in St. Paul's Parish at Adams Run existed in January 1861.[5] Since Hawkins S. King, its captain, is not listed in the CSR, the company was probably a militia unit.
5. The Newberry Chargers from Newberry District existed in February 1861.[6] No further information on this company appears in the record.
6. The Columbia Mounted Rifles was on duty in Charleston in April 1861.[7]
7. In June 1861, a Captain Lucas commanded a company of juveniles called the Lone Star Dragoons; it was probably a militia unit.[8]

8. The Ashepoo Guerillas, probably a militia company, was commanded by Charles Witsell, MD, in October 1861.[9]
9. The Black River Troop, commanded by W.J.N. Hammett, is listed in the index to the *Southern Historical Society Papers*, and Hammett's name appears as a sergeant in the Hampton Legion in the CSR. Hammett commanded the Black River Troop in the fall of 1860.[10]
10. The cavalry of the Western Battalion of the Sumter District South Carolina Militia, organized on July 25, 1863, elected South Carolina Senator F.J. Moses Jr. as its captain.[11] The Claremont Troop, probably the same unit, was a Sumter District militia company also called the Sumter Cavalry, South Carolina Militia. It was organized for home defense in November 1863 and was also commanded by Moses.[12] It is unlikely that this company and the Claremont Cavalry, Company A of the Holcombe Legion Cavalry Battalion, later Company I of the 7th Cavalry Regiment, were the same.
11. Captain Edward Avery commanded a company of boys under the age of eighteen in July 1863.[13] The company mustered in state service that month. When Avery's requests for active field service were denied, the company disbanded on January 1, 1864.[14] Avery is not listed in the CSR.
12. The Spartan Troop of Spartan Village was created by the General Assembly on January 28, 1861, and was attached to the Upper Battalion of the 9th Regiment, 5th Brigade, South Carolina Cavalry Militia.[15]
13. The South Carolina Executive Council authorized the creation of a company called the Combahee Rangers and accepted it for police duty and state service on May 26, 1862. Its captain was T.J. Allen.[16]
14. The Richland Rangers, which existed before the war, was commanded by Colonel R. Anderson, probably Richard Anderson who was elected lieutenant colonel of the 15th Infantry Regiment in September 1861. Its men tendered their services to the governor in January 1861, and they also offered themselves to the Confederacy. Although the company existed in April 1861 and was in Columbia the following October, any further activity is unknown.[17] It probably disbanded in the fall of 1861.
15. The Anderson Troop, commanded by Captain John W. Guyton, volunteered for service in the 4th Militia Regiment on January 3, 1861.[18]
16. The Mountain Cavalry, commanded by Captain Miles M. Norton, was in the 1st Regiment (probably the 1st Regiment, South Carolina Militia) in January 1861. Norton was later captain of Company E, Orr's Rifles.[19]

17. The Saluda Rangers, also called the Saluda Sentinels, existed in January 1861. Its captain was A.D. Bates.[20]
18. The Jefferson Nullifiers, which existed in February 1861, was commanded by Captain John F. Talbert.[21] The company, probably from Edgefield District, was disbanded at some point before September 4.[22] Governor Pickens ordered the company to return its arms by September 30. In 1862 and 1863, Talbert commanded Company F, 5th Regiment Reserves.
19. The Little River Rangers, commanded by Captain James L. Boyd, existed as a Home Defense Company in June 1861.[23]
20. The Salem Mounted Men, a Home Guard Company in Sumter District, commanded by Captain William Harris, existed in August and September 1863.[24]
21. Farmer's Rangers was commanded by Claus Volmer, who was elected captain on January 16, 1865.[25] Volmer served as first sergeant in the German Hussars when it was part of the South Carolina Militia earlier in the war.
22. Companies existing in Abbeville in April 1861 were: the Abbeville Light Infantry under Captain James C. Calhoun, the Mounted Minute Men under Captain J. Wardlaw Perrin, the Abbeville Squadron and the Southern Rights Dragoons.[26]

Appendix 3

Artillery Organizations with Unknown Regimental or Battalion Affiliations

1. Wood's Battery was based on the Black River. Whether it was a militia battery, a South Carolina battery called by an unrecognized name or, possibly, not a South Carolina battery at all, remains unclear.
2. There may have been a Captain Daniell or Daniell's Battery.
3. The McDuffie Artillery was probably a prewar militia organization from Newberry.
4. Moore's Battery was at Coosawhatchie in November 1861. We do not know if it was a militia battery, a South Carolina battery called by an unrecognized name or if it was not a South Carolina battery at all.
5. Thomas's Battery was engaged briefly at Columbia on February 15, 1865. It is described as "a small two-gun battery armed with obsolescent six pounders, which guarded the Congaree River Bridge at the foot of Gervais Street."[1] It was almost certainly manned by the Arsenal Cadets under the command of John Peyre Thomas.[2]
6. Nelson's Battery was engaged at Pocotaligo on October 22, 1862.[3] A Lieutenant Massie commanded the Nelson Light Artillery in January 1864.[4] It was probably a battery from Virginia.
7. Crenshaw's Battery was probably not a South Carolina battery.
8. The Camden Artillery Company was commanded by Captain A.W. Thames in June 1861.[5] Once again, it may have been a militia battery, a South Carolina battery called by an unrecognized name or one that was never accepted into service and was disbanded.
9. The Fairfield Artillery was commanded by Captain S.M. Smart, who was elected captain on September 14, 1861.[6] Whether this battery was a militia battery, a South Carolina battery called by an unrecognized name or a company that was never accepted into service and was disbanded is unclear.

10. From the fall of 1861 to December 1861, the Star Battery existed as a forty-man detachment of the 5th Regiment, South Carolina Infantry. It had two cannon detached from the Calhoun Artillery, probably indicating that it was Company A, Calhoun's Company, of the 1st Battalion, South Carolina Artillery (Regulars). The Star Battery was commanded by Lieutenant F.G. Latham of Company G.[7]
11. The Georgetown Artillery, also called Henning's Battery and the Georgetown Artillery Company, was commanded by Captain James G. Henning. This was a militia battery composed of older men of the community, many of whom had sons in Company A—the Georgetown Rifle Guards of the 10th Regiment, SCV. The General Assembly incorporated the battery on January 28, 1861.[8] That summer it participated in a brief expedition up the Waccamaw River with Company A of the 10th Regiment.[9] Although available for service, the battery had not been called up by late 1861 and early 1862.[10]

Appendix 4

Company Nicknames

1st Regiment, Infantry (Regulars) after May 1861

Company D, the Calhoun Light Infantry, Company K, Rivers's Battery

The 1st Regiment, South Carolina Volunteers (Hagood's)

Following are the companies that mustered in Confederate service on August 22, 1861:

Company A, the Edisto Rifles
Company B, the Jamison Guards
Company C, the Glover Guards
Company D, the St. Matthews Rifles or the Keitt Guards
Company E, the Allen Guards, later the Wee Nee Volunteers
Company G, the Johnson Guards
Company I, the Republican Blues, later the Pickens Sentinels and the Buford's Bridge Guards
Company K, the Bamberg Guards

Following are the companies of Hagood's regiment created at the reorganization on April 12, 1862:

Company A, the Bamberg Guards
Company C, the Buford's Bridge Guards
Company D, the Waxhaw Guards
Company F, the Dixie Guards
Company H, the Winsmuth Guards

The 1st Regiment, South Carolina Volunteers (Six Months) and the 1st Regiment, South Carolina Infantry, Provisional Army (Gregg's)

Gregg's 1st (six-month) Regiment was made up of the following companies:

Company A, the Richland Rifles, the Richland Volunteer Rifle Company, the Richland Volunteer Rifles, the Richland Riflemen
Company B, the Darlington Guards
Company C, the Edgefield Rifles, the Edgefield Riflemen
Company D, the Abbeville Volunteers, the Abbeville Minute Men
Company E, the Union Volunteers, the Union District Volunteers
Company F, the Wee Nee Volunteers
Company G, the Hamburg Volunteers, the Hamburg Company, the Hamburg Minute Men
Company H, the Cherokee Pond Volunteers, the Cherokee Pond Guards, the Meriwether Guards
Company I, the Monticello Guards, the Fairfield Volunteers, the Monticello Volunteers
Company K, the Marion Volunteers
Company L, the Rhett Guards
Company M, the Richardson Guard
Company N, the DeKalb Rifle Guards, the DeKalb Rifles, the DeKalb Guards, the Camden Rifle Guards
Company O, the Saluda Guard

Gregg's regiment, after the reorganization in the summer of 1861, was made up of the following companies:

Company A, the Gregg Guards
Company B, the Rhett Guards
Company C, the Richland Rifles, the Richland Volunteer Rifle Company
Company D, the Pee Dee Rifles
Company E, the Marion Rifles, the Marion Volunteers
Company F, the Horry Rebels, Horry Rifles
Company G, the Butler Sentinels, the Edgefield Company
Company H, Haskell's Rifle Corps, the Models
Company I, the Richardson Guards
Company K, the Irish Volunteers, the Irish Volunteers For The War
Company L, the Carolina Light Infantry Volunteers, the Carolina Light Infantry for the War, the Boy Company
Company M, the Furman Guards

THE 1ST REGIMENT, SOUTH CAROLINA RIFLES (ORR'S)

Company A, the Keowee Riflemen, the Keowee Rifles, the Keowee Volunteers, the Keowee Volunteer Company
Company B, the McDuffie Rifles, the McDuffie Guards
Company C, the Mountain Boys, the Pickens Boys
Company D, Orr's Rifles
Company E, the Oconee Riflemen, Oconee Rifles, the Mountain Cavalry, the Pickens Mountain Cavalry
Company F, the Blue Ridge Riflemen, the Blue Ridge Volunteers
Company G, the Marshall Riflemen, the Marshall Rifles, the Abbeville Riflemen
Company H, the PeeDee Guards
Company K, the Marshall Guards
Company L, the Calhoun Guards

THE 1ST REGIMENT, CHARLESTON (SOUTH CAROLINA) GUARDS

Company H, the Vigilant Rifles

THE 1ST (CHARLESTON) BATTALION, INFANTRY

Company A, the Charleston Riflemen
Company B, the Charleston Light Infantry
Company C, the Irish Volunteers
Company D, the Sumter Guards, the Sumter Guard Volunteers, the Gamecocks
Company E, the Calhoun Guards or Guard
Company F, the Union Light Infantry Volunteers, the Union Light Infantry Volunteers and German Fusiliers
Company G, the Charleston Light Infantry

THE 1ST BATTALION, SOUTH CAROLINA SHARPSHOOTERS

Company A, the Union Light Infantry and German Fusiliers
Company B, the Sumter Guards
Company C, the Charleston Sharpshooters, the Palmetto Guards

THE 2ND REGIMENT, SOUTH CAROLINA VOLUNTEERS

Following are the six companies that refused to go to Virginia in May 1861:
The Claremont Rifles
The DeKalb Rifle Guards, the DeKalb Rifles, the DeKalb Guards
The Lancaster Grays, the Lancaster Greys
The Richland Guards
The Salem Company, the Chicora Guards
The States Rights Guards, the Fork Troop

The following ten companies made up the 2nd Regiment after it entered Confederate service in April 1861:
Company A, the Governor's Guards
Company B, the Butler Guards
Company C, the Columbia Grays, the Richland Grays, the Columbia Greys
Company D, the Sumter Volunteers
Company E, the Camden Volunteers, the Camden Light Infantry, the Kershaw Guards
Company F, the Secession Guards, Perryman's Company, the Abbeville Volunteers, the Abbeville Guards
Company G, the Flat Rock Guards
Company H, the Lancaster Invincibles, the Lancaster Volunteers, the Lancaster Guards
Company I, the Palmetto Guard or Guards
Company K, the Brooks Guard Volunteers, the Brooks Guards, Brooks Home Guards

THE 3RD REGIMENT, SOUTH CAROLINA VOLUNTEERS

Company A, the State Guards, the State Guards Rifle Company, the Laurens Guards, the Garlington Rifles
Company B, the Williams Guard
Company C, the Pickens Guards, the Yahoo
Company D, the Cross Anchor Volunteers, the Cross Anchors
Company E, the Quitman Rifles, the Quitman Guard, the Quitman Riflemen, the Quitmans
Company F, the Wadsworth Guards, the Wadsworth Volunteers
Company G, the Briers, the Briars, the Laurens Briers, the Liars Briers

Company H, the Brooks Guards, the Brooks Palmetto Guards, the Dutch,
the Dutch Fork Boys
Company I, the Musgrove Volunteers, the Musgrove Guards, the Clinton Company, the Clinton Divers
Company K, the Blackstock Volunteers, the Blackstock Company
No letter designation, the Helena Guard
No letter designation, Company Raiborn, Company Rabun

The 3rd Battalion, South Carolina Infantry

Company B, the Williams Company
Company E, the Hunter Guards
Company F, the Harper Rifles
Company G, the Aiken Guards

The 4th Regiment, South Carolina Volunteers

Company A, the Butler Guards, Hoke's Rifle Company
Company B, the Palmetto Riflemen, the Palmetto Rifles, Whitner's Rifle Company
Company C, Dean's Infantry Company
Company D, the Piercetown Guards, Long's Infantry Company
Company E, the Calhoun Mountaineers, the Calhoun Guards, Kilpatrick's Infantry Company
Company F, the Tyger Volunteers, Poole's Infantry Company
Company G, the Saluda Volunteers, Hawthorne's Infantry Company
Company H, the Twelve Mile Volunteers
Company I, the Pickens Guards, Hollingsworth's Infantry Company
Company J, the Confederate Guards, Ashmore's Infantry Company
Company K, the Fort Hill Guards, Shanklin's Company

The 5th Regiment, South Carolina Volunteers

The following companies of the 5th Regiment existed from early March 1861 until the regiment was reorganized and mustered in Confederate service on June 4, 1861:
Company A, the Johnson Rifles, Johnson Riflemen
Company B, the Pea Ridge Volunteers

Company C, the Batesville Volunteers
Company D, the Pacolet Guards
Company E, the Jasper Light Infantry
Company F, the Lawson's Fork Volunteers
Company G, the Kings Mountain Guard
Company H, the Catawba Light Infantry
Company I, the Morgan Light Infantry, the Morgan Rifles
Company J, the Whyte Guards, the "Wild Geese"
Company K, the Tyger Volunteers, Tyger River Volunteers, the Goshen Hill Volunteers
Company L, the Spartan Rifles

Following are the companies of the 5th Regiment existing from June 4, 1861, to April 13, 1862:
Company A, the Johnson Rifles or Riflemen
Company B, the Kings Mountain Guards
Company C, the Lawson's Fork Volunteers
Company D, the Tyger River Volunteers, Tyger Volunteers, the Goshen Hill Volunteers
Company E, the Pea Ridge Volunteers
Company F, the Morgan Light Infantry, Morgan Rifles
Company G, the Pacolet Guards, the Limestone Spring Company
Company H, the Catawba Light Infantry
Company I, the Jasper Light Infantry
Company K, the Spartan Rifles
The Star Battery

Following are those companies of the 5th Regiment existing from April 23, 1862, to the end of the war:
Company A, the Lancaster Greys, the Lancaster Grays
Company B, the Catawba Light Infantry
Company C, the Limestone Southern Rights Guards
Company D, the Tyger River Volunteers, Tyger Volunteers, the Goshen Hill Volunteers
Company E, the Turkey Creek Grays
Company F, the Kings Mountain Guards
Company H, the Pea Ridge Volunteers
Company K, the Lawson's Fork Volunteers

THE 6TH REGIMENT, SOUTH CAROLINA VOLUNTEERS

The following companies were originally attached to the 6th Regiment from its inception on February 8, 1861, until it mustered in Confederate service in June:

The Boyce Guards
The Buckhead Guards
The Calhoun Guards
The Catawba Guards
The Cedar Creek Rifle Company, the Cedar Creek Rifles
The Chester Blues
The Chester Guards
The Fairfield Fencibles
The Little River Guards
The Monticello Guards, the Fairfield Volunteers
The Pickens Guards

Following are the ten companies of the 6th Regiment after they mustered in Confederate service in June and July 1861:

Company A, the Calhoun Guard or Guards
Company B, the Catawba Guards, the Catawba Light Infantry
Company C, the Buckhead Guards
Company D, the Boyce Guards
Company E, the Chester Guards
Company F, the Chester Blues
Company G, the Pickens Guards
Company H, the York Volunteers, the York Guards, the York Guard
Company I, the Limestone Springs Infantry, the Limestone Light Infantry, the Limestone Guards
Company K, the Carolina Mountaineers

Following are the companies created at the reorganization in the spring of 1862:

Company A, the Catawba Guards, Catawba Light Infantry
Company B, the Alston Riflemen
Company F, the Chester Blues
Company G, the Boyce Guards
Company H, the Buckhead Guards
Company I, the Chester Guards
Company K, the Dixie Guards

Manigault's Battalion South Carolina Volunteers

Company A, the St. James Santee Mounted Riflemen, the Mounted Rifles Company, Captain Thomas Pinckney's Company, Thomas Pinckney's Independent Mounted Riflemen
Company B, the Santee Light Artillery, Gaillard's Company of Light Artillery
Company C, the Trenholm Rifles, the Infantry Company–Trenholm Rifles, the Palmer Rifles
Company D, the Infantry Company–Chesnut Guards
Company E, the Kickapoo Riflemen

The 6th Battalion South Carolina Infantry

Company B, the Chesnut Guards
Company C, the Kickapoo Riflemen
Santee Light Artillery
St. James Santee Mounted Riflemen

The 7th Regiment, South Carolina Volunteers

Following are the companies of the 7th Regiment from its enlistment in state service in April 1861 until the reorganization in May 1862:
Company A, the Secession Guards, Perryman's Company, the Abbeville Volunteers, the Abbeville Guards
Company B, the Southern Guards, the Cokesbury Minutemen
Company D, Hester's Company
Company E, the Mount Willing Guards
Company F, the Davies Guard, Davies Guards, the Graniteville Riflemen
Company G, the Brooks Greys
Company H, the Ninety Six Rifles
Company I, the Red Hill Guard
Company K, the Ruffin Guards
Company L, the Horry Volunteers, the Horry Guards, the All Saints Riflemen, the All Saints Rifles

Following are the companies of the 7th Regiment after the reorganization in May 1862:
Company A, the Ninety Six Riflemen
Company B, the Southern Guards, Cokesbury Minutemen

Company E, the Mount Willing Guards
Company F, the Davies Guards
Company G, the Brooks Greys
Company H, the Ninety Six Rifles
Company I, the Red Hill Guard
Company K, the Ruffin Guards
Company L, the Horry Volunteers
Company M, the Saluda Riflemen

THE 7TH BATTALION, SOUTH CAROLINA INFANTRY

Company A, the Lucas Guards
Company B, the Lyles Rifles
Company C, the McCullough Rifles
Company D, the Kershaw Grays or Greys
Company F, the Lucas Rifles
Company G, the Moffatt Rifles
Company H, the Joe Johnston Rifles, the Johnston Rifles, the Partisan Rangers, the Brooks Infantry Partisan Rifles

THE 8TH REGIMENT, SOUTH CAROLINA VOLUNTEERS

Company A, the Darlington Rifleman
Company B, the Chesterfield Rifles
Company C, the Chesterfield Guards
Company D, the Jackson Guards
Company E, the Timmonsville Minute Men
Company F, the Darlington Grays
Company G, the Marlboro Guards, the Marlborough Guards
Company H, the Jeffries Creek Company, the Jeffries Volunteers
Company I, the Marion Guards
Company K, the McQueen Guards
Company L, the Spartan Band

THE 9TH REGIMENT, SOUTH CAROLINA VOLUNTEERS

Company A, the Lancaster Greys
Company B, the States Right Guards, the Fork Troop
Company C, the Clarendon Blues

Company D, the Chicora Guards, the Salem Company
Company E, the Kershaw Troop
Company F, the Sumter Grays
Company G, the Hartsville Light Infantry
Company H, the Blanding Blues
Company I, the Cowpens Guards or Guard, the Cowpens Cavalry
Company K, the Pickens Sentinels
Unlettered, the Clarendon Volunteers, Clarendon Riflemen, Clarendon Rifles

THE 9TH BATTALION, SOUTH CAROLINA INFANTRY

Company A, the Bull Creek Guerillas, the Bull Creek Rangers
Company C, the Irby Rifles
Company D, the Watchesaw Rifles, the Wachitaw Rifles
Company E, the Chesterfield Eagles
Company G, the Eutaw Rifles, the Floyd Guerillas

THE 10TH REGIMENT, SOUTH CAROLINA VOLUNTEERS

Companies attached to the 10th Regiment in early 1861:
Original Company D, the Wee Nee Volunteers, the Williamsburg Company
Original Company G, the Coast Guards
Original Company I, the Carver's Bay Palmetto Rifle Guards, the Carver's Bay Sharpshooters
Joshua Ward's Artillery Company, Mayham Ward's Company, South Carolina Light Artillery
The North Santee Mounted Rifles
The Sampit Rangers

Following are the twelve companies of the 10th Regiment after it mustered in Confederate service in August 1861:
Company A, the Georgetown Rifle Guards
Company B, the Brooks Guards, Brooks Rifle Guards
Company C, the Lake Swamp Volunteers
Company D, the Marion Volunteers
Company E, the Black Mingo Rifle Guards, Black Mingo Riflemen
Company F, the Pee Dee Rangers
Company G, the Horry Rough and Readys

Company H, the Liberty Volunteers
Company I, the Swamp Fox Guards
Company K, the Eutaw Volunteers
Company L, the Liberty Guards
Company M, the Horry Dixie Boys, the Horry Volunteers

The 11th Regiment, South Carolina Volunteers

Company A, the Beaufort Volunteer Artillery
Company B, the Calhoun Artillery, the St. Paul's Rifles
Company C, the Summerville Guards
Company D, the Whippy Swamp Guard
Company E, the Hamilton Guards or Guard
Company F, the Republican Blues, the Yemassee Volunteers
Company G, the Butler Guards, Butler Rifles
Company H, the St. George Volunteers, St. George's Volunteers
Company I, the Colleton Rifles
Company K, the Eutaw Volunteers
Bellinger's Company–the Colleton Guard, Colleton Rifles
Sheridan's Company–the Round O Guards

The 11th Battalion, South Carolina Infantry

The Beauregard Light Infantry
The Edisto Rifles
The Marion Light Infantry
The Ripley Guards, Gordon's Company
The St. Matthews Rifles, or Riflemen
The Washington Light Infantry, Company A
The Washington Light Infantry, Company B
The Wee Nee Volunteers, the Williamsburg Company
The Yeadon Light Infantry

The 12th Regiment, South Carolina Volunteers

Company A, the Palmer Guards
Company B, the Campbell Rifles, the Sevier Rifles, the Rock Hill Campbell Riflemen
Company C, the Cedar Creek Rifles

Company D, the Richland Guards
Company E, the Blair Guards
Company F, the Means Light Infantry, the Long Run Company, the Monticello Guards
Company G, the Bonham Rifles Volunteers, the Bonham Rifles, the Confederate Guards
Company H, the Indian Land Guards
Company I, the Lancaster Hornets
Company K, the Grisham Rifles
Unlettered, the Lancaster Guards

THE 13TH REGIMENT, SOUTH CAROLINA VOLUNTEERS

Company A, the Martin Guards
Company B, the Brockman Guards
Company C, the Forest Rifles, the Forest Guards
Company D, the Newberry Riflemen
Company E, the Cherokee Guards
Company F, the Pacolet Volunteers, Pacolet Guards
Company G, the DeKalb Guards
Company H, the Hope Guards
Company I, the Iron District Volunteers
Company K, the Johnson Rifles, Johnson Riflemen

THE 14TH REGIMENT, SOUTH CAROLINA VOLUNTEERS

Company A, the Lynch Creek Guards
Company B, the Dearing Guards
Company C, Company Raiborn
Company D, the Edgefield Rifles, the Confederate Light Guards
Company E, the Enoree Mosquitoes, the Enoree Rifles
Company F, the Carolina Bees, the South Carolina Bees
Company G, the McGowan Greys, Captain Jay's Company
Company H, Ryan's Guards, the Ryan Guard
Company I, the McCalla Rifles
Company K, the Meeting Street Saludas

THE 15TH REGIMENT, SOUTH CAROLINA VOLUNTEERS

Company A, the Columbia Rifles
Company B, the Gist Guards
Company C, the Lexington Rifles, the Lexington Guards
Company D, the Kershaw Guards
Company E, the Monticello Guards
Company F, the Thicketty Rifles
Company G, the Williamsburg Riflemen
Company H, the Mount Tabor Company, the Pinckney Guards
Company I, the Dutch Fork Guards
Company K, the Dorn Volunteers, the Dorn Invincibles, the Independent Guards

THE 16TH REGIMENT, SOUTH CAROLINA VOLUNTEERS

Company A, the Mountain Rebels, the Reedy Rifles
Company C, the Croft Mountain Rangers
Company D, the Elford Guards
Company E, the McCullough Lions
Company K, the Goodlett Guard, the Buttermilk Rangers, the Greenville Guard

THE 17TH REGIMENT, SOUTH CAROLINA VOLUNTEERS

Company C, the Defenders of Right, the Broad River Light Infantry
Company D, the Palmetto Rifles, the Palmettoes
Company E, the Indian Land Tigers, the Indian Land Rifles, the York Rangers
Company F, the Carolina Rifles
Company I, the Lancaster Tigers
Company K, the Lacy Guards

THE 18TH REGIMENT, SOUTH CAROLINA VOLUNTEERS

Company A, the Unionville Rifles
Company B, the Union District Volunteers, the York Rangers
Company C, the Cross Keys Company

Company G, the Mountain Guards
Company H, the Bethel Rifles
Company I, the Darlington Rifles
Company K, the Broad River Guards

THE 19TH REGIMENT, SOUTH CAROLINA VOLUNTEERS

Company B, the Lamar Guards
Company C, the Dorn Guards

THE 20TH REGIMENT, SOUTH CAROLINA VOLUNTEERS

Company C, the Evans Guards
Company D, the Bull Swamp Guards
Company F, the Kinard Phalanx
Company G, the Spring Hill Volunteers
Company I, the Edisto Guards
Company K, the Lexington Volunteer Rifle Company, the Lexington Riflemen Company L, the Ripley Rangers
Company M, Keitt's Company Mounted Riflemen, the Mounted Riflemen
Company N, the Peterkin Rangers
Company O, Venning's Company
Buist's Company Light Artillery

THE 21ST REGIMENT, SOUTH CAROLINA VOLUNTEERS

Company B, The Wilds Rifles
Company C, the Clarendon Guards
Company D, the Cheraw Guards
Company F, the Thomas Guards
Company G, the Williams Guards
Company K, the Timmonsville Minutemen

THE 22ND REGIMENT, SOUTH CAROLINA VOLUNTEERS

Company A, the Edgefield Riflemen, the Edgefield Reserves, the Edgefield Blues, the Confederate Light Guards
Company B, the Cedar Hill Guards

Company C, the Chapel Guards
Company D, the Hopewell Guards
Company E, the Lancaster Guards
Company F, the Hagood Guards

THE 23RD REGIMENT, SOUTH CAROLINA VOLUNTEERS

Company A, the Bee Rifles
Company B, the Chicora Rifles
Company C, the Johnson Rifles or Riflemen
Company D, the Duryea Guards, Duryea Coast Guard
Company E, the Marion Blues, the Marion Rifles
Company F, the Chester Grays
Company G, the Douglass Rifles
Company H, the Roberts Guards
Company I, the Sprott Guards
Company K, the Lee Guard

THE 24TH REGIMENT, SOUTH CAROLINA VOLUNTEERS

Company A, the Marion Rifles
Company B, the Pee Dee Rifles
Company C, M.T. Appleby's Company
Company D, the Evans Guard
Company E, the Colleton Guard
Company F, Hill's Company
Company G, Pearson's Company
Company H, Thomas's Company
Company I, the Edgefield Light Infantry, the Edgefield Guard
Company K, Tompkins's Company

THE 25TH REGIMENT, SOUTH CAROLINA VOLUNTEERS

Company A, the Washington Light Infantry, Company A
Company B, the Washington Light Infantry, Company B
Company C, the Wee Nee Volunteers

Company D, the Marion Light Infantry
Company E, the Beauregard Light Infantry
Company F, the St. Matthews Rifles or Riflemen
Company G, the Edisto Rifles
Company H, the Yeadon Light Infantry
Company I, the Clarendon Guards
Company K, the Ripley Guards

The 26th Regiment, South Carolina Volunteers

Company A, the Bull Creek Guerillas
Company D, the Irby Rifles
Company E, the Watchesaw Rifles
Company F, the Chesterfield Eagles
Company H, the Chesnut Guards
Company I, the Kickapoo Riflemen
Company K, the Eutaw Rifles, the Floyd Guerillas

The 27th Regiment, South Carolina Volunteers

Company A, the Calhoun Guards or Guard
Company B, the Charleston Light Infantry
Company C, the Union Light Infantry Volunteers
Company D, the Sumter Guards, the Sumter Guard Volunteers, the Gamecocks
Company E, the Union Light Infantry and German Fusiliers
Company F, the Sumter Guards
Company G, the Charleston Sharpshooters, the Palmetto Guard
Company H, the Irish Volunteers
Company I, the Charleston Riflemen
Company K, the Charleston Light Infantry

The Hampton Legion

Infantry Battalion

Company A, the Washington Light Infantry, the Washington Light Infantry Volunteers
Company B, the Watson Guards

Company C, the Manning Guards or Guard
Company D, the Gist Rifles, the Gist Guards, the Gist Riflemen
Company E, the Bozeman Guards
Company F, the Davis Guards
Company G, the Claremont Rifles
Company H, the German Artillery Volunteers, the South Carolina Zouaves

Cavalry Battalion

Company A, the Edgefield Hussars, the Edgefield Huzzars, the Edgefield Dragoons
Company B, the Brooks Troop, the Brooks Guards, the Brooks Dragoons, the University Riflemen
Company C, the Beaufort District Troop, the Beaufort Dragoons
Company D, the Congaree Troop, the Congaree Mounted Riflemen, Congaree Mounted Rifles, the Congaree Mounted Infantry, the Richland Light Dragoons

Artillery Battalion

Battery A, the Washington Artillery Volunteers, the Washington Mounted Artillery, the Washington Artillery for Confederate service, Lee's Battery, Hampton Horse Artillery
Company B, the German Artillery, the German Light Artillery, the German Flying Artillery, the German Volunteers, Hampton Legion, Bachman's Battery

THE HOLCOMBE LEGION

Infantry Battalion

Company A, Smith's Riflemen, the Palmetto Riflemen
Company B, the Batesville Volunteers
Company C, the Morgan Rifles
Company D, the Stevens Guards
Company E, the Spartan Guards
Company F, the Ripley Rifles
Company H, the Frog Level Scouts
Company I, the Fort Prince Guards
Company K, the Lucas Guards
Unlettered, the Stevens Light Infantry

Cavalry Battalion

Company A, the Claremont Cavalry
Company B, the Congaree Mounted Guard, the Congaree Mounted Riflemen, the Congaree Cavaliers
Company C, the Newberry Rangers, the Palmetto Light Dragoons
Company D, the McKissick Rangers, McKissick's Rangers
Company E, the Kirkwood Rangers, the Kirkwood Cavalry, the Kirkwood South Carolina Cavalry, The Kirkwoods, the Camden Rangers

THE PALMETTO SHARPSHOOTERS

Company A, the Johnson Rifles
Company B, the Calhoun Mountaineers
Company C, the Palmetto Riflemen
Company D, the Morgan Light Infantry
Company E, the Darlington Sentinels
Company F, the Pickens Sentinels
Company G, the Jasper Light Infantry
Company H, the Cowpens Guards
Company I, the Pickens Guards
Company K, the Spartan Rifles
Company L, the Confederate Guards
Company M, the Pacolet Guards

THE BATTALION OF SOUTH CAROLINA STATE CADETS, LOCAL DEFENSE TROOPS

Company A, the Citadel Cadets
Company B, the Arsenal Cadets

THE SOUTH CAROLINA COLLEGE CADETS

The South Carolina College Cadets, the College Cadets, the Third Cadet Company, the Stevens Light Infantry

Captain Rhett's Company, South Carolina

Captain Rhett's Company, the Brooks Home Guards, the Brooks Guards

Captain John Symons's Company, Naval Brigade, South Carolina Volunteers

The Sea Fencibles

Harlee's Legion, South Carolina Militia

The Black River Rangers
The Williamsburg Light Dragoons

Captain L.H. Charbonnier's Company, South Carolina Militia

The Pickens Rifles, the Pickens Guard, the Pickens Cadets

Shiver's Company–Local Defense Troops, South Carolina

The Rebel Guards

The Fire Companies of Charleston

The Aetna Fire Company, the Aetna Rifles, the Aetna Guard
The Phoenix Fire Company, the Phoenix Rifles
The Vigilant Fire Engine Company, the Vigilant Rifles, Vigilant Light Infantry

The (Columbia) Volunteer Battalion

The Cedar Creek Riflemen
The Columbia Artillery

The Emmett Guards
The Governor's Guards
The Richland Volunteer Rifle Company

1st Regiment Charleston Reserves, South Carolina Militia

Company A, the Hibernian Guard
Company B, the Charleston Home Guard
Company C, the Pickens Rifles

The 7th Regiment Reserves (90 Days 1862–1863)

Company B, the Rocky Creek Troop

The 9th Regiment Reserves (90 Days 1862–1863)

Company K, the Yemassee Volunteers

The 2nd Battalion South Carolina Reserves

Company C, the Spartan Rangers, the Spartanburg Rangers, the Spartan Rangers Independent Cavalry-Reserves
Company H, Captain Kay's Detachment, South Carolina Mounted Reserves the Palmetto Mounted Infantry

The 8th Battalion South Carolina Reserves

Company B, the Confederate Reserve Corps of Colleton District

2nd Regiment, Junior Reserves, South Carolina State Troops

Company B, the Saluda Company

3rd Regiment, Junior Reserves, South Carolina State Troops

Company K, the Bonham Guards

4th Regiment, Junior Reserves, South Carolina State Troops

Company B, the Union Laddies

South Carolina Militia Units-Cavalry

The 1st Regiment, South Carolina Mounted Militia
The Allendale Mounted Guard
The Beaufort District Guerillas, the Coosawhatchie Guerillas
The Beech Hill Rangers
The Bluffton Troop, the May River Troop
The Calhoun Minute Men
The Charleston Mounted Guard
The Colleton Rangers
The Dorchester Guerillas
The Etiwan Rangers
The Grey Riders of St. Bartholomew Parish, the Colleton Grey Riders, the Walterboro Home Guard
The Hardeeville Guerillas
The Marion Men of Combahee
The Marion Troop, the Marion Rangers, the Marion Scouts
The May River Troop, the Bluffton Troop
The Palmetto Hussars
The Palmetto Rangers
The Parish Mounted Rangers, the Parish Rangers
The Pickens Rangers
The Red Oak Rangers
The Salkehatchie Guerillas, the Saltketcher Guerillas
The Savannah River Guards
The South Carolina Rangers
The St. Helena Mounted Rifles, St. Helena Volunteer Mounted Riflemen

The St. Paul Home Guard, St. Paul Mounted Men
The St. Paul Rangers
The St. Peter's Guards

The 4th Regiment, South Carolina Militia

The Beaufort District Troop, Beaufort Troop
The Charleston Light Dragoons
The Combahee Troop, the Combahee Rangers
The German Hussars
The Hammond Huzzars, or Hussars, the Evans Light Dragoons
The Marion Troop
The McDonald Troop
The Palmetto Troop
The Wassamassaw Troop

The 1st Regiment Artillery, South Carolina Militia

Company A of the German Artillery Battalion
Company B of the German Artillery, the German Flying Artillery
The Lafayette Artillery
The Marion Artillery
The Rutledge Mounted Riflemen
The Vigilant Fire Engine Company, the Vigilant Rifles, Vigilant Light Infantry
The Washington Artillery of Charleston

The 1st Regiment Rifles, South Carolina Militia

The Beauregard Light Infantry
The Carolina Light Infantry
The Chichester Zouaves, the Charleston Zouave Cadets, the Zouave Cadets
The German Riflemen
The Jamison (or Jamieson) Riflemen
The Meagher Guards, the Emerald Light Infantry
The Moultrie Guard or Guards
The Palmetto Riflemen

The Pickens Rifles
The Sarsfield Light Infantry
The Washington Light Infantry, the Washingtons

THE 1ST REGIMENT, SOUTH CAROLINA MILITIA

Piney Mountain Company
The Saluda Battalion
The Tyger Battalion

THE 5TH REGIMENT, SOUTH CAROLINA MILITIA

The Pickensville Silver Greys

THE 7TH REGIMENT, SOUTH CAROLINA MILITIA

The Edgefield Riflemen

THE 13TH REGIMENT, SOUTH CAROLINA MILITIA

The Colleton Rifle Corps, the Colleton Rifle Company
The Palmetto Volunteers
The St. Paul's Rifles

THE 15TH REGIMENT, SOUTH CAROLINA MILITIA

The Lexington Rifle Company

THE 16TH REGIMENT, SOUTH CAROLINA MILITIA

The Jackson Guard
The Marion Rifles
The Pickens Rifles, Pickens Guards

THE 17TH REGIMENT, SOUTH CAROLINA MILITIA

The Brooks Guards or Brooks Home Guards
The Cadet Rifles or Riflemen
The Calhoun Guards or Guard
The Charleston Riflemen
The Emmet Volunteers
The German Fusiliers
The Highland Guards
The Irish Volunteers
The Jasper Greens
The Montgomery Guard or Guards
The Palmetto Guard
The Phoenix Rifles or Riflemen
The Richardson Guard
The South Carolina College Cadets
The Sumter Guards, the Gamecocks
The Union Light Infantry

THE 18TH REGIMENT, SOUTH CAROLINA MILITIA

Company E, the Dorchester Company
The Goose Creek Company

THE 26TH REGIMENT, SOUTH CAROLINA MILITIA

The Calhoun Guards
The Chester Rifles

THE 33RD REGIMENT, SOUTH CAROLINA MILITIA

The All Saints Riflemen, All Saints Rifles
Blantons Cross Roads Volunteers
Bull Creek Rangers
The Carolina Greys
Conwayboro Palmetto Guards
Cool Springs Home Guard
Dog Bluff Home Guards

Floyd Guerillas
Waccamaw Guerillas
The Waccamaw Light Artillery
Wachitaw Rifles
The Watchesaw Riflemen

THE 36TH REGIMENT, SOUTH CAROLINA MILITIA

The Johnson Volunteers
Lawson's Fork Volunteers
The Morgan Rifles
Pacolet Volunteers
The Spartanburg Light Infantry

THE 1ST BATTALION/1ST REGIMENT, SOUTH CAROLINA CAVALRY

Company A, the Abbeville Troop
Company B, the Ferguson Rangers, the Spartanburg and Laurens Rangers, the Enoree Rangers
Company C, the Edgefield and Barnwell Rangers, the Edgefield Rangers
Company D, the Chester Troop
Company E, the Fort Motte Rangers
Company F, the Allen Hussars
Company G, L.J. Johnson's Cavalry
Company H, Robin Jones's Cavalry
Company I, the Round O Troop

THE 2ND REGIMENT, SOUTH CAROLINA CAVALRY

Company A, the Boykin Rangers, the Hampton Scouts, Boykin's Independent Company, South Carolina Cavalry, the Mounted Rangers, the Independent Mounted Rangers
Company B, the Beaufort District Troop, Beaufort Dragoons
Company C, the Congaree Rangers
Company D, the Wassamassaw Cavalry, Wassa Massaw Rangers
Company E, Dean's Company
Company G, the Bonham Light Dragoons, Lipscomb's Troop

Company H, the Congaree Troop, the Congaree Mounted Riflemen or Rifles, the Congaree Mounted Infantry, the Richland Light Dragoons
Company I, the Edgefield Hussars, the Edgefield Dragoons
Company K, the Brooks Troop, the Brooks Guards, the Brooks Dragoons

THE 2ND BATTALION CAVALRY, SOUTH CAROLINA RESERVES

Company B, the Marion Men of Combahee
Company F, the Savannah River Guard or Guards
The Ashley Dragoons or Ashley Rangers
The Barnwell Dragoons
The Beaufort District Troop
The Calhoun Minute Men, Calhoun Mounted Men
The Colleton Rangers
The Spartan Rangers

THE 3RD REGIMENT, SOUTH CAROLINA CAVALRY

Company A, the Marion Men of Combahee
Company B, the Colleton Rangers
Company C, the Beaufort District Troop
Company C, Captain John H. Howard's Company
Company D, the Barnwell Dragoons
Company E, the Calhoun Minute, Calhoun Mounted Men
Company F, the St. Peter's Guards
Company G, the German Hussars
Company H, the Ashley Dragoons, Ashley Rangers
Company I, the Rebel Troop
Company K, the Savannah River Guards or Guard
Johnson's Section of Horse Artillery, Johnson's Mounted Artillery, Colcock's Light Artillery, Colcock's Section Light Artillery

THE 3RD BATTALION, SOUTH CAROLINA CAVALRY

Company B, the Congaree Rangers
Company D, the Wassamassaw Cavalry, Wassa Massaw Rangers

THE 4TH REGIMENT, SOUTH CAROLINA CAVALRY

Company A, the Chesterfield Light Dragoons
Company B, the Palmetto Rangers
Company C, the Calhoun Troop
Company D, St. James Mounted Riflemen, Company A
Company E, previously Company C of the 12th Battalion, South Carolina Cavalry
Company F, the E.M. Dragoons
Company G, the Evans Light Dragoons
Company H, the Catawba Rangers
Company I, the Williamsburg Light Dragoons
Company K, the Charleston Light Dragoons

THE 5TH REGIMENT, SOUTH CAROLINA CAVALRY

Company A, the St. Matthews Troop
Company B, the Dixie Rangers
Company C, the Beech Hill Rangers
Company D, the South Carolina Rangers, Carolina Rangers
Company E, the St. James Mounted Riflemen, Company B
Company F, the Lexington Light Dragoons
Company G, the Willington Rangers
Company H, the Santee Guerillas, Santee Rangers
Company K, the Mountain Rangers

THE 6TH REGIMENT, SOUTH CAROLINA CAVALRY

Company A, the Carolina Guerrillas
Company B, the Edgefield Rangers, the Edgefield Partisan Rangers
Company E, the Laurens Partizans
Company F, the Cadet Company, the Cadet Troop, the Cadet Rangers, the Citadel Troop
Company H, the Yeadon Rangers

THE 7TH REGIMENT, SOUTH CAROLINA CAVALRY

Company A, the Marion Men of Winyah, Company A
Company B, the Rutledge Mounted Riflemen
Company C, the McKissick Rangers, McKissick's Rangers
Company D, the Congaree Mounted Guard, the Congaree Mounted Riflemen, the Congaree Cavaliers
Company E, the Newberry Rangers, the Palmetto Light Dragoons
Company F, the Marion Men of Winyah, Company B
Company G, the Rutledge Mounted Riflemen
Company H, the Kirkwood Rangers, the Kirkwood Cavalry, the Kirkwood South Carolina Cavalry, the Kirkwoods, the Camden Rangers
Company I, the Claremont Cavalry
Company K, the Wateree Mounted Rifles, Boykin's Company Mounted Rifles, the Boykin Rangers

THE 10TH BATTALION, SOUTH CAROLINA CAVALRY

Company A, the Palmetto Rangers
Company B, the Calhoun Troop
Company C, the Evans Light Dragoons
Company D, the Catawba Rangers, the Lancaster Troop, the Lancaster Cavalry, the Catawba Guards

THE 12TH BATTALION, SOUTH CAROLINA CAVALRY

Company A, the Chesterfield Light Dragoons
Company B, the Williamsburg Light Dragoons
Company D, the E.M. Dragoons
The Waccamaw Light Artillery

THE 14TH BATTALION, SOUTH CAROLINA CAVALRY

Company A, the Santee Guerillas, Santee Rangers
Company B, the St. Matthews Troop
Company C, the Light Dragoons

The 16th Battalion, South Carolina Cavalry

Company A, the Carolina Guerrillas
Company B, the Edgefield Rangers, the Edgefield Partisan Rangers
Company E, the Laurens Partizans
Company F, the Cadet Company, the Cadet Troop, the Cadet Rangers

The 17th Battalion, South Carolina Cavalry

Company A, the South Carolina Rangers, Carolina Rangers
Company B, the Willington Rangers
Company C, the Dixie Rangers
Company D, the Beech Hill Rangers

The 19th Battalion, South Carolina Cavalry

Company A, Kirk's Company, South Carolina Partisan Rangers, the May River Troop
Company B, Captain E.S. Keitt's Company Mounted Riflemen, South Carolina Volunteers
Company C, Kirk's Squadron of Partisan Rangers, Company B
Company D, Captain J.J. Steele's Company
Company E, the Ripley Rangers

Independent Cavalry Organizations

Captain Manning J. Kirk's Company, South Carolina Partisan Rangers, Kirk's Partisan Rangers, the May River Troop
The Etiwan Rangers
The German Hussars
Keitt's Mounted Riflemen
The North Santee Mounted Rifles
The Pickens Rangers, the Aiken Mounted Infantry
The Ripley Rangers
The Stono Scouts, Stono Rangers

The 1st Battalion/1st Regiment, South Carolina Artillery Regulars

Company A, the Sumter Battery, the Calhoun Battery, the Calhoun Artillery, the Calhoun Flying Artillery, the Light Battery
Company B, the Brooks Flying Artillery

The 2nd Battalion/2nd Regiment, South Carolina Artillery

Company C, the Edisto Artillery
Company D, the Inglis Light Artillery
Company E, the Allen Guards
Company F, the Carolina Artillery
Company G, the Silverton Artillery
Company I, the Orangeburg Artillery

The 3rd Battalion, South Carolina Light Artillery

Company A, the Furman Artillery, Earle's Battery Light Artillery
Company B, the Columbia Flying Artillery, the Columbia Artillery, the Blake Artillery
Company C, the Wilson Light Artillery, Culpeper's Light Battery
Company D, the Wagner Light Artillery, Kanapaux's Light Artillery
Company E, the Yeadon Light Artillery
Company F, the Chesnut Light Artillery
Company G, the DeSaussure Light Artillery, the DePass Light Battery
Company I, Bowden's Battery Light Artillery
Company K, Richardson's Company

The 18th Battalion, South Carolina Artillery

The Beauregard Louisiana Artillery
The German Artillery, Company B
The Gist Guard, Gilchrist's Independent Company, South Carolina Heavy Artillery
The Horry Light Artillery, the Alston Light Artillery
Mathewes's Artillery

The McQueen Light Artillery, Gregg's Battery

The Palmetto Guard Artillery, the Palmetto Guards, the Buist Light Artillery

The Pee Dee Artillery, McIntosh's Battery

INDEPENDENT ARTILLERY BATTERIES

The Beaufort Volunteer Artillery

Beauregard's Battery–South Carolina Artillery, T.B. Ferguson's Company, Light Artillery

Brooks Guard Battery Artillery, Captain Fickling's Company, South Carolina Artillery, Fickling's Battery–Brooks Light Artillery, South Carolina; Rhett's Company, Rhett–Fickling's Battery

The Calhoun Artillery

The Chesterfield Light Artillery

The German Artillery Battalion, SCV

The German Light Artillery, the German Flying Artillery, the Charleston German Artillery, Captain Bachman's Company, South Carolina Artillery–German Light Artillery, Captain William K. Bachman's Battery

The Gist Guard Light Artillery, Captain Gilchrist's Company–the Gist Guard-South Carolina Heavy Artillery, Robert C. Gilchrist's Company, South Carolina Heavy Artillery

The Lafayette Artillery, Kanapaux's Battery—Lafayette Light Artillery—South Carolina, the Lafayette Light Artillery

The Macbeth Light Artillery, Captain Jeter's Company, South Carolina Light Artillery, Robert Boyce's Company, South Carolina Light Artillery

The Marion Artillery, the Marion Light Artillery, SCV

The Mathewes Artillery, Captain Mathewes's Company, South Carolina Heavy Artillery, Mathewes's Battery, Mathewes's Independent Company, F.N. Bonneau's Company Artillery, SCV, Confederate States Provisional Army

The McQueen Light Artillery

The Palmetto Light Artillery, Captain Garden's Company—the Palmetto Light Battery—South Carolina Light Artillery, the Palmetto Light Battery; Garden's Battery, SCV, Confederate States Provisional Army

The Pee Dee Light Artillery, Captain Zimmerman's Company, the Pee Dee Artillery, South Carolina Artillery, Captain McIntosh's Battery, Captain McIntosh's Company Light Artillery, Captain Brunson's Company, South Carolina Light Artillery

The Santee Light Artillery, Captain Christopher Gaillard's Company, Light Artillery, SCV, Gaillard's Light Artillery
Stephen D. Lee's Battery–South Carolina Artillery
The Waccamaw Light Artillery, Captain Mayham Ward's Battery, Captain Joshua Ward's Company, South Carolina Light Artillery
The Washington Artillery, Captain George H. Walter's Company, South Carolina Light Artillery, Walter's Battery–the Washington Artillery, Walter's Company–the Washington Artillery, Walter's Light Battery
The Washington Artillery, Captain Hart's Company of Horse Artillery, Hart's Battery, the Washington Light Artillery, Lee's Battery of Hampton's Horse Artillery, Halsey's Battery

Infantry Companies with Unknown Regimental or Battalion Affiliations

The Anderson Home Guard
The Anderson's Mills Home Guard
The Battleground Home Guard
The Bethel Guards
The Boy Cavalry
The Broad River Light Infantry
The Brooks Boys
The Bull Swamp Guards
The Burke Sharpshooters
The Carolina Greys
The Carolina Home Guards
The Charleston Guard
The Chesterfield Eagles
The Chichester Guards
The Citizen Guards
The City Guard of Charleston
The Claremont Vigilance and Military Volunteer Committee
The Confederate Guards
The Confederate Stars
The Davis Guards
The Dean Guards
The Edgefield Reserves
The Gasper Guards
The Georgetown Home Guard
The Georgetown Reserves
The Golden's Creek Company
The Greenville Home Guard

The Greenville Home Guards–State Troops
The Greenville Riflemen
Gregg Light Infantry
The Hanging Rock Home Guards
The Home Guard
The Home Guard of Charleston
The Home Guards of Edgefield District
The Home Guards of Yorkville
The Hope Guard
The Hudson Street Guard
The Independent Blair Guards
The Independent Men of Waxhaws
The Keitt Guard
The Lanham Guards
The Lynches Creek Home Guards
The Magrath Guard
The Manigault Guards
The Marion Men
The Mile Creek Home Guard
The Miles Grenadiers
The Mountain Creek Home Guards
The Mountain Guards
The Mountain Rangers
Old Men's Home Guards
The Palmetto Reserve Guards #6
The Pendleton Home Guard
The Pleasant Hill Guard
The Pleasant Lane Home Guards
The Port Royal Guards
The Pumpkin Town Home Guard, the Mountain Rangers
The Rebel Guard
The Rich Hill Guards
The Snow Creek Vigilant Committee
The Snow Hill Guards
The Southern Boys
The Southern Guards
The St. George's Volunteers
The St. Paul's Home Guards
The Sumter Cadets
The University Riflemen
The Village Creek Home Guard
The Walhalla Riflemen

The Walhalla State Guards
The Wild Cat Vigilant Company
The Yeadon Blues

Cavalry Organizations with Unknown Regimental or Battalion Affiliations

The Abbeville Squadron
The Anderson Troop
The Ashepoo Guerillas
The Black River Troop
The Claremont Troop, the Sumter Cavalry
The Columbia Mounted Rifles
The Combahee Rangers
Farmer's Rangers
Home Guard of Cavalry in St. Paul's Parish
The Horry Hussars
The Jefferson Nullifiers
The Little River Rangers
The Lone Star Dragoons
The Mountain Cavalry
The Mounted Minute Men
The Newberry Chargers
Patterson's Rangers
The Richland Rangers
The Salem Mounted Men
The Saluda Rangers, the Saluda Sentinels
The Southern Rights Dragoons
The Spartan Rangers, the Seneca Rangers
The Spartan Troop

Artillery Organizations with Unknown Regimental or Battalion Affiliations

The Camden Artillery
The Fairfield Artillery
The Georgetown Artillery
The McDuffie Artillery

Notes

Introduction

1. William J. Rivers, "Annual Report of the State Historian of Confederate Records For The Year 1899." Microcopy 13, Roll 29, South Carolina Department of Archives and History.

Overview

1. Charles E. Cauthen, *South Carolina Goes to War, 1860–1865*, 113. (Hereafter cited as Cauthen, *South Carolina Goes to War*.); Alexander S. Salley, comp., *South Carolina Troops in Confederate Service*, 1: 429. (Hereafter cited as Salley, *SC Troops*.)
2. *Acts of the General Assembly of the State of South Carolina, passed in November and December 1860 and January 1861*, 848. (Hereafter cited as *Acts*.)
3. *Acts*, 849.
4. Cauthen, *South Carolina Goes to War*, 114.
5. Confederate Historian, "Annual Report For The Year 1899, " 9, South Carolina Department of Archives and History. (Hereafter cited as Confederate Historian, "Annual Report.")
6. The county system of subdivision was not adopted until 1868.
7. Lockwood Tower, ed., *A Carolinian Goes To War, The Civil Narrative of Arthur Middleton Manigault, Brigadier General, C.S.A., R.*, 5. (Hereafter cited as Tower, *A Carolinian Goes To War*.)
8. Johnson Hagood, *Memoirs of the War of Secession, From the Original Manuscripts of Johnson Hagood*, 27. (Hereafter cited as Hagood, *Memoirs*.)
9. Charles E. Cauthen, ed., *Journals of the South Carolina Executive Councils 1861 and 1862*, 4. (Hereafter cited as Cauthen, ed., *Journals*.)
10. Cauthen, *South Carolina Goes to War*, 114.
11. Ibid.; Douglas Southall Freeman, *Lee's Lieutenants*, 1, 518. (Hereafter cited as Freeman, *Lee's Lieutenants*.)
12. Cauthen, ed., *Journals*, 17, 18; Salley, *SC Troops*, 1:1; United States War Department, *The War of the Rebellion: A Compilation of the Official Records of the Union and Confederate Armies*, series 4, volume 1, page 913. (Hereafter cited as *OR*. It should be noted that some volumes in this series are broken into parts, while some are not. Entries for volumes with parts are listed with a series, a volume, a part and a page number or numbers; entries for volumes without parts are listed only with a series, a volume and a page number or numbers.)

13. *Acts,* 854; *OR,* 4, 1, 914.
14. Confederate Historian, "Annual Report," 11.
15. *OR,* 4, 1, 914.
16. Ibid.
17. *Charleston Mercury,* 12-30-1861. (Hereafter cited as *CM.*)
18. *OR,* 1, 1, 265
19. Southern Historical Society Papers, 14, 51. (Hereafter cited as SHSP.)
20. Salley, *SC Troops,* 3:284; Cauthen, ed., *Journals,* 67, 68; Cauthen, *South Carolina Goes to War,* 135.
21. Confederate Historian, "Annual Report," 24.
22. Cauthen, ed., *Journals,* 77–79.
23. United Daughters of the Confederacy, South Carolina Division, *Recollections and Reminiscences, 1861–1865 through World War 1.* 9, 242. (Hereafter cited as *RR.*)
24. Confederate Historian, "Annual Report," 26.
25. Cauthen, *South Carolina Goes to War,* 116; *OR,* 4, 1, 412.
26. Confederate Historian, "Annual Report," 30.
27. *Lancaster Ledger,* 9-4-61. (Hereafter cited as *LL.*)
28. Cauthen, *South Carolina Goes to War,* 136.
29. *Camden Confederate,* 11-15-1861. (Hereafter cited as *TCC.*)
30. Cauthen, *South Carolina Goes to War,* 137.
31. *OR,* 4, 1, 779; *TCC,* 12-20-61.
32. Cauthen, *South Carolina Goes to War,* 138.
33. Confederate Historian, "Annual Report," 44.
34. *CM,* 12-18-61.
35. Confederate Historian, "Annual Report," 46.
36. Ibid.
37. *CM,* 2-19-62.
38. Ibid.
39. Cauthen, ed., *Journals,* 102
40. *CM,* 5-1-62; *Edgefield Advertiser,* 5-7-62. (Hereafter cited as *EA.*)
41. *OR,* 4, 1, 973; Cauthen, *South Carolina Goes to War,* 144; *CM,* 5-1-62.
42. *OR,* 4, 1, 963.
43. Cauthen, *South Carolina Goes to War,* 144.
44. *EA,* 3-19-62.
45. *CM,* 5-1-62; Cauthen, ed., *Journals,* 305.
46. *OR,* 4, 1, 975.
47. *CM,* 3-13-62; Cauthen, ed., *Journals,* 107.
48. *CM,* 3-13-62.
49. Cauthen, ed., *Journals,* 103; *OR,* 4, 1, 973–975; *EA,* 3-19-62.
50. *CM,* 5-1-62.
51. Cauthen, ed., *Journals,* 127.
52. *CM,* 4-21-62; Cauthen, ed., *Journals,* 154.
53. Ibid.
54. *OR,* 4, 1, 1062.
55. Confederate Historian, "Annual Report," 47, 57, 58; *CM,* 5-1-62.
56. *Yorkville Enquirer,* 9-17-62. (Hereafter cited as *YE.*); *EA,* 9-1-62.
57. D. Augustus Dickert, *History of Kershaw's Brigade,* 105. (Hereafter cited as Dickert, *Kershaw's Brigade.*)
58. *CM,* 4-21-62; *LL,* 10-8-62.

59. Dickert, *Kershaw's Brigade,* 332.
60. *Charleston Daily Courier*, 2-9-64. (Hereafter cited as *CDC.*)
61. *OR,* 1, 35, 1, 518, 577.
62. J.F.J Caldwell, *The History of a Brigade of South Carolinians*, 170.
63. *Daily Southern Carolinian*, 2-22-64. (Hereafter cited as *DSC.*)
64. *CM,* 7-12-62.
65. Confederate Historian, "Annual Report," 58
66. Ibid., 25.
67. Ibid., 57–58.
68. Cauthen, *South Carolina Goes to War*, 110.
69. Confederate Historian, "Annual Report," 25, 53.
70. *LL,* 10-8-62.
71. Cauthen, ed., *Journals,* 154.
72. Ibid.
73. *LL,* 7-30-62.
74. *CM,* 5-16-62; Cauthen, ed., *Journals,* 154–156; *TCC,* 5-2-62.
75. *YE,* 8-13-62.
76. Cauthen, ed., *Journals,* 154.
77. *CM,* 5-16-62; Cauthen, ed., *Journals,* 154; *YE,* 6-24-63.
78. Cauthen, ed., *Journals,* 228.
79. Ibid., 172.
80. Ibid., 173.
81. *CM,* 11-6-62.
82. Cauthen, ed., *Journals,* 154; *TCC,* 8-22-62.
83. *OR,* 4, 2, 155–56.
84. Ibid., 4, 2, 176.
85. *YE,* 11-12-62.
86. Cauthen, ed., *Journals,* 293; *TCC,* 11-14-62.
87. Cauthen, *South Carolina Goes to War,* 161.
88. *OR,* 1, 53, 281; Judith N. McArthur and Orville Vernon Burton, *A Gentleman and An Officer—A Military and Social History of James B. Griffin's Civil War*, 262. (Hereafter cited as McArthur, *Griffin.*)
89. McArthur, *Griffin*, 266.
90. *YE,* 2-11-63.
91. *OR,* 1, 14, 784–785.
92. Ibid., 1, 14, 816.
93. Cauthen, ed., *Journals,* 228.
94. *TCC,* 7-25-62.
95. Cauthen, *South Carolina Goes to War,* 146.
96. *TCC,* 11-14-62.
97. Cauthen, ed., *Journals,* 292.
98. *OR,* 4, 2, 580–582; *TCC,* 7-31-63; *Triweekly Watchman*, 7-18-63.
99. *OR,* 1, 28, 2, 145.
100. Ibid., 4, 2, 580.
101. Ibid., 1, 28, 2, 145.
102. *Greenville Southern Enterprise*, 7-30-63; Cauthen, *South Carolina Goes to War,* 192; *LL,* 6-24-63; *OR,* 1, 28, 2, 144.
103. *OR,* 1, 28, 2, 145; *YE,* 6-24-63.
104. *OR,* 1, 28, 2, 145.
105. *LL,* 7-15-63; *OR,* 4, 3, 38–39.

106. *OR*, 3, 38–39; 4, 2, 665; *YE*, 6-24-63; 7-29-63; *Carolina Spartan*, 8-27-63. (Hereafter cited as *CS*.)
107. *CM*, 8-14-63.
108. *OR*, 1, 28, 2, 339; 4, 2, 1058.
109. Ibid., 1, 28, 2, 339.
110. Ibid., 1, 35, 1, 562; 4, 2, 1058; *CM*, 2-15-64.
111. Lloyd Halliburton, *Saddle Soldiers, The Civil War Correspondence of General William Stokes 4th South Carolina Cavalry*, 125 (Hereafter cited as Halliburton, *Saddle Soldiers*.); *Sumter Watchman*, 1-18-63.
112. *OR*, 1, 35, 2, 456.
113. *DSC*, 3-15-64.
114. *LL*, 3-2-64; *EA*, 2-24-64.
115. *YE*, 3-2-64.
116. Cauthen, *South Carolina Goes to War*, 194.
117. *EA*, 2-24-64.
118. *YE*, 3-23-64.
119. *DSC*, 4-8-64.
120. *YE*, 6-15-64.
121. Ibid., 6-22-64.
122. Ibid., 7-13-64
123. Ibid., 7-20-64.
124. *EA*, 8-17-64; *LL*, 12-18-64.
125. *EA*, 1-4-65; *Compiled Service Records of Confederate Soldiers Who Served in Organizations from the State of South Carolina*, National Archives and Records Administration, M267, 391. (Hereafter cited as *CSR*.)
126. *RR*, 7, 27.
127. *CM*, 9-6-64.
128. *YE*, 3-29-65.
129. *EA*, 4-19-65
130. Ibid.
131. Ibid., 4-5-65.
132. Confederate Historian, "Annual Report," 84.
133. Ibid., 80.
134. Randolph W. Kirkland Jr, *Broken Fortunes—South Carolina Soldiers, Sailors & Citizens Who Died in the Service of Their Country and State in the War for Southern Independence, 1861–1865*, xiv. (Hereafter cited as Kirkland, *Broken Fortunes*.)
135. Confederate Historian, "Annual Report," 84.
136. *CM*, 4-21-62.
137. *Confederate Veteran*, 34, 221. (Hereafter cited as *CV*.)
138. *Due West Telescope*, 5-2-62. (Hereafter cited as *DWT*.)

Chapter 1

1. *OR*, 1, 28, 1, 537; *CM*, 7-3-62; *CSR*, M267, 110.
2. *OR*, 4, 1, 185.
3. *Keowee Courier (Walhalla)*, 2-16-61.
4. Ibid.
5. *CM*, 1-24-61.
6. SHSP, 48, 73; *CM*, 3-3-63.
7. SHSP, 48, 213; 49, 5, 76.
8. Ibid., 49, 99–100.

9. *OR*, 1, 28, 1, 536.
10. Ibid., 1, 35, 1, 518.
11. Ibid., 1, 35, 1, 577.
12. SHSP, 39, 146–52.
13. *YE*, 1-3-61.
14. *CM*, 1-24-61.
15. Ibid., 8-3-61.
16. Hagood, *Memoirs*, 92
17. *CM*, 8-3-61.
18. *EA*, 5-1864.
19. *RR*, 9, 587.
20. *CM*, 8-3-61.
21. South Carolina Department of Archives and History, *Roll of the Dead, South Carolina Troops Confederate States Service* (Hereafter cited as SCDAH, *Roll of the Dead.*); *CM*, 7-20-63, 7-23-63, 7-28-63.
22. *RR*, 5, 324; Warren Ripley, *The Battle of Chapman's Fort, May 26, 1864*, 14, (Hereafter cited as Ripley, *Chapman's Fort.*); *OR*, 1, 28, 1, 74.
23. *EA*, 7-22-63.
24. *Sumter Watchman*, 2-3-64.
25. Woodward, C. Vann and Elisabeth Muhlenfeld, *The Private Mary Chesnut, The Unpublished Civil War Diaries*, 18 (Hereafter cited as Woodward, *Mary Chesnut.*); *CM*, 2-13-64.
26. *Sumter Watchman*, 1-27-64.
27. Ibid., 2-3-64.
28. *Charleston Daily Courier*, 7-6-64; 7-18-64. (Hereafter cited as *CDC*.)
29. *OR*, 1, 47, 1, 1085.
30. *CDC*, 7-6-64; 7-18-64.
31. *CV*, 8, 32; Ulysses Robert Brooks, ed., *Butler and His Cavalry in the War of Secession, 1861–1865*, 474. (Hereafter cited as Brooks, *Butler.*).
32. *CV*, 4, 421.
33. *OR*, 1, 35, 1, 227; *CM*, 7-27-64; *CDC*, 7-23-64.
34. *CV*, 4, 421-22.
35. *CDC*, 7-23-64.
36. *Keowee Courier (Walhalla)*, 2-16-61
37. *CM*, 8-3-61.
38. Ibid., 8-3-61; *CV*, 4, 421.
39. Confederate Historian, "Annual Report," 12.
40. *Keowee Courier (Walhalla)*, 2-16-61.
41. *CM*, 1-24-61.
42. Ibid., 8-3-61.
43. *Keowee Courier (Walhalla)*, 2-16-61.
44. *CM*, 1-24-61.
45. *Keowee Courier (Walhalla)*, 2-16-61.
46. Salley, *SC Troops*, 1: 57.
47. Louise Haskell Daly, Alexander Cheves Haskell, *The Portrait of a Man*, 106. (Hereafter cited as Daly, *Portrait.*)
48. Salley, *SC Troops*, 1:79.
49. *Abbeville Press*, 7-17-63 (Hereafter cited as *AP.*); *CM*, 7-11-63, 7-13-63, 7-21-63; *CV*, 4, 6; John Johnson, *The Defense of Charleston Harbor including Fort Sumter and the Adjacent Islands, 1863–1865*, 91. (Hereafter cited as Johnson, *Charleston Harbor.*)

50. Johnson, *Charleston Harbor,* 91.
51. Harriet P. Lynch, *Reminiscences and Sketches of Confederate Times,* 18. 21.
52. *YE,* 3-22-65.
53. *CM,* 4-14-63.
54. *YE,* 3-22-65.
55. *OR,* 4, 1, 185.
56. Ibid., 1, 28, 2, 528; *CM,* 11-30-63.
57. *CDC,* 5-14-64.
58. *YE,* 3-22-65.
59. *CM,* 1-24-61.
60. *CV,* 25, 32.
61. C.M. Calhoun, "Liberty Dethroned," 29. (Hereafter cited as Calhoun, "Liberty.")
62. *OR,* 1, 28, 1, 536.
63. SCDAH, *Roll of the Dead*; *CM,* 7-20-63, 7-23-63.
64. *OR,* 1, 28, 2, 315; *RR,* 5, 325.
65. *LL,* 9-9-63.
66. *CM,* 9-8-63.
67. Ibid., 4-11-63.
68. Stewart Sifakis, *Compendium of the Confederate Armies—South Carolina and Georgia,* 55. (Hereafter cited as Sifakis, *Compendium.*)
69. *OR,* 1, 44, 875.
70. Ibid., 1, 44, 997.
71. Ibid., 1, 44, 2, 1070.
72. Ibid., 1, 47, 1, 1063; 1, 47, 3, 732.
73. Ibid., 1, 47, 1, 1063.
74. Ibid., 1, 1, 36.
75. Ibid., 1, 1, 36, 50.
76. Ibid.
77. *CM,* 1-30-62.
78. *OR,* 1, 14, 18.
79. Ibid., 1, 14, 269; Johnson, *Charleston Harbor,* Appendix A, v.
80. *OR,* 1, 14, 269.
81. Ibid., 1, 28, 2, 162.
82. Sifakis, *Compendium,* 55.
83. *OR,* 1, 28, 1, 413; Johnson, *Charleston Harbor,* 87.
84. *OR,* 1, 28, 1, 414; *CM,* 7-17-63; 7-28-63; Johnson, *Charleston Harbor,* Appendix F, lxxii.
85. *OR,* 1, 28, 1, 372.
86. Ibid., 1, 28, 1, 535; 1, 28, 2, 212; *CM,* 7-28-63.
87. Ibid., 1, 28, 1, 376.
88. Ibid., 1, 28, 2, 245, 325.
89. *OR,* 1, 28, 1, 520.
90. *CM,* 9-8-63.
91. *OR,* 1, 28, 2, 367.
92. Ibid., 1, 28, 1, 742.
93. Ibid., 1, 28, 1, 744.
94. Ibid., 1, 28, 2, 467, 1, 28, 2, 601; 1, 35, 1, 559.
95. Ibid., 1, 35, 2, 416, 457.
96. Ibid., 1, 35, 1, 169.

97. Ibid., 1, 35, 2, 598.
98. Ibid., 1, 35, 1, 220.
99. Ibid., 1, 35, 1, 231, 250.
100. Ibid., 1, 35, 1, 233, 250.
101. Ibid., 1, 35, 2, 644.
102. SHSP, 3, 267; *CM*, 12-16-64; *CDC*, 12-19-64.
103. Johnson, *Charleston Harbor*, 256.
104. Brooks, *Butler*, 474.

Chapter 2

1. SHSP, 14, 37–38.
2. Ibid.
3. Ibid., 14, 39.
4. *CDC*, 6-23-62.
5. SHSP, 14, 37–38.
6. *OR*, 1, 28, 2, 171.
7. Hagood, *Memoirs*, 207.
8. *CM*, 6-21-62; *CDC*, 6-23-62.
9. *CDC*, 6-23-62.
10. Ibid.
11. Ibid.
12. *CM*, 10-7-63.
13. *Triweekly Watchman*, 8-17-62.
14. *CDC*, 10-27-72.
15. *OR*, 1, 14, 289.
16. *RR*, 7, 17.
17. Ibid., 9, 400.

Chapter 3

1. *CM*, 6-3-63.
2. W.S. Dunlop, *Lee's Sharpshooters or, The Forefront of Battle*, 17 (Hereafter cited as Dunlop, *Lee's Sharpshooters*.); Susan Williams Benson, ed., *Berry Benson's Civil War Book, Memoirs of a Confederate Scout and Sharpshooter*, 56, 60. (Hereafter cited as Benson, *Berry Benson*.)
3. Caldwell, *History*, 130.
4. Dunlop, *Lee's Sharpshooters*, 23.
5. Daly, *Portrait*, 228.
6. *CV*, 19, 534; 21, 499; 6, 435.
7. Dunlop, *Lee's Sharpshooters*, 279.
8. *RR*, 6, 193.
9. Ibid., 194; Benson, *Berry Benson*, 178.
10. *CV*, 29, 534; *RR*, 1, 323.
11. *RR*, 1, 323.
12. *CV*, 31, 51.
13. *CM*, 7-19-64.
14. Ibid.
15. Ibid., 8-4-64; 8-23-64.
16. Dunlop, *Lee's Sharpshooters*, 280.
17. Ibid., 282.

Chapter 4

1. *CDC*, 6-24-62.
2. *CM*, 3-1-62.
3. Ibid., 6-16-63; 6-23-62.
4. *CDC*, 6-24-62.
5. Ibid.
6. Ibid., 6-23-62.
7. *CM*, 9-3-63.
8. SCDAH, *Roll of the Dead*; *CM*, 7-17-63.
9. *CM*, 10-11-62; 11-3-62.

Chapter 5

1. Eugene W. Jones Jr., *Enlisted for The War, The Struggles of the Gallant 24th Regiment, South Carolina Volunteers, Infantry 1861–1865,* ix. (Hereafter cited as Jones, *Struggles*.)
2. *CM*, 12-18-61.
3. Roster of Officers, Confederate Historian, South Carolina Department of Archives and History, S108079.
4. *CM*, 12-24-61.
5. Jones, *Struggles*, 7.
6. *CM*, 2-20-62.
7. Confederate Historian, "Annual Report," 51.
8. Jones, *Struggles*, 11.
9. *CM*, 3-20-62; 7-28-64.
10. Jones, *Struggles*, 9.
11. *CM*, 1-8-63.
12. Jones, *Struggles*, 59–60; Cauthen, ed., *Journals*, 208.
13. Jones, *Struggles*, 47.
14. *CDC*, 7-27-64.
15. Jones, *Struggles*, 4.
16. *CM*, 10-3-63.
17. *CDC*, 7-27-64.
18. *DSC*, 8-25-64; *CM*, 7-27-64.
19. *CM*, 7-28-64.
20. *DSC*, 8-25-64.
21. *CDC*, 7-27-64.
22. Jones, *Struggles*, 5.
23. Ibid., 7.
24. *CM*, 5-18-63.
25. Ibid., 10-3-63.
26. Ibid., 5-19-64.
27. Ibid., 12-28-64; *CDC*, 12-23-65.
28. *CV*, 7, 262; 14, 289.
29. Jones, *Struggles*, 42.
30. Ibid., 59.
31. *CSR*, M267, 341.
32. Ibid.
33. Robert K. Krick, *Lee's Colonels, A Biographical Register of the Field Officers of the Army of Northern Virginia*, 480. (Hereafter cited as Krick, *Lee's Colonels*.)
34. Jones, *Struggles*, 89, 100–101.

35. *CM*, 10-3-63.
36. Ibid., 12-24-64; 1-7-65; *CDC*, 12-27-64.
37. *CM*, 1-27-65; Jones, *Struggles*, 349.
38. Jones, *Struggles*, 230.
39. Ibid., 194.
40. SHSP, 11, 483.
41. *DSC*, 5-26-64.
42. *CDC*, 9-6-64; *CM*, 8-24-64.
43. Jones, *Struggles*, 374.
44. *CM*, 12-24-61; 1-1-62.
45. Ibid., 11-29-60.
46. Jones, *Struggles*, 13; *CM*, 12-24-61.
47. *CDC*, 3-22-61; *CM*, 12-25-61.
48. *CM*, 3-20-62.
49. *CDC*, 3-22-62.
50. *CM*, 10-3-63, 5-23-64.
51. *CDC*, 5-28-63.
52. *CM*, 6-3-63; *CDC*, 5-28-63.
53. *CDC*, 6-17-63.
54. *CM*, 5-18-64; 2-4-65; 11-5-64; *CDC*, 11-28-64.
55. Jones, *Struggles*, 207.
56. Ibid., 5.
57. *CDC*, 3-27-62.
58. *CSR*, M267, 341.
59. *CM*, 9-29-63.
60. Ibid., 8-24-64; *CDC*, 8-25-64.
61. *CM*, 3-20-62.
62. Jones, *Struggles*, 332.
63. *CM*, 10-3-63; 5-23-64; 8-24-64.
64. Ibid., 3-17-62; Jones, *Struggles*, 14.
65. *CM*, 3-17-62.
66. Ibid.
67. Jones, *Struggles*, 14.
68. *CM*, 8-9-62.
69. J.C. Garlington, *Men of the Time, Sketches of Living Notables, A Biographical Encyclopedia of Contemporaneous South Carolina Leaders*, 169. (Hereafter cited as Garlington, *Men of the Time.*)
70. *CSR*, M267, 337.
71. *CM*, 10-3-63.
72. Ibid., 7-1-64.
73. Ibid., 12-28-64; Kirkland, *Broken Fortunes*, 33.
74. *CM*, 3-20-62.
75. Ibid., 10-3-63.
76. Ibid., 10-20-63.
77. Jones, *Struggles*, 380.
78. Roster of Officers, Confederate Historian, South Carolina Department of Archives and History, S108079; Confederate Historian, "Annual Report," 50.
79. Jones, *Struggles*, 14.
80. *CDC*, 4-1-62.

81. *CM*, 10-3-63.
82. Ibid., 8-24-64.
83. *CDC*, 5-23-64.
84. *CM*, 8-24-64; *CDC*, 8-25-64.
85. *CM*, 2-4-65; 11-5-64; *CDC*, 11-28-64.
86. *CM*, 11-5-64.
87. Confederate Historian, "Annual Report," 50; Roster of Officers, Confederate Historian, South Carolina Department of Archives and History, S108079.
88. *CSR*, M267, 341.
89. Jones, *Struggles*, 50–51.
90. *CM*, 10-3-63.
91. Ibid., 8-24-64; *CDC*, 8-25-64.
92. Jones, *Struggles*, 335.
93. Roster of Officers, Confederate Historian, South Carolina Department of Archives and History, S108079.
94. *RR*, 8, 274; Robert J. Stevens, *Captain Bill, The Records and Writings of Captain William Henry Edwards (and others) Company A, 17th Regiment South Carolina Volunteers, Confederate States of America*, 2, 66. (Hereafter cited as Stevens, *Captain Bill.*)
95. *RR*, 8, 274.
96. *CSR*, M267, 342.
97. *RR*, 8, 274.
98. *CM*, 10-3-63.
99. Ibid.
100. Ibid., 7-1-64; Jones, *Struggles*, 392.
101. *CM*, 2-4-65; 11-5-64; *CDC*, 11-28-64.
102. *CM*, 11-5-64; *RR*, 8, 103.
103. Jones, *Struggles*, 14.
104. Steve Batson, Website on the 16th Regiment, S.C.V. <http://www.geocities.com/BourbonStreet/Square/3873/franklina.html. (Hereafter cited as Batson, Website.)
105. *EA*, 1-22-62.
106. Ibid., 1-22-62; 4-16-62.
107. *CM*, 5-23-63.
108. Jones, *Struggles*, 252.
109. Ibid., 414; *Cyclopedia of Eminent and Representative Men of the Carolinas of the Nineteenth Century*, 276. (Hereafter cited as *Cyclopedia.*)
110. Roster of Officers, Confederate Historian, South Carolina Department of Archives and History, S108079.
111. Jones, *Struggles*, 17.
112. *Confederate Military History Extended Edition, Volume 6, South Carolina*, 879. (Hereafter cited as *CMH.*)
113. *CSR*, M267, 342.
114. *RR*, 7, 214; *CMH*, 879.
115. *CM*, 6-19-62.
116. *RR*, 10, 214.
117. *EA*, 5-25-64; *DSC*, 5-26-64; *RR*, 9, 39, 392.
118. *CM*, 8-24-64.
119. Jones, *Struggles*, 374.
120. Sifakis, *Compendium*, 101.

121. *CM*, 2-12-63.
122. *OR*, 1, 47, 3, 735.
123. Jones, *Struggles*, 9.
124. *EA*, 4-9-62.
125. Ibid., 4-16-62.
126. Jones, *Struggles*, 17.
127. *OR*, 1, 14, 499; *CM*, 4-30-62; Jones, *Struggles*, 2.
128. *CM*, 5-21-62.
129. *OR*, 1, 14, 18.
130. *CM*, 6-5-62; 6-21-62; *CDC*, 6-21-62.
131. *CM*, 6-17-62; 6-19-62.
132. *OR*, 1, 14, 582; Jones, *Struggles*, 47.
133. *OR*, 1, 14, 742.
134. Jones, *Struggles*, 71.
135. *CM*, 10-11-62; 10-31-62.
136. *CDC*, 5-7-63; *YE*, 5-13-63; *OR*, 1, 14, 926.
137. *CM*, 5-6-63; 5-22-63; 6-3-63; Walter Brian Cisco, *States Right Gist, A South Carolina General of the Civil War*, 92. (Hereafter cited as Cisco, *States Right Gist.*)
138. *YE*, 12-9-63; Jones, *Struggles*, 138.
139. *CDC*, 7-21-64.
140. Jones, *Struggles*, 173.
141. *CM*, 8-20-64; 8-24-64; *EA*, 8-3-64.
142. *CM*, 11-5-64; *CDC*, 11-28-64.
143. *CM*, 11-5-64.
144. *EA*, 2-8-65.
145. Jones, *Struggles*, 248.

Chapter 6

1. *CM*, 1-7-65; *CDC*, 12-23-64.
2. *CM*, 8-24-64; Jones, *Struggles*, 374.

Chapter 7

1. Gary R. Baker, *Cadets in Gray*, 29. (Hereafter cited as Baker, *Cadets.*)
2. *Acts*, 870.
3. *CM*, 10-24-61; Baker, *Cadets*, 41.
4. *CM*, 10-3-61.
5. *CSR*, M267, 379.
6. *CM*, 9-25-62.
7. Ibid., 12-16-64.
8. Ibid., 5-3-61.
9. Ibid.
10. *OR*, 1, 47, 2, 1070.
11. Baker, *Cadets*, 12.
12. Ibid., 39.
13. Ibid., 40.
14. Ibid., 43.
15. *OR*, 1, 14, 835.
16. Ibid., 1, 28, 2, 326, 368, 382; Baker, *Cadets*, 68; *CMH*, 753.
17. Baker, *Cadets*, 84.

18. Ibid., 115.
19. Ibid., 119.
20. Ibid., 132.
21. *The Civil War in Southwestern South Carolina December 1864–January 1865*, 8. (Hereafter cited as *Civil War in Western South Carolina*.)
22. *CM*, 12-9-64, 12-16-64; *CDC*, 12-9-64, 12-19-64.
23. *OR*, 1, 44, 446.
24. Baker, *Cadets*, 155.
25. *OR*, 1, 47, 2, 1245; *RR*, 7, 31.
26. *OR*, 1, 47, 2, 1274, 1361.
27. *RR*, 7, 32; *CV*, 35, 307.
28. A.P Ford and M.J. Ford, *Life in the Confederate Army*, 45. (Hereafter cited as Ford, *Life*.)
29. *RR*, 7, 35.
30. *CDC*, 9-15-63.
31. Ibid., 10-3-63.
32. *CDC*, 10-27-64; 10-28-64; 11-3-64; 11-5-64; 11-7-64.
33. *OR*, 1, 35, 2, 599.
34. Ibid., 1, 35, 2, 644.
35. *CDC*, 10-27-64; 10-28-64; 11-3-64; 11-5-64; 11-7-64.
36. *OR*, 1, 44, 875, 985.
37. Sifakis, *Compendium*, 106.
38. *Daily Southern Guardian*, 2-17-63 (Hereafter cited as *DSG*.); *CM*, 3-17-63.
39. *YE*, 4-22-63.
40. *DSG*, 4-7-63.
41. Confederate Historian, "Annual Report," 82.
42. *CDC*, 9-15-63.
43. Ibid., 6-9-61; *YE*, 5-30-61; *LL*, 6-3-61.
44. *YE*, 5-30-61.
45. *EA*, 11-20-61.
46. *CDC*, 8-7-61.
47. Ibid., 9-21-61.
48. Ibid.
49. Ibid., 10-9-61; 11-8-61; 11-11-61.
50. Ibid., 11-13-61; 11-26-61.
51. Ibid., 11-13-61.
52. Ibid., 11-26-61.
53. Confederate Historian, "Annual Report," 73.
54. Ulysses Robert Brooks, ed., *Stories of the Confederacy*, 310. (Hereafter cited as Brooks, *Stories*.)
55. *OR*, 1, 44, 1008; 4, 3, 1083.
56. Brooks, *Stories*, 312.
57. Ibid., 311.
58. Ibid., 324, 325.
59. *RR*, 6, 185.
60. Brooks, *Stories*, 313.
61. Ibid., 325.
62. Ibid., 326.
63. *OR*, 1, 44, 923.
64. Confederate Historian, "Annual Report," 74.

65. Hagood, *Memoirs*, 472.
66. *OR*, 1, 44, 966.
67. *RR*, 5, 558.
68. Confederate Historian, "Annual Report," 74.
69. *OR*, 4, 3, 1083.

Chapter 8

1. *CM*, 11-6-62.
2. Ibid., 2-18-64.
3. Ibid., 8-1-62.
4. Sifakis, *Compendium*, 45.
5. *CDC*, 1-29-63; *CS*, 3-12-63.
6. Baker, *Cadets*, 97; Brooks, *Butler*, 244.
7. *CM*, 6-23-64.
8. Calhoun, "Liberty," 176.
9. Brooks, *Butler*, 549.
10. Calhoun, "Liberty," 144; Brooks, *Butler*, 346.
11. Calhoun, "Liberty," 170; Brooks, *Butler*, 342.
12. Calhoun, "Liberty," 131, 144.
13. Brooks, *Butler*, 339.
14. Ibid., 424.
15. Calhoun, "Liberty," 183.
16. A.B. Mulligan, *My Dear Mother and Sisters, The Civil War Letters of Captain A.B.* Mulligan *Company B, 5th South Carolina Cavalry, Butler's Division, Hampton's Corps, 1861–1865*, 156. (Hereafter cited as Mulligan, *My Dear Mother*.)
17. *EA*, 7-9-62.
18. *CV*, 22, 408; *EA*, 6-24-64, 6-29-64; *CM*, 6-23-64.
19. Calhoun, "Liberty," 119.
20. *CM*, 6-23-64.
21. *DSG*, 6-27-62.
22. *CM*, 6-23-64.
23. Ibid.; C.I. Walker, *Rolls and Historical Sketch of the Tenth Regiment, So. Ca. Volunteers in the Army of the Confederate States*, intro, 23. (Hereafter cited as Walker, *Rolls*.)
24. *CMH*, 648; *CV*, 2, 178.
25. Baker, *Cadets*, 58-59.
26. *CM*, 2-13-64.
27. Ibid., 6-23-64.
28. Baker, *Cadets*, 170.
29. Calhoun, "Liberty," 183; Brooks, *Butler*, 427.
30. *CDC*, 11-3-64.
31. *CM*, 12-16-63.
32. *CDC*, 10-11-64.
33. Ibid.
34. *CM*, 12-16-63.
35. *CDC*, 10-1-64.
36. *CM*, 6-23-64.
37. Brooks, *Stories*, 307.
38. *CM*, 6-23-64; *RR*, 1, 465.
39. Sifakis, *Compendium*, 45.

40. *OR*, 1, 47, 1, 1065.
41. *EA*, 9-24-62.
42. Brooks, *Butler*, 482.
43. *CM*, 11-6-62.
44. *OR*, 1, 28, 2, 169.
45. Ibid., 1, 28, 2, 169, 246, 326, 467, 544, 601; 1, 35, 1, 558.
46. *CM*, 7-15-63.
47. *OR*, 1, 28, 1, 196.
48. *CM*, 2-15-64.
49. *CM*, 3-12-64.
50. *OR*, 1, 35, 2, 458.
51. Ibid., 1, 35, 2, 362.
52. *DSC*, 5-5-64.
53. *CM*, 7-22-64.
54. Brooks, *Butler*, 190.
55. *CM*, 6-23-64.
56. Halliburton, *Saddle Soldiers*, 149; Brooks, *Butler*, 192.
57. *CM*, 7-15-64.
58. *CV*, 2, 178.
59. Calhoun, "Liberty," 139.
60. Brooks, *Butler*, 303.
61. Freeman, *Lee's Lieutenants*, 3: 589; Halliburton, *Saddle Soldiers*, 166.
62. *CM*, 10-12-64.
63. Ibid., 11-2-64; *CDC*, 11-3-64.
64. *CDC*, 12-8-64; Baker, *Cadets*, 129.
65. Halliburton, *Saddle Soldiers*, 184, 186.
66. *CDC*, 12-28-64; 1-6-65.
67. Calhoun, "Liberty," 170.
68. Brooks, *Butler*, 543.
69. Ibid., 418.
70. Sifakis, *Compendium*, 46.
71. Calhoun, "Liberty," 202.
72. *CV*, 2, 178.

Chapter 9

1. Daly, *Portrait*, xi.
2. Ibid., 130, 133, 134.
3. *CM*, 3-5-64.
4. Ibid., 4-2-64.
5. Daly, *Portrait*, 130.
6. Krick, *Lee's Colonels*, 342.
7. *CM*, 6-7-64.
8. Daly, *Portrait*, 125.
9. Ibid., 56, 61.
10. *CM*, 12-18-62.
11. Ibid., 5-6-63.
12. Daly, *Portrait*, 103.
13. Ibid., 132.
14. Ibid., 133.
15. *CM*, 10-8-64.

16. Krick, *Lee's Colonels*, 187; Daly, *Portrait*, xii.
17. R.A. Brock and Philip Van Doren Stern, *The Appomattox Roster*, 479. (Hereafter cited as Brock, *The Appomattox Roster.*)
18. Daly, *Portrait*, 164.
19. Ibid., 248.
20. Ibid.
21. *CM*, 6-6-64.
22. Brock, *The Appomattox Roster*, 479; *CV*, 5, 204.
23. *CV*, 5, 204.
24. *CM*, 6-6-64.
25. Edward Mortimer Boykin, *The Falling Flag*, 24. (Hereafter cited as Boykin, *The Falling Flag.*)
26. Brock, *The Appomattox Roster*, 479.
27. *For Love of a Rebel*, Arthur Manigault Chapter of the U.D.C., 139. (Hereafter cited as *For Love of a Rebel.*)
28. SHSP, 15, 479.
29. *CM*, 6-6-64; Daly, *Portrait*, 240.
30. *A Centennial of Incorporation*, 226.
31. *CV*, 4, 204.
32. *CM*, 3-5-64.
33. Ibid., 9-5-64.
34. Ibid., 4-30-61.
35. Ibid.; *DSG*, 7-7-63; *CDC*, 11-27-61.
36. *CM*, 4-13-61.
37. Ibid., 3-5-64.
38. Ibid., 6-6-64.
39. Brock, *The Appomattox Roster*, 481.
40. Samuel N. Thomas Jr. and Jason H. Silverman, eds., *A Rising Star Of Promise: The Civil War Odyssey of David Jackson Logan, 17th South Carolina Volunteers, 1861–1864*, 200. (Hereafter cited as Thomas, *Rising Star.*)
41. *Laurensville Herald*, 5-17-61. (Hereafter cited as *LH.*)
42. *CM*, 3-5-64.
43. Daly, *Portrait*, 243.
44. *CM*, 6-6-64.
45. Brock, *The Appomattox Roster*, 481.
46. *CM*, 9-5-64.
47. Daly, *Portrait*, 136.
48. SHSP, 15, 482.
49. *CM*, 6-6-64; 7-30-64.
50. Kirkland, *Broken Fortunes*, 217.
51. *CM*, 9-5-64.
52. Brock, *The Appomattox Roster*, 482.
53. *CM*, 8-31-61; 2-25-62; *TCC*, 7-4-62.
54. Mac Wyckoff, Website on South Carolina in the Civil War, <http://www.members.ripod.com/mwycoff. (Hereafter cited as Wyckoff, Website.)
55. *CM*, 3-5-64; 6-6-64; 9-5-64.
56. Ibid., 9-5-64; *CDC*, 8-29-64.
57. SHSP, 15, 483.
58. *Triweekly Watchman*, 9-17-62.
59. *CM*, 3-5-64.

60. Ibid., 6-6-64; *Sumter Watchman*, 6-8-64; *CDC*, 10-1-64.
61. *CM*, 9-5-64.
62. Brock, *The Appomattox Roster*, 483.
63. Confederate Historian, "Annual Report," 80.
64. Woodward, *Mary Chesnut*, 240.
65. *YE*, 11-28-64; *OR*, 1, 28, 2, 458.
66. *CM*, 6-6-64.
67. Brock, *The Appomattox Roster*, 479.
68. *CV*, 29, 332.
69. Daly, *Portrait*, 126.
70. *CM*, 6-6-64; *CDC*, 6-6-64.
71. *CM*, 6-7-64.
72. Ibid., 6-21-64; 7-15-64.
73. *DSG*, 7-14-64.
74. *CM*, 8-5-64.
75. *CDC*, 9-6-64.
76. *CM*, 9-5-64.
77. Sifakis, *Compendium*, 46.
78. *Jeremiah Smith and the Confederate War*, 144. (Hereafter cited as Smith, *Confederate War*.)
79. Boykin, *The Falling Flag*, 8.
80. *CV*, 29, 332.
81. Brock, *The Appomattox Roster*, 484.

Chapter 10

1. Krick, *Lee's Colonels*, 494.
2. Sifakis, *Compendium*, 48.

Chapter 11

1. *OR*, 1, 47, 2, 1249.
2. *CM*, 2-22-64.
3. *YE*, 11-28-64.
4. *OR*, 1, 35, 2, 457, 598, 644.
5. *CM*, 1-14-63.
6. Ibid., 6-2-62.
7. *OR*, 1, 47, 2, 1249.
8. Ibid.
9. *CMH*, 564.
10. *OR*, 1, 47, 2, 1249.
11. Ibid., 1, 47, 2, 1070-73.
12. Brooks, *Butler*, 478; *OR*, 1, 47, 1, 1065.
13. *OR*, 1, 44, 992, 44, 999; 1, 47, 2, 989.
14. Allan D. Thigpen, *Recollections of Potter's Raid*, 26. (Hereafter cited as Thigpen, *Potter's Raid*.)

Chapter 12

1. *OR*, 4, 1, 185.
2. Ibid., 4, 1, 317.
3. Ibid.
4. Ibid.,
5. Ibid., 1, 53, 170.

6. J.J. Lucas, "Sketch of Lucas's Battalion of Heavy Artillery," Miscellaneous Historical Sketches, 1868–1898, South Carolina Department of Archives and History, S108121. (Hereafter cited as "Sketch of Lucas's Battalion," SCDAH, S108121.)
7. Ibid.
8. Roster of Officers, Confederate Historian, South Carolina Department of Archives and History, S108079; *CM*, 7-18-63.
9. *CM*, 7-4-61; Confederate Historian, "Annual Report," 13; Cauthen, ed., *Journals*, 156.
10. *CMH*, 713.
11. *CDC*, 2-26-61; 9-18-63.
12. *CM*, 1-29-61.
13. Ibid., 4-8-62.
14. *CDC*, 9-18-63.
15. *Keowee Courier (Walhalla)*, 2-16-61.
16. Ibid.
17. *CM*, 7-4-61.

Chapter 13

1. Charles Inglesby, *Historical Sketch of the First Regiment of South Carolina Artillery (Regulars)*, 3.
2. Ibid., 5.
3. *OR*, 1, 35, 1, 577.
4. *CM*, 5-31-62.
5. Roster of Officers, Confederate Historian, South Carolina Department of Archives and History, S108079.
6. *South Carolina Historical Magazine*, 102: 1. (Hereafter cited as *SCHM*.)
7. *CDC*, 9-13-62.
8. Ibid.; *SCHM*, 102: 20.
9. *CSR*, M257, 58; Jones, *Struggles*, 51; *SCHM*, 102: 20.
10. Roster of Officers, Confederate Historian, South Carolina Department of Archives and History, S108079.
11. *CM*, 7-16-62.
12. Ibid., 7-17-62; 7-19-62.
13. *CDC*, 7-18-62.
14. Roster of Officers, Confederate Historian, South Carolina Department of Archives and History, S108079.
15. SHSP, 14, 39.
16. Johnson, *Charleston Harbor*, 131; *OR*, 1, 28, 1, 615.
17. SHSP, 7, 32; *OR*, 1, 47, 1, 1084.
18. *CV*, 1, 338.
19. *CM*, 7-6-64.
20. *YE*, 3-22-65; *OR*, 1, 47, 1, 1086.
21. Thigpen, *Potter's Raid*, 389.
22. *CM*, 7-4-64; *CDC*, 7-26-61; SHSP, Index; *RR*, 1, 225, 228.
23. *CM*, 7-4-64; SHSP, Index.
24. *CM*, 1-24-61; *Keowee Courier (Walhalla)*, 2-16-61.
25. *Keowee Courier (Walhalla)*, 2-16-61.
26. *CM*, 7-23-64.
27. Ibid., 5-12-63.

28. Ibid., 7-25-64.
29. Ibid., 1-24-61; 1-29-61.
30. *Keowee Courier (Walhalla)*, 2-16-61.
31. Krick, *Lee's Colonels*, 445.
32. *CV*, 1, 338.
33. *OR*, 1, 28, 1, 390, 613.
34. Ibid., 1, 28, 1, 615.
35. *YE*, 3-22-65.
36. *CM*, 8-3-61.
37. Ibid., 8-3-61; Roster of Officers, Confederate Historian, South Carolina Department of Archives and History, S108079.
38. *Keowee Courier (Walhalla)*, 2-16-61.
39. Roster of Officers, Confederate Historian, South Carolina Department of Archives and History, S108079.
40. *CM*, 12-10-63; Roster of Officers, Confederate Historian, South Carolina Department of Archives and History, S108079.
41. *OR*, 1, 28, 1, 6130.
42. *CM*, 11-25-63; 11-27-63; 12-10-63.
43. *OR*, 1, 28, 2, 522.
44. *RR*, 5, 326.
45. *CM*, 3-1-61.
46. *Keowee Courier (Walhalla)*, 2-16-61.
47. Roster of Officers, Confederate Historian, South Carolina Department of Archives and History, S108079.
48. *CM*, 7-11-63; 7-20-63.
49. Ibid., 11-30-63; *CDC*, 11-30-63.
50. *CM*, 10-18-64; 10-22-64.
51. *CDC*, 10-22-64.
52. John Mendinghall Gibson, *Those 163 Days; a Southern Account of Sherman's March from Atlanta to Raleigh*, 215. (Hereafter cited as Gibson, *Those 163 Days.)*
53. Roster of Officers, Confederate Historian, South Carolina Department of Archives and History, S108079.
54. Ibid.
55. *CM*, 8-19-63.
56. *OR*, 1, 47, 1, 1085.
57. Roster of Officers, Confederate Historian, South Carolina Department of Archives and History, S108079.
58. *CM*, 5-6-64; *OR*, 1, 35, 1, 207–27.
59. *CDC*, 7-30-64; *CM*, 7-21-64, 7-22-64; *CV*, 4, 6; *OR*, 1, 35, 1, 244.
60. *OR*, 1, 35, 1, 244.
61. Ibid., 1, 35, 2, 589.
62. Roster of Officers, Confederate Historian, South Carolina Department of Archives and History, S108079.
63. *OR*, 1, 28, 1, 390, 613.
64. Eleanor D. McSwain, ed., *Crumbling Defenses or Memoirs and Reminiscences of John Logan Black*, 81. (Hereafter cited as McSwain, *Crumbling Defenses.*)
65. Sifakis, *Compendium*, 5.
66. *CM*, 2-12-63.
67. *OR*, 1, 44, 875.

68. Ibid., 1, 44, 997.
69. Ibid., 1, 47, 2, 1070.
70. Ibid., 1, 47, 1, 1063; 1, 47, 3, 732.
71. Ibid., 1, 47, 1, 1063.
72. *CM*, 1-29-61.
73. Ibid., 2-1-61.
74. Ibid., 5-2-61.
75. *SCHM*, 102, no. 1: 9.
76. *CM*, 7-6-61.
77. *CDC*, 7-30-61.
78. *CM*, 7-23-64; *RR*, 1, 225–28.
79. *CM*, 6-11-62.
80. Ibid., 10-11-62.
81. *OR*, 1, 14, 742.
82. Ibid.
83. *CM*, 2-2-63; *CDC*, 2-3-63.
84. *OR*, 1, 14, 265.
85. Ibid., 1, 28, 2, 162.
86. *CM*, 7-11-63; 7-17-63; *OR*, 1, 28, 1, 527–29.
87. *CM*, 7-20-63.
88. *OR*, 1, 28, 1, 414.
89. Ibid., 1, 28, 2, 211.
90. Ibid., 1, 28, 1, 375; 1, 28, 2, 223.
91. Ibid., 1, 28, 2, 245.
92. Ibid., 1, 28, 1, 384.
93. Ibid., 1, 28, 2, 245.
94. Ibid., 1, 28, 1, 467, 494, 576.
95. *CM*, 9-1-63.
96. *OR*, 1, 28, 1, 393, 615.
97. Ibid., 1, 28, 1, 439, 499.
98. Ibid., 1, 28, 1, 617.
99. Ibid., 1, 28, 1, 397, 618.
100. Ibid., 1, 28, 2, 325.
101. Ibid., 1, 28, 2, 367–68.
102. Ibid., 1, 28, 2, 468.
103. Ibid., 1, 28, 1, 155.
104. Ibid., 1, 28, 1, 160, 634.
105. Ibid., 1, 28, 1, 176.
106. Ibid.
107. Ibid., 1, 28, 1, 187.
108. Ibid., 1, 28, 2, 603.
109. Ibid., 1, 35, 1, 558–59.
110. Ibid., 1, 35, 1, 198–200.
111. Ibid., 1, 35, 1, 194, 198.
112. Ibid., 1, 35, 1, 205.
113. Ibid., 1, 35, 2, 458.
114. Ibid., 1, 35, 2, 469.
115. *CM*, 7-4-64; *OR*, 1, 35, 1, 166.
116. *OR*, 1, 35, 1, 169.
117. Ripley, *Chapman's Fort*, 206; *OR*, 1, 35, 1, 249.

118. *OR*, 1, 35, 2, 598.
119. Ibid., 1, 35, 1, 251.
120. Ibid., 1, 35, 2, 644.
121. Ibid., 1, 44, 964.
122. Brooks, *Butler*, 474.

Chapter 14

1. *CM*, 1-29-61.
2. *OR*, 1, 53, 170.
3. "Sketch of Lucas's Battalion," SCDAH, S108121.
4. Ibid.
5. Roster of Officers, Confederate Historian, South Carolina Department of Archives and History, S108079; *CM*, 7-18-63.
6. *CM*, 7-4-61.
7. Confederate Historian, "Annual Report," 13; Cauthen, ed., *Journals*, 156.
8. *CMH*, 713.
9. *OR*, 1, 28, 2, 161.
10. *CMH*, 712.
11. "Sketch of Lucas's Battalion," SCDAH, S108121.
12. *CM*, 8-24-63; "Sketch of Lucas's Battalion," SCDAH, S108121.
13. *EA*, 8-26-63; *CM*, 8-15-63; *LL*, 8-19-63.
14. *CM*, 8-14-63; 8-19-63; 8-24-63.
15. *OR*, 1, 28, 1, 387.
16. *CM*, 8-24-63; 8-25-63.
17. *RR*, 5, 325.
18. Woodward, *Mary Chesnut*, 132.
19. *CMH*, 638, 713.
20. Ibid.
21. *OR*, 1, 1, 281.
22. Ibid.
23. Ibid., 1, 53, 268.
24. Krick, *Lee's Colonels*, 428.
25. *CMH*, 638, 713; *CM*, 8-8-63.
26. Ripley, *Chapman's Fort*, 311.
27. *OR*, 1, 44, 876.
28. Ibid., 1, 44, 997.
29. Ibid., 1, 47, 2, 1070.
30. Sifakis, *Compendium*, 8.
31. *OR*, 1, 47, 1, 1063; 1, 47, 3, 732.
32. Ibid., 1, 47, 1, 1063.
33. Ibid., 1, 6, 326.
34. Ibid., 1, 28, 1, 467.
35. *CM*, 2-2-63; *OR*, 1, 14, 202; *CDC*, 2-3-63.
36. *OR*, 1, 28, 2, 162.
37. Ibid., 1, 28, 2, 245, 325.
38. Ibid., 1, 28, 2, 211, 223.
39. *CM*, 7-25-63.
40. *CDC*, 8-24-63; *OR*, 1, 28, 1, 223, 470.
41. *CM*, 8-8-63; 8-24-63; 8-26-63; *OR*, 1, 28, 1, 499; 1, 28, 2, 249.
42. OR, 1, 28, 2, 367, 469.

43. Ibid., 1, 28, 2, 603.
44. Ibid., 1, 35, 1, 181, 189.
45. Ibid., 1, 35, 1, 559.
46. Ibid., 1, 28, 2, 603.
47. Ibid., 1, 28, 2, 603; 1, 35, 2, 469.
48. Ibid., 1, 35, 1, 230.
49. Ibid., 1, 35, 2, 645.
50. Ibid., 1, 35, 1, 168; 1, 35, 2, 598.
51. *CMH*, 713.

Chapter 15

1. *CMH*, 638, 713.
2. *OR*, 1, 53, 268.

Chapter 16

1. Confederate Historian, "Annual Report," 25, 53.
2. *LL*, 10-8-62.
3. Cauthen, ed., *Journals*, 154.
4. Ibid., 154.
5. *LL*, 7-30-62.
6. *CM*, 5-16-62; Cauthen, ed., *Journals*, 154-56; *TCC*, 5-2-62.
7. *YE*, 8-13-62.
8. Cauthen, ed., *Journals*, 154.
9. *CM*, 5-16-62; JSCEC, 154; *YE*, 6-24-63.
10. Cauthen, ed., *Journals*, 228.
11. *CM*, 11-6-62.
12. Cauthen, ed., *Journals*, 154.
13. *TCC*, 8-22-62.
14. CC 10-3-62; *CM*, 10-8-62.
15. Cauthen, ed., *Journals*, 279.
16. *OR*, 4, 2, 155–56.
17. Cauthen, ed., *Journals*, 282.
18. Ibid., 289; *CM*, 11-6-62; *CDC*, 11-6-62.
19. Cauthen, ed., *Journals*, 290, 291.
20. Ibid., 291.
21. *OR*, 4, 2, 176.
22. *YE*, 11-12-62.
23. Cauthen, ed., *Journals*, 293; *TCC*, 11-14-62.
24. Cauthen, *South Carolina Goes to War*, 161.
25. *OR*, 1, 53, 281; McArthur, *Griffin*, 262.
26. *CDC*, 1-26-63; McArthur, *Griffin*, 266.
27. *YE*, 2-11-63.
28. *OR*, 1, 14, 784–85.
29. Ibid., 1, 14, 816.
30. *CM*, 1-1-62.
31. Ibid., 10-11-61, 1-1-62; *CDC*, 10-17-61.
32. *CM*, 12-11-61.
33. Ibid., 12-24-61.
34. Ibid., 9-3-63.
35. Ibid., 12-24-61.

36. *CDC*, 12-4-61.
37. Ibid.,1-10-62; *CM*, 1-14-62.
38. *CM*, 1-1-62.
39. *CDC*, 8-22-62; *TCC*, 8-22-62.
40. Cauthen, ed., *Journals*, 87–89.
41. *TCC*, 8-22-62.
42. *CM*, 8-22-61.
43. Ibid., 10-4-61.
44. Ibid., 10-17-61; 12-11-61.
45. Ibid., 2-18-62; *CDC*, 11-25-62.
46. *CM*, 12-11-61.
47. Ibid.
48. Ibid., 2-18-62.
49. Ibid., 1-3-61, 2-25-61, 10-17-61; *CDC*, 10-17-61.
50. *CM*, 5-2-61, 10-17-61; *CDC*, 11-25-62.
51. *CM*, 10-17-61.
52. *CDC*, 12-11-61; 11-25-62.
53. *CM*, 9-3-61.
54. Ibid., 11-22-62.
55. Ibid., 9-26-61.
56. Ibid., 10-17-61.
57. Ibid.
58. *CDC*, 11-25-62.
59. *CM*, 11-22-62.
60. Ibid., 1-1-62.
61. *TCC*, 8-22-62; *CDC*, 8-22-62.
62. Cauthen, ed., *Journals*, 207.
63. Ibid.
64. *RR*, 9, 320.
65. Thigpen, *Potter's Raid*, 1
66. Sifakis, *Compendium*, 90.
67. Cauthen, ed., *Journals*, 240.
68. *CDC*, 11-21-62.
69. *OR*, 1, 14, 681.
70. *LL*, 1-7-63.
71. *OR*, 1, 14, 763.
72. *RR*, 3, 487.
73. *Greenville Southern Enterprise*, 1-8-63.
74. *CM*, 11-17-62; *LL*, 8-27-62; *EA*, 11-19-62; *CDC*, 8-22-62.
75. *TCC*, 8-22-62.
76. *CDC*, 8-22-62; *LL*, 8-27-62.
77. *CM*, 11-17-62.
78. *LL*, 8-27-62; JSCEC, 253.
79. *Greenville Southern Enterprise*, 2-26-63.
80. *CV*, 2, 98.
81. Ibid., 21, 305; *CMH*, 524.
82. *CDC*, 8-22-62.
83. Ibid., 7-21-64.
84. Ibid., 11-17-62.
85. Ibid.

86. Ibid.
87. *EA*, 11-19-62; *CDC*, 11-17-62.
88. *Greenville Southern Enterprise*, 1-8-63.
89. Ibid.
90. *Greenville Southern Enterprise*, 2-19-63; *CM*, 11-17-62.
91. *TCC*, 8-22-62; *CDC*, 8-22-62.
92. Cauthen, ed., *Journals*, 293; *TCC*, 11-14-62.
93. *CM*, 10-8-62; *LL*, 8-27-62.
94. Cauthen, ed., *Journals*, 279.
95. *LL*, 8-27-62.
96. Ibid.; JSCEC, 246.
97. Cauthen, ed., *Journals*, 279.
98. *TCC*, 8-22-62; *CDC*, 8-22-62.
99. McArthur, *Griffin*, 244.
100. Ibid.
101. Ibid.; *RR*, 11, 405.
102. *CSR*, M267, 201.
103. McArthur, *Griffin*, 244; *CM*, 10-8-62.
104. *RR*, 11, 405.
105. Bill Brasington, Website, "South Carolina State Troops Seed Corn Units, 1864–1865," wwww://geocities.com/sc_seedcorn. (Hereafter cited as Brasington Website); *RR*, 11, 405.
106. *Cyclopedia*, 292.
107. *EA*, 7-16-62.
108. Ibid., 10-8-62.
109. Ibid., 11-12-62.
110. McArthur, *Griffin*, 250.
111. *RR*, 11, 405.
112. *EA*, 12-3-62.
113. *CM*, 12-25-62; *EA*, 12-10-62.
114. *YE*, 10-1-62; *TCC*, 8-22-62; *CDC*, 8-22-62.
115. *YE*, 8-27-62.
116. Ibid., 11-19-62.
117. Ibid.
118. *TCC*, 8-22-62; *YE*, 10-1-62; *CDC*, 8-22-62.
119. *RR*, 11, 230; *CM*, 10-8-62.
120. *Cylcopedia*, 228.
121. *YE*, 8-27-62.
122. Ibid.
123. *CV*, 15, 102.
124. SHSP, Index.
125. *TCC*, 8-22-62.
126. *YE*, 10-1-62; 10-15-62.
127. McArthur, *Griffin*, 251.
128. *LL*, 1-7-63.
129. *TCC*, 8-22-62; *CDC*, 8-22-62.
130. *CM*, 11-6-62.
131. *Memory Roll: Rolls of South Carolina Volunteers in the Confederate States Provisional Army*, South Carolina Department of Archives and History, Microcopy No. 16. (Hereafter cited as *Memory Roll*.)

132. *Triweekley Watchman*, 1-16-63.
133. Ibid., 1-16-63.
134. *Sumter Watchman*, 2-3-64.
135. Cauthen, ed., *Journals*, 250; *CDC*, 1-26-63.
136. *Triweekly Watchman*, 1-16-63; *CDC*, 1-26-63.
137. *Triweekly Watchman*, 11-14-62; 1-5-63.
138. *Memory Roll.*
139. *DSC*, 11-28-62.
140. *Triweekly Watchman*, 11-14-62.
141. *TCC*, 10-3-62.
142. Ibid.
143. Ibid.
144. *Triweekly Watchman*, 10-14-62, 11-14-62; *TCC*, 11-14-62; *LL*, 11-19-62.
145. *TCC*, 11-3-62; *Triweekly Watchman*, 1-5-63.
146. *LL*, 1-7-63.
147. *Triweekly Watchman*, 1-16-63.
148. *LL*, 2-11-63.
149. Ibid., 8-27-62; *TCC*, 8-22-62; *CDC*, 8-22-62.
150. McArthur, *Griffin*, 251.
151. *CMH*, 581.
152. *RR*, 3, 23.
153. Ibid., 9, 314.
154. Brasington Website.
155. *CM*, 1-30-62.
156. *TCC*, 8-22-62; *LL*, 8-27-62; *CDC*, 8-22-62.
157. Cauthen, ed., *Journals*, 293; *TCC*, 11-14-62.
158. *CM*, 10-8-62.
159. Cauthen, ed., *Journals*, 250; *CDC*, 8-22-62.
160. Cauthen, ed., *Journals*, 250.
161. *CM*, 10-8-62.
162. Ibid., 10-9-62.
163. *Memory Roll.*
164. *CM*, 10-8-62.
165. Ibid., 7-28-63.
166. *Memory Roll.*
167. SCDAH, *Roll of the Dead.*
168. Brasington Website.
169. Ibid.
170. Ibid.
171. *CDC*, 11-21-62; *CM*, 2-10-63.

Chapter 17

1. *OR*, 4, 2, 580–82; *TCC*, 7-31-63; *Triweekly Watchman*, 7-18-63.
2. *OR*, 1, 28, 2, 145.
3. Ibid., 4, 2, 580.
4. Ibid., 1, 28, 2, 145.
5. *Greenville Southern Enterprise*, 7-30-63; Cauthen, *South Carolina Goes to War*, 192; *LL*, 6-24-63; *OR*, 1, 28, 2, 144.
6. *OR*, 1, 28, 2, 145; *YE*, 6-24-63.

7. *OR*, 1, 28, 2, 145.
8. *LL*, 7-15-63; *OR*, 4, 3, 38–39.
9. *OR*, 4, 2, 665; 4, 3, 38–39; *YE*, 6-24-63, 7-29-63; *CS*, 8-27-63.
10. *CM*, 8-14-63.
11. *OR*, 1, 28, 2, 339; 4, 2, 1058.
12. Ibid., 1, 28, 2, 339.
13. Ibid., 4, 2, 1058.
14. Ibid., 1, 35, 1, 562; *CM*, 2-15-64.
15. Halliburton, *Saddle Soldiers*, 125; *Sumter Watchman*, 1-18-63.
16. *OR*, 4, 2, 788.
17. Ibid., 1, 53, 296; 4, 2, 666.
18. Ibid., 1, 35, 1, 562.
19. Kirkland, *Broken Fortunes*, 186.
20. *CV*, 33, 185.
21. *AP*, 7-10-63.
22. *Greenville Southern Enterprise*, 7-16-63.
23. Brasington Website.
24. *AP*, 7-10-63.
25. Sifakis, *Compendium*, 57.
26. *OR*, 1, 53, 296; 4, 2, 803; *YE*, 9-9-63.
27. *DSG*, 9-8-63.
28. *OR*, 1, 28, 2, 368, 468, 603; 1, 35, 1, 558.
29. Ibid., 1, 53, 296; 4, 2, 666.
30. *CM*, 7-29-63.
31. *OR*, 4, 2, 788; *Memory Roll*.
32. Halliburton, *Saddle Soldiers*, 125.
33. *RR*, 12, 80.
34. *EA*, 9-16-63.
35. Brasington Website.
36. Sifakis, *Compendium*, 62.
37. *YE*, 9-9-63; *EA*, 9-16-63; *OR*, 1, 53, 296.
38. *OR*, 1, 28, 2, 467, 602; 1, 35, 1, 558.
39. Ibid., 1, 28, 2, 602.
40. Halliburton, *Saddle Soldiers*, 125; *CM*, 2-15-64.
41. *OR*, 1, 53, 296; 4, 2, 666.
42. *YE*, 1-27-64; *CDC*, 7-31-63.
43. *CDC*, 10-3-63; *CM*, 10-20-63.
44. *OR*, 1, 28, 2, 602.
45. *CM*, 1-11-61.
46. *CDC*, 10-7-63.
47. Ibid., 10-3-63.
48. Ibid.
49. Ibid.
50. Ibid.
51. *LL*, 7-8-63.
52. *CDC*, 10-3-63.
53. Sifakis, *Compendium*, 67.
54. *OR*, 4, 2, 788.
55. Ibid., 1, 53, 296; *DSG*, 9-8-63.
56. *OR*, 1, 28, 2, 468, 602; 1, 35, 1, 558.

57. *CM*, 8-27-63.
58. *YE*, 1-27-64.
59. Ibid.
60. *OR*, 1, 35, 1, 560.
61. *YE*, 9-2-63.
62. *OR*, 4, 2, 788.
63. Ibid., 4, 2, 666.
64. *LL*, 7-29-63.
65. Ibid.,10-21-63; *Triweekly Watchman*, 10-27-63.
66. *LL*, 7-29-63.
67. *Triweekly Watchman*, 10-27-63.
68. *LL*, 7-29-63.
69. *Triweekly Watchman*, 10-27-63.
70. *DSG*, 9-1-63.
71. *LL*, 7-15-63.
72. *TCC*, 7-10-63.
73. *Cylcopedia*, 448.
74. *Triweekly Watchman*, 1-18-64.
75. *DSG*, 9-2-63.
76. *Sumter Watchman*, 1-18-64.
77. *OR*, 4, 2, 666.
78. Sifakis, *Compendium*, 67.
79. *LL*, 9-2-63.
80. *Triweekly Watchman*, 10-27-63.
81. *OR*, 1, 28, 2, 468, 602; 1, 35, 1, 558.
82. *Triweekly Watchman*, 10-27-63.
83. *OR*, 1, 35, 1, 560.
84. *YE*, 8-19-63.
85. *OR*, 1, 53, 296; 4, 2, 666.
86. *YE*, 12-2-63.
87. Ibid.
88. Ibid.
89. *CM*, 10-23-63.
90. *YE*, 7-29-63.
91. Ibid., 10-28-63.
92. Ibid., 10-7-63.
93. Brasington Website.
94. Sifakis, *Compendium*, 71.
95. *OR*, 4, 2, 788.
96. Ibid., 1, 53, 296; *YE*, 9-9-63.
97. *OR*, 4, 2, 83; *YE*, 10-7-63.
98. *OR*, 1, 28, 2, 368.
99. *YE*, 11-11-63; *OR*, 1, 28, 2, 459.
100. *YE*, 11-25-63.
101. Ibid., 12-2-63.
102. Ibid.
103. Ibid., 1-27-64.
104. Ibid., 2-17-64.

Chapter 18

1. *OR*, 1, 35, 2, 456.
2. *DSC*, 3-15-64.
3. *LL*, 3-2-64; *EA*, 2-24-64.
4. *YE*, 3-2-64.
5. Cauthen, *South Carolina Goes to War*, 194.
6. *EA*, 2-24-64.
7. *YE*, 3-23-64.
8. *DSC*, 4-8-64.
9. *YE*, 6-15-64.
10. Ibid., 6-22-64.
11. Ibid., 7-13-64.
12. Ibid., 7-20-64.
13. Ibid., 11-9-64.
14. *OR*, 1, 35, 2, 598; 1, 44, 876.
15. Ibid., 1, 53, 344.
16. Ibid., 1, 44, 993.
17. *RR*, 3, 104; *CSR*, M267, 391.
18. Brasington Website.
19. Ibid.
20. *CDC*, 12-19-64.
21. *OR*, 4, 3, 1005.
22. Brasington Website; *OR*, 1, 44, 999.
23. *OR*, 1, 47, 2, 1071; 1, 47, 3, 692, 732, 786; *RR*, 3, 104.
24. *OR*, 1, 35, 2, 598.
25. Ibid., 1, 35, 2, 646.
26. Ibid., 1, 44, 876.
27. Ibid.
28. *Civil War in Western South Carolina*, 10.
29. *OR*, 1, 44, 993.
30. Ibid., 1, 44, 999.
31. Sifakis, *Compendium*, 51.
32. *Memory Roll*; *CMH*, 765.
33. *DSC*, 6-22-64.
34. *Memory Roll.*
35. *RR*, 11, 38.
36. *CV*, 31, 426.
37. *Memory Roll.*
38. *CV*, 21, 426; *RR*, 11, 355.
39. Brasington Website.
40. *Memory Roll*; *RR*, 7, 273.
41. *Memory Roll.*
42. *CV*, 33, 185.
43. *RR*, 2, 159.
44. *Memory Roll*; *RR*, 7, 273; 11, 58.
45. *Memory Roll*; *RR*, 12, 51.
46. *OR*, 1, 44, 993.
47. *RR*, 5, 468.
48. Ibid., 5, 475.
49. Brasington Website; *OR*, 1, 44, 999.

50. *OR*, 1, 47, 2, 1071; 1, 47, 3, 692, 786; *RR*, 3, 104.
51. *OR*, 1, 47, 2, 1071; 1, 47, 3, 732.
52. *RR*, 5, 475.
53. *OR*, 1, 44, 993.
54. Ibid., 1, 47, 3, 732.
55. Ibid., 35, 2, 644–46.
56. *Memory Roll*.
57. *RR*, 11, 58.
58. *OR*, 1, 44, 993.
59. Ibid., 1, 44, 999.
60. *YE*, 6-29-64.
61. Ibid., 4-20-64.
62. Ibid.
63. Ibid., 6-1-64.
64. Stevens, *Captain Bill*, 2: 100; *RR*, 11, 190.
65. *OR*, 1, 47, 3, 694.
66. Ibid., 1, 47, 3, 732.
67. *YE*, 7-20-64.
68. Ibid., 9-14-64.
69. Ibid., 9-28-64.
70. Ibid., 9-21-64.
71. Ibid., 9-28-64; *RR*, 6, 213.
72. *YE*, 10-5-64.
73. Ibid., 10-12-64.
74. *OR*, 1, 35, 2, 646; 1, 44, 876; *YE*, 10-19-64, 10-26-64, 11-2-64, 11-9-64, 11-15-64, 11-23-64, 11-30-64, 12-7-64, 12-7-64, 12-14-64, 12-21-64, 1-11-65.
75. *RR*, 6, 214.
76. *YE*, 2-1-65; 2-11-65.
77. Ibid., 3-16-65.
78. Ibid., 3-22-65.
79. *RR*, 6, 213.
80. *DSC*, 6-22-64.
81. *Cylcopedia*, 170.
82. Ibid.
83. *Sumter Watchman*, 3-30-64; *RR*, 3, 436.
84. *RR*, 5, 198.
85. Ibid., 7, 42.
86. *DSG*, 5-27-61.
87. *OR*, 1, 47, 3, 694.
88. Ibid., 1, 47, 2, 692; 1, 47, 3, 732.
89. *CM*, 7-12-64.
90. *RR*, 6, 302.
91. *OR*, 1, 35, 2, 646.
92. Ibid., 1, 44, 876; *YE*, 10-26-64.
93. *RR*, 5, 198.
94. Ibid., 6, 302.
95. *YE*, 3-22-65.
96. *RR*, 3, 211; 5, 198.
97. *DSC*, 6-22-64.
98. *OR*, 1, 44, 876.

99. *Sumter Watchman*, 4-20-64.
100. Ibid., 5-25-64.
101. *OR*, 1, 47, 3, 694.
102. Ibid., 1, 47, 3, 732.
103. *LL*, 9-20-64.
104. *OR*, 1, 35, 2, 646; 1, 44, 876; *YE*, 12-7-64.
105. *RR*, 3, 499.
106. Thigpen, *Potter's Raid*, 379.
107. *YE*, 3-22-65.
108. *RR*, 3, 499.
109. *EA*, 6-24-64.
110. Ibid., 6-22-64, 7-20-64.
111. Ibid., 7-20-64; *CSR*, M267, 391.
112. *EA*, 6-24-64.
113. Ibid., 4-27-64.
114. Ibid., 4-27-64.
115. *RR*, 1, 322, 354; *EA*, 7-20-64, 10-19-64.
116. *EA*, 7-20-64, 10-19-64.
117. Ibid., 7-20-64.
118. Ibid.
119. Brasington Website; *OR*, 1, 44, 999.
120. *OR*, 1, 47, 2, 1071; 1, 47, 3, 692, 732, 786; *RR*, 3, 104.
121. *EA*, 7-20-64.
122. *YE*, 9-28-64.
123. Ibid., 10-12-64.
124. *EA*, 10-19-64; *OR*, 1, 35, 2, 646.
125. *YE*, 10-5-64.
126. *OR*, 1, 44, 876, 884.
127. Ibid., 1, 44, 993.
128. Ibid., 1, 44, 999.
129. *RR*, 1, 354-55.
130. Ibid., 1, 354.
131. *OR*, 1, 47, 3, 732, 786.
132. *RR*, 8, 393.
133. Ibid.
134. *OR*, 1, 47, 2, 1073.
135. Ibid., 1, 47, 2, 1071; 1, 47, 3, 692, 732, 786; *RR*, 3, 104.
136. *OR*, 1, 35, 2, 646; 1, 44, 876; *YE*, 12-7-64.
137. *RR*, 3, 490.
138. Ibid., 6, 20.
139. Sifakis, *Compendium*, 75.
140. *CM*, 10-14-64.
141. Ibid.
142. SCDAH, *Roll of the Dead*.
143. *CM*, 4-27-64.
144. *OR*, 1, 47, 2, 1249.
145. Ibid.
146. Sifakis, *Compendium*, 78.
147. *OR*, 1, 47, 3, 694.
148. *OR*, 1, 47, 3, 732.

149. Ibid., 1, 35, 2, 646.
150. Ibid., 1, 44, 876.
151. Ibid., 1, 44, 993, 999.
152. *YE*, 3-22-65.

Chapter 19

1. *EA*, 8-17-64; *LL*, 12-18-64.
2. *EA*, 1-4-65, 4-19-65.
3. *CSR*, M267, 391.
4. *RR*, 7, 27.
5. *CM*, 9-6-64.
6. *TCC*, 10-9-63.
7. Ibid.
8. *YE*, 3-29-65.
9. *EA*, 4-19-65.
10. Ibid.
11. Ibid., 4-5-65.
12. Ibid., 4-19-65, *DSG*, 12-31-64.
13. *CM*, 9-6-64; *LL*, 9-20-64; *RR*, 3, 266.
14. *EA*, 1-4-65; *LL*, 1-10-65.
15. *EA*, 12-28-64.
16. Ibid., 12-28-64; *DSG*, 12-31-64.
17. *EA*, 12-28-64; *OR*, 1, 44, 993; *RR*, 12, 158.
18. *EA*, 12-28-64; *DSG*, 12-31-64.
19. *CV*, 29, 417; *RR*, 10, 213.
20. *RR*, 7, 27; 11, 38.
21. *OR*, 1, 47, 2, 1070.
22. *RR*, 6, 143.
23. *LL*, 9-20-64; *RR*, 3, 266.
24. McArthur, *Griffin*, 279–80; *RR*, 7, 27.
25. *EA*, 12-28-64.
26. *RR*, 7, 29.
27. *OR*, 1, 44, 992, 999.
28. McArthur, *Griffin*, 289.
29. Ibid., 291.
30. Ibid., 295.
31. *OR*, 1, 47, 2, 1274.
32. McArthur, *Griffin*, 79.
33. Ibid.
34. *RR*, 7, 27; *CMH*, 603; *RR*, 3, 266; 6, 143; 7, 1; 8, 396.
35. *EA*, 4-19-65; *DSG*, 12-31-64.
36. *CM*, 9-6-64.
37. *EA*, 1-4-65; *DSG*, 12-31-64.
38. *DSG*, 12-31-64.
39. Ibid.
40. Ibid.
41. *RR*, 2, 519; *Cyclopedia*, 310; *RR*, 11, 211.
42. *RR*, 11, 211.
43. Ibid., 8, 396; *CV*, 34, 185.
44. *RR*, 7, 1; Robert S. Seigler, *A Guide to Confederate Monuments in South Carolina*, 502.

45. W. Greer Albergotti, "Sketch of Company F, 2nd Battalion, South Carolina State Troops," Miscellaneous Sketches, 1868–1898, South Carolina Department of Archives and History, S108121. (Hereafter cited as Albergotti, "Sketch of Company F.")
46. Ibid.
47. *RR*, 6, 67; *CSR*, M267, 391.
48. Brasington Website.
49. *RR*, 2, 495.
50. Ibid.
51. Brasington Website.
52. *RR*, 10, 337.
53. Ibid., 6, 143.
54. *OR*, 1, 47, 2, 1070–71.
55. *LL*, 9-20-64; *RR*, 3, 266.
56. *RR*, 7, 1; 8, 396.
57. Ibid., 7, 1.
58. Ibid., 8, 397.
59. *Civil War in Western South Carolina*, 10.
60. *RR*, 8, 397.
61. *OR*, 1, 44, 971; *RR*, 7, 1.
62. *RR*, 8, 396.
63. *OR*, 1, 4, 923; 1, 44, 999.
64. *OR*, 1, 47, 2, 1274.
65. McArthur, *Griffin*, 79.
66. *RR*, 2, 519; 7, 3.
67. Ibid., 3, 266; 6, 143; 7, 27; 8,396; *CMH*, 603.
68. *EA*, 4-19-65; *DSG*, 12-31-64.
69. *CM*, 9-6-64.
70. Ibid., 12-10-64; *CMH*, 603.
71. *RR*, 6, 143.
72. *CM*, 12-10-64; *CMH*, 603.
73. *DSG*, 12-31-64.
74. *CM*, 12-10-64.
75. *RR*, 6, 53.
76. Brasington Website.
77. Ibid.
78. *Memory Roll.*
79. *RR*, 6, 53.
80. Ibid., 3, 271; *Memory Roll.*
81. *RR*, 3, 266.
82. Ibid., 3, 266; 6, 400; 12, 146.
83. *OR*, 1, 47, 2, 1070–71.
84. *LL*, 9-20-64; *RR*, 3, 266.
85. *RR*, 6, 143.
86. Ibid., 6, 143; 10, 18.
87. *OR*, 1, 44, 971; *RR*, 7, 1.
88. *OR*, 1, 4, 993, 999.
89. Albergotti, "Sketch of Company F."
90. *OR*, 1, 47, 2, 1274.
91. McArthur, *Griffin*, 79.

92. *CMH*, 603; *RR*, 3, 266; 6, 143; 7, 1, 27; 8, 396.
93. *EA*, 4-19-65; *DSG*, 12-31-64.
94. *CM*, 9-6-64.
95. *EA*, 1-4-65.
96. *RR*, 11, 540.
97. Ibid., 2, 607; *CV*, 37, 429.
98. *RR*, 1, 475.
99. Ibid., 12, 736.
100. Brasington Website; *RR*, 3, 436.
101. *OR*, 1, 47, 2, 1070–71.
102. *LL*, 9-20-64; *RR*, 3, 266.
103. *OR*, 1, 44, 970–71; *RR*, 7, 1.
104. *OR*, 1, 4, 993; 1, 44, 999.
105. Ibid., 1, 47, 2, 1274.
106. McArthur, *Griffin*, 79.
107. *CMH*, 603; *RR*, 3, 266; 6, 143; 7, 1, 27; 8, 396.

Chapter 20

1. Brooks, *Stories*, 276.
2. *CM*, 12-7-60; 7-18-61.
3. Ibid., 6-30-61.
4. Ibid., 12-7-60.
5. *CDC*, 8-22-61; *CM*, 8-22-61.
6. *CM*, 12-7-60.
7. Ibid., 8-22-61.
8. *CDC*, 9-10-61; *CM*, 10-2-61.
9. *CM*, 2-21-61.
10. Ibid., 6-20-61, 6-24-61; *CDC*, 8-14-61.
11. *CM*, 11-12-61.
12. *CDC*, 11-12-61.
13. *CM*, 5-21-60; *Acts*, 934.
14. *CM*, 2-22-60.
15. *CDC*, 8-14-61.
16. *CMH*, 721.
17. *CM*, 5-7-61.
18. Ibid., 5-28-61.
19. Ibid., 8-24-61; *CDC*, 8-24-61.
20. *CDC*, 1-29-62; *CM*, 1-29-62.
21. *CM*, 2-25-61.
22. Ibid., 9-17-60.
23. Ibid., 12-2-60.
24. "History of Charleston Zouave Cadets," Adjutant and Inspector General, South Carolina Department of Archives and History. (Hereafter cited as "History of Charleston Zouave Cadets," SCDAH.)
25. *CM*, 2-25-61; 4-22-61; 10-1-61.
26. *CDC*, 8-14-61.
27. *CDC*, 2-14-62.
28. *CM*, 2-23-60.
29. *CDC*, 10-17-61.
30. *CM*, 2-23-60; 4-17-60.

31. Brooks, *Stories*, 277.
32. *CDC*, 7-20-61; *CM*, 2-25-61, 7-30-61, 9-25-61.
33. *CDC*, 8-14-61.
34. Ibid., 9-25-61; C11-26-61.
35. *CM*, 10-2-61, 1-1-62; *CDC*, 9-21-61.
36. *CM*, 8-16-61.
37. Ibid., 10-2-61, 10-16-61, 1-1-62; *CDC*, 8-9-61.
38. *CM*, 10-1-62; 10-2-61.
39. Ibid., 2-25-62; *CDC*, 2-24-62.
40. *CDC*, 2-24-62.
41. Confederate Historian, "Annual Report," 9.
42. Ibid., 7.
43. *CM*, 12-29-60.
44. Ibid., 1-21-61; 2-18-61.
45. Ibid., 1-10-61.
46. Ibid., 1-19-61.
47. Ibid., 2-15-61.
48. Ibid., 3-7-61; 3-9-61.
49. Ibid., 4-9-61; *CV*, 8, 71.
50. *CM*, 4-23-61.
51. Ibid., 12-19-61.
52. Ibid., 1-28-62; 2-7-62; *CDC*, 2-7-62.
53. *CM*, 2-8-62.
54. Ibid., 2-14-62.
55. Ibid., 2-17-62.
56. Ibid., 2-24-62.
57. Ibid., 2-25-62; *CDC*, 9-23-62.
58. *Greenville Patriot and Mountaineer*, 1-3-61. (Hereafter cited as *GPM*.)
59. Ibid.
60. *Greenville Southern Enterprise*, 3-12-63.
61. Ibid., 7-16-63.
62. Ibid., 3-12-63.
63. *Memory Roll.*
64. *GPM*, 1-3-61.
65. Ibid.
66. *Anderson Intelligencer*, 1-3-61. (Hereafter cited as *AI*.)
67. *CM*, 1-17-62.
68. Ibid., 1-18-62; 1-23-62.
69. Ibid., 1-16-61.
70. *Keowee Courier (Walhalla)*, 6-15-61.
71. Ibid., 1-19-61.
72. *Acts*, 869.
73. *EA*, 2-19-62.
74. Ibid., 2-18-63.
75. Ibid., 1-18-65.
76. *CM*, 3-8-60.
77. *EA*, 3-6-61; *CM*, 3-8-1860.
78. *CM*, 3-9-61.
79. *EA*, 1-30-62.
80. Ibid., 2-18-63.

81. *CM*, 3-8-60.
82. *EA*, 7-15-63.
83. Ibid., 2-18-63.
84. *CM*, 2-4-62.
85. *CV*, 27, 107.
86. *CM*, 9-16-62.
87. *Acts*, 866.
88. Ibid., 877.
89. *OR*, 1, 47, 2, 1073.
90. *Acts*, 867.
91. *CM*, 7-20-63.
92. Ibid., 7-10-61.
93. *CDC*, 7-27-61.
94. *CM*, 7-6-60; 9-14-60.
95. Ibid., 10-2-61; *TCC*, 1-24-61.
96. *CDC*, 1-13-62.
97. *CM*, 9-28-61.
98. Ibid., 1-13-62; *CDC*, 1-13-62.
99. *CM*, 1-13-62; *CDC*, 1-13-62.
100. *CM*, 2-28-63; *OR*, 1, 28, 2, 370.
101. *CM*, 2-27-63.
102. Ibid.
103. Ibid., 10-2-61; 1-1-62.
104. Ibid., 1-13-62; *CDC*, 1-13-62.
105. *CDC*, 3-3-63.
106. Ibid., 1-13-62.
107. Ibid., 3-3-63.
108. *CM*, 1-13-62; *CDC*, 1-13-62.
109. *CDC*, 3-3-63.
110. Ibid., 1-13-62.
111. Ibid., 3-3-63.
112. Ibid., 1-13-62.
113. Ibid., 3-3-63.
114. *CM*, 6-14-60.
115. *CDC*, 1-13-62.
116. Ibid., 3-3-63.
117. Ibid., 1-13-62.
118. Ibid., 3-3-63.
119. *CM*, 7-4-61; *YE*, 8-16-61.
120. *CDC*, 7-4-61; *CM*, 7-2-61.
121. *CM*, 1-3-62.
122. Ibid., 1-13-62; *CDC*, 1-13-62.
123. *CM*, 7-10-61.
124. Ibid., 11-29-60.
125. *CDC*, 3-22-62.
126. *CM*, 8-23-61; *CDC*, 8-10-61.
127. *CM*, 11-14-61.
128. Ibid., 1-3-65.
129. Ibid., 7-24-61.
130. Ibid., 10-2-61.

131. *OR*, 1, 28, 2, 370.
132. *CM*, 4-16-61.
133. *CDC*, 7-10-61; *CM*, 7-9-61.
134. *CM*, 11-13-61.
135. Ibid., 12-25-60.
136. Ibid., 7-9-61; *CDC*, 7-10-61.
137. *CM*, 9-5-61; 10-2-61.
138. Ibid., 7-9-61; 7-15-61; *CDC*, 7-10-61.
139. *CM*, 10-2-61.
140. Ibid., 4-23-61.
141. Ibid., 7-2-60; 10-1-61.
142. Ibid., 8-8-61.
143. Ibid., 3-1-61; 3-19-61.
144. Ibid., 1-1-62.
145. Ibid., 4-16-61.
146. *CDC*, 7-2-61.
147. Ibid., 7-2-61; C7-3-61.
148. *CDC*, 7-29-61; *CM*, 7-26-61.
149. *CM*, 1-10-60.
150. Ibid., 1-1-62.
151. Kirkland, *Broken Fortunes*, 104.
152. *CM*, 4-16-61.
153. Ibid., 3-1-61; 4-23-61.
154. Ibid., 2-2-60.
155. Ibid., 4-16-61.
156. Ibid., 9-7-61; 1-1-62.
157. Ibid., 4-16-61.
158. Ibid., 8-16-61.
159. Record and Roll of the German Fusiliers, Confederate Historian, South Carolina Department of Archives and History, S108118.
160. *CM*, 4-16-61.
161. Ibid., 2-6-60.
162. Ibid., 3-13-61.
163. Ibid., 5-1-61; 5-9-61.
164. Ibid., 9-7-61.
165. Ibid., 5-10-61.
166. Ibid., 10-27-60; 5-11-61.
167. Ibid., 4-16-61.
168. Ibid., 1-9-61; 4-23-61.
169. Ibid., 5-21-61.
170. Confederate Historian, "Annual Report," 9; *CM*, 4-16-61.
171. *CM*, 4-23-61.
172. *DSG*, 7-24-61.
173. *CM*, 1-9-61; 4-16-61.
174. Ibid., 6-7-61.
175. Ibid., 10-7-61; 1-1-62; *CDC*, 10-7-61.
176. *CM*, 4-16-61; 4-23-61.
177. Ibid., 1-1-62.
178. Ibid., 1-11-61.
179. Ibid., 4-23-61; 7-11-62.

180. Ibid., 1-1-61; 7-11-62.
181. Ibid., 3-2-61.
182. Ibid., 4-23-61.
183. Ibid.
184. Ibid., 1-11-61.
185. Ibid., 4-7-63; *Memory Roll.*
186. *CM*, 4-16-61; 1-1-62.
187. *CDC*, 5-9-61; *CM*, 5-1-61, 5-9-61; Confederate Historian, "Annual Report, " 64.
188. *CM*, 4-23-61; 4-30-61; 9-11-61.
189. *CDC*, 9-25-61; *CM*, 9-17-61; *CM*, 10-5-61, 1-1-62.
190. *CDC*, 9-25-61; *CM*, 9-25-61.
191. Brooks, *Stories*, 277.
192. *OR*, 1, 1, 6–8.
193. *CM*, 12-29-60.
194. Ibid., 11-12-61.
195. Ibid., 2-1-61; 3-13-61.
196. Ibid., 3-16-61; 4-8-61.
197. *OR*, 1, 53, 1158.
198. *CM*, 4-15-61; 5-2-61.
199. Ibid., 5-2-61.
200. *OR*, 1, 1, 302.
201. *CM*, 4-15-61.
202. Ibid., 4-23-61.
203. *OR*, 1, 53, 158; *CM*, 4-29-61, 4-30-61, 5-1-61.
204. *CM*, 9-9-61.
205. Ibid.
206. Ibid., 9-27-61; 12-31-61.
207. Ibid., 1-28-62.
208. Ibid., 2-7-62; *CDC*, 2-7-62.
209. *CM*, 2-8-62.
210. Ibid., 2-17-62.
211. Ibid., 2-24-62.
212. Ibid., 2-25-62.
213. Ibid., 10-18-61.
214. Ibid., 4-5-60.
215. Ibid., 1-24-62.
216. Ibid., 4-24-63.
217. Ibid., 8-27-63.
218. *OR*, 1, 28, 2, 369; 1, 47, 2, 1070.
219. *CM*, 4-24-63.
220. Ibid., 9-29-63.
221. Ibid.
222. Ibid., 4-30-61; 9-29-63.
223. Ibid., 12-2-62.
224. *CDC*, 12-2-62.
225. *CM*, 12-6-61; *CDC*, 12-6-61.
226. *CDC*, 12-6-61.
227. *OR*, 1, 28, 2, 326, 368.
228. Ibid., 1, 28, 2, 370.

229. Ibid., 1, 47, 2, 1070.
230. *CM*, 3-5-63.
231. Ibid., 6-6-63; *OR*, 1, 35, 2, 497.
232. *CM*, 6-30-61.
233. Ibid., 6-6-63.
234. *OR*, 1, 35, 2, 497.
235. Ibid., 1, 47, 2, 1070.
236. *Sumter Watchman*, 12-26-61.
237. *CM*, 5-17-61.
238. Thigpen, *Potter's Raid*, 226.
239. Ibid., 267.
240. *LL*, 1-15-62.
241. Ibid.
242. Ibid., *LL*, 2-25-63.
243. Ibid., 9-14-61.
244. Ibid., 5-21-62.
245. *TCC*, 1-17-62.
246. Ibid., 2-6-63.
247. Ibid., 7-10-63.
248. Ibid., 11-1-61.
249. Ibid., 1-17-62.
250. Ibid., 2-6-63.
251. *CM*, 12-7-60.
252. Ibid., 2-28-63.
253. *Acts*, 865, 887.
254. *CM*, 3-23-60.
255. *Acts*, 865.
256. *CM*, 2-7-62.
257. *CDC*, 2-6-62; *CM*, 2-7-62.
258. *CM*, 11-5-60.
259. Ibid., 5-3-61.
260. Ibid., 1-18-62.
261. Ibid.
262. *CS*, 7-31-62.
263. *OR*, 1, 1, 310–11.
264. *Horry Dispatch*, 9-26-61.
265. *OR*, 1, 1, 310.
266. SHSP, Index.
267. *Horry Dispatch*, 5-23-61; 6-20-61.
268. *CM*, 4-9-61.
269. *Horry Dispatch*, 10-3-61.
270. *CM*, 7-7-61.
271. *YE*, 10-31-61.
272. Ibid., 8-24-64.
273. Ibid., 9-21-64.
274. *DSG*, 2-27-62.
275. *CS*, 10-17-61.
276. Ibid., 1-3-63.
277. Ibid., 3-3-63.
278. Ibid., 1-3-63.

279. Ibid., 1-23-62; 3-20-62.
280. *CM*, 1-14-62; Thigpen, *Potter's Raid*, 66–67.
281. Thigpen, *Potter's Raid*, 253.
282. *CM*, 3-2-61.
283. Ibid., 10-28-60.
284. *YE*, 5-7-61.
285. *CM*, 1-9-62.
286. *DSG*, 2-6-62.
287. Confederate Historian, "Annual Report," 43.
288. *CDC*, 11-13-61; *CM*, 1-13-62, 1-9-62.
289. *CDC*, 11-13-61.
290. *CM*, 1-9-62, 1-28-62.
291. *OR*, 1, 6, 351.
292. *CDC*, 1-27-62; *DSG*, 2-6-62.
293. *CM*, 9-16-61.
294. Ibid., 4-24-61; *CDC*, 6-1-61.
295. *CM*, 10-10-61.
296. Ibid.
297. Ibid.
298. Ibid., 9-18-61.
299. *CDC*, 8-5-61.
300. *CM*, 9-18-61.
301. Ibid.
302. *CDC*, 6-28-61; *CM*, 6-28-61.
303. *CM*, 9-18-61.
304. Brasington Website.
305. *CM*, 7-25-61.
306. Ibid., 10-10-61.
307. Ibid., 2-28-62.
308. Ibid., 11-30-61.
309. Ibid., 2-28-62.
310. Ibid.
311. *DSG*, 2-6-62.
312. *CDC*, 9-19-61.
313. Confederate Historian, "Annual Report," 35.
314. Ibid.
315. *CM*, 10-10-61.
316. Ibid., 9-18-61; Brasington Website.
317. *CM*, 4-24-61; 1-1-62.
318. Ibid., 9-16-61.
319. Ibid., 11-30-61.
320. *DSG*, 2-6-62.
321. Brasington website.
322. *DSG*, 2-6-62.
323. *CM*, 1-28-61.
324. Ibid., 12-10-60.
325. *DSG*, 2-6-62.
326. Brasington website.
327. *CM*, 9-18-61.
328. Ibid.

329. Ibid., 7-17-61.
330. Ibid., 2-20-61; Brasington Website.
331. *CM*, 1-28-62; Brasington Website.
332. *DSG*, 2-6-62.
333. *CM*, 9-17-62.
334. Brasington website.
335. *CM*, 6-11-61; 9-4-61.
336. Brasington website.
337. *CM*, 9-16-62; 9-17-62; 9-18-61; 2-17-62.
338. Ibid., 3-27-62.
339. Ibid., 8-8-61; 9-18-61.
340. Henderson, 21; E. Prioleau Henderson, *Autobiography of Arab*, 21. (Hereafter cited as Henderson, *Autobiography*.)
341. *DSG*, 2-6-62.
342. *CM*, 4-11-62.
343. Brasington website.
344. *CM*, 10-10-61.
345. Brasington website.
346. *CM*, 10-10-61.
347. Ibid., 6-27-61.
348. Brasington website.
349. *DSG*, 2-6-62.
350. Brasington website.
351. *OR*, 1, 6, 37, 38.
352. *CM*, 2-20-62.
353. *CDC*, 1-27-62.
354. *OR*, 1, 6, 24.
355. Brasington website.
356. *CM*, 3-10-64.
357. Ibid., 12-18-61.
358. Ibid., 1-7-62; *OR*, 1, 6, 68.
359. *CM*, 2-28-62.
360. Confederate Historian, "Annual Report," 36.
361. *CM*, 11-8-60.
362. *RR*, 12, 43.
363. *CM*, 12-10-60.
364. Ibid., 6-24-62.
365. Ibid., 5-6-61; Woodward, *Mary Chesnut*, 209.
366. Halliburton, *Saddle Soldiers*, 203.
367. Brooks, *Butler*, 62.
368. Cauthen, ed., *Journals*, 190.
369. Halliburton, *Saddle Soldiers*, 8.
370. *CM*, 10-2-61.
371. *OR*, 1, 28, 2, 370.
372. *CM*, 4-24-61; 7-18-61.
373. Ibid., 4-24-61.
374. *CM*, 7-26-61.
375. Ibid., 8-29-61.
376. Ibid., 4-24-61.
377. *Cylcopedia*, 616.

378. *CDC*, 9-6-61; *CM*, 9-7-61.
379. Bruce S. Allardice, *More Generals in Gray*, 230. (Hereafter cited as Allardice, *Generals.*)
380. *CM*, 4-26-61.
381. Ibid., 9-7-61.
382. *CDC*, 9-6-61; *CM*, 9-7-61.
383. *CM*, 10-2-61; 1-1-62.
384. Ibid., 10-9-61; *OR*, 1, 1, 34.
385. *CM*, 10-9-61.
386. Ibid., 8-18-60; 2-20-61; 6-17-62.
387. Confederate Historian, "Annual Report," 62.
388. *CM*, 6-17-62.
389. Ibid., 8-18-60; 7-24-61.
390. Ibid., 7-24-61.
391. Ibid., 11-11-61.
392. Confederate Historian, "Annual Report," 62.
393. *CM*, 3-26-60; 5-23-61.
394. Ibid., 3-14-61.
395. Ibid., 7-18-61.
396. Ibid.
397. Ibid., 3-4-64.
398. Ibid., 4-26-60; 4-24-61.
399. *CDC*, 4-8-62; *CM*, 12-30-61.
400. *CM*, 2-8-62.
401. Ibid., 2-27-62.
402. Ibid., 3-14-62; 2-24-64.
403. Ibid., 2-22-61.
404. *CV*, 9, 501; *CM*, 6-13-61, 7-10-61; *CMH*, 620.
405. *CM*, 6-28-61; 12-11-61.
406. Ibid., 3-12-64; 6-28-61.
407. Ibid., 11-6-60.
408. Ibid., 3-14-61; 4-24-61.
409. Ibid., 10-2-61; 1-1-62.
410. Ibid., 11-10-60.
411. Ibid., 4-26-61.
412. Ibid., 9-10-61.
413. Ibid., 10-2-61.
414. Ibid., 9-29-61.
415. Ibid., 10-22-61.
416. Ibid., 1-15-62.
417. Ibid.
418. Ibid., 2-17-62.
419. *OR*, 1, 28, 2, 362.
420. Confederate Historian, "Annual Report," 9.
421. *CM*, 4-16-61; Brooks, *Stories*, 277.
422. *CM*, 2-20-61.
423. Ibid., 1-9-61.
424. Ibid., 1-28-61.
425. Ibid., 1-12-61.
426. Ibid., 2-2-61.

427. Ibid., 2-11-61.
428. Ibid., 2-12-61.
429. Ibid., 3-14-61.
430. Ibid., 4-15-61; *OR*, 1, 1, 36.
431. *CM*, 4-24-61.
432. *OR*, 1, 1, 46; *CM*, 4-24-61.
433. *CM*, 4-17-61.
434. *OR*, 1, 1, 39.
435. *CM*, 4-24-61.
436. Ibid.
437. Ibid., 4-23-61.
438. Ibid., 5-1-61; *OR*, 1, 53, 158.
439. *CM*, 4-26-61.
440. Ibid., 4-30-61.
441. Ibid., 9-18-61.
442. Ibid., 10-3-61.
443. Ibid., 10-12-61; 11-11-61.
444. Ibid., 12-31-61.
445. *OR*, 1, 6, 326; *CM*, 2-17-62.
446. *CM*, 2-17-62; 2-18-62.
447. Ibid., 4-1-62.
448. Ibid., 3-18-62.
449. *OR*, 1, 28, 2, 326, 362.
450. Ibid., 1, 28, 2, 369.

Appendix 1

1. *CS*, 2-28-61; *CM*, 2-25-60.
2. *CM*, 1-11-61.
3. Ibid., 2-22-61.
4. Ibid., 3-1-61.
5. Ibid., 3-14-61.
6. Ibid., 3-27-61; *YE*, 4-4-61.
7. *CM*, 6-5-61.
8. *YE*, 1-24-61.
9. *CM*, 6-13-61.
10. Ibid., 7-13-61.
11. Ibid., 7-2-61.
12. Ibid., 8-16-61; *CDC*, 4-13-63.
13. *CM*, 8-19-61.
14. Ibid., 9-19-61.
15. Ibid., 9-23-61.
16. Ibid., 10-4-61.
17. Ibid., 12-25-61.
18. Ibid., 1-29-62.
19. Ibid., 4-14-62.
20. Ibid., 5-12-63.
21. Ibid., 6-3-64.
22. Ibid., 1-19-65.
23. SHSP, Index.
24. UDC, *RR*, 7, 23.

25. Ibid., 10, 337.
26. *DSG*, 9-4-63.
27. *YE*, 1-10-61.
28. Ibid., 1-17-61.
29. Thomas, *Rising Star*, 177.
30. *YE*, 1-24-61; *Keowee Courier (Walhalla)*, 1-12-61; 6-29-61.
31. *YE*, 1-24-61.
32. Ibid.
33. Ibid., 1-31-61.
34. Ibid., 2-21-61.
35. Ibid., 2-28-61.
36. Ibid., 4-25-61; *CM*, 5-6-61.
37. *YE*, 5-30-61.
38. *Keowee Courier (Walhalla)*, 2-2-61.
39. *EA*, 5-22-61.
40. Ibid., 6-12-61; 7-3-61.
41. Ibid., 6-19-61.
42. Ibid., 6-26-61.
43. Ibid., 7-3-61.
44. Ibid., 7-10-61.
45. Ibid., 8-7-61.
46. Ibid., 7-8-63.
47. Ibid., 7-21-64; *CDC*, 9-15-64.
48. *EA*, 3-22-65.
49. *Keowee Courier (Walhalla)*, 6-29-61.
50. Ibid., 6-29-61.
51. Ibid., 7-6-61.
52. Ibid., 7-13-61.
53. Ibid.
54. Ibid., 7-20-61.
55. Ibid.
56. Ibid.
57. *LL*, 5-1-61.
58. Ibid., 5-22-62.
59. Ibid.
60. Ibid., 5-29-61.
61. Ibid., 5-12-61.
62. Ibid.
63. Ibid., 9-18-61.
64. PM1-3-61.
65. *Greenville Southern Enterprise*, 7-2-63.
66. Ibid.
67. *LL*, 4-30-62.
68. *Anderson Intelligencer*, 2-7-61.
69. Ibid., 2-21-61.
70. *AP*, 9-20-61.
71. *OR*, 1, 47, 2, 1073.
72. *CDC*, 5-2-61.
73. Ibid., 5-31-61.
74. Ibid., 8-26-61.

75. Ibid., 8-30-62.
76. *For Love of a Rebel*, 50.
77. Ibid, 103.
78. Wyckoff, Website.
79. Brooks, *Stories*, 293.
80. Wyckoff, Website.
81. Ibid.
82. Ibid.

Appendix 2

1. Halliburton, *Saddle Soldiers*, 130.
2. *CM,* 1-12-61.
3. *Anderson Intelligencer,* 1-3-61, 1-10-61.
4. *Keowee Courier (Walhalla),* 1-19-61.
5. *CM,* 1-31-61.
6. Ibid., 2-22-61.
7. Ibid., 4-19-61.
8. Ibid., 6-1-61.
9. Ibid., 10-9-61.
10. UDC, *RR,* 7, 343.
11. *Triweekly Watchman,* 7-27-63.
12. *CM,* 11-14-63.
13. *CMH,* 687.
14. Ibid.
15. *Acts,* 878.
16. Cauthen, ed., *Journals,* 190.
17. *YE,* 1-10-61; *DSG,* 1-8-61; 5-4-61.
18. *Anderson Intelligencer,* 1-10-61; *Keowee Courier (Walhalla),* 1-19-61.
19. *Keowee Courier (Walhalla),* 1-12-61.
20. *EA*, 1-30-61.
21. Ibid., 2-27-61.
22. Ibid., 9-4-61.
23. *Keowee Courier (Walhalla),* 6-15-61.
24. *Triweekly Watchman,* 8-14-63; 9-18-63.
25. *CDC,* 1-17-65.
26. *AP,* 1-4-61.

Appendix 3

1. Baker, *Cadets in Gray*, 155.
2. *CMH,* 437.
3. *CM,* 10-29-62.
4. Ibid., 1-6-64.
5. Ibid., 6-27-61.
6. Ibid., 9-19-61.
7. James J. Baldwin, *The Struck Eagle—A Biography of Brigadier General Micah Jenkins, and A History of the Fifth South Carolina Volunteers and the Palmetto Sharpshooters*, 75.
8. *Acts,* 934.
9. *For Love of a Rebel*, 17.
10. Tower, *A Carolinian Goes To War*, 12.

BIBLIOGRAPHY

Abbeville Banner

Abbeville Press

Acts of the General Assembly of the State of South Carolina, passed in November and December 1860 and January 1861. Columbia, South Carolina: Charles P. Pelham, 1861.

Allardice, Bruce S. *More Generals in Gray*. Baton Rouge: Louisiana State University Press, 1995.

Anderson Intelligencer

Andrews, Robert W. *The Life and Adventures of Captain Robert W. Andrews of Sumter, South Carolina.* Boston, Massachusetts: E.P. Whitcomb, 1887.

Andrews, Welburn J. *Sketch of Company K, 23rd SCV in the Civil War from 1862–1865.* Richmond, Virginia: Whittet and Shepperson, n.d. Repr. South Carolina Division, United Daughters of the Confederacy. *Recollections and Reminiscences 1861–1865 through World War I.*

Armstrong, James. *The Carolina Light Infantry's Record in the Great War*. Charleston, South Carolina: Walker, Evans, and Cogswell, 1912.

Austin, J. Luke. *General John Bratton: Sumter to Appomattox In Letters to His Wife*. Sewanee, Tennessee: Proctor's Hall Press, 2003.

Baker, Gary R. *Cadets in Gray*. Columbia, South Carolina: Palmetto Bookworks, 1989.

Baldwin James J. *The Struck Eagle—A Biography of Brigadier General Micah Jenkins, and A History of the Fifth South Carolina Volunteers and the Palmetto Sharpshooters*. Shippensburg, Pennsylvania: Burd Street Press, 1996.

Barnwell Sentinel

Batson, Steve. Website on the 16th Regiment, SCV. http://www.geocities.com/BourbonStreet/Square/3873/franklina.html.

Baxley, Neil. *No Prouder Fate: The Story of the 11th South Carolina Volunteer Infantry*. Bloomington, Indiana: AuthorHouse, 2005.

Bell, L.M., ed. *Rebels In Grey, Soldiers from Pickens District 1861–1865*. Clemson, South Carolina: Joyce's Print Shop, 1984.

Benson, Susan Williams, ed. *Berry Benson's Civil War Book, Memoirs of a Confederate Scout and Sharpshooter*. Athens: The University of Georgia Press, 1992.

Boykin, Edward Mortimer. *The Falling Flag*. New York: E.J. Hale and Son, 1874.

Boykin, Richard Manning. *Captain Alexander Hamilton Boykin, One of South Carolina's Distinguished Citizens*. Repr. Camden, South Carolina: J.J. Fox, 1991.

Boyles, J.R., Lt. *Reminiscences of the Civil War, Company C, 12th Regiment, SCV.* Columbia, South Carolina: R.L. Bryan Co., 1890.

Boylston, Raymond P. *Butler's Brigade, That Fighting Civil War Cavalry Brigade from South Carolina*. Raleigh, North Carolina: Jarrett Press and Publications, 2000.

Bradshaw, Timothy E., Jr. *Battery Wagner, The Siege, The Men Who Fought and The Casualties*. Columbia, South Carolina: Palmetto Historical Works, 1993.

Brasington, Bill. Website "South Carolina State Troops Seed Corn Units, 1864–1865." Website deals with reserves and state troops. www://geocities.com/sc_seedcorn.

Brennan, Patrick. *Secessionville, Assault on Charleston*. Campbell, California: Savas Publishing Company, 1996.

Brock, R.A., and Philip Van Doren Stern. *The Appomattox Roster.* New York: Antiquarian Press, Ltd. 1962.

Brooks, Ulysses Robert, ed. *Butler and His Cavalry in the War of Secession 1861–1865, 1909*. Repr. Camden, South Carolina: J.J. Fox, 1991.

———. *Stories of the Confederacy.* Columbia, South Carolina: The State Company, 1912.

Brown, Joseph N., Col. "Account of the Battle of Gettysburg." Speech given in Anderson, South Carolina. March 23, 1901. (Available from the Greenville County Public Library. Microfiche SC 973.7457, Fiche 109.)

———. An Address Delivered on the Battle of the "Bloody Angle" at the November 1900 Meeting of the Robert E. Lee Chapter of the Daughters of Confederacy May 12, 1864. Anderson, South Carolina: The Association Publishing Company, 1900.

Brown, Varina D. *A Colonel at Gettysburg and Spotsylvania*. Columbia, South Carolina: The State Company, 1931.

Brunson, Joseph Woods, Sgt. *Pee Dee Light Artillery of Maxcy Gregg's (Later Samuel McGowan's) Brigade First South Carolina Volunteers (Infantry) C.S.A. A Historical Sketch and Roster*. University of Alabama: Confederate Publishing Company, 1983.

Buzhardt, Beaufort Simpson. "Diary of Beaufort Simpson Buzhardt." (Available from the Greenville County Public Library. Microfiche 973.7457, fiche 89.)

Caldwell, J.F.J. *The History of a Brigade of South Carolinians*. Philadelphia: King and Baird Printers, 1866. Repr. Dayton, Ohio: Morningside Press, 1984.

Calhoun, C.M. *Liberty Dethroned*. N.p., n.d. (Available from author.)

Camden Confederate

Carolina Spartan

Cauthen, Charles E. *South Carolina Goes to War, 1860–1865.* Chapel Hill: University of North Carolina Press, 1950.

———, ed. *Journals of the South Carolina Executive Councils 1861 and 1862*. Columbia: South Carolina Archives Department, 1956.

Centennial of Incorporation, 1783–1883. Charleston, South Carolina: News and Courier Press, n.d.

Charleston Courier

Charleston Daily Courier

Charleston Mercury

Chisolm, Robert. Papers. N.p., n.d. (Available from the Greenville County Public Library. Microfiche SC 973.7457, fiche 123.)

Cisco, Walter Brian. *States Rights Gist, A South Carolina General of the Civil War.* Shippensburg, Pennsylvania: White Mane Publishing Company, 1991.

The Civil War in Southwestern South Carolina December 1864–January 1865. Montmorenci, South Carolina: Western Carolina Historical Research, 1997.

Clary, James B. *A History of the 15th South Carolina Infantry 1861–1865*. Cary, NC: James B. Clary in cooperation with the South Carolina Department of Archives and History, 2007.

Coker, James Lide. *History of Company G, Ninth S.C. Regiment, Infantry, South Carolina Army and of Company E, Sixth S.C. Regiment, Infantry, South Carolina Army.* Greenwood, South Carolina: The Attic Press, Repr. 1979.

Confederate Military History Extended Edition, Volume 6, South Carolina. Wilmington, North Carolina. Broadfoot Publishing, 1987.

Confederate Veteran, Nashville, Tennessee. 40 vols.

Conrad, James L. The Sad History of 'Shanks' Evans." *The Civil War Times Illustrated*, Vol. 22 (Sept. 1983): 32–38.

Coward, Asbury, N.J. Bond, and O.L. Coward, eds. *The South Carolinians.* New York: Vantage Press, 1968.

Crute, Joseph H., Jr. *Units of the Confederate Army*. Midlothian, Virginia: Derwent Books, 1987.

Cyclopedia of Eminent and Representative Men of the Carolinas of the Nineteenth Century. Vol. 1. Madison, Wisconsin: Brant and Fuller, 1892.

Daily South Carolinian

Daily Southern Guardian

Daly, Louise Haskell. *Alexander Cheves Haskell, The Portrait of a Man*. Wilmington, North Carolina: Broadfoot Publishing Company, 1989.

Darlington Southerner

Davis, Nora M., comp. *Military and Naval Operations in South Carolina 1860–1865: A Chronological List, With References to Sources of Further Information*: South Carolina Archives, 1959.

Davis, Sam. Conversation with author.

Dedmondt, Glenn. *Southern Bronze, Captain Garden's (S.C.) Artillery Company During the War Between the States*. Columbia, South Carolina: Palmetto Bookworks, 1993.

Dickert, D. Augustus. *History of Kershaw's Brigade*. Dayton, Ohio: Morningside House, 1988.

Douglas, David G. *A Boot Full of Memories: Captain Leonard Williams, 2nd South Carolina Cavalry.* Camden, South Carolina: Gray Fox Publishing, 2003.

DuBose, Henry Kershaw. *The History of Company B, 21st Regiment (Infantry) SCV C.S.P.A*. Columbia, South Carolina: The R.L. Bryan Company, 1909.

Due West Telescope

Dunlop, W.S. *Lee's Sharpshooters or, The Forefront of Battle*. W.S. Dayton, Ohio: Morning House Inc, 1988.

Edgefield Advertiser

Edwards, W.H., Capt. *A Condensed History of the Seventeenth Regiment, SCV, C.S.A.* Columbia, South Carolina: The R.L. Bryan Company, 1908.

Elliott, Charles P., Maj. "Elliott's Brigade and how it held the Crater at the Battle of Petersburg. Speech given 5 December 1895. The Fitz William McMaster Collection. (Available from the Greenville County Public Library. Microfiche SC 973.7457, Fiche 113.)

Emanuel, S. "A Historical Sketch of the Georgetown Rifle Guards." Speech delivered on 17 November, 1909. (Available from the Greenville County Public Library. Microfiche 973.7457, fiche 100.)

Estilow, L.E., ed. "Doing My Duty—The Wartime Experiences of John S. Hard 1861–1863." Unpublished. (Available from author.)

Evans, Clement, ed. *Confederate Military History Extended Edition*, Vol. 6, *South Carolina*. Atlanta: Confederate Publishing Company, 1899. Repr. Wilmington, North Carolina: Broadfoot Publishing Company, 1987.

Everson, Guy R., and Edward H. Simpson Jr., eds. *Far, Far from Home—The Wartime Letters of Dick and Tally Simpson, 3rd South Carolina Volunteers*. New York: Oxford University Press, 1994.

Ewell, S.P.H. *Recollections of War Times*. Bamberg, South Carolina: The Bamberg Herald Printers, 1895.

Ford, A.P., and M.J. Ford. *Life in the Confederate Army*. New York: The Neale Publishing Company, 1905.

For Love of a Rebel. Georgetown, South Carolina: The Arthur Manigault Chapter of the U.D.C., 1964.

Freeman, Douglas Southall. *Lee's Lieutenants*. 3 vols. New York: Charles Scribner's Sons, 1944.

Garlington, J.C. *Men of the Time, Sketches of Living Notables, A Biographical Encyclopedia of Contemporaneous South Carolina Leaders*. Spartanburg, South Carolina: Garlington Press, 1902.

Gibson, John Mendinghall. *Those 163 Days; A Southern Account of Sherman's March from Atlanta to Raleigh*. New York: Bramhall House, 1961.

Greenville Mountaineer

Greenville Patriot and Mountaineer

Greenville Southern Enterprise

Hagood, James R. "Memoirs of the First South Carolina Regiment of Volunteer Infantry in the Confederate War for Independence from April 12, 1861 to April 10, 1865." Unpublished MS. Columbia: South Caroliniana Library.

Hagood, Johnson. *Memoirs of the War of Secession, From the Original Manuscripts of Johnson Hagood*. Columbia, South Carolina: The State Company, 1910.

Halliburton, Lloyd. *Saddle Soldiers, The Civil War Correspondence of General William Stokes 4th South Carolina Cavalry*. Orangeburg, South Carolina: Sandlapper Publishing Company, 1993.

Heller, J. Roderick, and Carolynn Ayres Heller, eds. *The Confederacy Is on Her Way Up the Spout, Letters to South Carolina 1861–1864*. Columbia: University of South Carolina Press, 1998.

Henderson, E. Prioleau. *Autobiography of Arab, E. Prioleau Henderson*. Oxford: The Guild Bindery Press, 1901. Repr. Camden, South Carolina: J.J. Fox, 1991.

Horry Dispatch

Howard, Robert M. *Reminiscences*. Columbus, Georgia: Gilbert Printing Company, 1912.

Hoyt, James A. *The Palmetto Riflemen, Company B, 4th Regiment SCV and Company C, Palmetto Sharpshooters*. Greenville, South Carolina: Hoyt and Keys Printers, 1886.

Hudson, Joshua Hilary. *Sketches and Reminiscences*. Columbia, South Carolina: The State Company, 1903.

Inglesby, Charles. *Historical Sketch of the First Regiment of South Carolina Artillery (Regulars)*. Charleston, South Carolina. Walker, Evans, and Cogswell, n.d.

Izlar, William Valmore. *A Sketch of the War Record of the Edisto Rifles, 1861–1865*. Columbia, South Carolina: The State Company, 1914.

Johnson, John. *The Defense of Charleston Harbor including Fort Sumter and the Adjacent Islands, 1863–1865*. Charleston, South Carolina: Walker, Evans, and Cogswell, 1890.

Jones, Eugene W. Jr. *Enlisted For The War, The Struggles of the Gallant 24th Regiment, South Carolina Volunteers, Infantry, 1861–1865.* Highstown, New Jersey: Longstreet House, 1997.

Jordan, Laylon Wayne, and Elizabeth H. Stringfellow. *A Place Called St. John's: The Story of John's Edisto, Wadmalaw, Kiawah, and Seabrook Islands of South Carolina.* Spartanburg, South Carolina: The Reprint Company, 2003.

Keowee Courier (Walhalla)

Kirkland, Randolph W., Jr. *Broken Fortunes—South Carolina Soldiers, Sailors and Citizens Who Died in the Service of Their Country and State in the War for Southern Independence, 1861–1865.* Charleston:The South Carolina Historical Society, 1995.

Krick, Robert K. *Lee's Colonels, A Biographical Register of the Field Officers of the Army of Northern Virginia.* 3d ed. rev. Dayton, Ohio: Morningside House, 1991.

Lancaster Ledger

Laurensville Herald

Lewis, Richard, Lieutenant. *Camp Life of a Confederate Boy.* Charleston, South Carolina: News and Courier Press, 1883.

Lexington Dispatch

Longacre, Edward G. *Gentleman and Soldier.* Nashville, Tennessee: Rutledge Hill Press, 2003.

Lynch, Harriet P. *Reminiscences and Sketches of Confederate Times.* Columbia, South Carolina: The R.L. Bryan Company, 1909.

Marion Star

McArthur, Judith N., and Orville Vernon Burton. *A Gentleman and An Officer-A Military and Social History of James B. Griffin's Civil War.* New York: Oxford University Press, 1996.

McDaniel, J.J. "Diary of the Battles, Marches, and Incidents of the 7th South Carolina Regiment." N.p., n.d. (Available from the Greenville County Public Library. Microfiche 973.7457, fiche 99.)

McSwain, Eleanor D., ed. *Crumbling Defenses or Memoirs and Reminiscences of John Logan Black, Colonel, C.S.A.* Macon, Georgia: J.W. Burke Company, 1960.

Melton, E. Frank. *War Between The States.* Hartsville: Old Darlington District, South Carolina Genealogical Society, 2002.

Mixson, Frank M. *Reminiscences Of A Private.* Columbia, South Carolina: The State Company, 1910.

Mulligan, A.B. *My Dear Mother and Sisters, The Civil War Letters of Captain A.B. Mulligan, Company B, 5th South Carolina Cavalry, Butler's Division, Hampton's Corps, 1861–1865.* Spartanburg, South Carolina: The Reprint Company, 1992.

Murray, J. Ogden. *The Immortal 600.* New York: The Neale Publishing Company, 1905.

National Archives and Records Administration. *Compiled Service Records of Confederate Soldiers Who Served in Organizations from the State of South Carolina* (CSR). Microcopy 267.

———. Register of Confederate Soldiers, Sailors, and Citizens Who Died in Federal Prisons and Military Hospitals in the North, 1861–1865. Microfilm publication. M918 (973.742).

Nichols, Wesley. *The Autobiography of Wesley Nichols.* N.p., n.d. (Available from the Greenville County Public Library. Microfiche SC 973.7457, Fiche 111.)

Phelps, W. Chris. *Charlestonians in War: the Charleston Battalion.* Gretna, Louisiana: Pelican Publishing Company, 2004.

Reid, Jesse W. *History of the Fourth Regiment, S.C. Volunteers, from the Commencement of the War until Lee's Surrender*. Greenville, South Carolina: Shannon and Company, 1891. Repr. Dayton, Ohio: Morningside Bookshop, 1975.

Rhea, Gordon C. *Carrying the Flag*. New York: Basic Books, 2004.

Ripley, Warren. *The Battle of Chapman's Fort, May 26, 1864*. Green Pond: Ashepoo Plantation, 1978.

———. *Siege Train, The Journal of a Confederate Artilleryman in the Defense of Charleston*. Columbia: University of South Carolina Press, 1986.

Rivers, William J. *Rivers's Account of the Raising of Troops in South Carolina for State and Confederate Service 1861–1865*. Columbia, South Carolina: The Bryan Printing Company, State Printers, 1899.

Salley, Alexander S., comp. *South Carolina Troops in Confederate Service*. 3 vols. Columbia, South Carolina: The R.L. Bryan Company, 1913, 1914, 1930.

Seigler, Robert S. *A Guide to Confederate Monuments in South Carolina*. Columbia, South Carolina: South Carolina Department of Archives and History, 1997.

Sellers, William W. *A History of Marion County, South Carolina, from its earliest times to present—1901*. Columbia, SC: R.L. Bryan Company, 1902.

Sifakis, Stewart. *Compendium of the Confederate Armies—South Carolina and Georgia*. New York: Facts on File, 1995

Smith, C.F. *Jeremiah Smith and the Confederate War*. Spartanburg, South Carolina: The Reprint Company, 1993.

South Carolina Department of Archives and History.

———. Adjutant and Inspector General. "History of Charleston Zouave Cadets." 1904. 1 vol. N.d.

Roster of 14th South Carolina Infantry. 2 vols. N.d.

———. Comptroller General. Confederate Pension Applications Division, 1910–1926. Nos. 1941–2202 (Charleston-Cherokee). Microfilm Roll CW1231 (AD1149), No. 1995.

———. Confederate Historian.

"Annual Report For The Year 1899." *South Carolina Reports and Resolutions 1868–1900, regular session 1900*. Microcopy 13, Roll 29.

Memory Roll: Rolls of South Carolina Volunteers in the Confederate States Provisional Army. 5 vols. Microcopy 16, 1993.

Record and Roll of the German Fusiliers. 1 vol. 1904.

Record and Roll of the Washington Light Artillery, 1905. 1 vol.

Roster of Officers. N.d. 1 vol.

———. Miscellaneous Historical Sketches, 1866–1898. S108121.

Albergotti, W. Greer. "Sketch of Company F, 2nd Battalion, South Carolina State Troops." N.d.

Alston, Butler P. "Sketch of the 6th South Carolina Infantry." 1878.

Fields, W.G. Unpublished Letter.

Griffin, James A. Unpublished Letter.

Hammond, W.A. "Sketch of Company B, 37th Virginia Cavalry." 1898.

"Historical Sketch of the 5th South Carolina Cavalry." 1866. S108121.

Hoyt, J.A. Unpublished Letter.

James, A.A. "Brief History of the 18th. South Carolina Volunteers." N.d.

Lucas, J.J. "Sketch of Lucas's Battalion of Heavy Artillery." 1882.

Rion, J.H. "History of the 6th Regiment, South Carolina Infantry," n.d.

Roll of Company G, 22nd South Carolina Infantry. 1884.

Roster of the 17th South Carolina Infantry (Partial). N.d.
Russell, D.H. Unpublished Letter.
"Sketch of Company F, 21st South Carolina Infantry." N.d.
"Sketch of the 2nd South Carolina Artillery Regiment." N.d.
"Sketches of the 23rd South Carolina Infantry." 1891.
Stokes, William. "Sketch of Company G, 4th South Carolina Cavalry." N.d.
———. *Roll of the Dead, South Carolina Troops Confederate States Service*. 1994.
South Carolina Historical Magazine
Southern Historical Society. Southern Historical Society Papers. 52 vols. Richmond, Virginia, 1876–1959.
Starr, Linda Sparks. *W.R. Rankin, Manassas to Appomattox*. Norman, Oklahoma: Linda Sparks Starr, 1990.
The State
Stevens, Robert J. *Captain Bill, The Records and Writings of Captain William Henry Edwards (and others) Company A, 17th Regiment, South Carolina Volunteers, Confederate States of America.* 3 vols. Richburg, South Carolina: The Chester District Genealogical Society, 1985–1990.
Stone, DeWitt Boyd, Jr. *Wandering to Glory.* Columbia: University of South Carolina Press, 2002.
Sumter Watchman
Taylor, John S. *Sixteenth South Carolina Regiment CSA from Greenville County, South Carolina*. Private printing, 1964.
Thigpen, Allan D. *Recollections of Potter's Raid*. Sumter, South Carolina: Gamecock City Printing, 1999.
Thomas, John P. *Career and Character of General Micah Jenkins, C.S.A.* Columbia, South Carolina: The State Company, 1903.
Thomas, Samuel N., Jr., and Jason H. Silverman, eds. *A Rising Star of Promise: The Civil War Odyssey of David Jackson Logan, 17th South Carolina Volunteers, 1861–1864.* Campbell, California: Savas Publishing Company, 1998.
Tolar, J.R. "A History of Company B, 10th Regiment, SCV" (Available from the Greenville County Public Library. Microfiche 973.7457, fiche 101.)
Tompkins, D.A. *Company K, 14th SCV* Charlotte, North Carolina: Charlotte Observer Printing Publishing House, 1897. (Available from the Greenville County Public Library. Microfiche SC 973.7457, Fiche 110.)
Toole, Gasper Loren. *Ninety Years in Aiken County*. Private printing, 1961.
Tower, Lockwood, ed. *A Carolinian Goes To War, The Civil Narrative of Arthur Middleton Manigault, Brigadier General, C.S.A., R.* Columbia: University of South Carolina Press, 1983.
Triweekly Watchman
United Daughters of the Confederacy. South Carolina Division, *Recollections and Reminiscences 1861–1865 through World War I.* 9 vols.
United States War Department. *The War of the Rebellion: A Compilation of the Official Records of the Union and Confederate Armies.* 128 vols. Washington, D.C.: Government Printing Office, 1891–1895. (It should be noted that some volumes in this series are broken into parts, while some are not. Entries for volumes with parts are listed in the endnotes with a series, a volume, a part, and a page number or numbers; entries for volumes without parts are listed only with a series, a volume, and a page number or numbers.)

Walker, C.I. *Rolls and Historical Sketch of the Tenth Regiment, So. Ca. Volunteers in the Army of the Confederate States by C.I. Walker, Late Lieut. Col. of the Regt. To which is added An Historical Sketch of the Georgetown Rifle Guards Company A, 10th South Carolina by Sol. Emanuel.* South Carolina: Walker, Evans, and Cogswell, 1881. Repr. Alexandria, Virginia: Stonewall House, 1985.

Warner, Ezra J. *Generals in Blue, Lives of the Union Commanders.* Baton Rouge: Louisiana State University Press, 1986.

———. *Generals in Gray, Lives of the Confederate Commanders.* Baton Rouge: Louisiana State University Press, 1986.

Welch, Spencer G. *A Confederate Surgeon's Letters to his Wife.* New York: Neale Publishing Company, 1911.

Wellman, Manly Wade. *Giant in Gray, A Biography of Wade Hampton of South Carolina.* New York: Charles Scribner's and Sons, 1949.

Wells, Edward L. *Hampton and His Cavalry in '64.* Richmond, Virginia: B.F. Johnson, 1899.

———. *A Sketch of the Charleston Light Dragoons, From the Earliest Formation of the Corps.* Charleston, South Carolina: Lucas, Richardson, and Company, 1888.

Wise, Stephen R. *Gate of Hell, Campaign for Charleston Harbor, 1863.* Columbia: University of South Carolina Press, 1994.

Woodward, C. Vann and Elisabeth Muhlenfeld. *The Private Mary Chesnut, The Unpublished Civil War Diaries.* New York: Oxford University Press, 1984.

Woodward, T.W. "History of the 6th Regiment, S.C. Volunteers." Speech. Columbia, South Carolina: Presbyterian Publishing House, 1883.

Wyckoff, Mac. *A History of the 2nd South Carolina Infantry 1861–1865.* Fredericksburg, Virginia: Sergeant Kirkland's Museum and Historical Society, 1994.

———. *A History of the 3rd South Carolina Infantry 1861–1865.* Fredericksburg, Virginia: Sergeant Kirkland's Museum and Historical Society, 1995.

———. Website on South Carolina in the Civil War. http://www.members.tripod.com/mwyckoff/.

Yorkville Enquirer

Index

C

N

Y